OTHER A TO Z GUIDES FROM THE SCARECROW PRESS, INC.

1. *The A to Z of Buddhism* by Charles S. Prebish, 2001.
2. *The A to Z of Catholicism* by William J. Collinge, 2001.
3. *The A to Z of Hinduism* by Bruce M. Sullivan, 2001.
4. *The A to Z of Islam* by Ludwig W. Adamec, 2002.
5. *The A to Z of Slavery & Abolition* by Martin A. Klein, 2002.
6. *Terrorism: Assassins to Zealots* by Sean Kendall Anderson and Stephen Sloan, 2003.
7. *The A to Z of the Korean War* by Paul M. Edwards, 2005.
8. *The A to Z of the Cold War* by Joseph Smith and Simon Davis, 2005.
9. *The A to Z of the Vietnam War* by Edwin E. Moise, 2005.
10. *The A to Z of Science Fiction Literature* by Brian Stableford, 2005.
11. *The A to Z of the Holocaust* by Jack R. Fischel, 2005.
12. *The A to Z of Washington, D.C.* by Robert Benedetto, Jane Donovan, and Kathleen DuVall, 2005.
13. *The A to Z of Taoism* by Julian F. Pas, 2006.
14. *The A to Z of the Renaissance* by Charles G. Nauert, 2006.
15. *The A to Z of Shinto* by Stuart D. B. Picken, 2006.
16. *The A to Z of Byzantium* by John H. Rosser, 2006.
17. *The A to Z of the Civil War* by Terry L. Jones, 2006.
18. *The A to Z of the Friends (Quakers)* by Margery Post Abbott, Mary Ellen Chijioke, Pink Dandelion, and John William Oliver Jr., 2006
19. *The A to Z of Feminism* by Janet K. Boles and Diane Long Hoeveler, 2006.
20. *The A to Z of New Religious Movements* by George D. Chryssides, 2006.
21. *The A to Z of Multinational Peacekeeping* by Terry M. Mays, 2006.
22. *The A to Z of Lutheranism* by Günther Gassmann with Duane H. Larson and Mark W. Oldenburg, 2007.
23. *The A to Z of the French Revolution* by Paul R. Hanson, 2007.
24. *The A to Z of the Persian Gulf War 1990–1991* by Clayton R. Newell, 2007.
25. *The A to Z of Revolutionary America* by Terry M. Mays, 2007.
26. *The A to Z of the Olympic Movement* by Bill Mallon with Ian Buchanan, 2007.

27. *The A to Z of the Discovery and Exploration of Australia* by Alan Day, 2009.
28. *The A to Z of the United Nations* by Jacques Fomerand. 2009.
29. *The A to Z of the "Dirty Wars"* by David Kohut, Olga Vilella, and Beatrice Julian, 2009.
30. *The A to Z of the Vikings* by Katherine Holman, 2009.
31. *The A to Z from the Great War to the Great Depression* by Neil A. Wynn, 2009.
32. *The A to Z of the Crusades* by Corliss K. Slack, 2009.
33. *The A to Z of New Age Movements* by Michael York, 2009.
34. *The A to Z of Unitarian Universalism* by Mark W. Harris, 2009.
35. *The A to Z of the Kurds* by Michael M. Gunter, 2009.
36. *The A to Z of Utopianism* by James M. Morris and Andrea L. Kross, 2009.
37. *The A to Z of the Civil War and Reconstruction* by William L. Richter, 2009.
38. *The A to Z of Jainism* by Kristi L. Wiley, 2009.
39. *The A to Z of the Inuit* by Pamela K. Stern, 2009.
40. *The A to Z of Early North America* by Cameron B. Wesson, 2009.
41. *The A to Z of the Enlightenment* by Harvey Chisick, 2009.
42. *The A to Z of Methodism* edited by Charles Yrigoyen Jr. and Susan E. Warrick, 2009.
43. *The A to Z of the Seventh-day Adventists* by Gary Land, 2009.
44. *The A to Z of Sufism* by John Renard, 2009.
45. *The A to Z of Sikhism* by W. H. McLeod, 2009.
46. *The A to Z of Fantasy Literature* by Brian Stableford, 2009.
47. *The A to Z of the Discovery and Exploration of the Pacific Islands* by Max Quanchi and John Robson, 2009.
48. *The A to Z of Australian and New Zealand Cinema* by Albert Moran and Errol Vieth, 2009.
49. *The A to Z of African-American Television* by Kathleen Fearn-Banks, 2009.
50. *The A to Z of American Radio Soap Operas* by Jim Cox, 2009.
51. *The A to Z of the Old South* by William L. Richter, 2009.
52. *The A to Z of the Discovery and Exploration of the Northwest Passage* by Alan Day, 2009.
53. *The A to Z of the Druzes* by Samy S. Swayd, 2009.
54. *The A to Z of the Welfare State* by Bent Greve, 2009.

55. *The A to Z of the War of 1812* by Robert Malcomson, 2009.
56. *The A to Z of Feminist Philosophy* by Catherine Villanueva Gardner, 2009.
57. *The A to Z of the Early American Republic* by Richard Buel Jr., 2009.
58. *The A to Z of the Russo–Japanese War* by Rotem Kowner, 2009.
59. *The A to Z of Anglicanism* by Colin Buchanan, 2009.
60. *The A to Z of Scandinavian Literature and Theater* by Jan Sjåvik, 2009.
61. *The A to Z of the Peoples of the Southeast Asian Massif* by Jean Michaud, 2009.
62. *The A to Z of Judaism* by Norman Solomon, 2009.
63. *The A to Z of the Berbers (Imazighen)* by Hsain Ilahiane, 2009.
64. *The A to Z of British Radio* by Seán Street, 2009.
65. *The A to Z of The Salvation Army* by Major John G. Merritt, 2009.
66. *The A to Z of the Arab–Israeli Conflict* by P R Kumaraswamy, 2009.
67. *The A to Z of the Jacksonian Era and Manifest Destiny* by Terry Corps, 2009.
68. *The A to Z of Socialism* by Peter Lamb and James C. Docherty, 2009.
69. *The A to Z of Marxism* by David Walker and Daniel Gray, 2009.
70. *The A to Z of the Bahá'í Faith* by Hugh C. Adamson, 2009.
71. *The A to Z of Postmodernist Literature and Theater* by Fran Mason, 2009.
72. *The A to Z of Australian Radio and Television* by Albert Moran and Chris Keating, 2009.
73. *The A to Z of the Lesbian Liberation Movement: Still the Rage* by JoAnne Myers, 2009.
74. *The A to Z of the United States–Mexican War* by Edward H. Moseley and Paul C. Clark Jr., 2009.
75. *The A to Z of World War I* by Ian V. Hogg, 2009.
76. *The A to Z of World War II: The War Against Japan* by Anne Sharp Wells, 2009.
77. *The A to Z of Witchcraft* by Michael D. Bailey, 2009.
78. *The A to Z of British Intelligence* by Nigel West, 2009.
79. *The A to Z of United States Intelligence* by Michael A. Turner, 2009.

80. *The A to Z of the League of Nations* by Anique H. M. van Ginneken, 2009.
81. *The A to Z of Israeli Intelligence* by Ephraim Kahana, 2009.
82. *The A to Z of the European Union* by Joaquín Roy and Aimee Kanner, 2009.
83. *The A to Z of the Chinese Cultural Revolution* by Guo Jian, Yongyi Song, and Yuan Zhou, 2009.
84. *The A to Z of African American Cinema* by S. Torriano Berry and Venise T. Berry, 2009.
85. *The A to Z of Japanese Business* by Stuart D. B. Picken, 2009.
86. *The A to Z of the Reagan–Bush Era* by Richard S. Conley, 2009.
87. *The A to Z of Human Rights and Humanitarian Organizations* by Robert F. Gorman and Edward S. Mihalkanin, 2009.
88. *The A to Z of French Cinema* by Dayna Oscherwitz and MaryEllen Higgins, 2009.
89. *The A to Z of the Puritans* by Charles Pastoor and Galen K. Johnson, 2009.
90. *The A to Z of Nuclear, Biological, and Chemical Warfare* by Benjamin C. Garrett and John Hart, 2009.
91. *The A to Z of the Green Movement* by Miranda Schreurs and Elim Papadakis, 2009.
92. *The A to Z of the Kennedy–Johnson Era* by Richard Dean Burns and Joseph M. Siracusa, 2009.
93. *The A to Z of Renaissance Art* by Lilian H. Zirpolo, 2009.
94. *The A to Z of the Broadway Musical* by William A. Everett and Paul R. Laird, 2009.
95. *The A to Z of the Northern Ireland Conflict* by Gordon Gillespie, 2009.
96. *The A to Z of the Fashion Industry* by Francesca Sterlacci and Joanne Arbuckle, 2009.
97. *The A to Z of American Theater: Modernism* by James Fisher and Felicia Hardison Londré, 2009.
98. *The A to Z of Civil Wars in Africa* by Guy Arnold, 2009.
99. *The A to Z of the Nixon–Ford Era* by Mitchell K. Hall, 2009.
100. *The A to Z of Horror Cinema* by Peter Hutchings, 2009.
101. *The A to Z of Westerns in Cinema* by Paul Varner, 2009.
102. *The A to Z of Zionism* by Rafael Medoff and Chaim I. Waxman, 2009.

103. *The A to Z of the Roosevelt–Truman Era* by Neil A. Wynn, 2009.
104. *The A to Z of Jehovah's Witnesses* by George D. Chryssides, 2009.
105. *The A to Z of Native American Movements* by Todd Leahy and Raymond Wilson, 2009.
106. *The A to Z of the Shakers* by Stephen J. Paterwic, 2009.
107. *The A to Z of the Coptic Church* by Gawdat Gabra, 2009.
108. *The A to Z of Architecture* by Allison Lee Palmer, 2009.
109. *The A to Z of Italian Cinema* by Gino Moliterno, 2009.
110. *The A to Z of Mormonism* by Davis Bitton and Thomas G. Alexander, 2009.
111. *The A to Z of African American Theater* by Anthony D. Hill with Douglas Q. Barnett, 2009.
112. *The A to Z of NATO and Other International Security Organizations* by Marco Rimanelli, 2009.
113. *The A to Z of the Eisenhower Era* by Burton I. Kaufman and Diane Kaufman, 2009.
114. *The A to Z of Sexspionage* by Nigel West, 2009.
115. *The A to Z of Environmentalism* by Peter Dauvergne, 2009.
116. *The A to Z of the Petroleum Industry* by M. S. Vassiliou, 2009.
117. *The A to Z of Journalism* by Ross Eaman, 2009.
118. *The A to Z of the Gilded Age* by T. Adams Upchurch, 2009.
119. *The A to Z of the Progressive Era* by Catherine Cocks, Peter C. Holloran, and Alan Lessoff, 2009.
120. *The A to Z of Middle Eastern Intelligence* by Ephraim Kahana and Muhammad Suwaed, 2009.
121. *The A to Z of the Baptists* William H. Brackney, 2009.
122. *The A to Z of Homosexuality* by Brent L. Pickett, 2009.

The A to Z of Japanese Business

Stuart D. B. Picken

The A to Z Guide Series, No. 85

THE SCARECROW PRESS, INC.
Lanham • Toronto • Plymouth, UK
2009

Published by Scarecrow Press, Inc.
A wholly owned subsidiary of
The Rowman & Littlefield Publishing Group, Inc.
4501 Forbes Boulevard, Suite 200, Lanham, Maryland 20706
http://www.scarecrowpress.com

Estover Road, Plymouth PL6 7PY, United Kingdom

British Library Cataloguing in Publication Information Available

Library of Congress Cataloging-in-Publication Data

The hardback version of this book was cataloged by the Library of Congress as follows:

Picken, Stuart D. B.
Historical dictionary of Japanese business / Stuart D. B. Picken.
p. cm. — (Historical dictionaries of professions and industries ; no. 1)
Includes bibliographical references.
1. Japan—Commerce—Dictionaries. 2. Business—Dictionaries. I. Title.
HF3824.P53 2007
330.952003—dc22 2006025473

ISBN 978-0-8108-6872-4 (pbk. : alk. paper)
ISBN 978-0-8108-7035-2 (ebook)

™ The paper used in this publication meets the minimum requirements of American National Standard for Information Sciences—Permanence of Paper for Printed Library Materials, ANSI/NISO Z39.48-1992.
Printed in the United States of America

For William and Lynn

Contents

Editor's Foreword *Jon Woronoff* ix

Preface xi

Reader's Note xiii

Acronyms and Abbreviations xv

Chronology xix

Introduction xxxiii

THE DICTIONARY 1

Glossary 1: Business Proverbs 327

Glossary 2: Traditional Business Expressions 333

Glossary 3: Modern Business Expressions 345

Bibliography 359

About the Author 387

Editor's Foreword

Although the Japanese economy has slowed down over the past decade or two, it has lost none of its edge, and Japanese companies remain among the toughest competitors any foreign company can face. In order to come out ahead, whether by beating one's Japanese competitors or cooperating with them, it would seem essential to know more about them, how they are managed and operate, what their strengths are, and also what their weaknesses are. Yet all too many foreigners remain blissfully unfamiliar with the Japanese business system and its many differences from how business is done in the West (and sometimes even in Asia) or seize on these differences as excuses. Considering that, admittedly, it is not easy to understand the inner workings of Japanese business, it should be a welcome relief to encounter a book that explains it in clear and simple terms and also traces its evolution from early times to the present.

This *Historical Dictionary of Japanese Business* starts at the very beginning, tracing the evolution from the earliest times to the present day in a chronology. Next, the introduction describes today's system and also inserts it in the broader history and culture so that it makes considerably more sense. Then the main portion, the dictionary, takes a closer look at the many features that make it distinctive, as well as outstanding business and other leaders and some of the most successful companies, one by one, starting with the abacus. But that is not all. The first glossary presents proverbial expressions used in business that help one understand what makes Japanese businesspeople tick. The second glossary, this one on traditional expressions, provides further insight into how the expresssions got that way, and the third, with modern expressions, sheds light on the mentality of today's employees and their bosses. Naturally, there is still much more to learn, and the bibliography points interested readers in the right direction.

This volume was written by Stuart D. B. Picken, who has spent decades living and working in Japan. For 25 years, he served on the faculty of the International Christian University in Tokyo before moving to the Nagoya University of Commerce and Business Administration, where he ended his career as dean of the Graduate School. His students have included large numbers of Japanese but also many foreigners, and this has helped him see Japanese business from both angles and realize just how confusing it can be for westerners and others. Meanwhile, he was also active outside of academia, functioning as a consultant to major Japanese corporations, including Mitsui Mining and Smelting, Kobe Steel, and the Japan Airlines Group. This allowed him to study Japanese business carefully from inside as he had done from outside. Finally, since many of today s practices are deeply embedded in earlier times and especially Japan's culture and religion, it certainly helps that Dr. Picken is also a specialist on Japanese religion and has written the *Historical Dictionary of Shinto*.

Jon Woronoff
Series Editor

Preface

It is always a privilege for anyone to have the opportunity to write about a subject in which they have a deep personal interest. My earliest encounters with Japanese corporate life and culture go back almost 40 years, when I began preparing to make my first trip to Japan. It is astonishing when I think back to the late 1960s that almost no literature on Japan was available in the average public library of the time and that what little there was proved frequently to be quite misleading. I still have in my possession a paper knife in the form of a samurai sword, bought in Belgium around 1961, and a minicamera that I bought in New York in 1958. The steel in the paper knife still shines, and the camera took excellent pictures, although film for it no longer exists. The quality of both little items speaks for itself. When I actually visited Japan, the word *quality* emerged spontaneously as the best adjective with which to describe what was before my eyes—of people, processes, and products.

In the introduction, I try to explain how Japan's cultural heritage has been quite un-self-consciously harnessed to meet the needs of industrialization and development. In contrast to the Western tendency to consign the past to the trash can of history in the name of progress, the Japanese have frequently used reverence for tradition as a point of departure for the future. It is often said that it is difficult to change things in Japan but always possible to add something new. The ability to massage continuity and change into an evolving continuum is a Japanese art that would benefit those Western societies dominated by a dialectical view of history that elevates change and considers tradition an obstacle to their ideal of progress.

Many aspects of Japanese business culture call for respect. The sense of commitment that permeates every business enterprise and that drives organizations in the direction of achievement and performance is one source of enormous strength. Another is the lack of the kind of cynicism that has eroded many Western societies. Tidiness, timekeeping, efficiency, following through, and attention to detail are deeply ingrained traits of the business culture as they are of the society as a whole. These are values that are central to the cultural system and, regardless of the often negative Western influences, remain central. It has been said frequently enough that Japan's greatest natural resource is its people. I would amend that to the quality of its people.

In spite of half a century of closer engagement with the West, Japan is still not adequately understood either as a society or as a business culture, even by those who make frequent visits there. The growing infatuation with China, while understandable as a source of short-term business benefits, has had the effect of moving attention away from Japan's achievements and the reason for them. In my view, regardless of how attractive China may seen (and its growth and future scale are not in question), Japan will remain, in many ways, the cornerstone of Asian business because of its experience, its Asian investment, and its inherent stability. I hope this dictionary, in addition to its many intended uses, may also serve as a source of information about one of the most successful and interesting business cultures in human history.

I have included a formal dedication to this book, but I would like to express my special appreciation to all those who helped this text see the light of day. I would single out the series editor, Jon Woronoff, whose patience has been almost saintly and who has been not only an editor but also a provider of guidance and encouragement. The editorial staff of the Scarecrow Press have been courteous, efficient, and supportive as in the past. I would also like to thank the teaching staff and the students of the Graduate School of Global Business Communication and the Faculty of Foreign Languages and Asian Studies at Nagoya University of Commerce and Business, of which I was privileged, in each case, to be founding dean, for their kindness and inspiration.

Reader's Note

ROMANIZATION

Romanization follows the *Kenkyusha New-Japanese English Dictionary* (1974). It uses a modification of the Hepburn system. The following exceptions to that system bring the text into line with the *Kodansha Encyclopedia of Japan*:

1. *m* instead of *n* is used before *p*, *b*, or *m*, as in *shimbun* or *kamban*.
2. *n* is retained where there is need to hyphenate a word, such as *han-batsu* (instead of *hambatsu*).
3. The final syllable *n* is distinguished with an apostrophe when it comes before a vowel or *y*, as in *San'in* or *San'yo*.
4. Macrons are used to indicate the long vowels *a*, *u*, and *o*, except for the following:
   * The seven place-names Tokyo, Kyoto, Osaka, Kobe, Kyushu, Honshu, and Hokkaido
   * Japanese words that have come into English usage, such as *samurai*, *sushi*, or *shogun*
5. For transliteration of Japanese names, the Library of Congress catalog cards are the standard of reference. Where no reference exists, the most common form in use is listed.
6. The order of names is as in Japanese, family name first and given name second (e.g., *Morita Akio*).
7. Italicization is used only for Japanese words that appear in isolation in the text (e.g., *konbini*).
8. Company names are not italicized (e.g., Toyota Jidosha).

Romanization may sometimes appear highly inconsistent. It should be remembered that no officially authorized system of romanization of the Japanese language has ever existed similar to the Hanyu Pinyin system that was created by the Chinese government. The older Hepburn system was widely used by Western scholars until other variants appeared. In practice, authors tend to use their own preference, and these usually reflect the era in which they lived. A name such as *Sato*, in the system used in this text, would be written with a macron over the *o*. In older forms, it can be found as *Satow*, *Satoo*, *Satou*, and *Satoh*. All these endings are devices used to lengthen the final vowel. There are also changes in how Japanese has come to be pronounced, partly through the increasing presence of English phonemes. *Mt. Fuji* was, in earlier texts, *Mt. Huji*, and *Edo*, like *Ebisu* beer, included a *y* at the beginning, hence *Yedo* and *Yebisu*. In modern romanized dictionaries of the Japanese language, the letter *l* is conspicuous by its total absence. It is hoped that there will not be too much confusion, but it is possible only to point to the evolution of both romanization and the pronunciation of Japanese under various influences since the Meiji period (1868–1912).

CROSS-REFERENCING

The system of cross-referencing is as follows:

1. Other entry titles referred to within individual entries are bolded (e.g., The ***kurofune*** [black ships] arrived in 1853).
2. Additional relevant entries are noted after each entry, indicated by *See also* MITSUBISHI GROUP.
3. Main dictionary entries included in the glossaries are bolded.

Acronyms and Abbreviations

ANA	All Nippon Airways
ANN	All Nippon News Network
ASEAN	Association of Southeast Asian Nations
ASLD	Asymmetric Digital Subscriber Lines
ATM	Automated Teller Machines
BA	Bankers' Acceptance Market
BOJ	Bank of Japan
CD	Certificates of Deposit Market
DDI	Daini Denden
DOMEI	Japan Confederation of Labor
EPA	Economic Planning Agency
FMS	Flexible Manufacturing System
GATT	General Agreement on Tariffs and Trade
HMMS	Hino Micro-mixing Systems
IATA	International Air Transportation Association
IBJ	Industrial Bank of Japan
IBM	International Business Machines
ICI	Imperial Chemical Industries
IDC	International Digital Communications
IDE	Institute of Developing Economies
ILO	International Labor Organization
IRCJ	Industrial Revitalization Corporation of Japan
ITJ	International Telecom Japan
JAL	Japan Airlines
JAMA	Japan Automobile Manufacturers' Association
JAS	Japan Air System
JCCI	Japan Chamber of Commerce and Industry
JDB	Japan Development Bank
JECC	Japan Electronic Computer Company

JETRO	Japan External Trade Organization
JIPM	Japan Institute of Plant Management
JIT	Just-in-Time
JMA	Japan Management Association
JNR	Japan National Railways
JPC	Japan Productivity Center for Socio-Economic Development
JR	Japan Railways Group
JRX	JAL Express
JTB	Japan Travel Bureau
JTUC-RENGO	Japan Trade Union Federation
JUSCO	Japan United Stores Company
JVC	Japan Victor Corporation
KDD	Japan International Telegraph and Telephone Corporation
KEIDANREN	Federation of Economic Organizations
KINTETSU	Kinki Nippon Railway
KONBINI	Convenience Stores
LDP	Liberal Democratic Party
LNG	Liquefied Natural Gas
LPG	Liquid Petroleum Gas
LTCB	Long Term Credit Bank of Japan
M&A	Mergers and Acquisitions
MEAF	Matsushita Electric Appliance Factory
METI	Ministry of the Economy, Trade, and Industry
MIPRO	Manufactured Imports Promotional Organization
MIS	Marketing Information System
MITI	Ministry of International Trade and Industry
MOF	Ministry of Finance
MSG	Monosodium Glutamate
MSK	Mitsubishi Shoji Kabushiki Kaisha (Mitsubishi Corporation)
NEC	Nippon Electric Corporation
NHK	Japan Broadcasting Corporation
NIKKEIREN	Japan Federation of Employers' Associations
NOKYO	Agricultural Cooperative Societies
NTT	Nippon Telegraph and Telephone Corporation
NYK	Nippon Yusen Shipping

ODA	Overseas Development Aid
OECD	Organization for Economic Cooperation and Development
OEE	Overall Equipment Effectiveness
QC	Quality Circles
R&D	Research and Development
SCAP	Supreme Commander Allied Powers
SECJ	Social and Economic Congress of Japan
SII	Structural Impediments Initiative
SMED	Single Minute Exchange of Die
SNG	Substitute Natural Gas
SOHYO	General Council of Trade Unions in Japan
TACSS	Takenaka Aquareactive Chemical Soil Stabilization
TEPCO	Tokyo Electric Power Company
TIFFE	Tokyo International Financial Futures Exchange
TPM	Total Productivity Management
TQC	Total Quality Control
TTNet	Tokyo Telecommunications Network
UFJ	United Finance Japan
WTO	World Trade Organization
YKK	Yoshida Kogyo

Chronology

10,000 B.C.E. The ancient Japanese used stone implements in areas where these do not exist in a natural state, suggesting a primitive form of barter trade between regions.

250 The *Yayoi* (Bronze-Iron) period artifacts include swords and mirrors. Yayoi culture marked the transition to a settled agricultural economy.

ca. 100 The island of Okinoshima (Fukuoka Prefecture) was a guardian *kami* of sailors traveling between Japan and Korea. Mirrors and beads, among some of the oldest artifacts known, resulted probably from trade with the Asian mainland.

ca. 250 Empress Jingu (r. 201–269) subdues Korea according to the *Nihon Shoki*, suggesting that strong central government existed.

ca. 300 Emperor Ojin (r. 270–310) introduces technology from the Asian mainland. The first recorded market, the Kara-no-ichi, was recorded as being established in Yamato.

552 Buddhism is brought probably by immigrants from the Korean peninsula who introduced a market system. References exist to a seller of rice wine from Korea and a seller of bearskins.

645–646 According to the laws contained in *Taika no kaishin*, all land came to be the property of the state. A controller of markets became responsible for all important trade and transport routes. He also had the power to levy taxes.

672–686 During the reign of Emperor Temmu (673–686), eastern and western markets are recorded in Asuka-Fujiwara-kyo and thereafter in the capital.

701 The *Taiho Ritsuryo* (Code) further regulated the market system in the capital city. Trading volumes required five carts to transport coins used in the markets.

708 The first known coins minted in Japan date to the Wado era (708–714).

710 Japan's first permanent capital, Nara, was built on the grid model of a Chinese city, and the first clearly documented signs of organized commerce date to this period.

724 Nara culture saw expanding foreign trade evidenced by imported luxury goods.

740 Eastern and western markets are recorded in Nara. These are subsequently moved to Kyoto in 794.

749 The great bronze Buddha of the Todai-ji is successfully cast in 752, evidencing the development of Japanese large-scale manufacturing and building technology.

797 Trade with Sung China (960–1279) is sponsored by major shrines and temples. Copper coins (*sosen*) from China were imported along with toiletries, medicines, silks, porcelain, books, and luxury goods. Japanese exports were gold, silver, mercury, fans, swords, lacquerware, screens, and timber.

807 First records of the Ikuno Silver Mine, which continued to produce copper and zinc after its silver had been exhausted. It was finally closed in 1973.

833 Earliest reference to the use of *kanban* (advertising boards) in Kyoto.

835 To assist in the economic development of western Kyoto, the government gave exclusive rights to sell 18 products, including brocades, damasks, and silks.

859–876 The eastern market in Kyoto grows in size and complexity. Shops appear outside the market areas, notably lumber merchants on the banks of the Horikawa.

1063 The *Uma-no-ichi* (day of the horse) market is established at Iwashimizu in Kyoto followed by the *ne-no-ichi* (day of the rat) market.

1100 Coins, imported from Sung dynasty (960–1126) China, are first used as the exchange medium in Japanese markets. Market towns along with *za* (guilds) appear.

1176 The Todai-ji in Nara was presented with gifts by the manager of the Minami-no-sho, who noted that while seafood items were available, expensive fabrics were not.

1220 Japanese pirates (*wako*) are recorded raiding China and Korea.

1226 Coins for trade exchange are reinstated with cloth being forbidden.

1254 Sung dynasty China requests a restriction of trade with Japan.

1334 The Iwanami Ginzan begins mining silver.

1462–1500 The *hyoromai* rice tax, dating from 1185, gradually increases from 2 percent to 50 percent of annual rice yield.

1540 European traders begin to appear bringing new firearms and European luxury goods such as silk, leather, and perfumes.

1601 Sado Mines first worked to support the Tokugawa economy. Sueyoshi Magozaemon sets up a government-authorized office in Edo known as the Ginza (now a popular downtown center in Tokyo) for minting silver coins.

1606 Recorded beginning of the whaling industry in Japan in Taji, a city in the modern Wakayama prefecture.

1610 Takenaka Komuten is founded as a construction company.

1672 Hachirobe Takatoshi, founder of the House of Mitsui, opens a shop in Edo.

1683 Hachirobe Takatoshi opens a second *echigoya* (dry-goods store) at Nihonbashi in Edo, the site on which Mitsukoshi Department Store now stands.

1690 The Sumitomo family acquires the Besshi Copper Mine in Shikoku.

1697 Opening of Osaka's wholesale rice market between the Shijimi and Dojima Rivers.

1715 Osaka records show 5,655 wholesalers operating in the city, which had become the principal commodity center of the nation with 24 rice wholesalers.

1717 Dry-goods store opens in Kyoto, the forerunner of Daimaru, the retailing chain, and became a joint-stock company in 1920.

1731 The world's first futures market for rice trading begins operation in Dojima Rice Market in Osaka.

1758 Store is founded in Edo that became Okadaya and eventually through a merger the supermarket chain JUSCO in 1969.

1791 Edo Chokaisho, forerunner of the Tokyo Chamber of Commerce, is formed. Matsudaira Sadanobu introduces the concept of *shichibukin tsumitate*, an emergency reserve fund to cover deficits that was eventually used to finance a substantial amount of infrastructure in the early Meiji period.

1804 Shimizu Kensetsu, one of the top five construction companies, is founded.

1830 Clothing store opens in Osaka, later to become the Sogo Department Store.

1831 Cotton goods store opens in Kyoto, later becoming Takashimaya Department Store.

1840 Kajima Kensetsu is founded, surviving as one of the oldest of the five main construction companies in modern Japan.

1842 Takara Shuzo is founded as a distiller of *shochu*, a low-classed distilled alcoholic beverage.

1853 U.S. naval Commodore Matthew Perry arrives in Edo Bay with a flotilla of black ships (*kurofune*), as the Japanese called them. Ishikawa Shipyard is built by the Mito *daimyo* at the mouth of the River Sumida in Edo, becoming in 1960 Ishikawajima-Harima Heavy Industries, after the merger of Ishikawajima Heavy Industries and Harima Zosenjo.

1858 Ito Chubei begins a hemp business in the provinces that became C. Itoh and Co.

1868 Ito Chubei opened a dry-goods store in Osaka called Benichu that in time became the foundation of Marubeni Corporation.

1867 The 15th shogun, Tokugawa Yoshinobu, resigns, and a new constitution is promulgated in 1868.

1869 *Kawase kaisha* (money-changing companies) replace the older *ryogaesha.*

1870 Hyogo Shipyards are built by the *daimyo* of Kanazawa and became part of Kawasaki Heavy Industries. Spring Valley Brewery became Japan Brewery in 1885, with Mistubishi's assistance using the Kirin (Chinese dragon) image. Tosa Kaisai Shosha is founded by Iwasaki Yataro and renamed Mitsubishi Shokai in 1873 and eventually Mitsubishi Corporation.

1871 The old mint equipment of the Hong Kong Bank is acquired by the Japanese government.

1872 First National Bank Ordinance becomes law. The first domestic railway line is laid between Shimbashi and Yokohama. A Western-style pharmacy opens in Ginza that eventually becomes cosmetics giant Shiseido.

1873 Oji Seishi (Oji Paper) is founded by Shibusawa Eiichi as the first joint-stock company formed in Japan. Taisei Kensetsu construction company is formed by Okura Kihachiro as part of the Okura Gumi group.

1874 The national Postal Savings System is introduced. Okura-Gumi Shokai becomes the first Japanese company to open a London office.

1876 Dai Nippon Printing is founded as Sueisha, taking its present name in 1934. Mitsui & Co. is founded as a trading house that became the core of the Mitsui *zaibatsu.* A Japanese business weekly starts, becoming a daily in 1885 and eventually the *Nihon Keizei Shimbun*, Japan's premier business newspaper after 1945. The Mitsui Bank is founded.

1877 Suzki Shoten is founded by Suzuki Iwajiro as a trading house. The Eleventh National Bank is founded, becoming Aichi Bank and later the Tokai Bank.

1879 The Senju Woolen Mill, Japan's first, is set up in Tokyo's Senju district. The Tokio Marine & Fire Insurance Company is founded.

1880 Money exchange founded by Yasuda Kenjiro becomes Yasuda Bank and eventually the Fuji Bank in 1948. Yasuda Fire & Marine Insurance begins as a fire insurance company, becoming a major seller of non–life insurance. Yokohama Specie Bank is established by the government to increase silver specie and to assist in international trade, being renamed the Bank of Tokyo after World War II.

1881 Osaka Iron Works is founded, later to become Hitachi Shipbuilding. Meiji Mutual Life Insurance is founded as Japan's first modern life insurance company.

1882 The Bank of Japan is established by law on 10 October.

1886 Kohodo, the earliest Meiji period advertising agency, is established. Iseya Tanji Dry Goods, renamed Isetan in 1930, is founded as a general retail store.

1887 Kanegafuchi Boseki (Spinning) Company is formed in Osaka, better known by its abbreviated name, Kanebo. Kao Sekken is founded as a soap maker by Nagase Tomiro. Government transfers Nagasaki Shipyards to Mitsubishi, becoming Mitsubishi Heavy Industries, the nation's largest heavy machinery and military contractor.

1888 Japan's oldest oil company, Nihon Sekiyu, is founded.

1896 Nippon Seifun, Japan's first Western-style flour producer, is founded. Nippon Sharyo Seizo Kaisha, maker of modern Shinkansen coaches, is founded to produce rolling stock.

1897 Nippon Gakki is founded by Yamaha Torakusu to produce musical instruments under the brand name Yamaha. Sumitomo Electric Company is formed to produce electric wire and cable.

1899 TA joint venture with the Western Electric Company of the United States is founded and develops into Nippon Denki (NEC), the leading electronics manufacturer. Wine manufacturer using the brand name Akadama is established by Torii Shinjiro, later to become drink maker Suntory.

1902 The Dai-Ichi Mutual Life Insurance, Japan's first, is founded. The Industrial Bank of Japan is founded.

1905 Suzuki Shoten creates a steel division that became a subsidiary in 1911 and eventually Kobe Steel.

1906 Kawasaki Steel Corporation, one of the five major steel producers, is founded.

1907 Asahi Glass corporation is founded. Daihatsu Motor Company is founded. Nihon Kokoku Kabushiki Kaisha and Dempo Tsushinsha merge to form Dentsu, the largest advertising agency in Japan.

1908 Ajinomoto company commences production of monosodium glutamate (MSG).

1910 Hino Motors, Ltd, is founded as a large-truck manufacturer that became affiliated with Toyota in 1966. Hitachi is founded as an electric machinery company that became a core member of the Nissan *zaibatsu*.

1912 Japan's first experimental car, the Dattogo, is built by Hashimoto Masujiro. The Japan Travel Bureau (JTB) is formed to bring tourists to Japan. Nara Railway Company opens a line from Osaka to Nara, extending to Nagoya in 1948, becoming Kinki Nippon Tetsudo (Kintetsu) in 1944. Musashino Tetsudo (later Seibu Tetsudo) is established. Yanmar Diesel Engine is founded as the world's first manufacturer of small-sized diesel engines for electric generators, agricultural machinery, and ships.

1913 Ito-Yokado retailing business starts.

1915 Hayakawa Electric Industry is formed by Hayakawa Tokukji, later becoming Sharp Corporation.

1916 Isuzu Jidosha is founded as a car manufacturer, taking its modern name in 1949.

1917 Fuji Heavy Industries is formed as an aircraft manufacturer (until 1945). Noda Shoyu, an Edo period soy sauce maker founded by the Mogi family, is incorporated, becoming Kikkoman Shoyu in 1964 and Kikkoman Corporation in 1980. Meiji Milk Products is founded. Mitsui & Co. forms a heavy industry company for shipbuilding (Mitsui Zosen in 1976). Nakajima Chikukei sets up his Airplane Research Institute that became the Nakajima Aircraft Company, manufacturer of the engine of the famous Zero fighter.

1918 Daiwa Bank is founded under the name Nomura Bank in Osaka. Matsushita Electric Appliance Factory is founded in Osaka by Matsushita Konnosuke, in time becoming Matsushita Electric Industrial (National Panasonic). Nippon Sheet Glass, advanced technology maker of plate glass, is founded.

1919 Sumitomo Shoji is formed as a real estate and construction business, later to become a trading house serving the Sumitomo Group. Tokyu Department Store is opened. A freight haulage company is formed in Kyobashi (in Tokyo) by Ogura Yasuomi that later became Yamato Takkubin.

1920 Ebara Corporation is founded to develop Inokuchi Ariya's theory of centrifugal pumps. Nippon NCR (National Cash Registers) is founded. Toyo Cork Kogyo is formed in Hiroshima, becoming Toyo Kogyo in 1927 and a maker of light trucks after 1931; it became known as Mazda Corporation. Mitsui Bussan cotton division becomes Toyo Menka (Tomen), later a general trading house.

1921 Mitsubishi Electric Corporation is formed.

1922 Tokyo Fish Market moves from Nihombashi to Tsukiji to become the largest fish market in Japan and possibly the world.

1925 Nippon Hoso Kyokai (NHK) is incorporated and radio broadcasting started. Nomura Shoken, one of the big three securities companies, is founded as an independent company from the securities division of the Osaka Nomura Bank.

1926 Toyoda Automatic Loom Works is founded by Toyoda Sakichi, from which Toyota Motor Corporation was later established in 1937.

1927 Financial Crisis is caused by the collapse of 37 banks. Victor Corporation of Japan (JVC) is incorporated as a wholly owned subsidiary of Victor Talking Machine Co., Ltd., of the United States.

1928 Ito Ham Provisions is founded in Osaka. Nihon Sangyo (Nissan) corporation is formed as a holding company and core activity of the Nissan zaibatsu.

1929 The Wall Street crash marks the beginning of the Great Depression of 1929. Hankyu Department Store chain is founded by Hankyu Corporation.

1930 Showa Depression (1930–1935) starts. Citizen Watch Company is founded.

1931 Bridgestone Tire company is established.

1933 Sanwa Bank is formed by the merger of the Konoike Bank, the Yamaguchi Bank, and the Sanushi Bank to be the central bank of the Sanwa Group.

1934 Brother Industries is established in Nagoya. Fuji Film is formed to produce photographic materials.

1935 Fujitsu is formed from Fuji Electric as a telecommunications manufacturer.

1937 IBM Japan is formed. Minolta Camera is founded to manufacture optical products, taking the business name Minolta in 1962. Nippon Tsuun (NITTSU), Japan's largest freight company, is formed. Toyota Motor Corporation is established.

1938 Asahi Optical corporation is founded. Fujiya Confectionery is founded. Kumagai Gumi is formed for public works and overseas construction projects.

1939 Daikyo Oil is created to explore and develop oil fields. Toshiba (Tokyo Shibaura Denki) is formed by the merger of Shibaura Engineering Works and Tokyo Electric.

1940 Musashino Railway Company is formed, becoming Seibu Railway in 1949.

1941 Eisai is founded as a pharmaceuticals manufacturer. On 6 December, Japan attacks Pearl Harbor, forcing the United States into World War II.

1945 In August, U.S. Army General Douglas MacArthur becomes Supreme Commander of the Allied Powers. Yoshida Kogyo (YKK), world famous zip-fastener manufacturer, is founded by Yoshida Tadao.

1946 Keidanren (Federation of Economic Organizations) is founded.

1947 Revised Constitution is promulgated. Former Yokohama Specie Bank becomes the Bank of Tokyo. House Food Industrial is founded. The Bank of Japan Policy Board is made the highest level decision-making body. San'yo Electric, the first Japanese manufacturer to produce radios in plastic casings, is formed. Sekisui Kagaku Kogyo is formed and uses Japan's first automatic injection molding machine.

1948 Chiyoda Chemical Engineering & Construction is founded. Honda Motors is founded as Honda Giken Kogyo. Japan Federation of Employers Associations (Nikkeiren) is formed. Yamazaki Baking is founded, becoming Japan's largest bread producer.

1949 Asahi Breweries, maker of the Asahi beer brand, is founded. The Ministry of Commerce is replaced by the Ministry of International Trade and Industry (MITI) to supervise the rebuilding of the economy. Japan National Railways (JNR) is created. Wacoal Corporation is formed to retail ladies clothing and accessories.

1950 Japan Export Bank is formed by the government and renamed the Export-Import Bank of Japan in 1952. Broadcasting Law permits the start of commercial broadcasting in Japan.

1951 Chubu Electric Power is founded. Japan Air Lines (JAL) is founded as a domestic carrier, becoming international in 1954. Nippon Shinpan (Nico's), is founded, marking the emergence of large consumer credit finance companies.

1952 The Treaty of San Francisco restores Japan's independence. Kokusai Denshin Denwa (KDD), Japan's largest international communications company, is formed. Denden Kosha (NTT), Nippon Telegraph and Telephone Corporation, is formed.

1953 Toyo Suisan Kaisha is founded to produce instant and frozen foods, growing to become Japan's largest company in the sector.

1954 The Bank of Tokyo is officially designated Japan's only specialist foreign exchange bank.

1955 The Japan Productivity Center is founded. Suzuki Jidosha Kogyo, founded as a loom company in 1920, makes its first small car.

1956 The Japan Highway Public Corporation is formed. Seiyu Stores group is formed.

1957 Japan's first supermarket is opened by Nakauchi Isao of Daiei.

1958 The Japan External Trade Organization (JETRO) is founded to assist in the promotion of exports from Japan.

1959 The world's first electronic organ is built by Nippon Gakki.

1961 Fuji Xerox is established to produce copying machines.

1964 Japan Domestic Airlines is founded, later TOA Domestic, and finally Japan Air System.

1967 Kanematsu Gosho trading house is formed by the merger of the Meiji period companies Kanematsu and Gosho.

1968 Iwai Sangyo, founded in 1862 as Iwai Shoten, merges with Nissho Co. to form Nissho Iwai, the major trading house (*sogo shosha*).

1969 JUSCO (Japan United Stores Company) is founded from the merger of three chain stores, including the Edo period store Okadaya.

1971 Dai-Ichi Kangyo Bank is formed through the merger of the Nippon Kangyo Bank and the Dai-Ichi Bank.

1972 McDonald's Japan opens its first outlet.

1974 Prime Minister Tanaka Kakuei resigns over his alleged involvement in the Lockheed Scandal. Large Store Retail Law revises the 1954 law to restrict the growth of large stores and supermarkets in local areas.

1983 Nintendo, the game manufacturer, is founded as the computer games business begins to develop.

1985 Bank of Japan deregulates the Bill Market as an early step in the process of financial liberalization and market opening. Plaza Accord is agreed in New York to bring down the value of the dollar, resulting in the rise in value of the Yen.

1987 Establishment of Japan's first commercial paper (CP) market.

1988 The economy starts to slow down during the months leading up to the death of Emperor Hirohito.

1989 Merger of the General Council of Trades Unions of Japan (SOHYO) with the Japan Trade Union Confederation (JTUC-Rengo). Crown Prince Akihito becomes emperor on 24 January on the death of his father, Emperor Hirohito. Consumption tax is introduced at 3 percent (and 6 percent for automobiles). Tokyo International Financial Futures Exchange (TIFFE) is formed by the Bankers Association of Japan. Recruit insider trading scandal is uncovered as involving former prime ministers Nakasone Yasuhiro and Takeshita Noboru. The "bubble economy" collapses as the government devalues land assets and non-performing loans begin to weaken the banking industry.

1995 Matsushita Electric Industrial Company sells MCA Inc. of Hollywood to Seagram Corporation for a loss of over U.S.$1 billion, marking the end of rash Japanese investments in the United States. Mitsubishi Bank merges with the Bank of Tokyo to become the Bank of Tokyo Mitsubishi. The economy enters a long period of low growth that came to be known as the recession of the 1990s. Corporate bankruptcies increase, putting more pressure on the banking and financial sectors, leading in turn to further collapses.

1997 Commencement of the deregulation of financial institutions in Japan known as the Big Bang. Hokkdaido Takushoku Bank becomes the only one of the 13 city banks to fail. New Bank of Japan Law gives it more independence from the government on matters of policy and personnel. Yamaichi Shoken, smallest of the big four securities companies, collapses. Yaohan, founded in 1930 and developed as an international store chain, declares bankruptcy. The Antimonopoly Law against holding companies is revised. Daiei forms the first post–World War II holding company.

1998 Collapse of the Long Term Credit Bank of Japan during the banking crisis. A district court in Okayama orders Kawasaki Steel to pay ¥52 million in the first successful lawsuit for compensation by a widow because of the death of her husband from overwork (*karoshi*).

2000 Chiyoda Mutual Life Insurance announces bankruptcy in October. Mizuho Financial Group is formed by the merger of the Dai-Ichi Kangyo Bank, the Fuji Bank, and the Industrial Bank of Japan (IBJ).

2001 Sakura Bank (formerly Mitsui and Taiyo-Kobe Banks) merges with the Sumitomo Bank to become the Mitsui-Sumitomo Bank. The Ministry of International Trade and Industry (MITI) becomes the Ministry of Trade, Economy, and Industry (METI) as part of a streamlining of government functions.

2002 The Japan Federation of Economic Organizations (Keidanren) and the Japan Federation of Employers Associations (Nikkieiren) merge to form the Japan Business Federation. Lebanese-born director of Renault, Carlos Ghosn, becomes president of Nissan Motor Corporation in 2002 in a restructuring drive. UFJ Bank (United Finance Japan) is formed by the merger of the Tokai and Sanwa banks. In May, Mori Hanae, one of Japan's largest and oldest international fashion houses of the postwar period, applies for court protection under the Civil Rehabilitation Law. Mitsui & Co. and an investment fund, Active Investment Partners, creates a new joint-venture that bought the trademark rights.

2003 The Industrial Revitalization Corporation of Japan (IRCJ) is formed in May to help with corporate restructuring. The first nonbank company to be rehabilitated is Mitsui Kozan. The Daiei Group seeks rehabilitation by the IRCJ after unsuccessfully attempting restructuring.

2004 Tsustumi Yoshiaki, head of the Seibu Group, steps down and is subsequently investigated for insider trading and falsifying Seibu Railway corporate accounts. Mitsubishi Tokyo Financial Group and the UFJ Group announced merger talks in July with the goal of becoming one of the world's largest financial groups. This completes the consolidation of Japan's major banks into three groups, the others being Mizuho and Sumitomo Mitsui.

2005 **August:** The Tokyo Stock Market shows signs of recovery. From a Mikkei Stock Average low of 7,000 in 2003, it rises to almost 13,000 after being trapped at 12,000 for the previous year. On September 11, Prime Minister Koizumi Junichiro wins a snap general election over the issue of privatization of the Post Office Savings Bank along with other urgent economic reforms. Following the election victory, real estate prices start picking up, suggesting that the deflation that has plagued the economy since the early 1990s is finally coming to an end.

Introduction

Japan, although still the world's second-largest economy in nominal terms after that of the United States, frequently appears to be overshadowed by China in media reporting and discussion. This is as unfortunate as it is unwise for a number of reasons. First, while China is growing and its markets are expanding, an enormous amount of the impetus for development as well as logistical support is coming from large numbers of Japanese corporations. Major Japanese enterprises such as Toyota, Sony, and Honda, to list but three household names, either are already in China or are in the process of establishing a presence there. The export of Japanese technology will have a profound influence on China's development.

Second, the benchmark of product quality within Asia has been set by Japanese industrial standards. Many shoddy products still emerge from Asia, but countries wishing to export to Japan or to be considered as sites for development know that they must meet the exacting requirements of the Japanese consumer. This in turn has forced them to examine their own production systems and their product standards. For example, Mitsubishi Motors in Malaysia has been producing the Mitsubishi Proton for export to third markets. The vehicle is marketed as combining "Japanese Technology with Malaysian Value," indicating that the basic designs and production systems are Japanese and therefore reliable.

A third point that should be noted is that Asian countries are more likely to adopt Japanese business practices than Western ones. One reason is simply the factor of proximity and regular business contacts. Influence through meeting can be a powerful factor. Another is that there is sufficient common cultural heritage for Japanese business practices to be more easily understood by Asians than by westerners, whose basic value orientations have a very different history. To these factors may be added the influence of the growing numbers of locals employed by Japanese corporations and trained in Japanese methods. Educational exchange is another source of influence. There are an estimated 30,000 Chinese students in Tokyo alone, studying Japanese language, business, and industry.

Japan has indeed slowed down compared to the dramatic expansion of the 1970s and early 1980s, and after the inevitable rise of the Chinese yuan, Japan may slip into third place in world rankings of trade and production. On matters of quality, efficiency, and productivity, however, Japan remains number two in some areas and number one in others. What is not always apparent also is that China's market growth is being supported by long-term Japanese investment, which goes back to the first public postwar rapprochement between Japan and China initiated by Prime Minister Tanaka Kakuei in 1972. If the Chinese find it necessary and beneficial to acquire an understanding of Japan's business culture, how much more essential is it for Western business interests? An examination of the origins and characteristics of that culture is therefore necessary.

THE ORIGINS OF JAPANESE CULTURE

The intellectual historian Ishida Ichiro has pointed out that the distinctive features of Japanese culture are derived from the character of Japanese civilization, namely, that of a wet-**rice** agrarian way of life that has existed and been practiced for more than 2,000 years. Everything in the culture has taken its meaning from this long history, and this must be contrasted with the relatively short period in which industrialization and economic development have been taking place. Therefore, it is necessary to have an adequate appreciation of the roots of Japanese culture. Three terms can be used for this purpose: Shinto,[1] Buddhism,[2] and Confucianism.

Shinto is the indigenous cult of the worship of *kami*, immanent divine beings that exist throughout the natural order. They protect the fields and the crops, and their benevolence is expressed in the harvest of rice, after which the most solemn festival of the year is celebrated. All major seasons of the year are marked by a Shinto festival, and the blessings of the *kami* are invoked at all stages of life, by individuals, families, communities, and by most major corporations.[3]

Buddhism, the immigrant religion that came from India via China, was transformed in Japan into the religion of ancestors. This is evidenced by the fact that the majority of funerals in Japan are conducted by Buddhist priests. Along with Buddhism, which was first recognized by the imperial court in the sixth century, came the Chinese value system known as Confucianism. This was adopted as the basis of social ethics but, like Buddhism, underwent modifications. Nevertheless, it is Confucianism that has had the greatest influence on social and moral values in Japan, an influence that can be seen at work even in modern business culture. But continuity in Japanese culture itself goes even further back, and traits of social behavior can be traced back long before the sixth century.

The following description is thought to have been written around 297 C.E. It is quoted here because some of the features of the profile painted of the Japanese are still recognizable today. If such an old document can demonstrate continuity in the civilization, it constitutes evidence for the argument that there is probably indeed more of Japan's preindustrial past alive in modern society than might be found in most other modernized societies. The document quoted is known as the *Wei Chih* (The History of the Kingdom of Wei):

> Father and mother, elder and younger brothers and sisters live separately, but at meetings there is no distinction on account of sex . . . it is their general custom to go barefoot.
>
> Respect is shown by squatting down. They are much given to strong drink. They are a long lived race, and persons who reach 100 are common.
>
> All men of high rank have four or five wives; others two or three. The women are faithful and not jealous. There is no robbery or theft and litigation is infrequent . . . they practice divination by burning bones, and by that means, they ascertain good and bad luck.
>
> When they undertake voyages, they appoint a man whom they style the "fortune keeper." He is not allowed to wash, eat meat or approach women. When they are fortunate and return safely, they make him valuable presents; but if they fall ill or disaster comes, they set it down to the fortune keeper's failure to keep his vows, and together they put him to death.
>
> They have distinctions of rank, and some are vassals to others. Taxes are collected. There are markets in each province where they exchange their superfluous produce for articles which they need.
>
> When men of the lower class meet a man of rank, they leave the road and retire to the grass. When they address him, they either squat or kneel

> with both hands to the ground. This is their way of showing respect. They express assent by the sound A![4]

Although 1,700 years old, several of the characteristics listed are still recognizable among the modern Japanese, such as the hierarchical system, the deference to rank, the proclivity for alcohol, the practice of bowing, and the penchant for the use of fortune-tellers, even by people of rank and education. Propitious days for starting a business, traveling, or commencing a new venture are often calculated meticulously from a cosmic calendar, not infrequently by a Shinto priest. And, of course, the tattoo marks on the backs of Edo period (1615–1868) personalities through to the modern yakuza (criminal syndicate member) is another sign of continuity. Towns still exist whose names indicate a specific market day, such as Yokka-ichi, meaning that markets are held on days bearing the number "four."

There is probably no simpler way to understand the role of Shinto, Buddhism, and Confucianism and their relationship to Japanese values and to Japan's modern business culture than to reflect on how they are identified and linked in a typical merchant house constitution of the Edo period (1615–1868). A sample follows:

> Clause 4: Far sightedness is essential to the career of a merchant. In pursuing small interests close at hand one may lose huge profits in the long run.
>
> Clause 22: It is each man's duty to believe in the *kami*, the Buddha, and follow the teachings of Confucius.
>
> Clause 24: The essential role of managers is to guard the business of the house. Since people become obtuse as they grow older, the age limit of around 55 should be considered proper for members of the Board.

Several important features are included in them that are still highly visible. Clause 4 states that sound business strategy should be long term in its thinking, a characteristic of Japanese business strategy that still exists. Clause 24 states that the task of management is the preservation of the business of the house, a principle that by implication suggests that the company belongs to the employees at least as much as it does to the shareholders. But most important, Clause 22 gives simple and specific instructions, to believe in the *kami* (a demand for the recognition of Shinto values), to believe in the Buddha (a call to revere ancestors), and to follow the teachings of Confucius (to practice harmony as a central virtue and to respect the order of heaven). These instructions, it should be noted, do not come from the pamphlet of a religious organization. They are stated in the House of Mitsui Constitution of 1722, one of many similar constitutions created from the late 16th century on, as Japanese business began to develop structural forms that contained expressions of older values. Consider the meaning of these individual requirements.

Reference to belief in the *kami* pointed members of the House to the spiritual roots of their culture. The mysterious creators and guardians of nature could be invoked in defense of the House. The universe of the divine could be protective, or it could be menacing if disregarded and therefore must be respected. Buddhism, the religion of the dead and the guardian of the long tradition of ancestral reverence, was to be observed. The souls of the House founders had to be pacified by appropriate rituals to ensure their continued protection. In modern Japan, both Shinto and Buddhism have maintained their independent identity in the form of the nation's 100,000 Shinto shrines and 80,000 Buddhist temples. The relationship between many old shrines, temples, and corporations continues to the present, a survivor of traditional practice.[5]

But while both Shinto and Buddhism continue to play a role in modern society, it is the reference to Confucianism in Clause 22 that is most important for this discussion. To understand the social order of Japan and some of the key values that underlie the business culture, it is necessary to pay attention to the origins, the development, and the influence of Confucianism as a basis for values in Japanese society and business. It is in this that one can best see the philosophical roots of continuity to be found within the business history of Japan. These ideas are usually referred to as the *Ie gensoku*, the "House Principle."

THE ROLE OF CONFUCIAN VALUES IN THE SOCIAL ORDER

Confucianism formed the basis of the Seventeen Clause Constitution created by Prince Regent Shotoku Taishi (574–622) and dictated the moral order on which early Japanese society was to be based. The importance of that constitution in Japanese history is most easily understood if it is considered as a parallel to the role of the Magna Carta in Anglo-American history, albeit noting that its objectives were almost antithetical. The Magna Carta was set out as a bill of rights out of which, for example, the law of habeas corpus emerged. In other words, the definitive concept for the development of the tradition that later found its way from England to the American colonies and became a paradigmatic concept of American law was the concept of rights. The reality of a right became the prime value. This, of course, led to other later notions of rights, such as consumer rights, animal rights, and the long list of rights to which various organizations and campaigns are dedicated.

The corresponding value in Japan, however, was not the concept of "right" but rather, derived from the Confucianism value system, the ideal of "harmony." Herein lies a key point of contrast between Japan and the West that is often overlooked in discussions involving comparisons and contrasts. While the issue of rights has been in the Anglo-Saxon tradition for 700 years, the value of harmony has been respected in Japan for twice that time, over 1,400 years. The importance of these definitive values cannot be overestimated. According to the Wei dynasty records, the Japanese were not, even then, litigious by nature. Confucian values merely gave them further cultural support for this tendency.

Just as society was influenced by Chinese values, so too the business culture of Japan took its moral color from the Confucian heritage. But it was taken far beyond its Chinese practice. The National Learning Scholars of the Edo period[6] frequently made the point that while China invented Confucianism, it never really worked there except in theory because Chinese history was never a model of harmony but rather one of dynastic wars and revolutions. Japan alone, they claimed, was peaceful and harmonious, and Confucianism worked there because Japan was ruled over by a line of emperors, unbroken, and descended from the *kami* of the sun. Japan was indeed the *kami no kuni*, the land of the *kami*. The early thinkers who came to this conclusion did so out of their study of ancient literature and history. Later thinkers saw the political merits of the idea and used it effectively in the modernization process, which will be discussed later.

CONFUCIANISM AND JAPAN'S BUSINESS CULTURE

The first and most important contribution to Japan's social development was the establishment of a stable hierarchical system based on the ideal of harmony. Harmony in the West is most frequently explained through the model of music. In Asia or Japan, harmony is conceived of as a consensus within a group that has taken a lot of work to achieve. Harmony is not natural. It is a state of affairs that must be cultivated. Many Japanese corporations have the characters for harmony (*cho-wa*) painted on a hanging scroll (*kakejiku*) prominently displayed in the corporate headquarters.

Respect for authority and tradition was the second value deemed necessary for social well-being. Confucius himself stated that his task was not to innovate but to conserve what was best in human civilization. The seeming innate conservatism of Japanese culture originates there or, if not originating there as a tendency, was certainly strengthened and reinforced. This links with the third great required value, namely, a sense of reverence for national history and life. Both Chinese and Japanese have a strong sense of their cultural identity and take pride in its preservation and in its practices. The difference between them lies in the detailed manner in which the Confucian order was implemented in Japan. Edo period government edicts on matters of diet and dress, for example, display a meticulous degree of micromanagement, to use modern terminology. The residue of this is still visible in many aspects of corporate practice, ranging from ceremonies and uniforms to specifics such as the correct way to place a document on the desk of a superior.

Esteem for the power of example is a fourth element of the Confucian legacy, a principle that translates into "Do what I do, not just do what I say." In Japanese corporations, managers set an example by their work hours, their dedication to the company, and their clearly determined order of priorities. Indeed, being part of a Japanese organization is not a job but rather a way of life. While in recent years nonmanagerial tracks have been created, anyone hoping to enter the managerial track must exhibit the attitudes and exude the values deemed proper for anyone aspiring to managerial status.

Allied to the appropriate attitude is the love of learning, from which the understanding of a manager is cultivated. Learning makes a man a saint, declared Confucius. This links with the idea of education as a form of broadly based moral cultivation rather than the idea of education merely as a means of acquiring specialized skills. If the contrast is drawn between a typical American curriculum vitae and a Japanese career history, it would probably show how the American had, within his or her specialty, moved upward through different corporations to ever-higher positions. The contrasting Japanese model would be of someone who moves through various specialties but all within one corporation. The point of moving through the specialties is the resultant ability to have a sympathetic and holistic understanding of the workings of the corporation. This in turn is derived from the sense of loyalty that calls for staff to know their company as thoroughly as possible. Doubtless, individuals may have a preference about where they like working and probably show more marked skills in one area than another. Nevertheless, the contrast remains between people who, when asked "What do you do?," answer either in the form "I am an accountant" or "I work for Mitsubishi Corporation."

Two final aspects of Confucian influence in Japanese culture and business relate to social change and to the distinctive way in which Japanese negotiate. Japanese culture shows a clear preference for non-violent methods of social change and for using prudence and caution, in short, demonstrating a preference for compromise. This is the hallmark of Japanese social development. Japan had only one long period of civil war, known as the Sengoku Jidai, which lasted for about 100 years starting around 1470 and during which time there was no effective central government. The emergence of three military leaders, Oda Nobunaga (1534–1582), Toyotomi Hideyoshi (1536–1598), and Tokugawa Ieyasu (1546–1616), resulted in the gradual unification of the nation and culminated in the establishment of the Tokugawa system of government and order that emanated from the city of Edo (modern Tokyo).

Some points of contrast with Western concepts should further clarify the significance of Confucian values. First, there is the stress on group harmony over individual desires. Individualism is a primary Western value and is acknowledged to be such in Japan. However, there is a deep-seated suspicion of it because it can easily become confused with self-assertiveness and often with plain selfishness. Buddhist and Confucian idealism define the individual as part of a group that engages in constructive cooperation for collective ends. The deferment of gratification, self-sacrifice, and group loyalty stressed in the training practices of *seishin shuyo* are designed to place limits on the demands of the individual self.

The Japanese concept of *aidagara shugi*, best translated as human betweenism, transforms the self into a meeting point within a network of human relations. This stands in sharp contrast to the idea of the self as an irreducible entity, which in turn makes the community or society merely the sum of the individuals in it.[7] In contrast, on the Japanese model, the individual is viewed as a resource. Hence, Matsushita Konosuke spoke of human resource management. Ninety percent of Japanese people polled on the subject indicated that they feel they all belong to the same middle mass of society, displaying no sense of the kind of the rigid class structure that is deeply rooted in British society, for example.

Second, there is the contrast between vertical and horizontal emphases in social structure. The Confucian order generated a hierarchical system with ranking according to seniority and experience. The concept of *sempai–kohai* (senior–junior) relations has roots in this structure. Relations become absolute and reflect the recognition of a natural hierarchy in the social order that can never change. The junior will for all his life be junior to those who came in before him and can be senior only to those entering the group or organization after him.

This is quite the opposite of the idea that "all men are created equal." Systems that have no formally recognized hierarchy can have all sorts of peculiar by-products. An obvious one is that it may lead to promotion based exclusively on short-term achievements rather than long-term overall demonstrated competence, which often means that people are put in positions that require greater ability than they possess. This is usually referred to as the "Peter principle" or, more cynically, as "promotion to failure." It can also have implications for corporate organization that could result in the risk of instability. There was actually a book in the "improve yourself" genre that had the question on the cover, "Could you do your boss's job for one day?" "If the answer is 'yes,'" it continued, "why is he still there?" The concept of undermining one's boss in order to replace him or her is quite simply unthinkable in the Japanese system. This is one clear surviving manifestation of its living feudalism, in this instance, feudal loyalty.

In modern business, these characteristics can still be seen. In matters of communication, tolerance for ambiguity, uncertainty, and indirectness as against the Western preference for clarity and finality have roots in a culture that prefers not to be too direct for fear of damaging important working relationships. It might be argued that the evolution of the Japanese language was based on the idea of it becoming a vehicle for that kind of communication. Japanese is not subject/object based, like English or Chinese, and is rather inexact on verb tenses. The use of nuance and the unspoken, or nonverbal communication, is enormously important. Indirectness and understatement are considered polite and appropriate. More attention is paid to people's actions and attitude or demeanor than to their actual words. Confrontation is avoided, and discussions can last long hours until unanimity is achieved. Contracts are usually short and are designed to reflect mutual trust that will work for both parties in the future rather than a set of binding restrictions. It is an agenda for cooperation first and foremost and is open to changed interpretation and ad hoc, case-by-case judgments. Most Western contracts are long and wordy and are designed to anticipate, predetermine, and limit likely areas of strife. In Japan, there is as yet only one lawyer per 10,000 people, as against one lawyer per 1,500 people in Europe or one lawyer per 700 people in the United States.

The very structure of Japanese corporations and what is referred to as "Japanese-style management" reflects this cultural heritage, in the manner of recruiting classes of workers as a group, gradual promotion, the role of seniority, and complex and subtle decision-making processes, combined with the demand for fierce and uncompromising loyalty.

EDO-PERIOD NEO-CONFUCIANISM

While Japanese business in the Heian period (794–1185) and in the Kamakura period (1185–1333) followed these general principles, it was not until the commencement of the Edo period in the early 17th century that the social structure that enforced them was put into place through the Baku-han system. This was in turn strengthened by the introduction of a new strain of Chinese neo-Confucian thought, associated with Chu Hsi (Zhu Xi, 1130–1200). The structure of society came to be based on the idea of four classes, known as *shi-no-ko-sho*, the samurai, the farmers, the artisans, and the merchants. The Edo period government was a military government but with token respect being given to agricultural communities. In reality, the farmers were at the bottom of the social scale, and by the late Edo period, it was the merchants who had claimed the right to carry swords, indicating how society had been transformed and how important the merchant class had become to the economy.

Two aspects of neo-Confucianism are very important to understand how the Japanese version differed from the Chinese original. First, there is the emphasis on loyalty over filial piety. Chinese revered the family, and Japanese expressed loyalty to the house and to the apex of all houses, the Imperial Household and that of the shogun. This meant in practice that the demands of the state took precedence over family matters or, in modern times, that corporate duties come first. Second, within Confucian values, society, the economy, and the entire feudal order were together encompassed as a single system. Therefore, to talk of reforming agriculture, as some well-intentioned scholars tried to do, for example, would be interpreted as presenting a challenge to what was perceived as a comprehensive quasi divine order.

The House Principle and the House Constitutions of the 17th century are manifestations of Confucian values. Following from the principle of loyalty, the houses were less consumed by the need for a genetic bloodline than for house survival. If a son was deemed incompetent or inadequate, an adopted son could succeed. Because of this, many houses survived a considerable number of generations. The merchants of Osaka were particularly adept in this regard. This has carried over into the modern period in what one scholar called the kin-tract system, a combination of kinship and contract. The modern Japanese employee does not have a contract or a job specification but, as the member of a family, has a wide range of moral obligations to fulfill.

CONTINUITY AND CHANGE IN JAPANESE BUSINESS CULTURE

Japan is an island nation, but unlike the British Isles, which were invaded successively by immigrants from continental Europe and Scandinavia, Japan did not receive waves of alien culture that gradually formed historical layers in the process of nation making and national development. Japan did import concepts and culture from its great neighbor, China, but these were swiftly adapted to meet specific needs. Consequently, the dynamics according to which business history unfolded in Japan, while drawing some influence from the outside world, were derived primarily from Japanese society itself as it developed.

This point is the key to understanding the interplay of continuity and change in Japanese cultural history.

Attention has already been drawn to the relatively short span within which industrialization and economic development have been taking place compared with the long history of the agrarian society imbued with Confucian values. One illustration of the point is that the year 2003 marked only the 150th anniversary of Japan's first serious public encounter with Western technology. While the Tokugawa shogunate maintained Nagasaki as a listening post, the information acquired was not publicly disseminated, a policy in keeping with the secretive nature of the government itself. The arrival in 1853 of Commodore Matthew Perry of the United States and the famous Black Ships (*kurofune*) in Tokyo Bay and the obvious inability of the shogun to prevent his landing and making demands became a public statement that the House of Tokugawa was, in reality, powerless and inept. It took a mere 15 years from that date to bring down the remains of the 300-year-old Tokugawa feudal system and to begin Japan's drive toward modernization. The entire political and social system had been steadily declining since the end of the 18th century, and the economy was suffering because of a debased coinage, a series of poor harvests, and consequent public protest movements. The arrival of Perry simply acted as a major catalyst in bringing about the revolutionary changes that ushered in the beginning of industrialization, the creation of a modern political and economic system, and the accompanying waves of social transformation.

Consequently, that ongoing process, the beginning of which is marked by the Meiji Restoration of 1868, is only a little over 130 years old, a very short period of time when compared first to the rise of industry in the Western world and, second and more important, to Japan's long cultural history. Small wonder that modern Japan exhibits many paradoxes that are difficult for outside observers to fully understand. In numerous areas of social and cultural life, continuity and change seem incongruously wedded to each other. Trends of tradition and innovation that prima facie should be in conflict in the modern world seem to be able to coexist in Japan.[8] Shinto priests in the court dress of the Heian period (794–1185 C.E.), borrowed from Tang dynasty China (618–907 C.E.), reciting *norito* composed 1,300 years ago, may be seen waving a purification wand over a jet aircraft newly built by Mitsubishi Heavy Industries or over a professional baseball team before the start of a new season. The popular imperial sport Sumo, which has fascinated many visitors to Japan, is itself an anachronism not only in its appearance but also in the fact that it perpetuates a social structure that theoretically vanished in the process of modernization.

While these kinds of anomalies can be seen in many areas, perhaps it is in the commercial and industrial life of the nation that their existence is the most glaring and puzzling. Reduced to one simple question, it might justifiably be asked, How indeed can a nation in which many farmers still plant rice by hand simultaneously be able to produce highly sophisticated goods and generate state-of-the-art technologies? To answer this question, it is necessary to discuss aspects of the history of Japanese business that help to keep the paradoxes alive.

The discussion can be opened by stating two simple but significant propositions that are widely agreed on by many influential historians of Japanese business and economic development. The first proposition is that there are many aspects of the Anglo-Saxon neoclassical model of the corporation that are not applicable to the understanding of Japanese corporate structure. James Abbeglen, Ronald Dore, George Stalk, Lester Thurow, and Robert Ozaki[9] have all made similar statements on this point. The second proposition is that more of Japan's preindustrial economic past has survived and been incorporated into Japan's industrial and economic present than would be found in modern Western business cultures.[10] The commentators listed have discussed the problem at the empirical level and have advanced their arguments from descriptive comparisons. It is, however, still necessary to probe a little more analytically to the conceptual roots that provide an un-self-conscious and sometimes invisible set of structures supporting the system. One element of that is the way in which traditional values in Japan have survived and been adapted to suit the needs of a modern society. That value system has remained a powerful influence on Japanese business culture, and it is with the examination of its content that one must begin.

THE PERIOD OF MODERNIZATION

The events of the Meiji Restoration of 1868 are well documented. With a stroke of genius, the new leadership gained popular support by representing its agenda as going back by restoring imperial prerogative while in fact they were undertaking a full-blown revolution of modernization, marked by a shift from an emphasis on agriculture to industry and to the creation of a modern military and the development of a modern economy. Unlike Britain and the United States, the world leaders of the age that had undergone several centuries of slow political change, Japan had to combine the change of a political system with industrialization at the same time, a complex undertaking. Three famous slogans explain the mood swings of Japanese society at that time.

First came *sonno-joi*, meaning "revere the Emperor—expel the barbarians." Modernization usually calls for some degree of nationalism to be developed in order to generate a national consensus. In this regard, Japan was no different from any other modernizing nation. However, that kind of attitude would not benefit Japan as a trading nation and was quickly replaced by the more positive and practical slogan *fukoku-kyohei*, meaning "rich economy—strong army." This slogan answered the psychological needs of modernization and led to a sense of security that Japan would not be invaded and humiliated like China. Finally, there emerged the more compromising philosophical slogan *wakon-yosai*, probably Chinese in origin, meaning "Asian spirit—Western techniques." This policy of adopt and adapt goes back to the Nara period (609–674) and typifies how, throughout Japanese history, alien concepts and cultural artifacts have been absorbed and transformed according to the nation's needs.

The one macrogoal was *bunmei to kaika*, or "Civilization and Enlightenment," in effect, catching up with the West. One problem of modernization that remains to the present in all Asian societies is their ambiguity toward change, expressed as the overwhelming desire not to lose traditional cultural characteristics in the process of importing the means necessary for national defense and survival. While debated less in Asian academic circles, which often reflect Western educational influences, this ambiguity appears to have gained some recognition in the writings of nonacademics and indeed among Asian politicians and businessmen. These people represent various countries, Japan included, but also the "Little Dragons" and, more recently, developing nations such as Malaysia under former Prime Minister Mahathir Mohamad. Awareness of this ambiguity, as described here, is one key to interpreting Asian attitudes that frequently puzzle Western observers.

As the process of industrialization commenced, the mass of cultural heritage began to exert its own influence on the way in which developments were taking place. There was relatively little preconceived planning or formal strategy, in the modern sense, to achieve the desired results. At a time when modern international financial institutions such as the International Monetary Fund or the World Bank did not exist, Meiji period Japan frequently benefited from the vision of leaders from the past. In the case of the new capital city of Tokyo, considerable financial resources were available for the development of essential infrastructure because of the *shichibukin tsumitate* tax that had accumulated over the years since it was first instituted by Matsudaira Sadanobu, an Edo period public official, in 1791. The growing wealth of the large commercial houses provided further capital, organizational structure, and management experience to help facilitate new developments.

For example, the expansion of business activities took place not in Western-style through new start-up companies but by already well-capitalized enterprises entering new sectors of commerce and industry and linking up with other "family groups" for mutual support. The kind of interlocking relationships these created eventually led to the formation of the *zaibatsu*, the large industrial combines that became the foundation of the modern economy. These were spearheaded, typically, by a large general trading house (*soga shosha*), a bank, and followed by a group of manufacturing companies that covered a wide range of products. The most prominent of the top-tier operations, still well-known names, were Mitsubishi, Mitsui, Sumitomo, Yasuda, and Furukawa. While the manner of the development was peculiar to each group's history, the resultant end product was similar, namely, a massive block of economic and industrial power that could be enlisted to aid in the modernization process and in whatever other needs the Meiji period (1868–1912) government saw as a priority at the time. Studies of individual *zaibatsu* show differences in the manner of formation, derived in part from the origins of each of the central houses. Mitsui was centered on a trading house, while Sumitomo started as a mining operation. Holding companies were formed that exercised control over all the enterprises, and, gradually, new activities were started and made into joint-stock companies. The Commercial Law of 1890 forced the *zaibatsu* to adopt new structures that in turn suited their development and expansion.

The joint-stock company system, adopted from the West, was adapted and modified to suit the needs of the growing corporations.

While the board technically had control of the enterprise in the interests of the shareholders, three important differences developed that remain visible in modern corporate structures. First, the board did not sit in a purely supervisory role over management but rather became involved in management. Second, the structure was rigidly hierarchical, and rank was given precedence on the basis of status over functional aspects of management. Third, a seniority system was introduced to control management promotions, to engender loyalty, and to guarantee future survival and expansion. This made mobility of management virtually impossible. While these features have survived into modern times and remain as three distinguishing marks of Japanese-style management, at the formative time of early industrialization, they contributed enormously to the creation of an industrial order that was designed to meet the needs of the emerging nation. That the system worked is beyond doubt, as history testifies, and although it was technically dismantled by the Supreme Commander Allied Powers in 1945 on the grounds that it fomented nationalism, in reality that impetus came more from education, government propaganda, and a manipulated and frenzied media. The *zaibatsu* contributed mostly to Japan's economic power. Even changes in the law in the postwar period did not prevent the *zaibatsu* reinventing themselves under other names such as *keiretsu* or *kigyo shudan*, or industrial groupings.

The change in the law in 1997 that permitted the formation of holding companies, banned since 1945, was deemed necessary to assist in major economic restructuring during the recession of the 1990s. The modern *keiretsu*, however, is quite different from the closed-circle activities of the old *zaibatsu*. Modern industrial groups may trade more freely than their historical antecedents and may belong to more than one group with respect to different areas of their business. They have adapted themselves to serve modern needs very effectively and are better suited to the rapidly changing climate of modern global business.

Another element of tradition harnessed to serve modern needs was the way in which loyalty was cultivated within the enterprise according to the House Principle discussed earlier. The rewards and benefits of long and loyal service generated both the modern idea of stable employment (*shushin koyo seido*) and a framework for business expansion. Branch houses were developed, and new and related areas of business were exploited and put into the hands of experienced managers loyal to the house. Out of this grew the need to create specific career tracks and a more clearly defined hierarchy of rank. It was these that evolved into the modern corporate structure, referred to now as Japanese-style management. The government at the end of the 19th and early 20th centuries became concerned with stabilizing the labor market and positively encouraged the large groups of specialized labor, or *gumi*, as they were known to affiliate themselves and indeed integrate with the major industrial groupings of the day. On the one hand, this added to the committed and loyal manpower of the growing *zaibatsu* but also led to the creation of structures that would ensure their loyalty. Modern management in Japan has been the beneficiary of all these developments.

Needs of later times resulted in the adaptation and updating of the basics of the old system, but the roots are quite apparent on closer examination. Recruitment directly from schools or colleges is the modern version of the *kodomo*, or young recruit of days gone by, an inexperienced boy with a tabula rasa mind as yet not written on. Moving staff around from section to section to gain experience helps to create the all-around educated Confucian manager. The modern subsidiaries and affiliated companies of the group, supplied usually with senior management from the core enterprise, strengthens the sense of family, a term still frequently employed in corporate circles. As has been said of Japanese society, the more it changes, the more it remains the same.

UNDERSTANDING MODERN JAPANESE BUSINESS CULTURE

Several features have been touched on, the most important being that authority in Japanese-style management remains largely value based as against functional. A manager should look like a manager, behave like one, and be the model for junior staff to follow. This is quite simply the way in which farmers taught their sons how to grow rice, the teaching method of preindustrial society. The normal manner of conducting business communication in Japan also draws its character from this personal style. Therefore, face-to-face encounter or direct contact by telephone is preferred to letter or e-mail. Visits to offices, sites, or plants are mandatory for good relations. This list could be expanded. In addition to Confucianism, however, there are other important characteristics that help to define and display the fundamental and unique character of Japanese business culture. Four in particular are worthy of mention. These also explain some misunderstandings about Japanese business history that have led foreigners to underestimate the formidable system they confront.

First is the complete absence of absolutes such as God, truth, rights, freedom, and justice. The Japanese social order was from the beginning based on relative role expectations, every one of which was concerned with receiving and handing on life, work, and traditions from one generation to the next in honor of the ancestors. It has implicitly argued that the potential development that came about in the Meiji period lay latent in the structures of the Edo period and that the enormous cultural power of the Edo heritage became disclosed in the transformation and continuity that survived into and influenced the Meiji period. This in itself goes a long way toward explaining some of the paradoxes experienced by Western observers when they view the perplexing tapestry of the intertwined threads of continuity and change in a highly modernized but still, in many respects, traditional society.

Second, there is the distinctive management role of central government at all stages of historical development, either to regulate markets to ensure order or to prevent exploitation and abuses, and ultimately in the management of the balance of change and continuity. The move from one phase to the next is always by orderly and carefully managed step-by-step transition. The Japanese penchant for market control may be analyzed in two quite opposite ways. One approach argues that distribution and price controls make life fairer for the population as a whole and are therefore justified. The antithetical approach claims that price controls, distribution restrictions, and volume limitations hinder fair and open trading and close the market. It has even been suggested that this aspect of economic policy may be labeled more Marxist than China. Regardless of the accuracy of this judgment, the state and business have always been close and, in modern terms, are mutually sympathetic to each other's objectives.

One can, however, take issue with those commentators who suggest that it is government ministries that have been primarily responsible for Japan's economic miracle. The entries, for example, on the computer industry and e-commerce in Japan demonstrate that the much-lauded Ministry of International Trade and Industry has been guilty of making several serious errors of judgment that have not been beneficial to the nation and in spite of this has been persistent in pursuing its own agenda. Entrepreneurship was what created modern Japan, and where government involvement was enlightened, it was beneficial. The dominant figures who forged modern Japanese industry were businessmen, not bureaucrats. To simply attribute success to government agencies is as naive as it is factually incorrect.

A third important characteristic of Japanese business is its innovative character. This forms a corrective to another popular Western misconception about Japanese business history, namely, that Japan has been merely a copier of others' ideas. Cultural borrowing has always been part of Japanese history, but anything borrowed is usually modified and refined, sometimes out of all recognition. With regard to new product development, one phenomenon that can be identified is the effective integration of invention and entrepreneurship that can be found in Japanese business history. Imaginative originality of product development and a large number of originals can also be found in the annals of Japanese business. Many examples could be cited, but one that immediately springs to mind is that of steel. Japanese made very powerful steel for swords several centuries ago, and from the techniques developed, it was able to create a world-class steel industry in a short space of time. Add precision engineering, and the high-speed Shinkansen trains become the result. The Japanese also grasped the principles of aerodynamics very quickly, and the famous World War II Zero fighter took the American military some 18 months to study before production of the F6F Hellcat became possible.[11]

In spite of accusations to the contrary, the Japanese have been quite astonishing innovators. The world's first operation under full anesthesia was performed in Japan during the Edo period. The world's first propelling pencil (sharp pencil, in Japanese) was invented by Hayakawa Tokuji (1895–1981), and the world's first electric organ was built by Nippon Gakki in Japan in 1959. Instant foods were pioneered by Nisshin. The first extraction of oil from beneath the seabed was a Japanese achievement. Such examples show that the judgment about mere copying is unbalanced. The famous bullet trains that debuted in 1964 have completed more than 40 years of service without serious accident.

Finally, there is the unique integrated balance of invention, entrepreneurship, and management. Honda Soichiro found a partner to manage the business and market his products. Matsushita of National Panasonic and Morita Akio of Sony managed their enterprises until they were no longer physically able to do so. Japanese entrepreneurs cared for their products, treated them as gifts of the *kami*, and developed them. The sense of appreciation and concern was never highlighted more forcefully than in the contrast between the sight of a small shrine inside the grounds of a Japanese company that manufactured industrial robots and a Scottish company that produced records. Enshrined in Japan was a model of the first robot produced. On the wall of what had been the Scottish company was its first golden disk, a 1-million-copy release. But the company had collapsed, and the golden disk hung on the wall of a deserted office, neglected, forgotten, and merely gathering dust.

JAPANESE BUSINESS CULTURE: PROBLEMS AND PROSPECTS

There is clear evidence that the recession of the 1990s and the pressures created by globalization have tested the resilience of the Japanese way of conducting business. This in turn has led to serious questions about its ability to survive in its present form. Subjects such as performance-related pay, the seniority system, and what is incorrectly described as lifetime employment (*shushin koyo seido*) became topics of debate in newspapers and in business circles during the 1990s. All the arguments were tied to Japan's competitiveness in global markets. Corporate responses varied. Some corporations felt that current practices encouraged inefficiency and should be placed under review, particularly, for example, in the banking and financial sector. While guaranteed incomes might encourage an easygoing attitude in some cultures, it was argued by others, there was little evidence that Japanese social psychology would react in the same way. Some corporations began to create dual employment tracks, regular and managerial. New employees could choose either a nine-to-five lifestyle or the more demanding (and rewarding) managerial track. This is perhaps a good example of accommodation to the needs of modern industry, typical of a culture that can blend continuity with change.

Certainly some of Japan's weaknesses became exposed. Most notable was the risk of authoritarian "one-man" styles of management that brought down Yaohan, Daiei, and the empire of Tsutsumi Yoshiaki, arrested in 2004. These cases exposed the lack of adequate corporate governance that was typical of the old system. Further, a chronic shortage of lawyers became seen as a major disadvantage to international corporations. Barriers to foreign lawyers practicing may have protected the Japanese legal system but was damaging business interests. Accordingly, over 60 new law schools were chartered by the Ministry of Education, Science, and Culture to start in academic year 2004. While more lawsuits are likely to be filed in the future, it is an open question if Japan will ever become as litigious as the United States. While at some levels it may become easier for foreign enterprises to enter Japan through merger and acquisition deals, this does not imply that functioning in Japan will be any easier or that foreign ownership of a Japanese enterprise will encounter fewer problems in management. Given its history, it seems highly unlikely that Japanese business culture will slavishly follow Western models. The underlying differences run too deep. Globalization may be forcing many changes on industry and society, but as long as global competitiveness is maintained, Japanese industry will instinctively prefer its own methods of operation. While systems may change, underpinning values will continue to survive.

The 21st century is producing unparalleled challenges, but it is the hallmark of Japanese ingenuity that continuity and change should be balanced. Both are always in evidence, and both constitute equally powerful driving forces in the business world. The Japanese are instinctively conservative, but they are also capable of dramatic leaps of change, after which they try to consolidate the gains acquired from these periods. Of great interest will be the relative success of contrasting approaches to the challenges being faced. In response to the problems of the automobile industry during the 1990s, different makers adopted different strategies. At one extreme, Nissan, under foreign ownership and leadership, embraced the challenge of globalization through using English as a tool of corporate communication, combined with radical labor strategies. On the other extreme stood Toyota, preferring a refinement of more traditional methods while demonstrating that Japanese manufacturing was still world class. The intriguing question is, Will the success or failure of one or the other signal major changes in Japanese management, or will both succeed? How these trends develop as the century progresses will be of concern to more than just historians of Japanese business. But for the foreign enterprise hoping to succeed in Japan, in the foreseeable future, there can be no escape from the efforts needed to acquire a solid understanding of what has been symbolically referred to as "Japan Inc."

NOTES

1. The *kami* are the divine beings revered in the rituals of Shinto celebrated at the nation's 100,000 shrines. The definition of Shinto and the role it plays in society is a matter of ongoing academic debate. For the purposes of this discussion, the Constitution of the House of Mitsui distinguished *kami* and Buddha, which constitutes adequate grounds for speaking of Shinto having an independent identity. See Stuart D. B. Picken, *Shinto: Japan's Spiritual Roots* (Tokyo: Kodansha International, 1980).

2. Buddhism arrived in Japan via China, where it had been transformed by Chinese culture to accommodate the concept of ancestral reverence. This northern transmission (Mahayana or *Daijo Bukkyo* in Japanese, the Buddhism of the great way) should be distinguished from the southern Buddhism of Thailand, Myanmar, and Southeast Asia (Hinayana or *Shojo Bukkyo* in Japanese, the Buddhism of the small way, also referred to as Theravada, the way of the elder monks). See Stuart D. B. Picken, *Buddhism: Japan's Cultural Identity* (Tokyo: Kodansha International, 1981).

3. A 1996 book titled, in Japanese, *Kigyo to Jinja*, on the theme of corporations and tutelary shrines, contained a list of all major corporations and their shrine affiliations. The cultic and the corporate are never far apart in Japan. Matsushita Konosuke, the founder of National Panasonic, for example, is enshrined at Tsubaki Grand Shrine in Mie prefecture as the *kami* of business management.

4. Text quoted from Ryusaku Tsunoda, *Japan in the Chinese Dynastic Histories*, ed. L. Carrington Goodrich (South Pasadena, Calif.: P.D. and I. Perkins, 1951), 8–16.

5. Ryusaku Tsunoda with William Theodore de Bary and Donald Keene, *Sources of Japanese Tradition* (New York: Columbia University Press, 1958), chap. 3.

6. Tsunoda, *Sources of Japanese Tradition*, chaps. 16–18, 22.

7. This extreme view is associated with Thomas Hobbes (1588–1679) in *Leviathan*, which defines society as in a state of natural war in which people seek to advance their own interests at the expense of all or any others.

8. Anyone interested in pursuing these theme visually should read Fosco Mariani's brilliant work *Patterns of Continuity* (Tokyo: Kodansha International, 1978), especially the photographic selections that graphically demonstrate the power of continuity.

9. To these may be added, as amplification, a related observation of former Finance Vice-Minister (later a professor at Keio University) Sakakibara Eisuke, found in his book on the subject, that capitalism in Japan is understood and practiced in a manner quite different from that in the West, referring specifically to the Anglo-Saxon neoclassical model. See also the bibliography under these names for relevant texts.

10. Mahathir Mohamad and Shintaro Ishihara, *The Voice of Asia* (New York: Kodansha International, 1995).

11. Ronald H. Spector, *The Eagle against the Sun* (New York: Macmillan, 1985), 178.

The Dictionary

– A –

ABACUS. *See* SOROBAN.

ABBEGLEN, JAMES C. Influential academic, writer, and consultant on Japanese business and management who came to Japan in 1945 and was a founding executive of the Boston Consulting Group (BCG) in 1950. His two main works were *The Japanese Factory* (1958) and *Kaisha* (1985), both of which sustain the argument that Japan's **modernization** process cannot be adequately explained simply by reference to Western models.

ACCOUNTING. The earliest evidence of basic accounting dates to the seventh century. Accounts ledgers are referred to in 1520, and books in existence date as far back as 1615. Double-entry accounting did not appear until Japan's closed country policy (***sakoku jidai***) began to break down. In the **Meiji period** (1868–1912), the older methods of accounting were superseded by Western methods. In 1871, old equipment from the Hong Kong mint was acquired by the Japanese government and sent to Osaka. Books were kept in English, and this policy was strengthened by the hiring of Alexander Allan Shand, a British specialist who taught and wrote a book on bank bookkeeping that was published in Japanese in 1873. **Fukuzawa Yukichi** (1835–1901), a leading Meiji period intellectual, led the drive toward both professionalizing accountancy and developing American methods. When foreign investment in Japan began to grow, so did the need for disclosure, in effect forcing the government to recognize accounting as a profession in 1909. This status became law in 1927, when the term "public accountant" was recognized. The then Ministry of Commerce and Industry (*Shokosho*) set out rules for financial statements in 1934 and applied this to the army and navy ministries in relation to their procurements.

After 1945, when the ***zaibatsu*** were providing financial past statements, it became clear that accounting was in need of both development and regulation. The Economic Stabilization Board of the Occupation, made up of academics, businessmen, and bureaucrats, gradually evolved into the Business Accounting Council (BAC) of the Ministry of Finance. In 1948, the Diet approved the Securities Exchange Law and the Certified Public Accountants Law.

Subsequently, Japan became a member of the Conference of Asian and Pacific Accountants in 1951 and a founding member of the International Accounting Standards Committee in 1973. In spite of the scale of the Japanese economy, the number of accountants in Japan is less than 1 percent of the 150,000 accountants in the United States. In the post-1945 period, fewer than 500 Japanese university graduates became accountants each year.

As Japanese business has become global, corporations functioning abroad have been forced to conform to international standards. Where they have not, they have faced tax evasion charges, frequently because of treating overseas subsidiaries in the same way they would treat domestic branches. The need for more internationally qualified accountants was recognized by the Ministry of Education in the closing years of the twentieth century. Various schools began offering preparatory courses for the American certified public accountant (CPA) examination, and, as with law, university-based professional schools slowly began to appear. *See also* CHOAI.

ADACHI TADASHI (1883–1873). Tottori-born business leader of the late **Meiji period** (1868–1912) through to the **Showa period** (1926–1989). After graduating from what is now Hitotsubashi University, he worked for **Mitsui & Co.** but moved to **Oji Paper Co.** in 1907 at the request of **Fujiwara Ginjiro** and became president in 1942. Although initially blacklisted by the **Supreme Commander Allied Powers (SCAP)**, his talents were in demand, and he became chairman of the **Japan Productivity Center** and the **Japan Chamber of Commerce and Industry** at a crucial time during the period of postwar reconstruction.

ADMINSTERED (REGULATED) PRICES. *See* KANRI KAKAKU.

ADMINISTRATIVE GUIDANCE. *See* GYOSEI SHIDO.

ADVERTISING AGENCIES. The oldest recorded agency, Kohodo, was established in 1886, primarily promoting newspapers and their potential for advertising. Magazines were added to newspapers in the early 1900s, but it was not until Japan's postwar economic expansion that advertising developed into its modern form. By 1990, over 4,000 agencies were registered. Similar to other sectors, over 90 percent of the companies employed 30 or fewer staff. In contrast, **Dentsu**, the largest, controlled a quarter of all advertising in the country.

As with the earlier agencies, the new entrants also functioned primarily as sales representatives of the media rather than as marketing representatives for corporations. Many agencies handle the accounts of firms that actually compete in the same sector. Where agencies specialize in a sector, all corporations that wish to advertise in that sector are virtually confined to the use of the one agency.

The unsatisfactory nature of this situation resulted in pressure to develop the United States account-executive system, under which, it was argued, clients would receive better service. In the United States, advertising agencies had begun, as in Japan, as agents for the media selling advertising space, but they soon evolved into representatives of the advertiser. Because of this change, clients could receive marketing advice as well as develop comprehensive media strategies. The gradual introduction of this system into Japan was facilitated by the fact that advertising agencies were bereft of marketing specialists because marketing was not adequately studied in business or economics departments of universities. Almost one-half of all agency staff were in sales rather than marketing because the two were kept separate. While there has been some transformation in the structure of advertising agencies, there are still traces of the oligopolistic controls of a market shared by a small number of large corporations and a larger number of small ones, still a distinctive feature of the Japanese economy as a whole. *See also* ADVERTISING INDUSTRY.

ADVERTISING INDUSTRY. Although likely older, advertising boards (*kamban*) are recorded as far back as 833 during the early Heian period (794–1185). They appear at a later date in art of the 15th century. The *noren* that carried the name of the shop or business, hanging in the doorway, made its appearance during the **Genroku period** (1688–1704). The **Edo period** (1615–1868) saw the development of handbills and advertisements inserted into popular books. From the **Meiji period** (1868–1912) on, the role of advertising began to be appreciated. The earliest advertisement in a Japanese newspaper dates to 1867, leading to expansion of press advertising from the 1870s on. **Fukuzawa Yukichi** (1835–1901), the academic advocate of modernization, preached the value of advertising as a public service. The advertising agency consequently began as a servant of the media, selling space for advertisements.

One important and distinctive feature of the development of advertising agencies in Japan was their links with the press. Kohodo, the earliest documented agency, appeared in 1886. Several of the major new ones grew out of wire services. In 1892, one of the oldest of these changed its name to Teikoku Tsushinsha, thus combining news and advertising. Others followed, including **Dentsu** (Nihon Dempo Tsushinsha) in 1907. Some new agencies were formed by newspapers that saw direct benefits in their creation. The whole field became unstable through rapid growth, resulting in the Osaka agencies and press organizing a press/advertising guild in 1916 followed by Tokyo in 1923. By 1924, one newspaper was read in every two households, a remarkable level of density resulting in escalating advertising revenues.

When commercial broadcasting began in 1951, it was aggressively adopted by Dentsu, coinciding with the period of high economic growth when the family dream was a TV, a refrigerator, and an air conditioner, plus a family car. Agencies then began to expand their range of activities to include managing exposition pavilions, producing television specials, and designing shopping malls and various types of building complexes. The integration of several functions and services within the objectives of an **advertising agency** is an example of a Japanese institution, externally viewed and defined as an advertising agency but being seen, on closer inspection, to be quite different in structure and function from its Western counterpart.

The industry in Japan is now the second largest in the world after the United States, consuming 1 percent of gross national product, about the same percentage as the national defense budget. Calculated in per capita terms, however, Japan ranks around number 13 in world terms among industrialized nations. Dentsu, Hakuhodo, and Daiko, the three largest agencies, have a market share of 37 percent, and if the next two are added, 42 percent belongs to them. The remaining 58 percent is divided among the other 4,000 smaller agencies, in a manner typical of Japan's dual-structure economy.

AGRICULTURAL BANK OF JAPAN. The Nippon Nogyo Ginko was the first of the specialized government-established banks that followed the creation of the Bank of Japan (Nippon Ginko) in 1882 as the central bank of the modern economy.

AGRICULTURAL BASIC LAW. The Nogyo Kihon Ho of 1961 revised the older **Meiji period** (1868–1912) Agricultural Reform Laws to bring them into line with the changing state of the postwar expanding economy and to promote the expansion of productivity. The motivating idea was to reduce the income and efficiency gaps between the industrial and agricultural sectors. *See also* AGRICULTURAL COOPERATIVES; AGRICULTURAL POLICY: AGRICULTURE IN JAPANESE HISTORY.

AGRICULTURAL COOPERATIVES. Cooperatives (*nokyo*) have a history dating back to the 1900 Industrial Cooperative Society Law. After the start of the postwar land reforms under the **Supreme Commander Allied Powers (SCAP)**, agriculture was singled out for special attention in order to tackle the food shortage facing the country. The Agricultural Cooperatives Act of 1947 transformed the prewar agricultural associations into a new category of cooperative to promote productivity for the national good. They have since grown into a powerful political lobby partly because of their nationwide presence but also because of their involvement in many aspects of rural life.

There are several ways they can be categorized, but broadly they can be divided into two types. One group is referred to as *sogo nokyo*, comprehensive cooperatives, that deal with wider concerns ranging from loans and credit financing to welfare, guidance, and services related to marketing and purchasing. The other type, *senmonren nokyo*, specialized cooperatives, deal with specific market sectors such as dairy farming, fruit farming, livestock, cereals, or vegetables. They are organized at local municipal level, in towns and villages; at the prefectural level, where local cooperatives are represented by regional federations; and at the national level. Groups such as the National Federation of Agricultural Cooperative Associations, the National Federation of Dairy Cooperatives, and the National Federation of Livestock Cooperatives make representation on issues arising at the local and prefectural levels. The whole system is supported by two major financial institutions, the Central Cooperative Bank for Agriculture and Forestry (Norinchukin Ginko), one of Japan's largest banks, and the National Mutual Insurance Federation of Agricultural Cooperatives. The political spearhead is the Central Union of Agricultural Cooperatives (Zenkoku Nogyo Kyodo Kumiai Chuoai, abbreviated to *Zenchu*), which also has many other roles in assisting regional and local federations to implement changes in agricultural and forestry-related laws, sometimes even acting on behalf of the government on a commission basis.

As the percentage of the population engaged in agriculture has decreased, so too have the number of cooperatives, from over 8,000 in 1965 to fewer than 2,000 in 1998. While this is accounted for in part by improved administration, it is also a reflection of steady changes in social and **industrial structure**. *See also* AGRICULTURAL POLICY.

AGRICULTURAL POLICY. The immediate goals of agricultural policy in the post–World War II period were to alleviate a national food shortage, to support the livelihood of farming communities, and to protect the domestic market from foreign companies wishing to export food products into Japan. Once the immediate crises of the late 1940s were over, changes in the Japanese economy began to affect farming quite seriously. To cope with these changes, the **Agricultural Basic Law** of 1961 became the cornerstone of policy between 1960 and 1990 by trying to support farmers' incomes through calculating the production cost of rice on a formula derived from the industrial sector. Import quotas were set on beef, citrus fruits, dairy products, beans, seafood, and processed foods. The import of rice was banned until 1993 and permitted only after a rancorous confrontation with the U.S. government during the **Structural Impediments Initiative**

(SII) negotiations. Heavy subsidies were also part of the law, in some cases amounting to as much as 80 percent. Such levels of subsidy are obviously important politically as well as economically.

The deregulation of the agricultural product business in the 1980s led to a shift in policy toward improvements in the agricultural environment through a variety of infrastructure projects ranging from roads to drainage systems. Since 60 percent of households living in agricultural communities are not engaged in farming of any kind, the future of farming itself is slowly coming to be the central matter of concern. The average farm size has dropped to 1.65 acres, and only 4 percent of the working population is engaged in agriculture, some of whom are only part-time farmers.

AGRICULTURE IN JAPANESE HISTORY. The original and definitive basis of Japanese society was formed with the introduction from the Asian mainland of rice cultivation. Community and religious cults (**Shinto**) developed around this, with **rice** growing being considered a sacred duty. The religious significance of rice has long been an unconscious psychological impediment to the introduction of foreign rice into Japan, just as much as the peculiar quality that differentiates it from the many other types found worldwide.

The role of agriculture in the **Edo period** (1615–1868) was central to the social order, with farmers placed in the rank immediately below the warriors (*bushi*), although in reality they were the lowest group in economic terms. For the first half of the Tokugawa era, agriculture seems to have been effective and productive. Rice became the de facto measure of economic value, with wealth and taxes being measured in the number of ***koku*** each area could produce.

Agriculture and its role was also tied to the political, economic, and moral values of neo-Confucianism. Because of this, even helpful proposed changes relating to agriculture implicitly represented a challenge to the omnipotent wisdom of the government itself. Kumazawa Banzan (1619–1691) and Yamaga Soko (1622–1685), both distinguished Confucian scholars who inclined toward various kinds of reform, found themselves on the wrong side of the government's policy by advocating improvements, particularly with regard to the economy as well as reforming ideas about the status of the emperor.

One significant contrast with the role of agriculture in Western feudal society is that rice cultivation was then, as it still is, labor intensive and seasonal. This meant that as manufacturing developed, it developed in rural areas where part-time labor was available. By way of contrast, the agricultural revolution in the West forced excess labor to move to the expanding cities to find work, which they readily did in the newly created factories of the 17th and 18th centuries. This also bequeathed to these cities their essential "industrial" character. In 1707, Edo was the bureaucratic center of Japan with a population of over a million. By contrast, preindustrial Glasgow, Scotland, had a population of less than 1,000. But within a century, the Industrial Revolution had transformed the city of Glasgow into a massive manufacturing center and trading market with a population of over a million. In 1776, Adam Smith, professor of moral philosophy at the University of Glasgow, published his famous *Wealth of Nations* to explain the process he was witnessing, and thus economic theory was born in the West.

Edo on the other hand did not change its character so radically, and even after becoming Tokyo, it remained fundamentally a bureaucratic capital. In the West, it is rare to find a factory in a rural area, not merely because of zoning but also because excess labor is found in cities. In Tokyo, Osaka, and Nagoya, it is possible to find small parcels of designated agricultural land still being farmed. In 2000, less than 4 percent of the total population of Japan was engaged in agriculture, often cultivating small plots in the midst of urban residences.

Ironically, it was successive harvest failures that weakened the shogunate and hastened its demise. However, government has always treated farmers with special consideration. Subsidies to rice farmers have a long history, and their importance for the modern **Liberal Democratic Party** is reflected in the disparity between the value of votes in urban and rural areas. *See also* AGRICULTURAL POLICY; LAND POLICY; TAXATION; TOKUGAWA FEUDAL SYSTEM.

AICHI STEEL WORKS. Aichi Seiko is an early core corporation of the **Toyota** group established as the steel manufacturing division of **Toyoda Loom Works** in 1934, becoming an independent company in 1940. Its present name was adopted in 1945. It supplies 40 percent of the steel, springs, and forged products for automobile manufacture to members of the Toyota group. At its peak, it also exported spring steel to 60 countries. Its head office is in Kariya City, Aichi prefecture.

AIKAWA YOSHISUKE (also GISUKE, 1880–1967). Founder of the Nissan zaibatsu and successful entrepreneur who took Nissan to Manchuria in 1937, renaming it Manchuria Heavy Industries Corporation. After World War II, under an Occupation Directive, he was forced to resign as president of Nissan along with all his other posts. He was elected to the House of Councilors in 1953 and in 1956 established the Japan Small and Medium Enterprises Political League and served as its president. *See also* NISSAN MOTOR CORPORATION.

AIRLINE INDUSTRY. Three major airlines serve Japan's domestic and international routes, the largest of which is **Japan Air Lines (JAL)**, the second **All Nippon Airways (ANA)**, and the third **Japan Air Systems (JAS)**. The national flag carrier, JAL, originally a government corporation, was privatized in 1986 as part of the deregulation of the industry that started in 1985. It almost collapsed as a result because it had been cushioned by subsidies over the years. After the privatization of JAL, competition became fierce as cut-price airlines quickly took to the air. Skymark began a daily Haneda-to-Fukuoka flight in 1998, charging a fare one-half that of the big carriers. Air Do (Hokkaido International Airlines) also opened in 1998 with three daily round trips from Haneda to New Chitose Airport in Hokkaido. These routes are two of the busiest in the world, Haneda-to-Sapporo flights being taken by 8 million people annually and Haneda-Fukuoka by 7 million. Developments like these forced JAL to expand the use of its lower-cost subsidiaries such as JAL Express (JE X) on domestic routes, JALways on international routes, and J Air and Japan Transocean Air of Okinawa for regional flights. Code sharing between airlines, initially resisted by Japan, became accepted after various types of tie-ups between domestic and foreign carriers were forced by economic necessity in the 1990s.

Apart from the airlines management and labor cost problems, the problem of airport location and high cost has affected the industry. The New Tokyo International Airport (Narita) is remote from Tokyo, and the hoped-for high-speed train link with Tokyo has never been developed. Narita, until the second terminal was opened and the second runway constructed, could handle only 20 million passengers a year compared to Haneda's over 40 million. Osaka's Atami airport handles only day flights, but the new Kansai Airport, built on an artificial island in Osaka Bay and opened in 1994, has helped to improve facilities. Nevertheless, it too is remote, and the airport tax is high. Nagoya Airport was supplemented by a new Chubu International Airport, completed in 2005, also on an artificial island 30 kilometers south of Nagoya. Landing a Boeing 747 at Narita costs almost ¥1 million, making it one of the most expensive landing sites in the world.

All these factors have had negative influences on Japan being selected as a venue for international events. The high costs are usually attributed to the long years of regulation and government dependence. This has forced the airlines to rethink their management policies. One new productivity term associated with the industry and developed by JAL is *kizuki*, referring to a system of management of engineers and mechanics assigned to specific aircraft for which they are responsible. This has helped to improve maintenance standards by taking advantage of the Japanese sense of group loyalty. Even innovations such as *kizuki* will not solve all the problems being faced, but the Japanese airline industry has been forced to rationalize to a degree never thought possible. It might be said that this is one exemplary impact of the **globalization** process.

AISIN SEIKI. One of the 12 core members of the **Toyota Group** founded in 1949 as a manufacturer of automobile components. It also produces sewing machines and knitting machines. It formed a **joint venture** with Borg-Warner of the United States in 1969, Aisin-Warner, which won the prestigious Deming Prize in 1972 for outstanding quality control. It has nine overseas offices and 10 subsidiaries and affiliates in the United States. Its head office is in Kariya City, Aichi prefecture.

AJINOMOTO. The largest manufacturer of L-monosodium glutamate (MSG) and amino acid products in the world, it is a well-known brand name of food seasoning. MSG was first extracted from *kombu*, a Japanese seaweed, by Ikeda Kikunae (1864–1936) in 1907. In 1908, commercial production was started by Suzuki Saburosuke, the founder of **Suzuki Shoten**. Suzuki acquired ownership of the formula in 1917, after which international expansion started with a New York office. By 1982, the company had 19 affiliates in 17 countries (including China, Myanmar, and Vietnam), manufacturing in eight of these. Ajinomoto has **joint ventures** with Knorr Foods and Ajinomoto General Foods. The company has several main areas of production, namely, processed foods, coffees and soft drinks, seasonings, cooking oils and vegetable proteins, and amino acids. Its sales of MSG represent about 30 percent of the global market. The head office is in Tokyo.

AKAI ELECTRIC. Akai Denki is a manufacturer of high-fidelity audio and video equipment founded in 1929. In 1969, the company research division developed the cross-field head and the high-quality GX (glass and crystal ferrite) head, and with this it developed the world's first portable video tape recorder, creating vast new markets. The head office is in Tokyo.

AKIHABARA. A district of central Tokyo famous for its estimated over 600 stores that retail electronic goods, computers, and accessories. Some manufacturers use Akihabara to test new models or technology, and it is a popular location for market research.

ALL NIPPON AIRWAYS (ANA). Zen-Niku is Japan's largest domestic airline, carrying more than 50 percent of passenger traffic, a larger share than that of Japan's largest carrier, **Japan Air Lines**. Nippon Helicopter Transport, the parent company, was founded in 1952, merging with Far Eastern Airlines in 1958. International flights were inaugurated in 1971. It joined the Star Alliance of international airlines led by Chicago-based United Airlines in 1999. *See also* AIRLINE INDUSTRY.

AMAE. A complex Japanese value centering on the idea of mutual dependence, analyzed by Professor Taeko Doi (1920–) in his best-selling book *Amae no Kozo* (The Anatomy of Dependence). It is a valuable concept for the understanding of Japanese social psychology and its influence on business culture. *See also* GIRI/NINJO; SEISHIN SHUYO.

AMAKUDARI. The term originates in the Japanese classics, referring to the descent to earth of divine beings (*kami*) in the mythological age. The symbolism refers now to the practice of retired senior members of government bureaucracies receiving lucrative positions in private industry with which they had connections when they worked for the government. The metaphor of the "golden parachute" is often used to refer to it. The practice is widely condemned but, like many such practices, is extremely difficult to eradicate. Some of the salaries and benefits paid to these parachutists from heaven are sufficiently large to create regular public outcry.

An **Asahi Shimbum** investigation of 1993 showed how **bureaucrats** from the Tokyo Metropolitan government found postretirement jobs. One post, chairman of the Tokyo Metropolitan Housing Supply Corp., carried a ¥1.01 million monthly salary and was given to a former bureaucrat. A **Yomiuri Shimbun** report of 1998 that concentrated on the financial sector disclosed similar findings. In spite of public criticism as well as a law that prevents central government officials from moving into the private sector for at least two years after retirement, financial institutions continued to employ retired bureaucrats as a result of indirect pressures from ministry officials. Some 160 retired **Ministry of Finance** staff and 300 former **Bank of Japan** employees were working for banks, securities houses, or insurance companies that were under supervision of either the ministry or the Bank (House of Representatives Finance Committee Report, February 17, 1998).

The most severe criticism was the observation that the *amakudari* system merely extended the government's employment system and that Bank of Japan branch managers' evaluations were based partly on the number of firms that could be persuaded to accept *amakudari*. It was reported that in 1998, 109 out of 417 former members of the inspection department of the Ministry of Finance were employed by private sector financial institutions. The same practices exist in almost all government ministries. While the banking scandals of the late 20th century along with the collapse of numerous financial institutions reduced the prospects of many potential *amakudari*, the need for smooth relations between businesses and bureaucracy will ensure that the practice does not completely disappear.

AMERICANIZATION. A popular expression that appeared postwar in reference to the seemingly unstoppable spread of American culture in the defeated nation. Constitutional changes, changing dietary habits, and new views of society, education, and life, plus changing social values, were regarded by many as part of the ongoing process of Japan's "Americanization." The influence was much less profound than the public realized. Americanization was also resisted as much by some of the Allied nations as it was by the Japanese.

During the 1970s, conceptual resistance to the concept grew as Japanese self-confidence was restored. Tokyo's Nogi Jinja (**Shinto** shrine), which houses the spirit of General Nogi, famous because he committed ritual **suicide** on the funeral day of Emperor Meiji in 1912, posted advertisements on the National Railways commuter lines with a photograph of a shrine wedding covered by the slogan in Japanese "We Japanese may be Americanized . . . but," implying that people still had a longing for tradition that they could express by having a Shinto wedding ceremony.

It was not the occupation that Americanized Japan but rather the emerging forces of **globalization**, symbolized for many by the "McDonaldization" of the world. By changing the eating habits of children, American culture became a fifth column of cultural invasion. Japanese resistance to American culture's frontal assaults has been strong, such as in dealing with market-opening pressures during the **Structural Impediments Initiative (SII)** negotiation period, but its resistance to investment projects such as Disneyland has been notably weak.

It is unlikely that Japan is any more Americanized than many other parts of the world, and, considering how much the United States depends on Japan for military logistics, it is surprising that cultural and other influences are not more powerful. However viewed, Japan is not a forced consumer of everything made in America, either products or policies, and is frequently accused by American corporations of maintaining complex and discriminatory trade barriers.

ANCESTRAL REVERENCE. This remains an important surviving part of Japan's **Confucian** tradition. Lafcadio Hearn (1850–1904), the **Meiji period** (1868–1912) authority on Japanese cultural behavior and customs whose work remains a helpful guide to understanding the classic roots of the Japanese tradition, declared that ancestral reverence was the core sentiment of Japanese religious feeling. The influence of Confucian values in general and the power of ancestral reverence have been passed over all too frequently by late 20th-century sociological theories that claim to explain aspects of Japanese culture.

Hearn's view of ancestral reverence has been supported by **Robert Bellah** in his suggestion that the ancestral line in both its collective form, nationally, through the ages, and its particular expression in individual houses is equal in conceptual influence to the transcendent God of the Judeo-Christian tradition, hence the silent power of **Shinto** that permeates the culture and that focuses on the *uji-gami*, the kinship-based group that obediently followed the rules of the ancestors, appreciating their blessings and benefits, and patiently accepting the punishment they administered.

At the apex of this system was the imperial institution, source of virtue and spiritual authority. Even the **Tokugawa government** required the mandate of the emperor in order to govern, which is one reason why the existence of the imperial institution was never questioned, no matter how tenuous the family line became.

Japanese business practices, past and present, make full use of the principle of ancestral reverence in a number of ways. First, the generations of a business were traditionally counted with great care. For example, during the **Edo period** (1615–1868), the ancestors of each house, a fact usually stated in the house constitution, were considered divine protectors of the house and its business. The head of the house, by virtue of his descent, could enforce the rules of the house as laid down by the founder without question. The head of the house derived his authority not as a parent in relation to his children or as an employer but as the direct descendant of the founder. He was the possessor and guardian of the family tablets, and he performed rituals for the souls of the ancestors. Such prerogatives empowered him to preside over both family and business. In other words, his authority was not functional but essentially moral and spiritual. For this system to function effectively, loyalty had to be considered the supreme virtue, even above the Confucian virtue of filial piety. While this may be decreasing, family control, such as in the case of the **Sumitomo House**, was virtually absolute until 1945.

During the **Meiji period** (1868–1912), although it was the age of **modernization**, the role of ancestors continued in ways similar to the practices of the preceding Edo period. However, with the creation of **joint-stock companies**, the role of ancestors became weakened, as companies became less and less family owned, although many continued to count the generations.

Mid- and late-20th-century research by Professor Robert J. Smith on ancestral reverence in postwar Japan has demonstrated over two research periods that despite social change, ancestral altars were still common even in a nuclear family environment such as Tokyo. His second period of study found that Buddhist statuary had all but vanished, suggesting that the tradition may not necessarily be dependent any more on **Buddhism**.

ANDO. Meaning literally "undisturbed possession," these were pieces of real estate granted by a feudal lord to vassals to guarantee subservience and loyalty. Ando became a political tool designed to maintain social stability and eventually a tax base for the government.

ANI COPPER MINES. One of a number of **mining** operations formerly owned by the **Tokugawa government** when it controlled all mines nationwide. It was subsidized by the new government after the **Meiji Restoration of 1868**. As part of a later policy to divest itself of operations it could not manage, the government sold it to **Furukawa Ichibei** (1832–1903) in 1885 for the sum of ¥338,000. Furukawa Mining grew out of this and subsequently the **Furukawa Zaibatsu**.

ANSHIN RITSUMEI. This doctrine, commonly believed in popular Japanese religion, teaches people not to worry about daily life concerns but to pursue their religious goals. It lies behind the idea of not making profit the first goal of business but rather pursuing the interests of the house, believing that all other things will fall into place. In modern times, pursuing market share has usually been as important as concern for profit.

ANTIMONOPOLY LAW. Enacted in 1947 at the behest of the **Supreme Commander Allied Powers (SCAP)**, it was intended to prevent the growth of large-scale monopolistic corporations following the dissolution of the prewar **zaibatsu**. Among its various provisions to prevent the growth of powerful combines, a phenomenon that the occupation leaders judged had contributed to the war effort, a ban was placed on the creation of **holding companies** (*mochikabu gaisha*). However, the Fair Trade Commission, established to implement the law, was unable to function as it would in the United States because the **Ministry of International Trade and Industry (MITI)** preferred to encourage the reconstruction of large industrial groupings and a return to prewar oligopolistic corporate structures. While opinions vary inside and outside Japan, the dismantling of the zaibatsu has been considered by many as the least relevant of all SCAP policies, especially when production was nonexistent and the population was hungry and restive. The persisting general preference for large financial groupings with centralized capital management resulted in the law being revised in December 1997, when holding companies were again permitted. Specific provisions required groups holding assets of over ¥300 billion to report to the **Fair Trade Commission** if they planned to set up a holding company. Three other rules are that ***keiretsu*** with assets of more than ¥15 trillion or with assets of more than ¥300 billion in each of five or more industrial sectors may not form a holding company. This effectively prevents the reemergence of diversified mass conglomerates. Further, no group may control both a financial company with assets in excess of ¥15 trillion or a nonfinance company with assets of over ¥300 billion. Finally, no individual company may control leading companies in more than five related areas, thus making it impossible for one single company to dominate an entire sector.

AOKI INTERNATIONAL GROUP. Men's clothing company founded in 1958 by the Aoki family that includes Aoki Men's Plaza, Suit Direct, and Torii along with ancillary businesses. They target the male salaried worker with less expensive but more fashionable suits than are usually found in department stores or tailoring shops. The result has been a steady change in the dress habits of younger businessman through the introduction of more color and style.

APPRENTICES. *See* DETCHI.

ARABIAN OIL CO. Founded in 1958 to help Japanese oil companies develop the oil fields of the Middle East, it became Japan's largest oil producer, having started initially in Saudi Arabia and Kuwait. As a result of a difference of opinion with the Saudi government, it lost the rights to drill in an offshore field that lay between Saudi Arabia and Kuwait, although it continued to drill from the Kuwait side. It also concluded an agreement with Iran in 2000 to drill in the Azadegan field, which it was believed could yield up to 400,000 barrels a day. The company has looked at Vietnam as well and is also involved in gas production offshore in China and in the Gulf of Mexico. Headquarters are in Tokyo. *See also* PETROLEUM INDUSTRY.

ASABUKI EIJI (1849–1918). Business leader of the **Meiji period** (1868–1912), born in what is now Oita prefecture in Kyushu. After graduating from the forerunner of Keio University, he joined Mitsubishi Shokai (now **Mitsubishi Corporation**) in 1878. In 1891, he became a director of Kanegafuchi Boseki (now **Kanebo**), a textile producer owned by **Mitsui & Co.** In 1894, he joined the **Mitsui Group** of companies and by 1902 was the leading figure within it.

ASAHI BANK. City **bank** dating to 1945 that was formed by the merger of the Kyowa Bank and the Saitama Bank in 1991. It had over 10,000 employees and around 360 offices nationwide when it merged with another city bank, **Daiwa Bank**, to form the **Resona Bank** during the restructuring of the **banking industry** at the end of the 20th century. *See also* BANKING HISTORY.

ASAHI BREWERIES. Manufacturer of beer, soft drinks, wines, and spirits, diversified into restaurants, pharmaceuticals, and glass products. It was founded in 1949 when Dai Nippon Breweries was split into two companies. For most of its history, it lagged behind the **Kirin** and **Sapporo** beer brands in market share until the launch of Asahi Super Dry, a brand that eventually overtook Kirin for the number one spot in the Japanese market during the 1980s.

ASAHI BROADCASTING CORPORATION (ABC). Commercial radio and television broadcasting station that serves the Osaka area founded in 1951 as a radio station funded by the Osaka office of the ***Asahi Shimbun***. After numerous changes, it became part of the All Nippon News Network (ANN) and is now part of **Asahi National Broadcasting** under control of the *Asahi Shimbun*.

ASAHI CHEMICAL INDUST. Asahi Kasei Kogyo is a chemicals manufacturer formed in 1823 as a manufacturer of ammonia. It diversified to manufacture rayon and other products. The present name was adopted in 1946, after which it began further diversification of interests. It heads a group of 200 affiliates, including Toyo Jozo and Asahi Organic Chemical Industry, along with 14 overseas **joint ventures**. Corporate headquarters are in Osaka.

ASAHI DENKA KOGYO. Part of the **Furukawa Group**, it is a chemical corporation producing a variety of items, including oils, fats, and foods. It was founded in 1917 to produce caustic soda, hardened oil, margarine, liquid chlorine, and ethylene glycol but moved into the petrochemical field after 1945. It formed a **joint venture** in 1972 with Procter and Gamble, Procter and Gamble Sun Home, to market soap and detergents in Japan. It owns a joint manufacturing company in Malaysia. Its corporate headquarters are in Tokyo.

ASAHI GLASS. A member of the **Mitsubishi Group**, it is Japan's largest glass manufacturer whose products are used in construction, automobiles, television sets, soda compounds, and ceramic products. It was founded in 1907 by Iwasaki Toshiya and was the first Japanese corporation to manufacture plate glass. It developed the basis of its own vertical manufacturing policy by manufacturing firebrick in 1916 and soda ash in 1917, thus ensuring a guaranteed supply of raw materials. In 1944, it merged with Nihon Kasei Kogyo under the name Mitsubishi Kasei Kogyo but renamed itself Asahi Glass after the merger was dissolved in 1950. It thereafter expanded its product range to include safety glass and halogenous compounds. The company's technology has been successfully exported, specifically its drawing process used for plate glass and its ion-exchange membrane electrodialysis process for manufacturing caustic soda. Both have received international recognition. Its headquarters are in Tokyo.

ASAHI NATIONAL BROADCASTING. Commercial broadcasting corporation founded in 1959 with support from the ***Asahi Shimbun*** to serve the Kanto region. It was intended to be an educational network, known initially as Nippon Educational Television (NET), but its goals clashed with the Japan Broadcasting Corporation (Nippon Hoso Kyokai, or NHK, as it is better known), which also had an educational channel. Asahi began general programming in 1973 and adopted its present name in 1977. It is affiliated with the All Nippon News Network (ANN), which includes 10 stations. It is remembered for the aggressive way in which it obtained sole rights for the broadcast of the Moscow Olympics in 1980 and is known for giving its name to Terebi Asahi Dori in Roppongi, Tokyo.

ASAHI OPTICAL. Manufacturer of cameras and optical and medical equipment founded in 1938, using the trade name Asahi Pentax. In 1954, it developed the world's first mechanism for the quick return of the camera mirror, making possible the era of the single-lens reflex camera. Its headquarters are in Tokyo.

ASAHI SHIMBUN. Started in 1879, it is now one of Japan's largest national daily **newspapers**. It has been in Tokyo since 1888 and is involved in a range of media activities, including magazines and broadcasting. It has four main offices in Tokyo, Osaka, Nagoya, and Kita Kyushu, and a branch office in Sapporo. It has overseas bureaus in Washington, London, Cairo, and Singapore with offices in 21 other countries. It carries the Associated Press, Reuters, and Tass wire services and subscribes to the *New York Times* and *London Times* news services. It is known for its progressive and careful coverage of domestic and international events. Circulation exceeds 7 million copies daily.

ASANO SOICHIRO (1848–1930). Meiji period (1868–1912) entrepreneur and founder of the **Asano Zaibatsu**. Born in what is now Toyama prefecture, he moved in 1871 to Tokyo, where he made a lot of money in coal and coke. He bought a cement factory in 1884 that became **Nihon Cement**. From this, Asano, expanded into many other areas of business, including **shipbuilding**, **iron**, and **steel** as well as trading and water power development. He formed a holding company, Asano Dozoku Kaisha, in 1918, thus creating the core of the Asano financial combine.

ASANO ZAIBATSU. Financial and industrial combine created in 1918 by **Asano Soichiro** (1848–1930) when he placed 30 subsidiaries and 50 affiliated companies under control of Asano Dozoku Kaisha, the holding company he created for the purpose. He was on good terms with **Yasuda Zenjiro** (1838–1921), founder of the **Yasuda Zaibatsu**. The present-day successor of the Yasuda Zaibatsu, the **Fuyo Group** includes members of the former Asano Zaibatsu as well as numerous other large corporations such as **Showa Denko**, **Marubeni**, and **Nissan Corporation**.

ASANUMA GUMI. An Osaka construction company started in Nara in 1892, specializing in schools, hospitals, and other public works projects that included prewar installations for the Japanese Imperial Army. It worked with the U.S. military in Okinawa after 1945. It began civil engineering projects after 1950 and moved to prefabricated housing in the 1970s. It has one overseas subsidiary located in Guam.

ASHIO COPPER MINE. Located in Tochigi prefecture, it was the major source of copper in the **Meiji period** (1868–1912). Although older, it was not being seriously worked at the **Meiji Restoration of 1868** and was acquired by **Furukawa Ichibei** (1832–1903). He installed modern equipment and later electric pumps. The result was an increase in production from 53 tons in 1877 to 6,400 tons in 1901. By 1917, this had risen to 15,000 tons each year.

The mine was also the cause of the first major industrially induced environmental problem during the process of **modernization** caused by polluting the nearby rivers. From 1890, floods in the North Kanto Plain covered thousands of hectares and consequently spread pollution all over the region. In 1897, by order of the government, the **Furukawa Mining Company** installed antipollution equipment that had little overall effect.

Pollution continued until the mine was finally closed. In 1974, after lengthy litigation, the farmers on the Watarase River received the equivalent of U.S.$7 million in compensation. It was the first such successful appeal managed by the government's Environmental Disputes Coordination Commission. The incident was known as the Ashio Dozan Kodoku Jiken.

The mine was also at the center of a labor dispute that boiled over into violence in 1907 when irate miners cut telephone lines and stormed company buildings before being contained by police. On 6 February, miners placed explosives and blew up the main gate and then set fire to 130 buildings. Some 181 miners were arrested, of whom 82 were convicted and imprisoned. Further trouble flared up in 1919 and again in 1921. The dispute at Ashio became a precedent for similar disputes in mines around the country, ushering in a long era of disputes over liability for pollution that appeared in many protracted legal actions against major corporations. *See also* ENVIRONMENTAL PROBLEMS.

ASIAN FINANCIAL CRISIS OF 1997. The *Asia keizei kinyu kiki* was the simultaneous collapse of several developing economies in Asia, principally Thailand, South Korea, and Indonesia, although other economies were also affected. The International Monetary Fund (IMF) took drastic action, imposing currency devaluation and economic reforms that resulted in mass dismissals and extreme hostility to Western interference in the economies of Asia. It was perceived by many observers as one of the first clear consequences of the growing **globalization** of the world economy. Subsequent academic discussion and opinion was divided over whether the crisis was the result of bad management and corruption in Asia or whether the crisis was the result of the flight of capital from the region to the cash-starved markets of the West. Japan was only minimally affected, and in spite of pressure, China did not devalue the yuan.

ASSOCIATION OF SOUTHEAST ASIAN NATIONS (ASEAN). Founded in 1967, ASEAN was created to promote cooperation between the nations of Southeast Asia. Its present membership includes Brunei, Cambodia, Indonesia, Laos, Malaysia, Myanmar, the Philippines, Singapore, Thailand, and Vietnam. Together they have a population of about 500 million, a combined gross domestic product of U.S.$737 billion, and a total trade of U.S.$720 billion.

The first Japanese prime minister to visit ASEAN was Fukuda Takeo in 1977, after which relations became close through cooperation in economic, social, academic, and cultural activities. Since 1997, ASEAN has periodically held meetings with Japan, China, and South Korea known as "ASEAN plus Three." The year 2003 was designated ASEAN-Japan Exchange Year, during which events were held to strengthen mutual understanding and cooperation, ranging from economic dialogue to pop music concerts.

ASUKA PERIOD. The early phase of Japanese cultural growth from around 552 to 710 C.E., during which many Korean and Chinese cultural forms entered Japan. The cult of **Buddhism** and the Chinese model of bureaucracy were introduced and established during this period, leading to the creation of the city of Nara, built on the Chinese grid system, symbolically initiating the ensuing **Nara Period** (710–794).

ATAKA SANGYO. Ataka & Co. is a large second-tier trading house established in 1904 as an importer of pulp, lumber, and sugar but that diversified in 1927, making steel trading its main business. It collapsed in 1992. *See also* SOGO SHOSHA.

ATOGIME. This is one typical example of Japan's unusual and complex **pricing** system, in this case a deferred price setting arrangement in the paper and petrochemical industries that permits the seller to renegotiate prices after delivery.

AUTOMATION. *See* ROBOTICS.

AUTOMOBILE INDUSTRY. In 1902, an automobile company was founded by Yoshida Shintaro and Uchiyama Komanosuke that produced Japan's first car using a 12-horsepower American engine. In 1904, Yamaha Torao produced a two-cylinder steam car in Okayama. In 1912, Kaishisha, a company created by Hashimoto Masujiro, produced a car that he named the Dattogo. Various other trial cars were produced before Hakuyosha manufactured the Otomogo in 1920. By 1923, it had produced 250 vehicles, justifying the use of the designation "manufacturer."

Although Japan was not far behind the United States in starting to manufacture cars, local makers could not compete with cheap American imports. After the 1923 earthquake in Tokyo, the government imported Model T Fords that were rebuilt as buses (known as Entaro buses) for public transport. Ford and General Motors production, sales, and marketing systems gave them massive advantages, and both set up Japanese subsidiaries between 1925 and 1926. They built facilities to manufacture trucks and cars from imported parts. Consequently, domestic production was limited and did not reach even 1,000 cars per year until 1933, while imported cars exceeded 16,000 in 1929. This fact, plus Japan's backward technology, discouraged even the ***zaibatsu*** from entering the sector.

The initiative for manufacturing was taken by the Japanese military as early as 1918 with the Gunyo Jidosha Hojo Ho (Military Vehicle Subsidy Law) intended to produce trucks for military use. From the beginning of the **Showa period** (1926–1989), the changing international environment made it necessary to develop domestic production. Some newer *zaibatsu* saw the potential of the business, but the real initiative came from start-up companies, two of which grew into giants, **Nissan Motors** and **Toyota Motor Corporation**. Both were licensed under the Automotive Manufacturing Industries Law (Jidosha Seizo Jigyo Ho) of 1935. By 1940, with foreign manufacturers closed down, domestic production focused on military needs. The two major manufacturers were joined by Diesel Jidosha Kogyo, successor of Tokyo Jidosha Kogyo (now **Isuzu Motors**), as a diesel truck and bus manufacturer.

During the war years (1941–1945), **Mitsubishi Heavy Industries** and **Hino Motors** joined the expanding list of makers. After 1945, the principal objective of manufacturing was trucks and buses for public transport. The shattered state of Japan's factories limited production to only 20,000 vehicles in the first year. The Korean War, however, added impetus to manufacturing, and domestic car manufacturers began on a larger scale in 1952, principally for taxis. Private cars came later. Brief affiliations with European makers produced alliances such as Nissan-Austin and Isuzu-Hillman (both British companies), facilitating technology transfer that was fed into passenger car manufacture. The alliances were of brief duration, after which the **Ministry of International Trade and Industry (MITI)** began a policy of protecting domestic manufacturers. One aspect of the policy was to form links with foreign makers. Another was to create domestic industrial groupings. After 1960, Japanese society warmed to the car with the *mai-ka-shugi* as a slogan, and large-scale manufacturing began in earnest.

Several new names joined the original three prewar corporations. Mitsubishi had manufactured trucks prewar and joined the new group that also included Hino (which produced diesel trucks), **Fuji Heavy Industries** (the maker of the Subaru), **Toyo Kogyo** of Hiroshima (the maker of Mazda), **Daihatsu**, and **Honda**. New factories were built, and production in many of these could exceed 100,000 units. By 1977, Nissan and Toyota had produced 1 million units each, and by 1980, Toyota exceeded 3 million. Pressure from America forced Honda to sell heavily abroad, transforming it in practice into an American corporation.

The cash-rich era of the **bubble economy** that lasted through the 1980s resulted in many corporations being unprepared for the leaner times that followed. The recession that began around 1989 affected all car makers. Mazda, which had formed a strategic alliance with Ford, intending to market Ford cars in Japan, found itself de facto taken over when Ford appointed an American as chief executive officer. Nissan was on the verge of bankruptcy when Renault stepped in and appointed a Lebanese-born director, Carlan Ghosh, as president. Drastic restructuring followed in each case, with positive consequences. By 2002, Nissan was turning a profit, and Mazda had survived the worst. Toyota restructured itself and became financially very sound, drawing up plans for East Europe and China as it continued its overseas expansion. The same was not true for Mitsubishi and smaller companies that ran into serious financial difficulties.

AVIATION AND AEROSPACE. Apart from the creation of excellent aircraft for military purposes, production for civil aviation has never been developed seriously in Japan. Poor sales in 1973 stopped production of the YS11, Japan's first domestically developed aircraft, a turboprop first manufactured in 1961. At the time when manufacture ceased, only 182 planes had been produced.

The **Ministry of the Economy, Trade, and Industry (METI)** announced in January 2003 that it would join a private-sector group to produce jointly a small passenger aircraft capable of carrying 30 to 50 people by 2007 since the decrease in the defense budget affected aircraft production. The plan to produce a small passenger plane was considered feasible since Boeing and Airbus Industries concentrate on larger aircraft and desirable in order to maintain a high level of aviation technology. The research-and-development cost was estimated at ¥50 billion, half of which the government was to provide. Among companies in the private sector that have experience in aircraft manufacturing, the principal is **Mitsubishi Heavy Industries**.

AZUCHI-MOMOYAMA PERIOD (1568–1615). The brief period immediately preceding the **Edo period** (1615–1868), marked by the lavish building of castles and fortifications by military leaders **Oda Nobunaga** (1534–1582) and **Toyotomi Hideyoshi** (1536–1598) and the steady secularization of the culture as it moved away from **Buddhism**. The defeat of Toyotomi's son Hideyori (1593–1615) by **Tokugawa Ieyasu** (1546–1616) in 1615 is usually considered the decisive event that marked the close of the period.

– B –

BABA KEIJI (1897–1961). Tokyo University professor of business administration credited with introducing post–World War II American organizational theory of management into Japan, particularly the Barnard-Simon school of management.

BAKUFU. Literally "curtain government," the term conveyed the image of concealed power, an expression used by the military government of **Minamoto Yoritomo** (1147–1199), the founder of the **Kamakura period** (1185–1333) shogunate. The expression continued into the **Edo period** (1615–1868) and was used of the **Tokugawa government**, although it was infinitely more refined, organized, and subtle than that of the Minamoto clan. *See also* TOKUGAWA FEUDAL SYSTEM.

BAKU-HAN SYSTEM. The *Bakuhan Taisei* was the **Edo period** (1615–1868) ***bakufu*** system, by means of which it and the 250 ***daimyo*** of the various ***han***, or domains, ordered the social life and political order of the nation beginning at village level. Villages were placed under the administration of officials responsible for collecting taxes and keeping public order. Village headmen who were usually from important local families kept records, enforced the law locally, and ensured that tax revenues were forwarded to the regional official.

Since public order depended on uniformity and obedience, the *daimyo* imitated the *bakufu* in issuing regulations about what clothes peasants could wear, what fabrics and colors were permitted, how a house could be designed, what furnishings were permissible, and what foods could be consumed. In addition to ensuring general conformity, this system prevented peasants from consuming more than a small percentage of the gross national product of the age.

Three other features of the early Baku-Han system enabled the economy of the first century of the Edo period, between around 1600 and about 1700, to be economically productive. First was an extensive program of land reclamation that was designed to increase rice production and consequently tax revenues. Diligent peasants who took advantage of government-supported projects by accepting lower tax revenues from such reclaimed land were able to become landlords themselves, helping to create a moneyed class that was able to diversify its economic interests and that eventually produced merchants, entrepreneurs, and local leaders for the future.

A second factor, a by-product of the peaceful country created after the long period of civil wars (*Sengoku Jidai*), symbolized by the ***Tenka-Taihei*** (great peace under heaven) slogan, was the emergence of a market economy, with all its merits and demerits. Creation of niche products and specialization began to emerge, reflected in distinctive products becoming associated with different regions. This in turn stimulated the development of agricultural science and technology. Better strains of rice were identified, new crops were developed, and even fertilizer became commercially available. While agriculture was advancing, costs were rising, and the peasants had to learn to budget carefully so as to avoid debt to ruthless merchants who could quickly appropriate land in lieu of debt.

This led to the third important consequence of the system, namely, a level of economic rationality within which commercial activities could be regulated. This gave rise to the need for the development of bookkeeping (***choai***) along with basic literacy taught in temple schools known as ***terakoya***. Such skills enabled both farmers and merchants to survive and to keep their affairs in order. *See also* ACCOUNTING; TOKUGAWA FEUDAL SYSTEM.

BANKING HISTORY. Now one of the world's major economic forces, the earliest evidence of banking in Japan was the appearance of *ryogae* (money changers) in the 13th century. Merchants known as *ryogaesha* appeared from the early **Edo period** (1615–1868) on in Osaka and Edo (modern Tokyo). Restrictions were placed on these activities, and ***kawase kaisha*** (exchange companies) replaced them from 1869 (just after the **Meiji Restoration of 1868**) as forerunners of the modern banks. These were organized by the Bureau of Commerce (Tsuhoshi), which was abolished in 1871 to the detriment of the *kawase kaisha*, which then began to fail. Only one in Yokohama survived and was restructured as the Second National Bank in 1884. The failure of the *kawase kaisha* created an opportunity for the major merchant houses such as **Mitsui** to commence the establishment of private commercial banks.

Several attempts were made to create a banking system. First was the National Bank Ordinance (Kokuritsu Ginko Jorei) of December 1872 to establish a system modeled on that of the United States. "National" banks were chartered by the government but were privately capitalized. Government banks were 100 percent state owned and controlled. Convertibility requirements for bank notes were abolished in 1876 to release bonds used as pensions for former **samurai** that in turn could become capital for new national banks. By 1879, when permission for new banks was stopped, 153 had been formed. The European model of a central bank was copied in 1882 with the establishment of the **Bank of Japan**. All banks were required to replace their own promissory notes (***tegata***) with Bank of Japan bank notes within 20 years of their charter date. The national banks became regular banks (*futsu ginko*) under a subsequent Bank Ordinance (Ginko Jorei). The reorganization of national banks was completed by 1899.

The **postal savings** bank movement started in 1874 with the government encouraging savings through the post office network. By 1880, a European-style savings bank had been formed. By 1883, 21 savings banks had been established. Bad business practices led to the closure of many of these, and restrictions were enforced until the Savings Bank Ordinance (Chochiku Ginko Jorei) had been issued in 1890.

The government also created a special group of banks to deal with foreign exchange and loans for development. The Yokohama Specie Bank (Yokohama Shokin Ginko) was the first in 1880 in the foreign exchange field, while the Nippon Kangyo Bank followed in 1987 to service industry and agriculture with loans. Similar banks (*nokyo ginko*) were established in each prefecture between 1898 and 1900. The Hokkaido Takushoku Bank was established in 1900 to serve the island of Hokkaido. The Industrial Bank of Japan (Nippon Kogyo Ginko) was in operation by 1902. Its focus was the development of heavy industry.

The number of regular banks peaked at 1,867 in 1901, after which the number slowly decreased. Post–World War I economic conditions forced mergers involving around 400 banks between 1921 and 1926, leaving only 1,417. The Kanto earthquake of 1923 created waves of inflation as the government engaged in massive expenditure to deal with the damage and the general social chaos. The **Financial Crisis** of 1927, followed by the **Great Depression** of 1929, forced the government to enact a new bank law that specified minimal capital requirements. Since many banks could not meet the requirements, mergers occurred that reduced the number to 693 by 1931 and finally to 418 in 1936. The Bank of Japan Law (Nippon Ginko Ho) of 1942 permitted the Bank of Japan to engage in coordinating and providing industrial funds for wartime purposes.

After World War II, the Bank of Japan Law was revised to create a policy board to encourage its autonomy. The specialized banks were turned into ordinary banks. The Nippon Kangyo Bank later merged with the Dai-ichi Bank to become the Dai-Ichi Kangyo in 1971, which in turn merged in 1973 with the Taiyo Kobe Bank (itself a merger of the Taiyo and the Kobe banks). The Industrial Bank of Japan became a long-term credit bank, and the Yokohama Specie Bank became the **Bank of Tokyo** in 1947 and a designated foreign exchange bank in 1954.

As Japan's economy grew stronger from the 1960s on, the banking system began to expand again. The period was marked by an enormous appreciation of the yen from the fixed rate of ¥360 to U.S.$1 after the war to a mid-1980s peak of around ¥65 to U.S.$1. Banks were besieged by loan requests, construction, overseas business expansion, and consumer financing, particularly for the purchase of homes. Credit cards, virtually unseen before the 1970s, and a whole wave of consumer credit swelled at the same time. Economists are not yet agreed on what actually led to the collapse, but the Bank of Japan acted in 1991 to deflate the **bubble economy**, as it was called.

The seeds of recession had already been sown during the period leading up to the death of Emperor Showa, with the cancellation of all social events, such as weddings, end-of-year parties, New Year parties, and any celebratory events from the fall of 1988 until well after his death in 1989. As corporations were unable to service their debts, the term "nonperforming loan" became the phrase of the day, and although it forced many organizations into liquidation, it also affected the value of bank reserves and capitalization. Numerous scandals were exposed involving payoffs to ***sokaiya*** (corporate racketeers) to conceal information about nonperforming loans as well as questionable behavior by corporate leaders.

This set in motion a chain reaction of arrests, followed by a further wave of bank mergers. Between 1991 and 1997, 112 banks had merged, a process that continues into the 21st century. The **Mitsui Bank**, which had merged with the Taiyo-Kobe Bank to become the **Sakura Bank**, revived its old name when it merged with the **Sumitomo Bank** to become the **Mitsui-Sumitomo Bank** in 2001. The **Dai-ichi Kangyo Bank** merged with **Fuji Bank** and the Nippon Kogyo Bank to become the **Mizuho Financial Group**. The **Bank of Tokyo** merged with the **Mitsubishi Bank** to become the **Bank of Tokyo Mitsubishi**. The **Sanwa Bank** merged with **Tokai Bank** to become the **UFJ Ginko** (United Finance Japan Bank), cynically referred to as "another underfunded Japanese bank." Subsequently, two more **city banks**, the **Asahi** and the **Daiwa** banks, merged to form the **Resona Banking Group**. In 2004, the UJF and Tokyo-Mitsubishi opened negotiations toward a merger that took place on January 1, 2006, when Mitsubishi UFJ Ltd. was formed. This reduced the number of major banks to three.

One major shock was the collapse of the **Long-Term Credit Bank of Japan** in December 1998, again through scandals, and its subsequent rebirth as the Shinsei Bank (New Life Bank). These events of the last quarter of the 20th century transformed both the face and the character of Japanese banks, whose credibility was severely damaged by the events of the period. *See also* BANKING INDUSTRY; MONEY HISTORY; TEGATA.

BANKING INDUSTRY. Besides the **Bank of Japan (BOJ)**, the **Export-Import Bank**, and the **Japan Development Bank (JDB)**, the banking industry is divided into three main categories: **city banks** (five), regional banks (64 first tier and 65 second tier), and foreign banks licensed by the Ministry of Finance. Alongside these are four other types of financial institutions specializing in different kinds of loans and deposits.

1. Long-term credit banks (three). The **Industrial Bank of Japan (IBJ)**, the **Long-Term Credit Bank of Japan** that failed in 1998 and reopened as the Shinsei Ginko, and the **Nippon Credit Bank**.
2. Trust banks (Shintaku Ginko, eight), dealing with pension and trust fund management, the largest of which are Mitsubishi Trust & Banking, Mitsui Trust & Banking, Sumitomo Trust & Banking, and Yasuda Trust & Banking.
3. Banks designed to serve small and medium-sized enterprises (***chu-sho kigyo***). These are mutual banks (*sogo ginko*), credit associations (*shinkin ginko*), Zenshiren Bank (national federation of *shinkin* banks), credit cooperatives, and labor credit associations.
4. Financial institutions designed to serve the agricultural, forestry, and fishing industries. There are three levels that parallel the levels of **agricultural cooperatives**. The cooperatives function at village and town level. There are prefectural-level credit associations, and nationally there is the Central Cooperative Bank for Agriculture and Forestry (Norin Chukin Ginko).

The complexity and segmentation of the banking industry is the result of massive government regulation of activity dating back to the **Meiji period** (1868–1912), with bank deposit rates regulated until 1994. In the early postwar years, it was an effective way of directing funds toward growth industries at low interest rates and ensuring that weak sectors were adequately served. With the coming of deregulation, banks, **securities** firms, and **insurance** companies have less clearly defined boundaries between them. The burst of the **bubble economy** in 1989 and the subsequent recession of the 1990s affected many banks that had been lending too much for real estate speculation. In November 1997, the Hokkaido Takukshoku Bank went bankrupt, the largest financial collapse since 1945. The banking industry began a period of reorganization and realignment from the mid-1990s in the face of domestic problems as well as the advancing force of **globalization** in financial markets. *See also* BANKING HISTORY.

BANK OF JAPAN. The Nippon Ginko (Nichi-gin) was established on 10 October 1882 as the nation's central **bank** along the lines of the Bank of England as the bank of banks for the nation. It was reorganized during World War II in 1942 to give the war cabinet full control. A 1949 amendment to the law drafted by the **Supreme Commander Allied Powers (SCAP)** designated the Policy Board as its highest level decision-making body. A further revision, the New Bank of Japan Law in 1997 gave it more independence from the government in the conduct of monetary policy and on personnel. Under the previous law, the minister of finance was required to approve the bank's budget and had power to dismiss officials of the bank, including even the governor. The influence of the **Ministry of Finance (MOF)** over the bank proved inappropriate and excessive during the **bubble economy** period that lead into the protracted recession of the 1990s.

As the central bank, only the Bank of Japan issues banknotes, whose value must be supported by gold and silver bullion, government bonds, commercial bills, and other tangible assets. The bank deals only with financial institutions, accepting deposits, providing loans, buying and selling securities, and acting as the settlement institution for interbank transactions. It also acts as a mediator between public and private sector activities. Government receipts and payments are drawn from government deposits at the bank. The 1947 Finance Law, however, prohibits the bank from extending other than short-term loans to the government. It also handles government bonds and acts for the government in foreign exchange market intervention.

The bank's principal task is to ensure price stability and a stable financial system as the key to sound economic development. To achieve this, it employs, in common with other central banks, a range of policy instruments that include control of the official discount rate (the interest rate of the bank's loans to other financial institutions), open-market operations (involving buying and selling securities and bills directly to affect liquidity in the financial system), and reserve deposit requirements from financial institutions that must deposit a percentage of their liabilities with the bank. The ratio required depends on the type of institution. One other policy instrument, unique to Japan in the form in which it was conducted, was that of ***madoguchi shido*** (window guidance, a form of ***gyosei shido***), or guidance from the bank, issued quarterly, as to the extent of lending to be conducted by commercial banks. From 1954, when it started, until the early 1980s, when financial deregulation began, it seemed to work quite well. However, changes in the banking world as a result of deregulation provided corporations with many alternative sources of capital, and in 1991 the bank ended the system.

In terms of maintaining the stability of the financial system, the bank has a solid track record. The **Suzuki** Shoten collapse of 1927 was the harbinger of a major banking crisis in which over 500 banks collapsed, but over 1,400 were saved. **Yamaichi Securities** (but not its brokerages) was rescued in 1965, and in 1994 the bank helped credit unions and banks that were suffering from **nonperforming loans**. Nonetheless, during the 1990s and even later, many banks were forced to merge or close. *See also* BANKING HISTORY; FINANCIAL CRISIS OF 1927; GREAT DEPRESSION; MONEY HISTORY.

BANK OF KOREA. The Chosen Ginko was so named in 1911 to manage the Korean economy during the Japanese colonial period (1910–1945). Originally established in 1909 as the Kankoku Ginko, it replaced the Japanese First National Bank (Daiichi Kokuritsu Ginko), which opened a Korean branch in 1878. The name Chosen was the Japanese colonial name for Korea. It was managed by the Japanese governor-general of Korea until 1924, when the Japanese **Ministry of Finance** took direct control. It was dissolved by the **Supreme Commander Allied Powers (SCAP)** in 1945.

BANK OF TAIWAN. The Taiwan Ginko was the pre–World War II Japanese colonial bank created in 1899 to regulate and develop the economy of Taiwan. Local currency unification and standardization was completed by 1909, after which the bank began lending to Taiwan's main business leaders in sugar, tea, and camphor. By the 1920s, because of its perceived strength, it became a source of finance for Japanese corporations even more than for Taiwanese enterprises. Its virtually unlimited but unsecured credit to **Suzuki Shoten** helped precipitate the **Financial Crisis of 1927**. It was closed down after 1945 by order of the **Supreme Commander Allied Powers (SCAP)** and finally liquidated in 1957.

BANK OF TOKYO. The Tokyo Ginko was designated by the Foreign Exchange Bank Law of 1954 as Japan's only **bank** specializing in foreign exchange and was established in 1946 to replace the **Yokokama Specie Bank**. The bank was limited in the number of its domestic branches as policy, but its international network was comparable to major foreign banks, with representation in 39 countries in the form of 29 branches, 24 offices, and 26 affiliated banks. One of its best-known early branches was Ka-Shu-To-Gin (California State Bank of Tokyo). More than half the bank's staff of 14,000 at its peak were foreign nationals. Its business created relationships with trading houses (***sogo shosha***) and major manufacturers.

The financial liberalization of the 1990s resulted in all banks becoming involved in foreign exchange, and as other banks established overseas branches, the position of the Bank of Tokyo became less relevant and more precarious. Consequently, a merger with the **Mitsubishi Banking Corporation** was a logical step to integrate the large international network of the Bank of Tokyo with the large domestic structure of the Mitsubishi Bank. The result was the **Tokyo Mitsubishi Bank**, incorporated in 1996.

BANK OF YOKOHAMA. The Yokohama Ginko is the largest of the regional banks and was established in Yokohama in Kanagawa prefecture in 1920. At its peak, it had 155 branches in Tokyo and in other major cities as well as in London, New York, and Hong Kong. *See also* BANKING HISTORY.

BANKRUPTCY LAW. The Hasan Hao, still in effect, is the 1922 law that provides for legal proceedings to liquidate the assets of an insolvent debtor and for the possibility of financial rehabilitation, provided there is an agreement among creditors. *See also* CORPORATE REORGANIZATION LAW.

BANTO. This was the highest administrative position within a **merchant house** of the **Edo period** (1615–1868), to be distinguished from ranks held by senior family members. Small houses usually had only one, while larger houses often had several, with one designated as the *shihainin* (senior manager). *Banto* were permitted to apply their savings to new businesses and, if successful, could be permitted to set up a *bunke* (branch house) or a *bekke* (new house), independent of the *honke* (the main house). Similar to what is still recognizable in modern practices, youths joined as *kodomo* and held the rank of ***detchi***. Through proven skill and loyalty, they could rise to the rank of *tedai*, and finally, after a sufficient number of years, they could advance to *banto*. The modern equivalent of the *bunke* would be a *kogaisha* (subsidiary), and the equivalent of the *bekke* would be a *kanrengaisha*, an affiliated firm. *See also* EDO PERIOD APPRENTICE SYSTEM; EDO PERIOD MANAGEMENT; IE GENSOKU.

BELLAH, ROBERT (1927–). American sociologist and Japanologist famous for his study of the relationship between the values of Tokugawa Japan of the **Edo period** (1615–1868) and the modernization process. He drew attention to the degree to which the role played by continuity in the **modernization** process of Japan had been overlooked.

BENEDICT, RUTH FULTON (1887–1948). Author of the famous book *The Chrysanthemum and the Sword* (1946), she was the first non-Japanese cultural anthropologist to write about Japanese society, albeit based solely on English-language sources, plus interviews with Japanese Americans, diaries of prisoners of war, and Japanese media materials. She never visited Japan or studied the language, but she was able to provide some background that was of assistance to the **Supreme Commander Allied Powers (SCAP)** in the formation of postwar policy. While a little simplistic in several respects, given the time within which she was required to produce the text, it provided valuable material for the occupation to better understand the culture and values of the defeated nation.

BESSHI COPPER MINE LABOR DISPUTES. The **Sumitomo Corporation** Copper Mine at Besshi in Ehime prefecture was the subject of a furious dispute in 1907 and again in 1925–1926. Workers in 1907 demanded better wages and improved working conditions. Disgruntled miners rioted, and the Japanese military was called in to restore order. The company dismissed all the miners but rehired only 96. Thirty of the leaders were convicted of criminal acts.

A local branch of the Japan Federation of Labor (Sodomei) was dealing with complaints about working conditions and poor treatment of injured miners in 1925 that had been rejected. In December 1925, rioting started, in response to which the company fired 172 miners. They destroyed the mine's generating plant, and union members attacked the Sumitomo family residence in Osaka. The strike failed, but the governor of the prefecture intervened and ordered the dismissal of the leaders of the riot with only token severance pay (*taishokukin*). *See also* ASHIO COPPER MINE; LABOR UNIONS.

BIG BANG. The name given to the deregulation of Japanese financial institutions that took place between yen fiscal years 1997 and 2001. Modeled on the similar liberalization policy implemented in Great Britain during the 1980s, it was far from as radical and was hampered by institutional infighting as well as by natural Japanese anxiety over lack of order and regulation. Revision of the **Antimonopoly Law** to permit the creation of **holding companies** was the first stage, and from 1 April 1988, control mechanisms were lifted on foreign transactions. March 2000 was set as the date after which **insurance** companies could enter the **banking** sector, with March 2001 as the corresponding date when banks and **securities** companies could enter the insurance sector.

The goal was to achieve free competition in the market by allowing different groups to enter other market sectors. However, pressure from each industry's representative associations impeded free implementation from the start, giving rise to great skepticism that the whole plan could come to nothing. The **Insurance Council** bitterly resisted the sale of insurance by banks but finally agreed on limiting the number to two. Other sectors also bemoaned the loss of profits, with some saying they would take advantage of a more liberal system. Small and medium-sized securities companies were driven to the Internet to attract new investors. The financial crisis of the 1990s, plus the near collapse of the Japanese banking industry, has meant that a complete evaluation of the process must wait until Japan's finances have been reconstructed and the situation of the Japanese economy becomes clearer than it was in 2001, when the final reforms were due to be realized. *See also* DEREGULATION.

BON-MATSURI. This festival, celebrated from mid-July to early August, welcomes back the souls of ancestors and is found also in other parts of Asia, derived most likely from these Asian origins. It is linked with **Buddhism** in Japan, and its celebration involves lighting a *mukae-bi* (welcoming fire) and later an *okuri-bi* (sending fire). Between these occurs the Bon Odori, the dance with the ancestors that is intended to be a form of communal entertainment.

In modern Japanese society, the (normally) early August Bon festival ranks second only to the celebration of the New Year, when around 80 percent of the population visit shrines and temples. These two events are the only two for which most Japanese corporations officially close down and take a very short vacation.

BONUS. Japanese employees do not receive their salaries in 12 equal monthly amounts. The annual amount is usually divided into 18 parts, of which 12 are paid monthly as basic salary (*honpo*). The remaining six are divided in two and paid in mid-June and mid-December. Therefore, they are not a bonus in the Western sense of an additional payment for success or productivity. They are also separate from *teate*, or special allowances for responsibilities or special tasks undertaken.

The bonus began as a profit-sharing system in the early part of the 20th century, but after 1945 it came to be a de facto method of enforced saving. Employees usually **bank** these with a retirement home or children's education in mind. This system is also one reason why Japan's rate of savings is the highest in the world, a factor that has greatly assisted the development of the Japanese economy because of the large amount of capital available to the government since so much of the total amount saved was traditionally lodged with the **Post Office**, which offered preferential rates over normal commercial banks. *See also* TAISHOKUKIN.

BOSHIN SHOSHO. This was one of numerous imperial rescripts issued at different times in the name of **Emperor Meiji** (r. 1868–1912), in this case promulgated on 13 October 1908, on the themes of thrift and diligence. It urged the people of the nation to unite and to show both economic and personal self-restraint. The main objective was to raise capital to cover the cost of Japan's very costly wars against China and Russia by stimulating national savings, a familiar device of Japanese governments dealing with cash-flow problems.

However, it was also a key theme built into prewar moral education. It further became linked with the values of the **Hotoku** movement based on the ideals of repayment of and indebtedness to ancestors, founded by **Ninomiya Sontoku** (1787–1856), the **Edo period** (1615–1868) farmer and philosopher. The government promoted the creation of Hotoku societies nationwide in order to stimulate patriotism and self-restraint. The Ministry of Home Affairs (Naimusho) was so vigorous in this exercise that it earned the tag "Hotoku Naimusho." *See also* TOKUGAWA ECONOMIC POLICY.

BRIDGESTONE TIRE. Company founded by **Ishibashi Shojiro** (1889–1976) in 1931 in Kurume, Fukuoka prefecture, as a manufacturer of rubber products, including automotive tires (and tubes in the early days), chemical products, and golf balls. Bridgestone relied only on Japanese capital and Japanese technology but quickly came to occupy the top spot in the Japanese market. It expanded to four overseas manufacturing facilities and exports to over 150 countries. The company also pioneered the development of rayon-cord tires, nylon-cord tires, and steel-cord ties in Japan. The company has technology cooperation with Goodyear Tire and Rubber Co. of the United States. The name "bridge" and "stone" is one of the few instances where the modified translation of a Japanese name was successful, being the English rendering of the Japanese characters *ishi* (stone) and *hashi* (bridge). Corporate headquarters are in Tokyo.

BROTHER INDUSTRIES. Established in 1934 as a manufacturer of sewing machines, the company expanded into household electrical appliances, musical instruments, and office machines. Diversification began in 1954, and by the late 1970s it was the largest manufacturer of sewing machines, knitting machines, and typewriters. The present name was introduced in 1962. The Brother Machine Sales company handles domestic sales. Brother International handles overseas business that is conducted in over 100 countries. Corporate headquarters are in Nagoya.

BUBBLE ECONOMY. A term used in the popular Japanese media to refer to the Japanese economy during the high inflation of the 1980s, ending when the **Bank of Japan** took drastic action and devalued assets to what were perceived as realistic levels. To numerous commentators and critics, the intervention proved to be excessive interference in market mechanisms that led to deflation, in turn creating the conditions for the protracted **recession of the 1990s**.

BUCHO. Normally translated as division manager, a *bucho* carries responsibilities similar to a vice president in large U.S. corporations or even the president of a member enterprise of an American conglomerate. The presidents of Japanese overseas subsidiaries are usually *bucho* from the head office. Not infrequently, a *bucho* may also be a board member, a phenomenon typical of the manner in which the distinction between upper management and the board is often vague and ill defined in the structure of **Japanese-style management**.

The principal duties of a *bucho* are to report to the president or his appointed deputy, to participate and chair intradivision meetings, and to liaise with the board. The *bucho* normally delegates tasks that would be handled by a secretary in a Western company. If a letter has to be sent, he will explain what is needed but has the draft written at a lower level. It then comes to him for his approval and signature via the ***kacho*** responsible for that business. In the sense in which the *kacho* can initiate proposals, the *bucho*, by virtue of his experience in different roles in the company, has the function of an overseer.

BUDDHISM. An Asian religious cult that began in India around the sixth century B.C.E. and entered Japan through China and Korea.

Based on information in the Nihon Shoki (720), the year 552 C.E. is normally acknowledged as the date of imperial court recognition. The interaction with Japanese culture took six centuries to complete, after which Buddhism became fully indigenized as distinctively Japanese forms of Buddhism began to develop. In its beginnings in India, Buddhism was deeply concerned with the problem of individual enlightenment, but through its travels north into China, it changed radically because of its encounter with the eastern Asian tradition of **ancestral reverence** and the values of **Confucianism**. Hence, in Japan it became a religion of the ancestors and eventually, after the gradual withdrawal of state patronage, the religion of the funeral.

BUKEHO. The Military House Code governed the behavior and obligations of the military houses owned by ***bushi*** of the Kamakura period (1185–1333) and the **Edo period** (1615–1868).

BUNMEI-KAIKA. A slogan of the pro-Western modernizing movement of the **Meiji period** (1868–1912) meaning "civilization and enlightenment." *See also* MODERNIZATION.

BUREAUCRACY. Internationally recognized as simultaneously being one of Japan's great organizational strengths, it is also condemned for its excessive rigidity and for being time consuming, but nowhere in such extreme form as in government bureaucracy. Japan, for example, still has around 10,000 industrial regulations with which every corporation must comply.

Applications for permission to engage in new and regulated areas of business require the generation of vast amounts of paperwork, much of which is repetitive and of marginal value. The same is true of all government departments and ministries. The government bureaucracy is self-perpetuating, and in spite of attempts to reduce its size, it has demonstrated remarkable powers of survival. *See also* JAPANESE MANAGEMENT; NEMAWASHI; RINGI-SEIDO.

BUSHIDO. The way of the ***bushi*** is the general name given to the warrior cult that emerged at the time of the civil wars in the 16th century and that was institutionalized in the Military House codes (**Bukeho**) of the period and the subsequent **Edo period** (1615–1868). **Zen Buddhism**, the preferred cult of the *bushi*, cultivated deep aesthetic sensitivity about the concept of **death** as a form of "purification" (*harai*) since a noble death could atone for lost innocence. Willingness to die was the essence of the warrior spirit. The most famous text of Bushido, the *Nabeshima Rongo* (Analects of the Nabeshima House), contains in the opening page the famous line, "I have learned that the way of the warrior is the way of death" (*Bushido to wa shinu koto to mitsuketari*).

The values of the *bushi*, placing loyalty above all personal considerations, continued to inspire disciplined obedience in Japanese corporate social psychology long after the institution of the warrior class had ceased to exist. The continuity of its existence may also be seen in the acts of **suicide** committed by employees, sometimes to protect their company from disgrace, from the **Meiji period** (1868–1912) to modern times, although it is less common than it once was. The kind of dedication that leads to death from overwork (***karoshi***) probably originates in the same mind-set. *See also* CONFUCIANISM; MEIJI RESTORATION; MODERNIZATION; TOKUGAWA FEUDAL SYSTEM.

– C –

CALL MONEY MARKET. This is the core of the interbank money market in which short-term borrowing and lending for less than one year is conducted among financial institutions in Tokyo, Osaka, and Nagoya. Call loans are short-term loans made between financial institutions in the call money market. *See also* MONEY MARKETS.

CAPITAL MARKETS. In a modern economy, they serve the dual functions of being a device for investing savings and a source for funding projects that will contribute to long-term economic growth and development. Where the lending/borrowing period is up to one year, traditionally this has been known as a **money market**, a common feature of Western banking practice. Normally, for money markets, interest rates are higher than standard interest rates, increasing in proportion to the amount invested. Beyond one year becomes a capital market.

Decisions made after 1945 to center the postwar financial system on **banks** rather than on financial markets meant that investors could deal only with banks. This in turn made it easier for the government to access household **postal savings** for various types of investment. This system was deemed easier to control but took from consumers any rights to choose. This has been referred to by some observers as a "nonmarket" type of financial system. Depending on one's viewpoint, it could be equally be argued that Western-type capital markets really do not exist in Japan.

During the rapid growth period that lasted into the mid-1970s, the system served Japan well in that priorities could be identified and financed with ease. In the absence of other options, families were encouraged to deposit their twice-a-year **bonus** in a bank or the post office, a form of enforced saving, to contribute capital to the banking system or to the government.

Western capital markets rely heavily on stock and bond markets, which are often easily destabilized. That is not to say that these markets did not develop in Japan. Both emerged, but very much as submarkets, although bearing in mind the scale of the Japanese economy, these are still among the largest in the world, although they are considered in Japan only as secondary sources of financing. The relationship between these secondary markets and their international counterparts has been the subject of strict regulation, a source of frustration to overseas investors. It was to loosen some of these strictures that the **big bang** was implemented between 1997 and 2001.

Japan's three specialized long-term banks and the trust banks were created to be the providers of working capital for major operations in contrast to the **city banks**, which specialized in short-term project finance. The bond market, again one of the largest in the world, has functioned only as a secondary source of finance, although it was increasingly used since the 1970s to finance local and central government debts. Deficit financing was a new idea in Japan and one that led to the emergence of a government bond market that subsequently grew in importance.

The stock market differs similarly from Western markets in that the proportion of institutional investors far outnumbers that of individual investors. For example, in 1980 the management of all pension funds was in the hands of around 30 banks and insurance companies. The corresponding figure in the United States was more than 1,000.

From 1980 on, various aspects of Japan's capital markets began to interface with the international financial system to permit countries in need of finance to borrow from Japan's surplus. This factor lay in the background to the big bang. The collapse of the Long-Term Credit Bank of Japan in 1998 and the general financial malaise that grew out of the protracted recession slowed down these developments. The dramatic intervention of the **Bank of Japan** in the early 1990s, when it pricked the economic bubble, has been the subject of considerable controversy. Some critics allege that it was less an attempt to curb inflation than an attempt to bring Japan's capital markets under the control of the banks as in 1945. The collapse of numerous major banks and the realignment of the banking system around 2000 threw the process into disorder, leaving the world's second-largest economy looking frighteningly like a frail and faltering giant. *See also* BUBBLE ECONOMY; SECURITIES INDUSTRY.

CAPITAL STRUCTURE. Also known as a **corporation**'s capital-liability ratio, the term refers to the ratio of capital to liabilities. A high ratio implies strength and stability. Prior to 1945, ratios in Japan averaged 50 to 60 percent, compared to a much lower required post-war ratio because borrowing was much more easily financed by the major credit **banks**. The net result is that Japanese corporations became used to lower capital-liability ratios, notably banks themselves, which resulted in ratings agencies in the United States lowering their status, to the overall detriment of the economy. *See also* CAPITAL MARKETS; MONEY MARKETS.

CAREER ESCALATOR. Unlike a typical American curriculum vitae that lists the various organizations for which someone has worked in his or her specialty, the comparable Japanese curriculum vitae (which is usually presented on a standardized form) would list all the specialties in which the individual has worked, all within the same company. In keeping with the **Confucian** heritage, Japanese business education is broad and comprehensive and covers most key areas of business. The progression through the company is paralleled by the steady progression upward as the individual, on the basis of evaluation by managers and other senior staff, slowly moves up in seniority, salary, and rank. In the public sector, this might climax in being invited to the private sector for a **postretirement** post.

This upward progression has been affected by impeded growth, restructuring, the strong yen, and cheap foreign competition. As new developments force change, some companies even try to assist staff with midlife career changes, something frowned on until almost the 1980s. By the mid-1990s, government surveys showed that over 11 percent of all employees (approximately 7.4 million) were fed up and hoped for a job change. This has been induced by changes in the economy as well as in social aspirations.

CHICHIBU CEMENT. Founded in 1923, it became a leader in cement equipment technology, working with **Ishikawajima-Harima Heavy Industries** to develop new technology, including the SF-type (suspension preheater and flash furnace) cement calcination process. It provides technical advice to numerous international clients. Its plant is located in Chichibu City in Saitama prefecture, and its corporate headquarters are located in Tokyo. In October 1994, it merged with **Onoda Cement** to form Chichibu-Onoda Cement, Japan's largest cement maker.

CHINDOYA. During the **Edo period** (1615–1868), it was a form of advertising a new business in which costumed people, usually three, beat a drum and announced the opening date and place, carrying a banner displaying the same information. It is still used in street advertising campaigns in some cities.

CHISSO CORPORATION. Founded originally as Nippon Nitrogen Fertilizer Co. (Nippon Chisso Hiryo), the core operation of the Nitchitsu group led by Nogushi Shitagau (1873–1944), it controlled 50 chemical companies in Japan and Korea before World War II. It continued as a manufacturer of industrial chemicals and fertilizers and became notorious over the discharge of chemical waste, particularly mercury, into the ocean from its factory in Minamata (Kumamoto prefecture). The Minamata disease first appeared in the 1950s, forcing residents to take legal action when the company denied any wrongdoing. The Kumamoto District Court ruled in favor of the plaintiffs in 1973 and again in 1981, ordering damages of over U.S.$200 million. The head office is in Tokyo. *See also* ENVIRONMENTAL PROBLEMS.

CHIYODA CHEMICAL ENGINEERING & CONSTRUCTION. Chiyoda Kako Kensetsu, the nation's largest builder of oil and natural gas plants, was founded in 1948 by former members of Mistubishi Oil. It began building seaport oil refineries and started its overseas operations in Brazil in 1959, after which it quickly expanded into Korea, Southeast Asia, the Middle East, and Eastern Europe. Its main customers are oil-producing regions of the world, and subsidiaries have been set up in the United States, Singapore, Iran, and Saudia Arabia. While its principal corporate shareholders are members of the **Mitsubishi group**, its management is quite independent. Its headquarters are in Tokyo.

CHOAI. The **Edo Period** (1615–1868) bookkeeping system used in shops and merchant houses. *See also* ACCOUNTING.

CHOREI. Motivational rituals characteristic of **Japanese-style management** that takes the form of a company morning assembly at which the president or section leader gives greetings and an exhortation for the day. It may also include some physical exercises to music, singing the company anthem (*shaka*), or reciting the company creed (*shakun*). *See also* SHAZE.

CHORI CO., LTD. A late **Edo period** (1615–1868) Osaka-based trading house established in 1861 that handled textiles, chemical products, machinery, and a variety of general goods. Its products in the field of synthetic fibers were made principally by **Toray Industries**, **Asahi Chemical Industry**, and Teijin. It currently engages in life sciences research. At its peak, it had 22 overseas offices and was engaged in 14 **joint ventures**. The head office is in Osaka. *See also* SOGA SHOSHA.

CHUBU ELECTRIC POWER. Chubu Denryoku was established in 1951 and serves Shizuoka, Aichi, Gifu, Mie, and Nagano prefectures. Capitalization was drawn from the Chubu Power Distribution Co. and the Japan Electric Generation & Transmission Co. and was created as part of the postwar rationalization of the industry. It ranks third in size behind the **Tokyo Electric Power Company (TEPCO)** and the **Kansai Electric Power Company**. Corporate headquarters are in Nagoya.

CHUGEN. Formally referred to as *ochugen*, these are midyear gifts exchanged between people and organizations. *See also* GIFT-GIVING CULTURE.

CHU HSI or ZHU XI (1132–1200). He was the founder of a neo-Confucian intellectual movement in China that was imported by the **Tokugawa government** as the basis of its sociopolitical system of thought. It was known as Rigaku (the Study of Rational Principles). Chu Hsi's social thought became the basis of the entire **Edo period** (1615–1868) social order, and, with some changes, it also became the foundation of Yoshikawa Shinto. Until the Edo period, Confucian values had been closely linked to **Buddhism** from the time of the Seventeen Clause Constitution of Shotoku Taishi (574–622). After the early Edo period, **Confucianism** and **Shinto** became linked as the values and cosmology of Chu Hsi became associated with Shinto, which fitted the **Tokugawa Feudal Government**'s preference for syncretism over the discrete identity of religious groups.

CHU-SHO KIGYO. The term refers to the small to medium-sized enterprises that account for over 90 percent of all Japanese corporations. While many are independent, a large percentage belong to a ***keiretsu***, or some kind of hierarchically structured industrial grouping that provides them with their core business. Small businesses usually number 20 or fewer employees, while medium-sized corporations may employ from 30 to over 100 employees. There are only around 2,000 major **corporations** employing more than 1,000 staff. Most of the remainder, either directly or indirectly, depend on them.

CITIZEN WATCH. Established in 1930, it is one of the three largest domestic watchmakers. It expanded into lens shutters, adding machines, and machine tools. During World War II, it manufactured weapons parts but reverted to watches after 1945. It formed a tie-up with Bulova, the American watchmaker, after which it expanded into South Korea, Taiwan, Hong Kong, and Mexico. Headquarters are in Tokyo.

C. ITOH & CO. Itoh-chu Shoji is a major comprehensive trading house (***sogo shosha***) that traces a common origin with **Marubeni** to a company founded in 1858 by Itoh Chubei, who began the business of selling hemp to the outlying provinces. During the **Meiji period** (1868–1912), he expanded into cotton and textile trading and in 1884 moved into international trade. After the war, the company was divided into C. Itoh & Co. and Marubeni Corporation. Thus, it was not until 1949 that their modern identity was established following the breakup of a wartime merger of corporations known as Taiken Industries. C. Itoh ranked third in size among the top houses in the 1940s and diversified into machinery and chemicals in support of postwar reconstruction. It expanded to 70 overseas branches and 43 overseas affiliates. Headquarters are in Osaka and Tokyo.

CITY BANKS. The largest commercial banks in Japan. In 1980, there were 13, which had been reduced to 10 by 1997 and eight by 2000. Following the principle enunciated by the Bank for the International Settlements in 1992 that banks should have a minimal capital adequacy of 8 percent (net worth in relation to deposits), the Japanese **banking industry** was forced to restructure. By 2002, the number had been further reduced to five. These were the **Resona Holdings**, the **Mizuho Financial Group**, the **Sumitomo-Mitsui Financial Group**, the **Mitsubishi Tokyo Financial Group**, and **UFJ Holdings**. The Mitsubishi Tokyo Financial Group and UFJ Holdings merged in 2006 as the Mitsubishi UFJ Bank, creating a megabank with assets of ¥190 trillion, sufficient to give it global status. The only one of the original 13 to collapse was the smallest, the **Hokkaido Takushoku Bank**, which failed in 1997. *See also* BANKING HISTORY.

COCA-COLA (JAPAN) LTD. A U.S. soft-drink maker that grew successfully in Japan after World War II and expanded its range to include sports drinks and the popular bottled Chinese tea, *uroncha*.

Its primary task has been to market the Coca-Cola brand in Japan and in neighboring Asian countries, which it has done to outstrip its main U.S. domestic rival, Pepsi.

COMMERCIAL CODE. The Shoho was one instrument of the policy that lay behind Japan's **modernization** process that commenced in earnest after the **Meiji Restoration of 1868**. It is comprised of the Constitution, the Civil Code, and the Criminal Code. Like many institutions developed in Japan at the time, after an initial flirtation with Anglo-Saxon ideas, the German model was followed, Germany being perceived in socioeconomic terms as more similar to Japan in the stage of its development. Philosophical thought, principally the philosophy of law, jurisprudence, and military discipline and strategy, were notable examples. The Commercial Code was also based on the German Commercial Code. The old Commercial Code was drafted by Karl Friedrich Hermann Roesler in 1890. A newer code was approved in 1899 that more adequately reflected existing Japanese business practices.

The post–World War II changes were influenced by a number of factors, including the **Antimonopoly Law of 1947**, the abolition of **holding companies**, the dissolution of the ***zaibatsu***, and longer-term moves to standardize **accounting** practice. The Commercial Code is under the administration of the Ministry of Justice, while other commercial laws and rules are under the **Ministry of Finance**.

COMMERCIAL HIGH SCHOOLS. Shogyo Kotogakko are commercial high schools that usually date to the **Meiji period** (1868–1912) in which engineering, accounting, and business courses were taught to prepare students for careers in these fields. Although postwar educational reform tried to liberalize and broaden the base of **education**, many of these schools continued to follow their specialized practices while combining them with other studies. Many still have links with **corporations** that traditionally recruited from them.

COMMERCIAL INSTRUMENTS. Both Tegata Ho (Bills and Notes Law) and Kogitte Ho (Checks Law) have existed since 1934 and were based on international conventions agreed in 1930 and 1931 and remain fundamentally in line with them to the present.

COMMERCIAL PAPER MARKET. Unsecured promissory notes (CPs) began to be issued by corporations with high credit rankings in November 1987 to raise short-term funds. With a face value of ¥100 million and a maturity date of between two weeks and nine months, it is a convenient and inexpensive way of raising capital. Sale is through official dealers such as banks and security houses, and they are bought only by large corporations and major trading houses (***sogo shosha***). *See also* CAPITAL MARKETS; MONEY MARKETS.

COMMODITY MARKETS. Japan boasts the world's first futures market, the **Dojima Rice Market**, opened in Osaka in 1731. Modern commodity markets are relatively small if judged by New York or London standards, although the largest volume of platinum in the world is traded in Japan. There are a total of 12 markets, the major being the Tokyo Commodity Exchange for Industry (TOCOM) and the Tokyo Grain Exchange, which together deal with 70 percent of total commodity trading nationwide. The remainder are comparatively small. The former **Ministry of International Trade and Industry (MITI**, now **METI)** oversees the trading of metals and industrial products, while the Ministry of Agriculture, Forestry and Fisheries covers agricultural products.

The Nikkei Commodity Futures Index reflects the overall price level of traded commodity futures. Precious metals showed the greatest increase in volume traded between the mid-1980s and the end of the 20th century. In 1992, a commodity fund market was opened to the subsidiaries of **banks** and brokerages that were thus enabled to set up funds, sell shares to investors, and manage the funds in the commodity futures market. A preference exists for this kind of investing because it is less risky than securities, and it matures within five years. *See also* STOCK EXCHANGES.

COMPUTER INDUSTRY. Japan's first computer development program dates to 1947 and was set up by Osaka University. The first digital computer was not produced until 1956. Sperry Rand had developed the first in the United States in 1946. After the first export of American computers to Japan in 1954, the **Ministry of International Trade and Industry (MITI)** set up a Research Committee on the

Computer to coordinate industry development. It was not until the 1960s that the computer industry was given serious attention. **IBM** was the first foreign firm to be permitted to manufacture computers in Japan under conditions that included licensing agreements. Thirteen Japanese corporations immediately entered cross-licensing agreements with IBM, and the basis of the modern industry had come into existence.

Four instruments of policy were employed to develop the industry. These were protectionism, financial support, state-sponsored research-and-development projects, and a quasi-governmental computer leasing company, Japan Electronic Computer Company (JECC), created in 1961 to facilitate computer usage. The company bought computers that were requested by users and rented them for at least 15 months at reasonable fees. The maker was asked to buy the computer back when the lease ended. This gave Japanese manufacturers some return on investment. The company was busiest between 1961 and 1981, the early years of expansion in the industry. The rate of subsidy of the industry was not high by American standards, for example, but was high in comparison to what corporations were spending.

The period 1960–1970 was devoted to improvement of hardware with IBM as the ideal being pursued. Through shared research and cooperative projects (e.g., the New Series Project of 1972–1976 and the VSLI Project of 1976–1979), **Fujitsu**, **Hitachi**, and **Nippon Denki (NEC)** made enormous strides forward. This in turn created the need for a semiconductor industry of matching quality. American corporations were working on bipolar semiconductors from the 1960s on, while Japanese corporations guided by MITI began to work on memory semiconductors (DRAMS), which were used in calculators and timepieces. Generally, software was less a priority than hardware, a characteristic that remained until the 1990s. An incident in mid-1982, when Fujitsu and Hitachi were caught in an FBI sting operation, stealing technology from IBM brought such borrowing to an end, and licensing fees had to be paid to IBM. Various strategies were attempted, including the creation of a Japanese operating system (TRON) that was minimally successful. The real change of fortune came with the move of the Japanese manufacturers into the realm of supercomputers, supported by government funds for research and development. A further development that disadvantaged the Japanese manufacturers was the growing demand for smaller and compact computers. Other aspects of the **electronics industry** kept the corporations alive until they could catch up with the trend. One further handicap they faced was their locked-in disparate systems in a market environment where fragmentation and internationally accepted standards of compatibility were being preferred. Japanese computer manufacturers finally decided to pursue international standards in the industry. This was compounded by the explosion of the Internet and many new forms of software development.

Toward the end of the 20th century, Japanese manufacturers found themselves struggling to resist Western domination of the industry. The LINUX operating system was developed and made available as a give-away to buyers, but various problems in LINUX that led to it being branded not user friendly placed limitations on its potential. Some argue that Japan has failed in the computer industry through lack of creativity, India and China being cited as being more progressive in respect of nurturing software producers.

Nevertheless, Japan's enormous business in semiconductors, supercomputers, and component supply is second only to the United States. Apart from the United States, Japan remains the only country with a truly viable and competitive computer industry. The real competition began coming from South Korea and Taiwan because of their cheaper production of component and memory chips. The industry at the turn of the century was facing the challenge of how to make the transition from success in hardware to success in software for telecommunications and Internet-related technologies. The recession of the 1990s has had the effect of slowing down the pace of development, a factor that may cost the industry dearly in the future.

CONFUCIANISM AND NEO-CONFUCIANISM. Confucian values entered Japan with **Buddhism** and are evident in the Seventeen Clause Constitution of Shotoku Taishi (574–622), in reality a set of moral guidelines for national well-being. The emphasis on harmony is one of the lasting traces of Confucian influence in Japanese culture.

Confucianism may never have existed independently after its initial entrance to Japan along with Buddhism, and it may also have been more closely linked to Buddhism during its first few hundred years in Japan. However, by the **Edo period** (1615–1868), a Shinto–Confucian synthesis had begun to emerge that came to be highly influential in creating the values of premodern Japan and that helped to provide the foundations of modern Japanese social values. This integration of Shinto and neo-Confucian values began during the early Edo period and was based on the thought of **Chu Hsi** (1132–1200), whose system of thought was most congenial to the goals of the **Tokugawa government**. It was encouraged and developed by the government philosopher Hayashi Razan (1583–1687), who created a syncretistic system that linked Confucian values with Shinto ***kami***. One basic shift of emphasis within the Confucian hierarchy of values implemented by the Tokugawa government was to place the ruler/subject relation above that of husband/wife, making the loyalty of vassal to master the ultimately most important social value.

As the era progressed, various expressions of the basic concepts began to appear at the popular level and in this way seeped into popular consciousness. Thinkers such as Ishida Baigan (1685–1744), Kaibara Ekken (1630–1714), and **Ninomiya Sontoku** (1787–1856) created movements and fostered ideals that reflected Confucian values, distilled for consumption at the popular level. It is through the values created by these thinkers that Japan found the ideological and psychological basis for the development of the **modernization** program of the **Meiji period** (1868–1912). Scholars such as **Robert Bellah** have even tried to draw comparisons between these and the Protestant work ethic that the early sociologist Max Weber (1864–1920) identified as an essential ingredient of the modernization of the Western world. (See also the introduction to this volume.) *See also* HUMAN NATURE IN CONFUCIANISM.

CONSTRUCTION INDUSTRY IN JAPAN. This is the largest sector by number of companies in the Japanese economy (over 550,000) but the most complex because of many kinds of links, not least of all with ***yakuza*** and other corrupting influences that have a long history. The industry represents 15 percent of gross domestic product and in actual size is larger than those of the United States and Western

Europe combined. It is also the nation's largest employer (over 10 percent of the labor force). The modern industry dates largely to the **Meiji period** (1868–1912), although **Shimizu Kensetsu** (founded in 1804) and Kajima Kensetsu (founded in 1840) can trace their origins to the **Edo period** (1615–1868). The five major firms are Kajima, Obayashi Gumi, Shimizu, **Taisei Kensetsu**, and **Takenaka Komuten**.

All of the older major firms were able to draw on a legacy of building and civil engineering projects that date back to the 17th century, such as the buildings of bridges, roads, castles, temples, and land reclamation. All of these projects entail complex socioeconomic management for their execution, competence in which has proven a major asset in the modern period. At the lower end of the small subcontractors, many are still *gumi* (small groups) of carpenters in the traditional sense, who do piece work for a living along with subcontracted projects from the next tier up. Below the top five is a large tier of second-level corporations, the biggest of which is **Kumagai Gumi**, Japan's largest overseas contractor.

In the post–World War II period, the industry was largely financed by the government as the nation rebuilt its infrastructure. By the 1970s, the proportion of government contracts had dropped to 50 percent and by the 1990s to 30 percent. The industry is considered one of the most difficult for foreign companies to enter largely because of a traditional practice known as ***dango***, by means of which there is "consultation" between companies entering bids for projects to ensure a degree of work sharing among all the levels of the industry. This has been criticized, especially by the U.S. government, as bid rigging that violates the **Antimonopoly Law** of 1947. This was also one of the items on the agenda of the **Structural Impediments Initiative (SII)** talks of the late 1980s.

CONSUMER CREDIT FINANCE. Until around 1980, **banks** concerned themselves primarily with corporate customers, while consumers tended to deposit their twice-yearly salary **bonus** in the **Post Office savings system**, which offered better rates of interest than banks. When consumer credit began to expand, apart from housing loans, credit was categorized into sales credit, for payment of goods and services to be repaid in installments, and consumer finance, meaning cash paid directly to the consumer. Four types of organizations provide credit. They are banks; credit sales companies (*shinpan*); retailers, many of which own finance companies and issue credit cards; and consumer finance companies (***sarakin***), commonly referred to as loan sharks because of their exorbitant interest rates and their use of ***yakuza*** in many cases to threaten people slow in repayment. Their activities were widely reported in the early 1980s, when there were over 220,000 charging interest rates of over 100 percent. Successive laws reduced the legal rates of interest they could charge to 40 percent in 1991. Lowered interest rates and alternative sources of loans reduced their influence to around 5 percent of the loan market.

CONSUMPTION TAX. *Shohizei* was introduced in 1989 by the Tax Reform Act of 1988. It is a value-added tax levied at each stage of the distribution of goods and services and now accounts for 20 percent of national tax revenues.

CONVENIENCE STORES. *Konbini* are normally 24-hour retail stores that began to spring up in the late 1970s and early 1980s, located on main roads for pedestrian customers or at junctions or corners for mobile customers. The Japanized version of the expression "convenience store," *konbini*, dates to the late 1980s. They are now a major part of the retail industry for daily necessities including ready-to-eat meals, packaged foods, magazines, toiletries, bottled drinks, magazines, and basic household needs ranging from batteries for appliances to paper clips. Their range of activities has expanded to include automated teller machines (ATMs), pickup and delivery of luggage and packages (*takkyubin*), sale of postage stamps, copying and fax services, and online reservations for train and air transport. Bills for telephones and other services may also be paid in convenience stores.

Initially popular only with young people—and especially students since many were located close to university campuses—their role came more to resemble the old-fashioned small shops that carried various foodstuffs that housewives traditionally preferred to buy fresh on a daily basis. This consumption style was readily adapted to the convenience store. Another market they commandeered was that of the carryout instant hot food chains usually calling themselves Hoka-Hoka Bento stores. Since these were restricted to freshly prepared meals, they did not provide the range of services found in the convenience stores. While some survived, few remained once the convenience stores had gained a local foothold.

According to government research toward the end of the 20th century, 30 percent of sales in convenience stores was of boxed meals (*obento*). A further 30 percent was accounted for by other types of foods, bottled drinks, and snacks. The remaining percentage consisted of sales in magazines, media, and the various services listed. Electronic services, although initially accounting for less than 5 percent, have shown enormous capacity for growth. Busy and successful stores in prime locations can draw up to around ¥1 million per day, which has made them the targets of many robberies.

The largest chain is 7-11 (Seven-Eleven), owned by **Ito Yokado**, the major supermarket chain. It bought out the Southland Corporation of the United States, creator of the 7-11 franchise. The second largest is Lawson, which is owned by the major retailer **Daiei**. There are other regional chains, such as Circle K and Family Mart. 7-11 is noted for its effective "just-in-time" supply-chain management system, which called for deliveries frequently more than once a day to busy outlets. The technological expertise and supply infrastructure that has been created by these chains has led to many older small businesses, such as grocery stores, corner shops, liquor stores, and even **rice** stores seeking franchises and converting themselves into convenience stores. Consequently, many small-sized family businesses have been able to survive by taking advantage of the ready-made management that the chains have created. Convenience stores, however, are not without their critics, who see them as destroyers of local culture and tradition, while others denounce them as a threat to health because of the quality of food they purvey. The demand for ready-made meals will only continue to rise as people become busier. Research in 1990 in one area of Tokyo revealed that less than half the households polled owned or ever used a traditional chopping board for preparing meals. Not only have convenience stores fitted into the pattern of consumption, but they are coming to exert their own influence and have become part of the lifestyle of an entire generation.

CORPORATE REORGANIZATION LAW. *See* BANKRUPTCY LAW.

CORPORATIONS (or Companies, Kaisha). Four types of companies are identified in the **Commercial Code**. *Gomei kaisha* are commercial partnerships with unlimited liability to creditors. *Goshi kaisha* are limited partnerships that have both limited and unlimited liability partners. *Yugen gaisha* are liability companies where the total capitalization is no less than ¥3 million and the contribution per member is no less than ¥50,000. *Kabushiki kaisha* are joint-stock corporations with minimal capitalization of ¥10 million. At the turn of the century there were an estimated 2,800,000 registered companies in Japan, of which 27,000 were *gomei kaisha*, 850,000 were *yugen gaisha*, and over a million were *kabushiki kaisha*, of which only 2,000 were listed in the first and second sections of the Tokyo Stock Exchange.

The majority of companies in Japan are small and medium-sized enterprises (***chu-sho kigyo***). The number of very large companies is relatively small, with NTT Docomo and **Toyota Motor Corporation** the largest two at the onset of the 21st century. A 1997 revision of the **Antimonopoly Law of 1947** permitted the reestablishment of the formerly banned **holding companies** (*mochikabu gaisha*) to assist in the financial control of industrial groupings (***keiretsu***). Within such groupings, corporations fall into three classes depending on the nature of their relationship to the parent company. There are *ko gaisha* (wholly or partly owned but at least 50 percent subsidiaries), *kanren gaisha* (affiliates that are between 20 and 50 percent owned by the main company), and *shitauke gaisha* (subcontractors, especially in the **automobile** and **construction** industries).

Other legally constituted businesses fall into different categories. There are 3,000 **foreign** companies in Japan (*gaishike*), including Japanese subsidiaries of overseas enterprises, **joint ventures**, and wholly owned foreign enterprises. Companies set up as cooperatives (*kumiai*) are not regarded as regular companies and are constituted and administered for tax and other purposes under different laws. The **insurance industry** in Japan is also in a special category. Insurance companies are defined as *sogo kaisha*, mutual companies in which customers holding policies are considered members of the company. Their premiums are considered contributed capital for which they receive dividend payments.

Government and **public corporations** are referred to as *tokushu hojin*, specially incorporated legal persons. These are usually created to perform some specific industrial or economic role. There are also *tokushu gaisha*, which that are usually jointly government/private sector financed. **Nippon Telephone and Telegraph (NTT)**, **Japan Tobacco and Salt Corporation**, and several of the privatized **Japan Railways (JR)** companies are in this category.

CROSS SHAREHOLDING. Known as *kabushiki mochiai*, it is the system by means of which companies own each other's shares for the purpose of maintaining stability and strengthening long-term business relations. It is a specific form of the more general concept of stable stockholding (*antei kabunushi*). The practice dates to the dissolution of the ***zaibatsu*** by order of the **Supreme Commander Allied Powers (SCAP)** after World War II.

There are various analyses of its development, but it is generally agreed that three phases can be distinguished. The first phase includes the early years after the Treaty of San Francisco had restored Japanese sovereignty in 1952. What American business refers to as "greenmail," speculative purchase of stock for resale to management at exorbitant prices, was rife then.

The **Antimonopoly Law** of 1947 therefore prevented companies from trading in shares. A 1953 revision of the act made it possible for corporate ownership of shares provided it did not affect competitiveness. Shareholding by financial institutions, limited to 5 percent, was increased to 10 percent. This enabled the development of the **Mitsubishi Group**, the **Mitsui Group**, and the **Sumitomo Group**. Members of the former *zaibatsu* regrouped into industrial conglomerates (***keiretsu***), horizontally structured enterprise groups (***kigyo shudan***), with their general trading houses (***sogo shosha***) and **banks** as the twin central pillars.

The stock market crisis of 1964–1965 is usually identified as marking the beginning of the second phase. **Yamaichi Shoken** was forced to face bankruptcy in 1964, in response to which the **Ministry of Finance** intervened by jointly setting up the Nihon Kyodo Shoken

Gaisha with the **securities industry** to buy large amounts of shares. In the same year, Japan joined the Organization for Economic Co-operation and Development (OECD), one stipulation of which was market deregulation. This heightened fears of hostile **takeovers** by foreign enterprises. The Commercial Code was amended to permit boards of **corporations** to allocate shares to other corporate investors as well as individuals. As a direct result of this, the **Sanwa Bank**, the **Daiichi Kangyo Bank**, and the **Fuji Bank** created the second wave of industrial groupings. This phase was brought to an end by the oil crisis of 1973 when it was disclosed that prices had been artificially increased through collusion. The 1977 Antimonopoly Reform Bill reverted bank shareholding from 10 percent back to the pre-1953 level of 5 percent.

The third phase took place during the late 1980s **bubble economy**, when rising equity prices encouraged many corporations to offer new issues to raise capital. Theoretically this should have increased the proportion of shares available for trade, but the cross-holding system limited this considerably. Coincidental with this was a period of financial engineering, ***zaitech***, that was purely speculative. Corporations acquired other corporations' shares and built up portfolios, and if these were not traded, they were added to those they already held for cross-shareholding purposes. After the stock market crashed, those shares did not move in value, and in the ensuing period, corporations began shedding many as useless cross holdings. They became a handicap in the banking industry where the capital adequacy ratio had been raised by the Bank of International Settlements (BIS) to 8 percent. This started a process in which financial institutions became less inclined to be cross shareholders if the paper value of such shares was unrealizable.

Over the years, two types of cross shareholding emerged. There is cross shareholding between members of an industrial grouping (*kigyo shudan* or *keiretsu*), and there is the type between suppliers and customers in various sectors. According to the Anglo-American view of shareholding, this is considered an improper act of corporate governance. This complaint was lodged as part of the **Structural Impediments Initiative (SII)** in 1990. In response, the **Economic Planning Agency (EPA)** set out its position arguing in general terms that application of the assumptions of the Western model leads to misunderstanding. Far from implying ownership rights, Japanese-style cross shareholding is little more than a framework for continuing business relationships. In particular, three arguments were employed. First, the EPA pointed out that cross shareholding provided a stable source of capital because new issues of stock would be bought by corporations that were part of the issuer's overall business strategy. Second, cross shareholding acted as a defense mechanism against hostile takeover bids. Western corporations can be dramatically affected by stock prices, in turn having an impact on long-term business planning. Japanese corporations do not face this kind of pressure because the stock market in Japan is a secondary **capital market**. Third, it was argued that the system strengthens business relations through creating a scenario of what it called "mutual hostage taking." Some Japanese economists argued along the lines of the EPA position that cross shareholding was simply a method of risk management in the Japanese economy. The EPA did admit that this structure created a closed system, in effect making it difficult for foreign corporations to enter. However, since there is nothing inherently illegal about the practice, it can hardly be condemned simply because it differs from Western practice. More serious has been its impact on what Western business now refers to as corporate governance.

Since a Japanese company's principal shareholders are its business partners, management accountability is seldom discussed. The implications of this were demonstrated in the 1990s in a series of financial scandals, bank failures, and corporate collapses in which the absence of a braking mechanism permitted bad managerial practices to continue unchecked until an irreversible situation had been reached, as in the case of the **Daiwa Bank** problem in New York. But Western-style corporate governance did not save the United Kingdom's Baring's Bank from a similar collapse. Lack of return on equity has also been listed as a negative side effect of cross shareholding. The protracted recession of the closing decade of the 20th century did force some corporations to make demands for a reasonable financial return on their investments. However, the most serious criticism of the system is that it actually defeats its own purpose by not really generating new capital. New issues of stock become paper transfers only, resulting in the value of shares declining since more shares have been issued without a corresponding increase in profitability. Allied to this as a further consequence is that prices of linked corporations on the stock market become interdependent and therefore artificial in a way that effectively defrauds shareholders who are not involved in cross shareholdings, namely, third-party investors. Since the bulk of cross-holding shares are not traded, the remainder that is traded represents only a small percentage of a corporation's value. Talking shares up or down is thus made easier for speculators.

The debate over cross shareholding is a long one, and while it is unlikely that Japanese business will abandon it completely, the various financial crises of the closing years of the 20th century made it abundantly clear that, whatever its merits, reform in various aspects of corporate governance in Japan was overdue. However, the fact that business in Japan is conducted in what some observers have described as highly contextualized structures of relationship governed by procedures that are far from clear, it is unlikely that cross shareholding will disappear entirely.

CURRENCY. *See* MONETARY HISTORY; RYO; YEN.

– D –

DAICEI CHEMICAL INDUSTRIES. Daiseru Kagaku Kogyo was established in 1919 as an affiliate of **Mitsui & Co., Ltd,** for the manufacture of cellulose derivates, organic synthetic materials, plastics, wrapping film, and related products. The company became one of the world's largest producers of cellulose products before expanding its product range during the 1930s. **Fuji Photo Film** became a successful independent business development of the company. It has offices in New York and Dusseldorf. Its principal Japan offices are in Tokyo and Osaka.

DAIDO STEEL (Daido Tokushuko). Founded in 1916 as a manufacturer of special steel products such as cast steel and forged steel, it also produces industrial furnaces, antipollution devices, and other products. Its name came about through a merger with Nihon Tokushuko Ltd and Tokushuko Seiko Co. in 1976. Around 60 percent of its products are sold to the **Nissan Motor** company. Its head office is in Nagoya.

DAIEI GROUP. Founded by the family of **Nakauchi Isao** (1922–) in 1949 as Daiei Pharmaceutical Industries, selling cheaply priced products. Nakauchi opened Japan's first modern supermarket in 1957 targeting housewives in Osaka. A major store was opened in Kobe in 1958, out of which grew what became the largest supermarket chain in the country. The Daiei name first appeared in 1970 and by 1972 had exceeded **Mitsukoshi** in sales volume. The company expanded aggressively both domestically and internationally, especially during the period of supermarket growth, but like its competitors, its expansion was affected by the protracted recession of the 1990s.

The Large Supermarket Law was extended to cover supermarkets to protect small family business, a change that forced Daiei to expand into new businesses. It developed various new retail enterprises, creating Lawson (a **convenience store** chain), D-Mart (a discount store), Maruetsu (a supermarket chain), Robella (a specialty store), and Printemps (a **department store** created in cooperation with Au Primtemps of France). It also became involved in hotels, property development, finance, restaurants, fast food, and travel and in so doing overextended.

Daiei was forced to file for protection and entered a period of restructuring in the late 1990s. It rationalized by transforming its nine divisions into independent companies. To manage these, it created Japan's first postwar **holding company**, Daiei Holding Co., in December 1997, taking advantage of changes in the **Antimonopoly Law**. The objective was to split capital and management in such a way that capital would be centrally managed but that more managerial decision making would be delegated to subsidiary companies in different areas of business. Nakauchi retired as president in 1999, becoming chairman, to make way for Takagi Kunio, who struggled with corporate rehabilitation. Bank loans of ¥400 billion were extended, but by October 2004 it was clear that debt levels were such that Daiei could not continue. It agreed to be put into the hands of the **Industrial Revitalization Corporation of Japan (IRCJ)** for restructuring in October 2004.

Daiei became a symbol of the problem of bad bank loans that plagued the banking industry throughout the 1990s. The hypergrowth model of expansion, made possible by excessive borrowing and unchecked by cross-shareholding companies, exposed one of the basic defects of Japanese-style consensual capitalism, namely, lack of adequate corporate governance.

DAIHATSU. Daihatsu Kogyo was founded in 1907 for the manufacture of internal combustion engines. It began producing small-size passenger cars, on an order/consignment basis, for the **Toyota Group**, which it joined by an agreement signed in 1967. Its reputation as a manufacturer was guaranteed by its most famous model, the Charade, which it eventually exported successfully to over 100 countries. It is also a pioneer of technology in the field of electric cars, which became of great interest in the last decade of the 20th century. It is headquartered in Ikeda, Osaka prefecture. *See also* AUTOMOBILE INDUSTRY.

DAI-ICHI KANGYO BANK. At one time Japan's largest commercial bank, it was founded as the Dai-ichi Bank, Ltd, in 1873 with **Shibusawa Eiichi** (1840–1931), the famous **Meiji period** (1868–1912) entrepreneur, as is first president. It became a commercial bank in 1896 and merged with the **Mitsui Bank** in 1943, taking the name Imperial Bank (Teikoku Ginko). The merger ended in 1948, and the Dai-ichi name was restored. It merged in 1971 with the Nippon Kangyo Bank, which had been established in 1897 as a special bank to provide funds for industrial development during the late Meiji period.

At its peak, the bank had over 300 domestic branches and eight overseas with 11 liaison offices. The problem of **nonperforming loans** that bedeviled the **banking industry** during the mid-1980s and 1990s forced the bank to restructure, after which it became the **Mizuho Bank** in 2000 through merging with the **Fuji Bank** and the **Industrial Bank of Japan (IBJ)**. *See also* BANKING HISTORY; BANKING INDUSTRY; SANKIN-KAI.

DAI-ICHI MUTUAL LIFE INSURANCE (Dai-Ichi Seimei Hoken Sogo Kaisha). The oldest mutual **insurance** company founded in 1902 by Yano Tsuneta, second only to **Nippon Life Insurance** in policy sales.

DAIKO ADVERTISING. An Osaka-based agency founded in 1944 that controls much of the business in Kansai. It formed Grey-Daiko in 1956 with the Grey Advertising Agency of New York, which assisted its overall development in the 1960s as the industry expanded. It grew to become third behind **Denstsu** and Hakuhodo. *See also* ADVERTISING INDUSTRY.

DAIKOKUTEN. Thought to have originated in India, this deity was introduced into Japan by Saicho (767–822) as a guardian of the Buddhist Treasures. Because readings are homophonous with O-kuni-nushi-no-kami (of Izumo Taisha), the identification led to the association of the two figures. During the **Edo period** (1615–1868), he gradually became transformed into a *kami* of prosperity, being associated with **Ebisu** as one of the seven *kami* of prosperity (*Shichifukujin*). In southwestern Japan, he is known as Ta-no-kami, *kami* of **rice**-fields. He is portrayed holding a mallet and a sack and wearing a black cloth cap. He was particularly patronized by the merchants of Edo.

DAIKYO OIL. Established in 1939 as a merger of eight companies in Niigata to explore and develop oil fields, the company imports, refines, and retails oil products. Along with **Maruzen Oil** and **Nippon Mining**, it created the Abu Dhabi Oil Company to drill for and pump crude oil in the United Arab Emirates in 1968. The Daikyo Oil Hong Kong Corporation and the Singapore Daikyo Corporation were established in 1974. The Mubarras Oil Company was set up as a subsidiary to develop oil fields in Abu Dhabi. The head office is in Tokyo. *See also* PETROLEUM INDUSTRY.

DAIMARU. Kansai-based department store that evolved from a Kyoto dry-goods and clothing shop opened in 1717. It became a **joint-stock company** in 1920 and began to expand into restaurants, supermarkets, and general trading and manufacturing under its own brand name. It opened a store in Hong Kong in 1960 and thereafter in France, Thailand, and Singapore. It has seven main stores, several affiliated stores, and a further group that retails Daimaru products. The head office is in Osaka.

DAIMYO BONDS. Yen-denominated bonds sold in Japan to investors in Europe by nonresident firms. *See also* CAPITAL MARKETS; MONEY MARKETS; SAMURAI BONDS; SHOGUN BONDS.

DAI NIPPON INK & CHEMICALS. Dai Nippon Inki Kagaku Kogyo was founded in 1908 as Kawamura Ink Manufacturing, producing chemical products before World War I and synthetic resins shortly after 1918. It acquired Kohl & Madden Printing Ink Corporation of the United States in 1951 and in 1952 added P. T. Sydney Cooke, a printing ink manufacturer in Indonesia. In the same year, it formed a joint affiliate with Reichold Chemicals, also of the United States, leading to a merger 10 years later, when the company's current name was introduced. The new company then acquired the Polychrome Corporation of the United States, a company that manufactured information-related products. This gave it a total of 28 overseas facilities. Its head office is in Tokyo.

DAI NIPPON PRINTING. Dai Nippon Insatsu is the largest of Japan's 2,000-plus printing companies. DNP, as it is known, was founded in 1876 as Shueisha and became a **joint-stock company** in 1894. Its present name was announced in 1935. It covers a substantial range of printed products and became an early manufacturer of precision electronic components for color, TV tubes, as well as photomasks for integrated circuits. Its interests include advanced electronics and computer-related products. Its overseas activities extend from Hong Kong, Singapore, Jakarta, and Sydney in Asia to San Francisco, New York, London, and Dusseldorf. Corporate headquarters are in Tokyo.

DAI NIPPON SUGAR MANUFACTURING. Dai Nippon Seito was founded in 1896 and guided by **Fujiyama Raita** (1863–1938), who made it a leading corporation in the sugar refining business during the 1930s and 1940s. The modern company dates to 1950, when the prewar facilities were put under its management. The liberalization of the sugar market in 1963 resulted in the company's decline in parallel with the decline in the price of the commodity itself; as a result, it elected to become a member of the **Mitsubishi Group**. Its head office is in Tokyo.

DAIWA BANK. Daiwa Ginko was founded in Osaka as the Nomura Bank in 1918. It was the ninth largest of the 13 **city banks** at the peak time of the postwar banking system. It was the only one of the main banks that handled trust business, normally the province of trust banks (*shintaku ginko*). Its **securities** division became independent as **Daiwa Securities**. It acquired undesirable notoriety in 1995 when a rogue trader lost U.S.$1.1 billion in bond trading in the United States; as a result, the bank was ordered out of the country and lost its U.S. banking license. *See also* BANKING HISTORY; BANKING INDUSTRY.

DAIWA SECURITIES. Daiwa Shoken was founded as a bond trader in 1902, growing to become one of the "big four," which was reduced to three when **Yamaichi Shoken** collapsed in 1997. The modern name dates to 1943. After 1945, it expanded and was an early entrant to the international market. *See also* SECURITIES INDUSTRY.

DANGO. A form of bid rigging used by **construction** companies to "divide the spoils" of major construction projects announced for public bidding. Companies engage in "consultations" to agree on prices and work sharing that will distribute contracts in an orderly manner. Because of the clandestine way in which it takes place, in practice it closes the Japanese market to any non-Japanese corporations that might wish to bid for public works projects. The U.S. Defense Department, in making use of Japanese contractors to bid for contracts, has claimed to be victimized several times. On at least one occasion, it set up a sting operation to prove its point in relation to projects at Yokosuka Naval Base. *Dango* is also considered a nontariff barrier to the Japanese market. *See also* STRUCTURAL IMPEDIMENTS INITIATIVE (SII).

DEBENTURES. From the **Meiji period** (1868–1912) on, the government authorized a small number of **banks**, such as the **Bank of Tokyo** or the **Long-Term Credit Bank of Japan**, to issue debentures, certificates of indebtedness issued to raise long-term funds for capital and investment. While these may now be issued by private corporations, the Ministry of Finance ranks the creditworthiness of debentures to issued, and they are restricted to terms of seven, 10, or 12 years. The major **securities** companies underwrite them.

DECISION-MAKING PROCESS. *See* NEMAWASAHI; RINGI-SEIDO.

DENTSU. Japan's largest advertising agency, founded by Mitsunaga Hoshio as Nihon Kokoku Kabushiki Kaisha in 1901. He also founded in 1901 a news agency called Dempo Tsushinsha. The companies were amalgamated in 1907 as Nihon Dempo Tsushinsha, becoming abbreviated to Dentsu, as it is still known. After a merger in 1936 of the news agency with Domei Tsushinsha, the advertising and telecommunications functions were separated. Dentsu was announced as the official name in 1955. The company operates 30 offices in Japan and eight overseas branches. In conjunction with its affiliate, Dentsu Corporation of America, it provides services in Europe, the United States, and Southeast Asia. It also has substantial influence on numerous television companies through shareholding and seats on the board.

DEPARTMENT STORES. Known in Japanese as either *hyakkaten* or *depato* (an abbreviation of department store), these large retail units (defined in law as having a minimum 3,000 square meters of floor space in cities and 1,500 square meters in rural areas) became popular in the early 20th century. At its peak time, the Japan Department Stores Association had 122 **corporations** and 230 stores in its membership. The evolution of the store is an illuminating part of modern Japanese business history. The original stores began as dry-goods stores in the **Edo period** (1615–1868), the leading name of which remains **Mitsukoshi** (located for over 300 years at Nihonbashi in Tokyo), followed by Matsuzakaya, **Takashimaya**, and **Daimaru**. A second type emerged from the 1930s as stores at major terminal stations of private railway companies, such as **Hankyu**, **Tokyu**, and later **Seibu** and **Tobu**. The third group grew up as stores in various localities, such as Yamagata and Temmaya, and in more recent times this list has come to include names such as **Ito-Yokado**, **Yaohan** (now liquidated) and **Jusco**, although these are normally designated as supermarkets.

The hallmark of the stores has always been value-added service, such as elevator girls, delivery services, and, of great importance, the store wrapping paper used for gifts. The stores also specialized in brand names such as Dunhill, Louis Vuitton, Burberry, or Givenchy, for which they charged premium prices. A Hermes necktie, for example, wrapped in Takashimaya paper and placed in a Takashimaya carrier bag, could cost twice as much as it would cost in an airport duty-free shop and therefore became more prestigious as a gift.

The protracted **recession of the 1990s** brought to an end the free-spending 1980s, with the result that numerous stores began to face dramatic decreases in income. The Kansai-based Yaohan chain overextended and moved to Hong Kong, where it collapsed completely after planning to open 2,000 stores in China. The **Sogo** chain faced bankruptcy and was forced to close nine of its major outlets. The Sogo store in Nara, for example, was taken over by Ito-Yokado in the spring of 2003. The rehabilitation of the remaining 13 of the company's 22 stores was completed in February 2003. Other stores were forced to cut costs by using more part-time workers and by lowering prices.

From the 1970s on, the older stores have faced services competition from existing supermarket chains, such as Ito-Yokado and Jusco, as well as the expansion of discount specialist stores, such as **Aoki** or its affiliate Torii, the men's clothing specialists. **Convenience stores** have also had an effect on the supermarket chains as the entire retailing and **distribution system** was steadily revolutionized in the latter part of the 20th century.

DEREGULATION. An integral part of the **big bang** in the financial world that affected primarily the **banking** and **insurance industries**.

DETCHI. Edo period (1615–1868) business apprentice. *See also* IE GENSOKU.

DIESEL KIKI. Jizeru Kiki is an **automobile** parts maker founded in 1939 by **Mitsubishi Heavy Industries** and Tokyo Jidosha Kogyo (later renamed **Isuzu Motors**). It produces fuel pumps for diesel engines as well as car air-conditioning systems. It is still linked to Isuzu Motors but has links with Bosch of Germany and the Bendix Corporation of the United States and has a **joint venture** in Canada. The head office is in the Shibuya district of central Tokyo.

DISTRIBUTION SYSTEM. The multilayered distribution system at work in Japanese business gained enormous notoriety from the late 1960s onward as foreign corporations tried to penetrate the market. They found a highly fragmented system heavily regulated by government licensing. Well-known international exporters of wines and spirits discovered that Japanese importers could not wholesale or retail and that retailers could not procure an import license. In Western economies, where the middleman role has long been considered parasitical, the problem of wholesalers' margins became a serious issue of dispute at international governmental level as a **nontariff barrier** to imports.

The distribution system in Japan has a long history, which is one explanation of its unique form. During the **Edo period** (1615–1868), when many of Japan's commercial structures were put into place, wholesalers and merchants developed a professional guild orientation toward their activities. Wholesalers worked with retailers on a regional basis, often customizing requirements from producers on behalf of retailers. This relationship is the key to understanding how the system developed after Japan began the process of **modernization**.

One reason for the large number of modern wholesalers is the very large number of small independent retailers as compared with most Western nations, where consolidation of manufacturing and wholesaling developed vigorously particularly since the end of World War II. While the expansion of companies such as Wal-Mart has been an ongoing trend in the United States and Europe, Japanese retailing has strongly resisted the pattern. Discount liquor stores in some areas of Japan even became the victims of arson, presumably by disgruntled local older sake retailers. A 1970s survey reported that Japan had over 1.6 million retail stores as compared to 1.5 million in the United States. It also revealed that 70 percent of wholesalers and 95 percent of retails employed 10 or less staff. Japan had 340,000 wholesalers as compared to 370,000 in the United States, which has twice the population and double the size of economy.

While the situation may be condemned by foreign exporters, its existence derives less from any conspiracy to block imports than from the long-ingrained habits of Japanese consumers. Housewives traditionally preferred—and in many cases still prefer—to shop locally and on a daily basis because space restrictions at home prevent the use of large freezers and refrigerators. Japan has less than 4 percent of the land space of the United States but nearly half the population. Compactness has always been considered a virtue, and small is indeed beautiful, as the bonsai demonstrates. Small independent shops account for over 70 percent of all consumer sales, although **convenience stores** and discount chains began making inroads in the 1980s. The personalized charm of the small family business and the convenience of its locality have enabled it to survive. If the nonuse of automobiles can be factored as a plus to the environment, the case for local shopping grows stronger. The Japanese preference for fresh items, such as fruit, vegetables, or fish, means daily deliveries of small amounts to convenient localities, which is the reason that wholesaling has remained so central to the economy.

The whole future of retailing in Japan has been thrown into disorder for many reasons. First, the 1990s recession radically altered spending habits. Customers became extremely price conscious. This had a devastating effect on **department stores**. Once consumer spending habits alter radically, it is very difficult to turn the clock back. A second factor has been the involvement of supermarket chains in convenience stores. Seven-Eleven in Japan is owned by **Ito-Yokado**, as one example, and future trends suggest more streamlining. A third factor has been the rise of **e-commerce** as a challenge to all traditional distribution systems and TV sales programs, both of which have again eroded retail outlet sales. The diversification of retailing has proceeded on a dramatic scale. There are strong arguments for the view that supermarkets will reach a volume beyond which they will be unable to move, and a case has been made that there will always be a place for the local retailer, even in a reinvented form. What will happen in the future will be subject to the factors listed as well as to the principle that the application of the law of supply and demand in Japan will continue to function according to its own specific variables.

DIVINATION. Uranai, or Bokusen, are terms that refer to communication with the supernatural in order to determine propitious times and places for events to ensure their success. Numerous traditional methods exist, such as *futomani*, performed by interpreting the cracks on the heated shoulder bone of a deer; *kiboku*, which uses turtle shells;

and the practice of consulting shamanistic mediums. The first two of these can be traced to Chinese origins. The latter appears to be local to Japan, although similar forms exist in other cultures, notably Korea.

At **Shinto** shrines, there are numerous versions still in use, such as *yabusame*, *matoi*, and *omato-shinji*, all forms of fortune-telling that use archery. Many shrines provide fortune-telling guides based on the traditional Oriental (originally Chinese) Zodiac, which runs in cycles of 12 years, each one named after an animal. There are also *omikuji* (fortunes printed on sheets of paper).

Even today at cultural events at universities, the fortune-teller regularly appears, and many are found on the streets of big cities such as Tokyo or Osaka, advising clients on their way home from work. It is not unknown that some **corporations** employ fortune-tellers on an ad hoc basis for advice.

DOGEN (1200–1253). Buddhist priest and poet, philosopher and scholar of the Zen tradition, and author of the famous treatise *Shobogenzo*. He was an important contributor to the austere perception of life and nature found in the values of **Zen Buddhism**, which in turn had a profound influence on Japanese values, particularly in encouraging the virtue of self-sacrifice. It has been argued that this is one source of the psychological power of Japanese **corporations** over their employees, making them place corporate obligations before family or personal concerns.

DOJIMA RICE MARKET. Originally established in 1697 on a site between the Shijimi and Dojima rivers in Osaka as a wholesale market for **rice**. After some years of disorder, in 1731, Osaka merchants were officially licensed to manage the business of the market. Money changers (*ryogae*) and warehouse (*kurayashiki*) companies began to spring up on the island. The early **Edo period** (1615–1868) government permitted 531 seats on the rice exchange (*nakagai kabu*) but increased the total to 1,351. Seat holders were permitted a range of activities typical of modern commodity trading, including speculating on rice futures, bulk buying and wholesaling, and managing financial transactions. The market continued to function until the closing stages of the Edo period but had to face competition from other Kansai traders who were strong enough to ignore the faltering government. The early **Meiji period** (1868–1912) government issued new regulations in 1876, and the market became the Osaka Dojima Komeisho Kaisho. It was renamed Osaka Dojima Beikoku Torihikisho in 1893 and finally, in 1939, was integrated into the government-directed Nihon Beikoku Kabushiki Kaisha (Japan Rice Corporation). *See also* COMMODITY MARKETS.

DOKO TOSHIO (1896–1988). Business leader and graduate of what is now Tokyo Institute of Technology whose career began as a turbine designer in the Ishikawajima Shipyard. By 1950, he had become president of Ishikawajima Heavy Industries, at that time in financial straits, but under his leadership and by supporting the United States in the Korean War, it prospered. He became president of **Ishikawajima-Harima Heavy Industries** and was responsible for the building of the *Idemitsu Maru*, the world's largest oil tanker during the early period when Japan's **shipbuilding industry** was expanding and replacing the United Kingdom as leader in the field. Doko was thereafter was invited to take over **Toshiba Corporation**, which he successfully rehabilitated. In 1974, he became the fourth president of **Keidanren** (Federation of Economic Organizations). During this time, he opposed proposed changes to the **Antimonopoly Law**, which that would have forced the breakup of large **corporations**. The dissolution of these was perceived by the **Supreme Commander Allied Powers (SCAP)** as integral to the dissolution of the ***zaibatsu***, the industrial conglomerates that were the core of prewar Japanese business. Doko's position was validated by the passage of a law in 2002 that permitted the creation of **holding** companies as they existed before 1945.

DOMEI. Known by its full title Zen Nihon Rodo Sodomei or in English as the Japanese Confederation of Labor, it is next in size to **Sohyo** (General Council of Trade Unions of Japan). It came into being in 1964 as a result of a group of unions breaking away from Sohyo in 1953 along with a group of civil service unions. Taking a firm anti–left wing stance, it advocated conciliation between management and labor, disdaining industrial action as a tool of policy. It was very influential during the period of high economic growth, claiming at its peak over 2 million members. Domei was dissolved to make way for the Japan Trade Union Confederation (JTUC-Rengo) in 1987, a private sector union with 5.5 million members. Sohyo also dissolved, two years later, increasing JTUC-Rengo to over 8 million members. *See also* ENTERPRISE UNIONS; LABOR LAWS; LABOR–MANAGEMENT RELATIONS.

DORE, RONALD P. (1925–). British sociologist and senior research fellow, Centre for Economic Performance, London School of Economics and Political Science. A graduate of the University of London, he has written extensively in the area of Japanese society, business, and industrial relations. His pioneering work after World War II elevated him to being Europe's foremost authority on the subject.

DUTCH TRADE. Dutch trade in Japan began in 1609 with the establishment of the Dutch Factory in the city of Hirado (in Kyushu) with the approval of the **Shogun Tokugawa Ieyasu** (1543–1616). It was moved to Deijima, a small island in Nagasaki Harbor, in 1641 and kept under strict control. A maximum of only 20 traders were permitted to live there, and their movements were severely restricted. The post was Japan's only window to the outside world prior to the **Meiji Restoration of 1868**, when the policy of seclusion was ended and the nation entered the modern world. During the period, several officials of the factory made considerable contributions to the growth of Rangaku, Dutch learning, giving Japan some perspectives on Western civilization during the three centuries of isolation. Among the names of the traders of the era may be found those of Hendrik Doeff, Philipp F. von Siebold, and Carl P. Thunberg.

– E –

EBARA CORPORATION. Ebara Seisakusho is a manufacturer and distributor of air and hydraulic machinery and a leading maker of pumps. The inspiration for the founding of the company in 1920 was the theory of centrifugal pumps developed by Inokuchi Ariya. The company supplies equipment to numerous different enterprises, including water supply and sewage systems, agriculture, and nuclear power plants. Ebara has links with Borg-Warner Corporation and Westinghouse in the United States and has several subsidiaries around the world, including the United States, Brazil, and Indonesia. Its head office is in Tokyo.

EBISU. Also known as **Daikokuten**, this deity is one of the **Shinto *kami*** respected particularly by the merchants of the **Edo period** (1615–1868). There is a district in central Tokyo that bears his name, as does one of the brand names owned by **Sapporo Beer**.

E-COMMERCE. While still new on the global business stage, e-business made its debut in Japan in the 1990s. Its growth was impeded by the highly regulated telecommunications system controlled by the Ministry of Post and Telecommunications through a complex licensing system. The development of **Internet** technology was a key factor in weakening government control, in particular the introduction of broadband systems that enhanced speed and volume of transmissions.

The Japanese government, on its part, having little understanding of how the speedy development of technology can induce change, tried to impose itself on developments by setting up the Electronic Commerce Promotion Council of Japan in 1996. The **Ministry of International Trade and Industry (MITI)** and the Council invested the equivalent of almost U.S.$500 million to develop e-commerce technology with little significant impact on what had become a consumer-driven industry. The Ministry of Posts and Telecommunications issued a White Paper in 2000 that reported the value of the e-commerce market as more than U.S.$200 billion. Business-to-business transactions were the majority, while individual consumer transactions accounted for just over 6 percent of the market. By the end of 2003, Japan's almost 40,000 virtual shops were being joined by an average of 20 new entrants every day. Many other innovative types of e-commerce were developing, such as Internet auctions on sites posted by individuals. Sales taxes could not easily be imposed on short-term sites.

One factor that initially impeded the progress of e-commerce was the reluctance of Japanese consumers to the online use of credit cards. Consequently, **convenience stores** that had sprung up in the previous decade and a half started becoming sites for e-commerce transactions. First in the field was **IBM**'s Loppi system, which enabled consumers to buy online but pay and pick up at the store. The most serious impediment, however, was the absence in Japan of a nationwide policy about information technology. In the very area where the government's role was desirable (if not necessary), it was absent, leaving Japan behind developing nations such as Singapore and Malaysia, which placed higher priority on being connected to the world.

Why should this be so? Government intervention in Japan is broadly for two reasons. One is revenue; if a system can be successfully taxed, regulations will be created. The other, slightly less transparent, is government fear of social instability. It is probably not incorrect to say that the government prefers to control information flow at its source, where possible. But as with satellite broadcasting, regulation was at worst impossible and at best ineffective. Some anxiety existed also in business circles that Japan's traditional **distribution system** would be affected through short-circuiting middlemen and wholesalers (***tonya***).

In spite of reservations, the industry continued to be propelled by developments that the government could not control. Since 40 percent of Internet users in Japan were women, who were much more adventurous than their male counterparts, the desire for access to foreign companies and products along with new entertainment and services continued to expand, and a new dimension was added to e-commerce.

E-commerce was a central part of the new economy that was growing inside the traditional one, but it was neither amenable nor responsive to the kind of regulatory style that Japanese governments traditionally like to impose on industry. Critics have observed that it is an example of Japanese **bureaucracy** using 19th-century logic to deal with a 21st-century industry. The difference between e-commerce and traditional business lies in the interaction of the twin factors of the technology, the development of which is fast and not easily predicted, and the consumer base, the tastes and preferences of which drive the virtual shop business. How this unparalleled phenomenon will play itself out in Japan is not yet known, but there is no doubt that Japan possesses the technology, the business experience, and the consumer demand to make it successful. At any rate, the growth of e-commerce has opened a new chapter in the history of Japanese business.

ECONOMIC DECONCENTRATION LAW (1947). One of the laws inspired by the **Supreme Commander Allied Powers (SCAP)** designed to break down large industrial and financial combines that were held responsible, in part, for Japan's militarism. *See also* ANTIMONOPOLY LAW.

ECONOMIC PLANNING AGENCY (EPA). Known in Japanese as the Keizai Kikaku Cho, it is an agency of the Prime Minister's Office that reports to the cabinet and is responsible for generating economic proposals for the nation's future. The power to recommend to the cabinet belongs to the Economic Council, a nongovernmental committee that studies EPA reports and makes recommendations on the basis of these reports and their own deliberations.

A question that frequently occurs in international discussions about the EPA is how the Japanese version differs from the central planning systems of state-controlled economies as formerly existed in Eastern Europe or in North Korea and China. The role of the EPA in Japan was never to enforce or implement but rather to suggest courses of action. It is for the Economic Council to make actual proposals to submit them to the government for deliberation and, if thought desirable, action. *See also* MINISTRY OF INTERNATIONAL TRADE AND INDUSTRY (MITI).

EDO CHOKAISHO. The city of Edo (now Tokyo) town assembly that dates to 1791 and that was the forerunner of the **Tokyo Chamber of Commerce** formed in the **Meiji period** (1868–1912).

EDO PERIOD (1615–1868). Dating varies according to different criteria, from the early 1600s, but certainly lasting from 1615, when **Tokugawa Ieyasu** (1584–1635) established himself as shogun through defeating the son of his great rival Toyotomi Hideyoshi (1536–1598), to 1868, the time when a group of young revolutionary **samurai** ended almost 300 years of isolation. They declared the emperor "restored" and replaced the feudal government with a modern one. During the Edo period, the country was rigidly controlled by the Tokugawa shogunate, technically ruling in the name of the emperor and isolated from the rest of the world. Political and economic power was concentrated in Edo (renamed Tokyo after 1868), and the **Tokugawa Feudal System** ordered all aspects of the life of the nation. *See also* BAKUHAN-SYSTEM; TOKUGAWA ECONOMY.

EDO PERIOD MANAGEMENT. The merchant houses of the **Edo period** (1615–1868) were managed in a standardized form, based on a system of apprentices known as *kodomo*, children brought in to grow up within the house. They could rise through the rank of *joza* to *kumigashira* by means of seniority. Beyond that rank to *tsukin shihainin*, promotion was by merit and performance. The top two positions of *omotojime* and *motojime* below it were the peak of the hierarchy. *See also* BANTO.

EDUCATION. The modern educational system was introduced in the early **Meiji period** (1868–1912), building on the ***Terakoya*** (temple schools) of the **Edo period** (1615–1868). Japan's introduction of compulsory education was almost simultaneous with the introduction of compulsory education in the West, a fact often overlooked by observers puzzled by the speed with which Japan's **modernization** was successfully initiated and completed. In spite of often uninformed Western criticism, Japan's system has been an overall effective servant of society, reflecting Japanese society's character and goals.

Primary and secondary education stress rote-learning memorization that is designed to help students prepare for entrance examinations for the next stage of their career. Socialization, as with preschool activities, stresses the virtues of diligence and loyalty. Classroom discipline, however, began to erode during the last decade of the 20th century with "classroom breakdown," as it was called, becoming a concern of teachers nationwide. While a matter of concern, the problem remains manageable when compared to similar problems in the United Kingdom or the United States.

Tertiary education has been its weakest feature, primarily because **corporations** traditionally saw it as their task to educate new staff in their own corporate culture, the organizational patterns peculiar to each corporation. This has led to students not being serious about education. Indeed, the common image of the Japanese students in the postwar period was that of a nighttime Majhongg player who slept during the day. While there is still some truth in that portrayal, it is also true to say that because of the **recession of the 1990s** small to medium-sized companies (***chu-sho kigyo***), having less budget for training programs than they did in the past, began to expect more skills from graduates in areas such as accounting, foreign languages, and management-related disciplines.

Another consequence of the tradition of corporate in-house training has been the backwardness of graduate programs in all areas except the natural sciences. In the early 1990s, educational reform for the needs of an internationalized Japan became a concern of the Ministry of Education (Monbusho) in the early 1990s, without whose recognition no academic qualification earned in Japan is considered valid. The proportion of the population in graduate studies in Japan is one-twentieth of that in the United States, a percentage that may increase in the future because of corporate demands for more practical skills and the emulation of professional standards in the future. The name of the ministry was altered in 1998 to the Ministry of Education, Science, Sport, and Culture (Monbu-kagakusho).

ELECTRIC POWER INDUSTRY. A regionally controlled network of **public corporations** that provide for commercial and domestic energy needs nationwide. **Tokyo Denroku** is the largest of the nine national power companies.

ELECTRONICS INDUSTRY. One of the most advanced in the world and a pillar of the Japanese economy, Japanese electronics gained global recognition in the postwar surge in the area of consumer electronics, focusing on television sets, air conditioners, refrigerators, and washing machines. These were later replaced by fax machines, copy machines, and personal computers in the 1980s, known colloquially as the "three treasures" of the businessman, analogous to the three pieces of the imperial regalia: the mirror, jewel, and sword.

The industry dates to the **modernization** of Japan in the **Meiji period** (1868–1912), when technology was imported from Europe. Radio broadcasting began in 1925, and thereafter scientific and commercial developments followed one after another. It was not until after 1945 that growth and export became possible. The Korean War, which began in 1950, acted as a catalyst for development since Japanese companies were part of the procurement process by the U.S. military. Private broadcasting was permitted in 1951, and television broadcasting started in 1953, creating a huge domestic market. The invention in 1948 of the transistor in the United States led to the development of **semiconductors** and the consequent revolution in circuit technology.

While consumer needs drove the industry until the 1970s, commercial needs began to take precedence in the 1980s, after which it became the story of names that began to dominate the industry. These may be listed as the three principal manufacturers of electronics, **Hitachi**, **Toshiba**, and **Mitsubishi Electric**; the four home appliance manufacturers, **Matsushita Electric**, **San'yo Electric**, **Sony Corporation**, and **Sharp Corporation**; and the three telecommunications specialists, **Nippon Electric**, **Fujitsu**, and **Oki Electric Industry**.

However, there can be no doubt that government economic planning and policy had an enormous impact through its guidance and support and must be considered a major success story in modern industrial development, Japanese style, in which government, semigovernmental organizations, and the private sector work in harmony.

The two major electronics industry organizations, the Electronics Industry Development Association (JEIDAO) and the Electronics Industry Association of Japan (EIAJ), merged on 1 November 2000, to form the Japan Electronics and Information Technology Industrial Association of Japan (JEITA). Headquarters are in the Mitsui Sumitomo Kaijo Building Annex, Chiyoda Ward, Tokyo. *See also* ECONOMIC PLANNING AGENCY (EPA); MINISTRY OF INTERNATIONAL TRADE AND INDUSTRY (MITI).

EMPEROR SYSTEM. The *Tennossei*, the imperial system of Japan, while a central organ of the Japanese sociopolitical system and an integral part of Japanese national identity, is still the focus of conflicting attitudes. Historically dating to at least the second century C.E., it probably originated much earlier in a shamanistic sacerdotal role according to which the emperor (or empress, as has been suggested by some scholars) came to be viewed as the high priest of the nation, a role that modern emperors continue to fulfill in the performance of various rituals throughout the year.

According to the Constitution imposed after World War II, the role of the emperor is symbolic, and, indeed, emperors in the past seldom exercised political power, which was traditionally delegated elsewhere. During the **Edo period** (1615–1868), although the imperial institution was weak, it was nevertheless required as an imprimatur for the right of the **Tokugawa Feudal System** to function. In modern times, the most controversial event was the so-called 1945 renunciation of divinity by Emperor Showa, known also by his personal name, Hirohito. In Japanese it was called the *Tenno Ningen Sengen*, meaning a "declaration of humanity." It was read by the emperor and couched in the style of a traditional imperial rescript, although the language was rather less formal. Its intent was to dissolve any mythological status of divinity in the Western sense and to provide reassurance that Japan desired to return to the family of nations purified of extremism.

According to the mythological register, Emperor Heisei (Akihito) is the 125th emperor. His father, Emperor Showa (r. 1926–1989), had the longest reign in Japanese history. While debate may continue about Emperor Showa himself, there is no serious indication of public feeling seeking to end the system. As with other aspects of Japanese culture and society, the sense of continuity it provides is one element that helps maintain social stability.

EMPLOYMENT, HISTORY OF. The history of employment in Japan can be divided into the pre- and post-**Meiji periods** (1868–1912). In the earlier period, the oldest records date to the **Ritsuryo Seido** (Ritsuryo System) implemented in the mid-seventh century. Government officials were empowered to recruit forced labor (*kyoko*) that had to be paid fixed wages. A system called *wako* (peacefully agreed terms of employment) was developed to implement the payment of labor. From the Muromachi period (1333–1568), indentured service was known, and it evolved into a one-year system during the 16th century.

During the **Edo period** (1615–1868), employer–employee relations were formalized. Employers came to be known as *hokonin* and were of three types. There were *fudai* (hereditary vassal families of the **samurai**), *nenki* (indentured servants who worked for a specified time for agreed wages), and *hiyo* (day laborers). A special class of *shichiken hokonin* existed, people forced to work to pay back loans. The class of *fudai* began to disappear toward the end of the 17th century and to merge with the *nenki hokonin* because of structural changes in the economy. Alongside these was the category known as *tsutome hoko*, which included prostitutes and entertainers. The government identified and defined these categories, and while it did not permit slavery, it did not exercise strict control over the manner in which such people were recruited or treated. The rise of the merchant class did not immediately affect employment conditions, but eventually the rise of the great houses resulted in the development of analogous employment practices to those of the samurai class, except that the merchants were the rising economic class, while in terms of wealth and influence, the samurai class was in serious decline.

After the **Meiji Restoration of 1868**, the modern employment system did not come about immediately. Groups of laborers (*gumi*) were able to sell their services to the highest bidder, a situation that displeased the government because it destabilized the labor market. The Labor Laws of 1910 encouraged the integration of these *gumi* into established companies. Groups joined in return for guarantees of employment. Out of this, the modern concept of *shushin-koyo-seido* started. This term is incorrectly translated as "lifetime employment" and should really be called "stable employment" or "career-long employment." This, combined with the seniority system and **enterprise unions**, provides the three pillars that support the employment structure. Career-long employment remained a central characteristic of Japanese employment until the late 20th century, when the protracted **recession** forced less successful companies to rethink their employment policies. Although many implemented changes, for people on the managerial track, the old system remained in force, and given Japan's innate conservatism, it is unlikely to change completely into the Western contract basis of employment. *See also* CAREER ESCALATOR; EDO PERIOD MANAGEMENT; JAPANESE-STYLE MANAGEMENT; KATATATAKI; KIBO TAISHOKU; KODOMO; NENKO JORETSU; SHUSHIN KOYO SEIDO; TAISHOKU; TEINEN; TOKUGAWA FEUDAL SYSTEM.

ENDAKA. Literally "high-value yen," the term refers to what Western observers would call the weakening of the yen against other currencies but what the Japanese refer to as its value rising.

ENTERPRISE GROUPS. The term *Kigyo Shudan* refers to two principal types of industrial associations designed to support the structure of the economy and the coordination of business activities. The existence of these groups is one explanation of Japan's economic power and growth. Each of the two major groupings is based on solid and traditional institutions, one deriving from the prewar *zaibatsu*, such as the **Mitsubishi**, **Mitsui**, and **Sumitomo Groups**. The other type has traditionally been led by banks. There was, for example, the Fuyo group (now led by the **Mizuho Bank**) and the **Sanwa Bank** group, which merged with the **Tokai Bank** to form the **UFJ Bank**. There is a newer, third type, led by a major company in a sector. The Furukawa Group is led by **Furukawa Electric**, the Kawasaki group by **Kawasaki Heavy Industries**, and the **Seibu Group** by **Seibu Railway**, and there are other groups led by other big-name enterprises, such as **Nissan** and **Toyota**.

Relations between group members are strengthened by informal meetings of presidents, **cross shareholding**, cross appointments of board members, intragroup finance and business, and joint entry into new projects and markets. There are no restrictions on forming nongroup business partnerships, nor are there any overall or obligatory management policies. While the number of **corporations** belonging to these groups is little more than 150, they account for almost 20 percent of national corporate assets and almost the same percentage of sales. It should be remembered that each group sits on top of a vast hierarchy of small and medium-sized corporations, subsidiaries, and affiliated enterprises of the larger corporations. Consequently, their influence is enormous, and while their collective share of employees is only 5 percent nationwide, this figure rises dramatically when the employees of all the smaller corporations are added to each group. At its peak, the Mitsui group controlled the employment of almost 3 million workers. *See also* KEIRETSU.

ENTERPRISE UNIONS. Unlike most Western labor unions that are trade or craft centered, Japanese unions are formed within enterprise structures or industrial sectors. Their forerunners were the Sangyo Hokoku Kai (Patriotic Industrial Associations), which date to the years of World War II and were intended to ensure cooperation between labor and management. Enterprise unions are normally independent of national or nationally organized unions, such as Zensen Domei in the textile industry with over 550,000 members and Nikkyoso, the teachers' union with over 350,000 members. If the traditional annual wage negotiations that were part of the **shunto** (spring labor offensive) are taken as a basic function of unions, most of these were conducted at enterprise level, using the national level as a negotiating tactic.

The key points of difference between Japanese enterprise unions and those in Western nations are first that they are more comprehensive in membership. Both blue- and white-collar workers can belong to the same union, although blue-collar workers rising to a foreman's position normally remain in the union, while white-collar workers rising into the managerial ranks lose their union status. In Great Britain and the United States, for example, these groups would belong to two separate unions. A second difference is that enterprise unions in Japan are organized in alignment with the structure of the company. Separate skills do not call for separate unions; hence, all the staff of a hospital, from senior medical staff to cleaners, belong to the same union. The third aspect of Japanese enterprise unions is that they fulfill two apparently contradictory functions. On the one hand, they are involved in collective bargaining with management over wages and salaries; on the other, they participate in joint consultation committees that exist to improve efficiency, competitiveness, and profitability. This is one by-product of the fact that labor and management in Japan are distinguishable only in very fuzzy manner. *See also* LABOR–MANAGEMENT RELATIONS; LABOR UNIONS.

ENVIRONMENTAL PROBLEMS. The **Ashio Copper Mine** near Nikko in Tochigi prefecture was the first seriously contended case of pollution in the **Meiji period** (1868–1912). The symbols of later problems were the notorious chest ailments in the city of Kawasaki, caused by air pollution, and **Minamata disease**, caused by mercury poisoning. Although much criticism was directed at Japan, in reality the nation's pollution problems were no worse than those of other industrial nations at the same stage of development. Proper waste disposal and recycling have since come to the forefront of national and regional policies, with regions requiring households to separate their garbage into numerous categories to avoid waste and to promote recycling. The government monitors air and water quality, resulting in enormous improvement since the last quarter of the 20th century. *See also* CHISSO CORPORATION.

EQUAL EMPLOYMENT OPPORTUNITY LAW. A 1986 law passed to conform to the principles of the UN Convention on All Forms of Discrimination against Women, which Japan signed in 1980. Its basic provisions forbid discrimination by employers on grounds of gender in respect of training, retirement, and benefits and expects employers to offer the same conditions of employment to **women** as they offer to men. Restrictions caused by marital status, age, or childbirth were to be eliminated, and pregnancy leave, determined by the Labor Standards Law of 1947 as 12 weeks, was to be increased to 14. The downside from the female perspective was the removal of protective restrictions in order to ensure equality for both men and women. The revised law that took effect in 1999 was more strict and detailed and threatened "name and shame" punishment for companies in violation of its provisions.

The effects of the law are somewhat less certain than its objectives. There is no doubt that some of the worst manifestations of discrimination, such as unequal starting pay, have been curbed. Women (along with men) in some **corporations** are invited to choose between being *ippan shokuin*, general employees, with a nine-to-five job, or *sogo shokuin*, which entails acquiring comprehensive experience in different divisions of the organization with an eye to the managerial track. The law also specified **sexual harassment** as an offense and required all organizations employing women to deal with the problem with assistance from the Ministry of Labor if necessary. This, said, however, the fact remains that women make up less than 10 percent of corporate managers. This looks poor if compared to the figure of over 40 percent in the United States. On promotion and related matters, not a great deal appears to have changed. In the public sector, only around 5 percent of career **bureaucrats** are women. This is another example of how much traditional mind-sets remain influential in modern Japanese society. It is also a fact that large numbers of women are quite happy with their traditional role as homemakers, and it is a further reminder that the aspirations of some Western woman are not necessarily shared by Japanese women.

EURODOLLAR WARRANTS. Denominated in U.S. dollars, these warrant bonds are issued by Japanese **corporations** and are traded on the Euromarket and in Japan. The warrants themselves are certificates that give investors the right to buy new issues of stock for a fixed price and within a considerably long window of time, in some cases three to four years. They are, in fact, corporate bonds with equity warrants attached that compensate for lower interest rates and are therefore a convenient way of raising capital at low cost. *See also* CAPITAL MARKETS IN JAPAN; MONEY MARKETS IN JAPAN.

EUROYEN BONDS. Denominated in yen, these are bonds issued by Japanese corporations. However, since 1986, as part of Japan's financial liberalization, they have also been issued by foreign companies, national governments, the World Bank, and even foreign banks. *See also* DAIMYO BONDS; SAMURAI BONDS; SHOGUN BONDS.

EUROYEN FUTURES. These are contracts to trade short-term three-month deposits on a future date in the Euromarket at a fixed interest rate. *See also* CAPITAL MARKETS IN JAPAN; MONEY MARKETS IN JAPAN.

EXPORT-IMPORT BANK OF JAPAN (JEXIM). This is a government bank formed in 1950 as the Japan Export Bank, which changed its name to the Export-Import Bank of Japan in 1952 and is engaged in financing export and import projects. It supplies credit to Japanese exporters and to foreign buyers and bank-to-bank loans to foreign governments, particularly those of developing nations, to assist Japanese exporters enter foreign markets.

While a successful instrument of government policy, the bank drew widespread criticism because of the resultant trade surpluses that were growing in Japan's favor. After the Plaza Accord of 1985, the yen strengthened, and the bank began to recycle its surpluses to promote the development of poorer nations. From 1986, it worked in this area with the World Bank and the Asian Development Bank. In 1998, the Export-Import Bank of Japan was merged with the Overseas Economic Cooperation Fund to create the **Japan Bank for International Cooperation (JBIC)** to develop cross-border economic transactions and general development cooperation. Its charter states clearly that it is not to compete with commercial banks and is responsible primarily for the promotion of Japan's export and import activities and for socioeconomic development in emerging economies worldwide.

– F –

FAIR TRADE COMMISSION (FTC). A body created to oversee the implementation of the **Antimonopoly Law of 1947**, which that prohibited **holding companies**, excessive **cross shareholding** by financial institutions, and cartel formation. The FTC was weakened by the reversion of Japanese sovereignty in 1951 and was completely overshadowed by the creation of the **Ministry of International Trade and Industry (MITI)**. The entire postwar trend was back to mergers and oligopolies. Significantly, one solution to the economic turmoil created by the protracted **recession of the 1990s** was an act of the National Diet in 1997 lifting the ban under the 1947 law that forbade the formation of holding companies, bringing history full cycle.

FARMERS' MOVEMENT. The name given to attempts by poor owner farmers and tenant farmers to achieve social and economic security that began in the mid-**Meiji period** (1869–1912) and lasted until Japan became embroiled in the war in the Pacific, after which the **Supreme Commander Allied Powers (SCAP)** began a process of land reforms to give tenant farmers property rights. The government of the period followed a deflationary policy suggested by Masukata Masayoshi, inducing a severe depression that produced chaos in farming communities, resulting from the price of raw silk being halved. In 1885, for example, over 100,000 farming households were bankrupted, and almost 400,000 households were forced to sell their land to pay taxes. This meant that 40 percent of all land was being worked by tenant farmers. Riots ensued in various parts of the country, one of the most radical being in the silk-growing area of Chichibu in present-day Saitama prefecture.

After World War I, from 1918 on, cheap imports of **rice** from Korea and Taiwan (both part of the Japanese Empire) hit mainland farmers severely. Unions began to spring up to fight for farmers' rights, and in 1922 the Nihon Nomin Kumiai (Japan Farmers' Union) came into being. The union, however, attracted less than 10 percent of the estimated 4 million tenant farmers. The union membership lacked positive policy directions and had more the character of a protest movement. Mobilization of resources for war after 1937 resulted in various changes. It was, nevertheless, only after 1945 that the reform process was initiated. *See also* AGRICULTURAL BANK OF JAPAN; AGRICULTURAL BASIC LAW; AGRICULTURAL COOPERATIVES; AGRICULTURE; FARMERS' ORGANIZATIONS.

FARMERS' ORGANIZATIONS. The modern Agricultural Cooperative Societies (*nokyo*) arose out of the prewar Agricultural Association (*Nogyokai*). The Agricultural Association Law (Nogyo Dantai Ho) of 1943 forced the merger of the two farmers' associations that had a history going back to earlier in the century, the Farmers' Assembly (*nokai*) and the Producers' Organization (*noso*). Wartime necessity required that all agricultural products be controlled by the government to prevent a black market from being created through private sales. Government responsibility for agriculture remains a serious issue for all Japanese politicians. In spite of the fact that the number of farmers continued to decline in the postwar years, the power of the lobby they represent was well demonstrated by the response to the pressure from President George H. W. Bush's administration to import American rice during the **Structural Impediments Initiative (SII)** talks of 1989–1990. The World Trade Organization's proposals on liberalization of agricultural products was greeted with great disdain in Tokyo. *See also* AGRICULTURAL BANK OF JAPAN; AGRICULTURAL BASIC LAW; AGRICULTURAL COOPERATIVES ACT; AGRICULTURE; FARMERS' MOVEMENT.

FEDERATION OF ECONOMIC ORGANIZATIONS. *See* KEIDANREN.

FEDERATION OF EMPLOYERS' ORGANIZATIONS. *See* NIKKEIREN.

FINANCIAL CRISIS OF 1927. Known in Japanese as the *kin'yu kyoko*, it refers to the largest **banking**-system collapse prior to the **Showa Depression** (1930–1935), when 37 banks failed and the government was forced to resign. It came on the back of a boom period between 1915 and 1920, during which many business overextended. Then came the 1923 earthquake with its resultant economic consequences. The **Bank of Japan** acted as guarantor by means of government-issued loans. These loans, however, became suspect, and there then occurred the crisis of the **Bank of Taiwan** (Taiwan Ginko) and the Suzuku Shoten catastrophe, bringing the economy almost to a standstill. The failure of numerous regional banks, however, simply strengthened the control of the major *zaibatu* banks over national finances. *See also* GREAT DEPRESSION.

FINANCIAL DEREGULATION. This followed the gradual liberalization and **deregulation** of Japan's financial system that began in the late 1970s, when the yen began the process of internationalization. The next stage included the introduction of new kinds of financial instruments and markets, gradual decontrol of foreign exchange transactions, and loosening of control over interest rates and **banking** businesses. The process continued into the closing years of the 20th century, culminating in the **big bang** of 2001, which was intended to be analogous to the big bang in London of the mid-1980s.

It consisted of a timetable for various changes and reforms that were to bring the financial system more into line with that of Western nations, to whom the flexibility it afforded gave them clear advantages over Japan's cumbersome and heavily regulated system. As with all attempts at reform in Japan, the **bureaucracy** was less enthusiastic than the **corporations**, although rivalry between sectors was also a serious obstacle, particularly between banking and **insurance**.

FINANCIAL FUTURES MARKET. The Tokyo International Financial Futures Exchange (TIFFE) was established in 1989 by the Federation of Bankers Associations of Japan to trade three financial instruments, namely, yen–dollar currency futures, three-month Euroyen, and Eurodollar interest-rate futures. *See also* CAPITAL MARKETS; MONEY MARKETS.

FISHING INDUSTRY. As a great consumer of seafoods, the Japanese fishing industry is the largest in the world, representing 15 percent of the global catch. Its traditions stretch back in history but, like the **whaling industry**, began to become structured into the economy through the **distribution system** that evolved during the **Edo period** (1615–1868). Catches are auctioned at the **Tsukiji Shijo**, the largest wholesale fish market in Japan and probably in the world.

Since 1970, the fishing industry has undergone fundamental structural changes brought about by a number of factors. First was the contentious issue of the worldwide introduction of the 200-mile fishing limit that brought a number of nations into conflict over fishing rights. A second factor was the general change in the Japanese economy that resulted in increased labor costs and the demand for a more rational system of distribution. A third factor that became a long-term trend was the increased consumption of meat products by younger Japanese. However, even in 1975, a government survey showed the nation as 100 percent self-sufficient in seafood production, a figure that dropped to 60 percent by 1997. Data from 1980 showed that the volume of domestically generated seafood was seven times that of imported seafood (10.6 million metric tons to 1.7 million metric tons). By 1999 the volumes had become almost equal. The large and older fishing **corporations** have been steadily moving away from fishing itself to importing, processing, and distributing seafood products to restaurants and to supermarkets.

FIVE FAMILY GROUPS. The *Gonin-gumi* made up the smallest administrative unit in a village during the **Edo period** (1615–1868). Responsibilities of supervision and cooperation were strictly imposed. The groups were responsible for **rice** delivery and for monitoring behavior in moral and legal matters. Thus grew up the tradition of enforced conformity to avoid trouble within the group, a feature of Japanese society's lingering feudalism, which still survives.

FLEXIBLE MANUFACTURING SYSTEM (FMS). Computer-aided design, or small-lot order-based manufacturing, was introduced to widen product variety but also to cut labor and inventory costs. FMS is implemented in different ways according to individual industries. Machine tools can be used to change production lines, as in the case of some electronics manufacturers. **Toyota**'s famous **just-in-time** system and **Shingo Shigeo**'s SMED method allows the same **automobile** production line to change to a new model through a single-minute exchange of die.

FOREIGN COMPANIES. Over 3,000 foreign **corporations** were functioning in Japan as of the late 1990s, usually referred to as *gaishike*. The largest included **IBM Japan** (which has a history dating back to 1937), Ford Motor Corporation, Exxon Corporation, Esso Sekiyu, and Citibank. Successful new postwar entrants from the United States include **Coca-Cola Japan** and **McDonald's**. The first wave of entrants to the Japanese market date to the 1960s, when IBM, for example, revived its presence in the form of a subsidiary wholly owned by the IBM World Trade Corporation. In reality, few were able to enter successfully, partly because they did not know the market well enough but more so because of the complex system of **cross shareholding** between members of industrial group (***keiretsu***). Some foreign **petroleum** companies were able to enter Japan, but usually to meet strategic needs in the industry. Many of them were required to license some of their technology as the price of entry. **Joint ventures** account for another large group, including Hewlett Packard and Yokogawa Electric, Xerox, and Fuji, plus a number of other big names. The catalog of failed joint ventures is equally impressive.

Studies of the operations of foreign companies in Japan suggest that the majority struggle, although some have performed well. Reasons cited for the mixed levels of success include high running costs, excessive government regulation, finding qualified Japanese staff, access to **distribution** routes, finding and negotiating with potential customers, the *keiretsu* system, and the peculiar character of many Japanese business practices. American corporations, in other studies, were criticized for short-term thinking and obsession with the quarterly balance sheet; their lack of understanding of the Japanese market and consequent inability (or refusal) to modify products accordingly; failure to recognize the high standards and specifications to which Japanese products are made, presented, and packaged; and lack of a after-sales service. Well-qualified Japanese were reluctant to become staff in foreign companies, even in the mid-1990s, because management practices were different, although many foreign corporations have been adopting Japanese practices. Studies of Asian corporations in Japan have disclosed their difficulties in meeting Japanese standards and expectations in matters ranging from product quality to simply adhering to schedules.

In the closing years of the 20th century, the acquisition of Japanese corporations became a new and attractive way of entering the market. Renault acquired an important share in **Nissan**, while **Merril Lynch** acquired the remains of **Yamaichi Securities** when the brokerage collapsed in 1997. This enabled it to set up a network of branches with little difficulty. However, it still faced numerous internal management and customer relations problems. Generally, successful foreign companies are led by people who have taken the study of the Japanese language and business culture seriously and who engage in the kind of networking, exchanging of business cards, and informal meetings that are indispensable to success in any area of Japanese business life. Conditions in the early 21st century are probably more favorable to foreign companies than at any previous time. It remains to be seen whether many can rise effectively to meet the challenge. *See also* INVESTMENT, INWARD; JAPANESES-STYLE MANGEMENT; OYATOI GAIKOKUKJIN.

FORTUNE-TELLING. *See* DIVINATION; INTRODUCTION.

FREETERS. A term coined from "free" to suggest an activity that refers to an increasing number of young people in the early 21st century who prefer **part-time employment** to regular membership of a **corporation**. The implications for the economy become serious if they never make contributions to the **pension** system or pay any sizable amount of tax.

FUJI BANK. Fuji Ginko was originally founded in 1864 by Yasuda Kenjiro as a money exchange agency and became the **Yasuda Bank** (Yasuda Ginko) in 1880. It slowly began to acquire small local **banks**, and by 1923 it had grown substantially through mergers and acquisitions, which it continued to engage in until it had become the nation's largest bank in terms of volume of deposits. With the breakup of the ***zaibatsu*** after 1945, it left the hands of the Yasuda family and was renamed the Fuji Bank in 1948. It was seriously affected, as were all Japanese banks, by the nonperforming loans problem that was part of the background to Japan's economic slowdown during the closing months of the **Showa period** (1926–1989) and the recession of the 1990s. It merged with the **Daiichi Kangyo Ginko** and the **Nippon Kogyo Bank** to form the **Mizuho Financial Group** in 2000.

FUJI ELECTRIC. Fuji Seizo Denki was formed in 1923 to manufacture heavy electrical machinery with both technology and capital coming from **Furukawa Electric** and Siemens of Germany. It now produces equipment for hydroelectric and geothermal power generators as well as reactors for atomic power generation and sewage and water systems. It has also become the world's largest manufacturer of vending machines. **Fujitsu** grew out of its **telecommunications** division in 1935. The head office is in Tokyo. *See also* ELECTRONICS INDUSTRY IN JAPAN; FURUKAWA ZAIBATSU.

FUJI HEAVY INDUSTRIES. Fuji Jukogyo was originally an Airplane Research Institute created by **Nakajima Chikuhei** (1884–1949) in 1917 during World War I and became an aircraft manufacturer, which it remained until 1945. The postwar dissolution of large **corporations** resulted in its fragmentation into numerous small companies. These reunited in 1955 under its present name. Fuji began as a maker of scooters, graduating thereafter to small cars (under the **Subaru** brand name), buses, and, once more, light aircraft for both private and military use. The company has overseas interests in the United States and in Belgium and is affiliated with the **Nissan Motor Corporation**. Its head office is in Tokyo. *See also* AUTOMOBILE INDUSTRY.

FUJI HEIGO (1906–1980). Business leader who was born in Gifu prefecture and who graduated from Waseda University in Tokyo. Following a short career as a reporter for the *Asahi Shimbun*, he joined the **Nippon Steel Corporation** in 1937 and became secretary to the president. After 1945, Nippon Steel was broken up into Yawata Steel and Fuji Steel. Fuji became vice president of Yawata Steel in 1962. He also became vice chairman of the **Keizai Doyukai** (Japan Committee for Economic Development). When Nippon Steel was reconstituted in 1970, he became vice president. He ended his career as a politician after being elected to the House of Councilors in 1974.

FUJI PHOTO FILM. Fuji Shashin Firumu was established in 1934 as an independent company from the photo division of Dai-Nippon Celluloid (renamed **Daicei Chemical Industries**). It grew to become the nation's largest producer of film and photographic materials and has progressively expanded and developed both its new products and its advanced technology. Fuji introduced color film in 1946 and began producing cameras in 1948. It branched into magnetic tapes in 1960 and in 1962 formed **Fuji Xerox** as a **joint venture** with Rank Xerox of the United Kingdom. It expanded overseas to the United States, Canada, Brazil, Germany, France, and the United Kingdom and has representative offices in Hong Kong, Seoul, Taipei, Singapore, Bangkok, Mannila, and Sydney. Corporate headquarters are in Minami-Ashigara, Kanagawa prefecture, although it has a large liaison office in Tokyo.

FUJISAWA PHARMACEUTICALS. Fujisawa Yakuhin Kogyo was formed in 1894 to develop medical products, especially antibiotics. It also began to produce medicines for the nervous system, vitamins, and a diversified range of medical products. Its most famous development was the antibiotic Cefazolin sodium. Its head office is in Osaka.

FUJISAWA TAKEO (1910–1988). Business entrepreneur who worked with **Honda Soichiro** (1906–1991), the founder of **Honda Motors**, to develop a franchise store system nationwide for the sale of Honda motorcycles.

FUJITA DENZABURO (1841–1912). A leading **Meiji-period** (1868–1912) entrepreneur from the Choshu fiefdom (present-day Yamaguchi prefecture). He was the son of a sake and soy sauce maker who joined the antishogunate movement prior to the **Meiji Restoration of 1868**. He moved to Osaka and as a supporter of the government was awarded various procurement contracts for the army. His major achievement was the founding of the Fujita-Gumi, which in time became the Dowa Mining and which was involved in land reclamation and forestry as well as mining. He was elevated to the House of Aristocrats as a baron for successfully selling government bonds during the 1904–1905 Russo-Japanese War.

FUJITSU. Formed in 1935 from the telephone division of **Fuji Electric**, it grew into an electronic data processing and **telecommunications** manufacturer. It branched further into the field of electronics and in 1954, without relying on acquired technology, became the first Japanese corporation to produce a relay computer. As the telex became obsolete with the development of the fax, it began to manufacture copy machines, facsimile machines, and computers. It continues to produce these and has production and marketing operations in the United States, Australia, Brazil, Germany, Korea, Ireland, Singapore, and Spain. Headquarters are in Tokyo.

FUJIWARA GINJIRO (1869–1960). He was a business leader from Nagano prefecture whose career spanned the **Meiji** (1868–1912), **Taisho** (1912–1926), and **Showa** (1926–1989) periods. After graduating from what is now Keio University, he entered **Mitsui Bank** in 1894 and **Mitsui & Co** in 1899. In 1911, he moved to an affiliated company of the **Mitsui Group**, **Oji Paper**, which he restructured and of which he became president. He subsequently acquired Fuji Seishi and Karafuto Kogyo, enabling Oji Paper to become the largest paper producer in Japan. After retiring in 1940, he devoted himself first to politics and then to educational projects.

FUJI XEROX. Capitalized in 1961 by **Fuji Photo Film** and the Rank Xerox Corporation of the United Kingdom as a **joint venture**, it grew rapidly to become the nation's largest manufacturer of medium- and high-speed copying machines. Its research and innovation has made it a key company within the Xerox group worldwide. It is also engaged in the development of various kinds of office systems. The head office is in Tokyo.

FUJIYA CONFECTIONERY. Founded by the Fuji family in 1938, the company is now a major confectionery producer that also has a brand name as a nationwide franchise in the field of shops, tearooms, and restaurants. It developed associations with Rowntree-Macintosh of Great Britain and Hershey Foods Corporation of the United States, whose products it began importing and retailing nationwide. Its head office is in Tokyo.

FUJIYAMA RAITA (1863–1938). He was a distinguished **Meiji period** (1868–1912) entrepreneur from Saga prefecture in Kyushu and graduate of Keio University in Tokyo, a university that now boasts the largest number of graduates who hold positions as presidents of major corporations. He worked initially for **Mitsui Bussan** and helped the company acquire **Oji Paper**. He was also involved in various start-ups, such as the Tokyo Municipal Tramway Company (Tokyo Shigai Dentesu), the Nippon Fire Insurance Company (Nippon Kasai Hoken), and the Imperial Theater (Teikoku Gekijo) in the Marunouchi district of central Tokyo. His major achievement was the restructuring of **Dai Nippon Sugar Manufacturing** and the development of the sugar industry in Taiwan. He became president of the **Tokyo Chamber of Commerce and Industry** and was greatly respected in business circles until his death.

FUKIMI. Term used when the market prices exceed the book value of a **corporation**'s assets and the capital is considered to be like a lucky windfall.

FUKOKU-KYOHEI. "A rich country and a strong military," one of the popular ideological slogans of the **Meiji period** (1868–1912) that set out some of the goals of the group that was advocating Japan's need for speedy **modernization**. The goal was to prevent the country from facing the same tragic fate experienced by a weakened China, when it was unable to resist the depredations of Western nations such as Britain and Germany during the 19th-century wave of European colonialism. *See also* INTRODUCTION; KUROFUNE.

FUKUZAWA YUKICHI (1835–1901). He was the most famous of all **Meiji period** (1868–1912) educators and innovative intellectuals whose many accomplishments include the founding of what is now Keio University, from which many business leaders have emerged over the years. His face appears on the current ¥10,000 bill.

FURUKAWA ELECTRIC. Furukawa Denki Kogyo was formed when **Furukawa Kogyo** bought the Yokohama Wire Manufacturing Company in 1908, which it merged with its own Nikko Copper Works and Honjo plant in 1920. The new company formed was Furukawa Denki Kogyo, the name by which it is still known. The company not only mined and refined copper but also produced cable and wire from it. Its battery division evolved into the Furukawa Battery Co., Ltd, in 1950, while the light metal division was transformed into Furukawa Aluminum in 1971. The rolled copper division developed into Furukawa Metals in 1971. The company also created **Fuji Electric**, **Nippon Light Metal**, and the **Yokohama Rubber**, all of which became household names in Japan because of the products they supplied for domestic use. The head office is in Tokyo.

FURUKAWA ICHIBEI (1832–1903). Leading **Meiji period** (1868–1912) entrepreneur who founded the **Furukawa zaibatsu**. He was born in Kyoto, the son of a tofu maker called Kimura. Having learned his business skills at home, he left and went to work for the Morioka branch of the **Konoike Family** in 1849 as a silk purchasing agent. He left Morioka and moved to the **Ono-Gumi**, which that was based on Kyoto, where he met a silk merchant named Furukawa Tarozaemon, who subsequently adopted him, giving him the Furukawa name. He rose in the ranks of the house of Ono, becoming chief buyer in 1862, after which he helped set up the house's silk trade in Yokohama. In 1871, with the assistance of two European experts, he imported various pieces of equipment and built Japan's first mechanical silk filature. He became chief manager of the group, and he remained with it until its financial collapse in 1874.

Furukawa thereafter moved to Tohoku as the manager of a mining company that belonged to the Soma family. With capital borrowed from **Shibusawa Eiichi** (1840–1931), the business expanded into silver and copper. The Soma family withdrew its interest in the business, and Furukawa continued as owner and received further help from Shibuswa. He also acquired the **Ashio Copper Mine** and developed other mines as government enterprises. He introduced the most advanced technology he could import from abroad, and through the intelligent use of existing infrastructure, his mines produced nearly half of all Japan's copper requirements. Out of this business base grew the Furukawa ***zaibatsu***.

Furukawa was decorated twice by the emperor with the Imperial Order of Merit for his contribution to Japan's economic development. Unfortunately, careless and irresponsible handling of industrial waste at the Ashio mine created Japan's first serious pollution problem, producing numerous repercussions that somewhat tarnished the name of the group.

FURUKAWA KOGYO. Created in 1918 as the mining division of the **Furukawa Zaibatsu**, it began as a copper refiner that manufactured various types of industrial machinery. It eventually grew into Japan's largest manufacturer of rock drills and the world's largest producer of high-purity metal arsenic for use in the electronics industry. The technology it developed in the field of refining is internationally acclaimed. It is now a leading member of the Furukawa Group (***keiretsu***).

FURUKAWA ZAIBATSU AND GROUP. This is a typical example of the second-tier group of financial combines that included the **Yasuda** ***zaibatsu***, the Okura, and the Asano groups. It was founded by **Furukawa Ichibei** (1832–1903), and its beginnings in the **Meiji period** (1868–1912) can be traced to his acquisition of the Tochigi prefecture **Ashio Copper Mine** in 1877. He successfully developed the mine and became producer of almost half of Japan's copper requirements and also launched new companies in the fields of silver mining, electric power, light metals, and rubber. After his death, the various businesses he created were merged into **Furukawa Kogyo** in 1905. By the end of World War II, under the ***Zaibatsu*** **Dissolution** order of the **Supreme Commander Allied Powers (SCAP)**, the 84 companies were declared independent. In the 1970s, they reorganized into the ***keiretsu*** known as the Furukawa Group, with Furukawa Kogyo being a leading member. *See also* FUJI ELECTRIC; FURUKAWA ELECTRIC; NIPPON LIGHT METAL; YOKOHAMA RUBBER.

FUYO GROUP. This is a large postwar ***keiretsu*** of former Yasuda Bank–related corporations that replaced the **Yasuda *zaibatsu*** after World War II, including **Fuji Bank**, **Yasuda Trust & Banking**, and **Marubeni Corporation**. The Fuji Bank merged with the **Daiichi Kangyo Bank** and the **Industrial Bank of Japan** in September 2000 to form the **Mizuho Bank**.

– G –

GENDER ISSUES. *See* WOMEN.

GENERAL AGREEMENT ON TARIFFS AND TRADE (GATT). Organization formed in 1947 to bring about the standardization and reduction of tariffs that were impeding world **trade** at the time. Japan joined in 1955 but was greatly feared because of the nation's dramatic recovery from the war and its subsequent remarkable economic development. Several member nations imposed discriminatory restrictions on Japan soon after it became a member, but these were lifted during the 1960s.

Japan has tried to cooperate with the member countries and has worked consistently at lowering tariffs by giving preferential duties to exported products of developing nations. While this went a long way to stemming criticism, Japanese policies nevertheless still face some hostility over **nontariff barriers** to imports. Some complaints may be considered legitimate in the sense that because of **industrial groupings**, the Japanese market is perceived as extremely difficult to penetrate or indeed simply closed. Other criticisms are of practices that are in some respects causally rooted in cultural traditions, as in the case of **rice** and the **distribution system**. While the process of overcoming nontariff internal barriers has been slow, a number of **foreign corporations** have established themselves as brand names in Japan, such as Mercedes-Benz and BMW of Germany. In 1995, GATT was replaced by the **World Trade Organization (WTO)**.

GENERAL SEKIYU. Petroleum products sales company established in 1947 that adopted its present name in 1967 and is affiliated with the U.S. giant Exxon. It is also a member of the General Sekiyu Group, which is engaged in the refining, transportation, and retailing of oil and liquid petroleum (LP) gas, used particularly by taxis. Its head office is in Tokyo.

GENERAL TRADING CORPORATIONS. *See* SOGO SHOSHA.

GENROKU PERIOD (1688–1703). Part of the **Edo period** (1615–1868) marked by a lavish and decadent merchant-dominated culture of excess in lifestyle that provoked a puritan reaction by Shogun Yoshimune (1716–1745) in the form of the **Shinki Hatto** edict intended to restore neo-Confucian values. *See also* CONFUCIANISM.

GENSAKI MARKET. Market for trading bonds that were sold with a repurchase agreement. *See also* CAPITAL MARKETS; MONEY MARKETS.

GIFT-GIVING CULTURE. Because of the centrality of harmonious human relations in Japanese culture, the custom of gift giving evolved over the centuries to help cultivate and maintain relationships at all levels of the sacred hierarchy. During the **Edo period** (1615–1868), gifts for all occasions were prescribed and presented according to the dictates of custom as handed on from one village head to the next. In modern times, similar rules exist, and organizations will advise what is appropriate for events such as weddings and funerals, where paper money (new for a wedding and used notes for a funeral) placed in the appropriately colored envelope is standard. Red and white are considered congratulatory colors. Black is the only color, along with white, that symbolizes mourning.

The busiest gift-giving times are midyear (***chugen***) and the end of year (***seibo***), when valued customers, group leaders, persons of consequence, and their clients exchange gifts. People making domestic or international trips are often feted with gifts before leaving and are expected to bring back souvenirs.

The value of a gift is also enhanced by the name of the **department store** on the packaging in which it is wrapped. Prior to the burst of the **bubble economy**, lavish gift giving was common, and highly priced imports were at the top of the list. The lengthy

recession of the 1990s brought the excesses to an end, and the general value of seasonal gifts declined considerably, hurting the department stores that depended heavily on them for revenue. Still, however it may be modified, the gift-giving culture of Japan will remain an important device used to help maintain smooth human relations.

GIRI-NINJO. *Giri* means "obligation" or "duty," and *ninjo* means "human feeling." *Giri/ninjo* refers to a conflict between a duty to someone and a feeling of being drawn in a different direction. This is a particularly complex psychological as well as moral problem for Japanese to face because it can create an intense internal crisis. At bottom it is a conflict between the **Confucian** virtue of duty and basic human emotion.

During the **Edo period** (1615–1868), this was the substance of great dramas, particularly those written by **Chikamatsu Monzaemon** (1653–1725). Invariably, it was a conflict faced by a **samurai** who had to choose between the love of a geisha and his duty to his feudal master. The preferred denouement of these dramas was the double **suicide** of both the samurai and the geisha, an act that was seen as degrading the highly honorable status of *seppuku*, the ritual act of suicide that was restricted to the warrior class.

GLOBALIZATION. This term came into vogue in the closing decade of the 20th century, referring to the growing interconnectedness and interdependence of many aspects of the world socioeconomic structure as well as the emergence of problems that can be defined or analyzed only in global terms. Many theories have been advanced to give meaning to the term. If the question is raised as to what makes a problem "global," among the obvious criteria would be that it can seriously affect millions of people who are far from its source, like the **Asian Financial Crisis of 1997**, the Chernobyl nuclear accident in the former Soviet Union, or the 2002 outbreak of SARS in China. Global problems, once identified, move immediately to the center stage of world events and gain a momentum of their own and a media identity. Another aspect of global problems, to take terrorism as an example, is that they call for strategies rather than simplistic "solutions" because of their complex character.

Globalization should be seen in the first instance as one inevitable result of technological advance. From supersonic aircraft to the **Internet**, people and information can move at high speed, and while there are positive benefits, there are also negative side effects. From a business perspective, globalization offers various opportunities for wider markets but has also forced changes, for example, in Japanese business styles. In the **computer** industry, the emergence of the USB system makes possible the interchangeability of products. Manufacturers must take account of this. In finance, **accounting**, and legal services, Japan is being compelled to embrace global standards in order to remain competitive. Such global standards and systems are as much consumer driven as they are the product of corporate planning.

One major causal factor in the development of globalization is the enormous power wielded by multinational **corporations** in dominant industries such as oil, transport, and defense. The activities of Japan's huge trading companies, the ***soga shosha***, are prime examples of the dramatic rate at which the interpenetration of economies through trade, investment, and **joint ventures** in third markets accelerated during the last two decades of the 20th century. These factors have fed the need for agreements on intellectual property rights, trademarks, and action against piracy through illegal copying.

Proponents of globalization point to the savings that it makes possible through the best use of labor and resources. However, critics are not slow to point out that cheap resources and low labor costs are actually a form of exploitation of the developing nations by the developed ones. Environmental destruction, global warming, a new wave of economic "colonization," and excessive interference in traditional ways of life have all been listed as the downside of globalization. Developed nations have also faced problems, such as the inability to compete with cheap globally produced goods. By 2004, China was rocking world markets by supplying goods that underpriced those in any developed nation, just as Japan had disrupted the U.S. **textile** market in the 1950s and 1960s. With developed nations honing more advanced skills, jobs that were classified in Japan as "dirty, dangerous, and, difficult" had to be delegated to imported labor. On the other hand, in order to compete in some industries, Japan has been forced into offshore manufacturing, resulting in domestic unemployment and the further hollowing out of Japanese industry.

The **World Trade Organization (WTO)** has been targeted as a source of unwelcome globalization, as has been the International Monetary Fund (IMF) because of its interference in numerous Asian economies during the Asian Financial Crisis of 1997. Regardless of the antiglobalization protests at the G8 meetings, globalization is a tide that cannot be turned back. Like **modernization** in the 19th century, cultures and economies must come to terms with it or else face the consequences.

GLOVER, THOMAS BLAKE (1836–1911). British trader, born in Peterhead, Scotland, and active in Japan during the closing years of the **Edo period** (1615–1867) and the early years of the **Meiji period** (1868–1912). He formed Glover and Co. in Nagasaki in 1859 and developed a business through exporting gold, silver, and marine products to pay for the import of ships and weapons that he sold to the fiefdoms of Satsuma (now Kagoshima) and Choshu (now Yamaguchi prefecture). His company imported a steam locomotive from Shanghai in 1865 and experimented with makeshift tracks along the Oura shoreline. His company also helped develop the **Takashima Coal Mine** and the building of the Kosuge Shipyards in 1868, which subsequently became the **Mitsubishi** Shipyards. The business expanded with offices in Kobe and Osaka but collapsed in 1870, mainly because of the absence of the need for weapons once the **Meiji Restoration of 1868** had removed the **shogunate**. In 1908, Glover was awarded the Order of the Rising Sun (second class), an award normally reserved exclusively for Japanese nationals, and died in Tokyo in 1911. His famous Western-style wooden house in Nagasaki still stands and remains a local tourist attraction.

GOLDEN WEEK. The name given to a 10-day holiday period that begins on 29 April, known as Midori-no-hi, or Green Day, formerly a holiday because it was the birthday of the late emperor Showa (r. 1926–1989), and ending on 5 May, Kodomo-no-hi (Children's Day). Not all the 10 days are holidays, and many corporations take only the official holidays as days off. Others close down for the entire period. Usually upward of a quarter of a million Japanese take the opportunity to travel abroad.

GOTO KEITA (?–1989). Business leader and founder of the **Tokyu Group**, known for his aggressive business style and his equally tough approach to management. A homonyn for the name "Goto" carries the meaning of robber bandit, which helped give Goto his harsh public image. Lifelong rivalry with the Tsustumi family of the **Seibu Group** created the scenario of the Tokyu Kingdom versus the Seibu Empire, evoking the model of a feudal age struggle between two great military houses. Goto was succeeded on his death by his son Goto Noboru.

GOVERNMENT BONDS. A part of central government financial policy to raise funds for various projects is the issuance of bonds (*kokusai*), regulated by the Public Finance Law. **Public corporations** also finance themselves through bonds in much the same way as private **corporations** sell share issues. Although from time to time questions are raised about the necessity of the sale of bonds, their issuance remains a central part of public finance. *See also* CAPITAL MARKETS; MONEY MARKETS.

GREAT DEPRESSION. The 1929 collapse of the U.S. stock market had effects all around the world. Prior to the collapse, Japan was having structural economic problems. It had benefited from minimal involvement in World War I, but after the war, the Western powers resumed trading with Asia and Africa, resulting in a loss of Japan's market share. Smaller companies began to go under, making more room for the survival of the larger ones. The economy was rapidly differentiating, and unemployment suddenly began to rise. Violent strikes became common, but the government failed to act effectively because of its lack of a relevant and appropriate economic policy. Instead of forcing rationalization on industry and returning to the gold standard of pre–World War I days, it tried to buy its way out of the crisis. Military expenditures were increased, and money was poured into industry, railways, and **education** to ease unemployment. Economic problems became further aggravated by the long-lasting effects of the Kanto earthquake of 1923. Further expenditure on damaged infrastructure merely served to stimulate inflation against the background of a depressed world market.

In trying to prevent the collapse of high-cost businesses, the government encouraged support of major enterprises. The **Suzuki**

Shoten incident became symbolic of the encroaching realities of the era. While **Mitsui Bussan** and **Mitsubishi Corporation** had been successful in the war period, Suzuki Shoten had shown the most dramatic expansion. It was therefore one of the high-cost operations that the government wished to save. At the time, it was being financed by the **Bank of Taiwan**, which collapsed in 1927, resulting in 36 lower-tier **banks** collapsing, including the major Bank 15. This produced a chain reaction that reduced the number of banks from 1,417 in 1926 by 541, to 876, still a large number, as subsequent historical events have shown. All bank trading ceased for three weeks in the wake of these events. In 1929, the government was forced to adopt a policy aimed at curbing deflation. Japan returned to the gold standard in 1930, exports were promoted, and production was rationalized. Unemployment grew on a massive scale, and prices fell further, by 17 percent between 1925 and 1929 and by a further 15 percent between 1930 and 1931. Some 1.3 million people were officially recorded as unemployed, a figure that belied the reality of hundreds of thousands of others who were forced back to the countryside or who labored in sweatshops for minimal wages.

All these factors began playing out against the background of increasing militarism and decreasing control over the military. In 1931, the Manchurian Incident, initiated by the Kwantung (Guangdong) Army, resulted in the annexation of Manchuria. The government cautioned the army but could do no more. Japan left the gold standard, and the yen devalued from 2:1 against the dollar to 5:1. The government promoted an export policy and restricted imports. By 1932, there was an export surplus, and by 1936, the value of exports had doubled. Recovery from recession was one step toward the creation of the **Greater Asia Co-Prosperity Sphere**. The China Incident of 1937 was the decisive event in the process that led to the outbreak of war.

GREATER EAST ASIA CO-PROSPERITY SPHERE. The name given by Foreign Minister Matsuoka Yosuke to the region of Japan's domination, which included Japan, Taiwan, China, Manchukuo (Manchuria), French Indochina, and the Dutch East Indies. It was more of a slogan than a reality but was represented internationally as being the concept of an order created by Asians without Western influence. Japan had acquired three main territories in the region. First there was Taiwan in 1895, with cooperation from British missionaries in achieving the surrender of Taipei. Second was the Korean peninsula, annexed in 1910 with tacit American support. Finally, the culminating act was the occupation of Manchuria in 1933. A number of small Pacific islands had been acquired after World War I in 1919: the Mariana Islands, the Caroline Islands, and the Marshall Islands. Sakhalin was acquired in 1905. Still controversial are Japan's claims to the Kurile Islands, dating to 1875.

GROUP DYNAMICS. *Seishin Shuyo* is a distinctively Japanese character-building process that is intended to cultivate group harmony. It teaches self-discipline that accepts deferment of gratification, physical hardship even when sick, loyalty to the group (organization or **corporation** above all else), self-sacrifice when necessary, and unlimited commitment to work. New employees have this instilled into them by being taught it when they join as well as seeing it in their managers' behavior. The main point of contrast with Western styles of management is that the basis of group dynamics is derived from the belief that the fate of the corporation is the direct result of staff and worker effort rather than examining external factors. The employees, however, if the company is successful, expect to share in the benefits of success. **Loyalty** and self-interest are not mutually exclusive. *See also* AMAE; GIRI-JINJO; JAPANESE-STYLE MANAGEMENT; SEMPAI/KOHAI.

GROUP HIRING. *Shudan Shushoku* was first recorded in 1954 when a local association of stores in the Setagaya Ward of Tokyo decided to hire a group of junior-high and senior-high graduates as a group rather than as individuals by enticing them from Niigata with offers of good working conditions, better benefits, and reasonable wages. In 1955, the Tokyo Metropolitan Labor Bureau and Public Employment Security Office jointly engaged in group hiring. Within a decade, over 12,000 people had been hired this way. The acute labor shortages of the 1960s resulted in increased group hiring, which peaked around 1970, after which it declined until 1977, when it was finally abandoned.

GUILDS. *Za* were **trade** guilds organized during the late Heian period (794–1185) and the subsequent Kamakura period (1185–1333) that resembled the guilds of medieval Europe with regard to their social role. The term referred originally to the relationship that a trade group formed with either courtiers or a famous shrine or temple, but it also came to mean the allied group resulting from the relationship. Members paid fees to the patron of the *za* in return for which they received authentication of status, along with the right to perform services for the patron, latterly in the form of either products or monetary gifts. On average, a *za* contained around 10 to 12 members, although larger groups existed. Records show more than 60 Oyamazaki *za* oil merchants doing business in Kyoto in the 14th century.

There were many kinds of *za*, and various classifications existed at various times. As well as business *za*, there were *za* for professions such as acting or entertaining, and there were *za* that dealt with production of goods and other *za* that dealt with the sale of goods. *Za* leaders were referred to as *zato*, master of the *za*.

Regardless of type, all *za* fulfilled two important functions. One was to provide members with protection of their privileged status, which was achieved because of the patronage of the politically powerful families that supported them. More important, however, was the role of the *za* in guaranteeing the monopolistic rights of the members over specific professional or commercial activities. Shrines and temples hired *za* that were affiliated with them for all construction projects. Monopolistic practices were common, and on major projects there was usually cooperation and collusion among *za*, probably not dissimilar to bid-rigging practices among modern construction firms, referred to as ***dango***.

Monopolies over the sale of products were maintained and, where necessary, enforced strictly. Control was also maintained over the supply of raw materials. In contrast to the *za* monopolies, there were "untied" or "free" merchants whose activities were perceived as threatening to the *za* and their members. Frequently, these independent merchants were forced to contract with the *za* in order to ensure a supply of raw materials. Restrictions were placed on the sale of specific items, and members who did not observe the rules in force were punished by having their goods confiscated and had heavy fines levied on them.

While the purpose of the *za* was to facilitate business transactions in an orderly manner, rivalry did exist among *za* that handled similar products. Beyond stressing their lineage or qualifications, some *za* even produced fake documentation from government or court officials. Physical violence was not unknown either, as in the case of the infamous rivalry between the *sake-za* of east Kyoto and the maize-*za* of west Kyoto that bordered on gang warfare.

GYOSEI SHIDO. This terms means the administrative guidance issued by agencies of the Japanese government to assist **corporations** and individuals to understand and adhere to policies considered by the government to be in the best interests of the economy and society. While such guidance cannot be enforced by law, the moral pressure to conform voluntarily is enormous, and failure to comply may have negative consequences in the future. Ministries use a combination of persuasion, advice, and inducements to achieve the desired results. The **Ministry of International Trade and Industry (MITI)** was particularly famous for its advice to corporations, another example of how **Confucian** values continue to function in indirect ways. In some instances, such advice has been sound and beneficial, such as in the cases of **automobiles** and **steel**, while in other areas, it has been either bad or useless. Aerospace, **computers**, and the attempted management of the **Internet** are obvious examples.

GYOSHA. This is the general term for a merchant or business supplier. While the **Meiji period** (1868–1912) *gyosha* were considered people of dubious moral standing, the term came to be used by the government or **corporations** to which specific projects were contracted. Large corporations now refer to subcontractors as *gyosha*, who in turn refer to their suppliers or retailers as *gyosha*.

– H –

HACHIROBE TAKATOSHI (1622–1694). An early **Edo period** (1615–1868) entrepreneur and founder of the **House of Mitsui**, he was born son of a masterless **samurai** (***ronin***) in Matsuzaka near Ise.

His mother was the daughter of a merchant who ran a sake and miso (soybean paste) business. Hachirobe spent much of his youth with his elder brother in Edo (now Tokyo) returning at age 21 to Matsuzaka. In 1772, he elected to move back to Edo with his family of six sons and opened his first shop there. He opened a supply shop in Kyoto in 1673. In 1673 he also opened his first Echigoya dry-goods store, which was followed by a second in 1683, in Nihombashi, on the site of what is now Mitsukoshi Department Store, still the nation's largest retailer. His business policy was "cash payment, low prices, and no markups." By having customers visit his shop, he could satisfy their needs more effectively and even customize clothing by measuring his clients in person. Hachirobe also supplied many small shops and in so doing weakened the rigid distinction between wholesaler and retailer. He both recognized and responded to the growing mass market of Edo and in spite of opposition became recognized as a leading business figure among the merchants of the city. He was succeeded after his death by his eldest son, Hachiroemon, and thereafter all heads of the house took that name.

HAN EI SEMBAI. These were businesses operated as monopolies by domainal (*han*) governments during the later stages of the **Edo period** (1615–1867), covering a wide range of economic activities, such as rice, silk, cereals, textiles, and even armaments. They were the forerunners of the idea that money, finance, and the management of industry by government are functions of the state, a concept that was readily understood and employed after the **Meiji Restoration of 1868**.

HANKYU CORPORATION. Private **railway** corporation founded by **Kobayashi Ichizo** (1873–1957) as Mino Arima Railway to provide transport in the Kinki region, the Kobe–Kyoto–Osaka area. One innovative aspect of business policy was the idea of housing developments along the railway tracks to make travel more attractive and practical. Another feature followed by other railways was the idea of locating a **department store** at the railway terminal station. The railway owns 141 kilometers of track and has been consistently one of the best performers in the sector. *See also* HANKYU DEPARTMENT STORES.

HANKYU DEPARTMENT STORE. Hankyu Hyakkaten was established by **Hankyu Corporation** in 1929 as a project designed for the convenience of passengers. The concept of a **railway** terminal store became the model for most other regional private railways. Although the stores became independent in 1947, when large business conglomerates were broken up by order of the **Supreme Commander Allied Powers (SCAP)**, it remains a core company within the Hankyu Group covering transportation, distribution, real estate, and travel and leisure industry companies. Hankyu operates six stores in Japan in Tokyo, Osaka, Kyoto, and Kobe as well as overseas stores in London, Paris, and Milan. The main store is in Osaka.

HAYAKAWA TOKUJI (1895–1981). He was the entrepreneurial founder of **Sharp Corporation** who invented the snap-in belt buckle and the mechanical propelling pencil, known in Japan as a "sharp pencil" because it never required to be sharpened. After losing his first factory during the Kanto earthquake of 1923, he moved to Osaka and engaged in research into radio technology. He succeeded in making his first crystal radio in 1925. With this product as a start, he began to produce more inventions. Hayakawa's management was not merely in product invention but also in maintaining an efficient and high-quality workplace. This was one feature that influenced the next generation of entrepreneurs, such as **Morita Akio**, founder of **Sony Corporation**, in its formative years. By the time of his death, Sharp had become a worldwide household name for quality **electronic** products.

HEIBONSHA. Founded in 1914 by **Shimonaka Yasaburo** (1878–1961) as a publishing company specializing in encyclopedias, dictionaries, and academic texts in the fields of science and philosophy. It pioneered the production of encyclopedias in Japan, has published many famous series, and has expanded to the fields of the art and literature of Asia.

HINO MOTORS. Hino Jidosha Kogyo was founded in 1910 and affiliated with the **Toyota Motor Corporation** since 1966. It manufactures diesel- and gasoline-engine vehicles under the brand name Hino. It is the largest Japanese corporation producing trucks 8.4 tons and over. Its engines are known for the Hino micromixing system

(HMMS), which is considered one of the most efficient fuel–air mixing combustion engine designs. It has numerous overseas activities and is a continuing pioneer in antipollution technology. Its headquarters are in Hino City.

HITACHI. Hitachi Seisakuso takes its name from the town of Hitachi in Ibaraki prefecture. It was founded in 1910 as an electric machinery repair company to serve Kuhara Kogyosho, a company founded by Odaira Namihei (1874–1951). It broke away from the parent company in 1920 and by the early 1930s was well established as a producer of electrical machinery. It also became one of the key businesses of the Nissan ***zaibatsu*** that was dissolved in 1945 by order of the **Supreme Commander Allied Powers (SCAP)**. Before and after World War II, it created a variety of new businesses. It is now one of the central companies of the **Hitachi Group** of over 800 **corporations**. Its main business has been generators, transformers, industrial machinery, and electric locomotives. It also builds industrial plants for specific purposes, such as for copper wire production and parts for cast-iron products. It entered the **computer** industry in 1959 and expanded to other advanced **electronic** products and is ranked among the world's most sophisticated corporations in its sector. Its headquarters are in Tokyo.

HITACHI CHEMICALS. Hitachi Kasei Kogyo was founded in 1962 as an independent company although originally the chemical products division of **Hitachi**. The company produces a wide range of organic and inorganic products, principally electrical equipment, synthetic resins, housing equipment, and construction and environmental preservation–related products. Worldwide exports include copper-clad laminated sheets for printed circuits and laminated varnish. Subsidiaries operate in the United States, Germany, Hong Kong, Singapore, and Taiwan. The head office is in Tokyo.

HITACHI GROUP. A large group of almost 800 **corporations** that are linked to the parent company, **Hitachi**, led by three major ones, Hitachi Cable, **Hitachi Chemicals**, and **Hitachi Metals**. Each of the three has four or five large subsidiaries specializing in different areas of electronics manufacture. These cover industrial equipment, transport-related equipment, household appliances, and electronic communications equipment. Each group has supporting companies that handle their sales and marketing, after-sales, and other types of service, including Hitachi Credit Corporation. The group image is often likened to a *ronin* (the name given to a **samurai** who had no master) because of its image as a maverick known to pioneer unusual technologies. It introduced consolidated accounting within the group in the late 1950s, permitting individual firms to pursue their own entrepreneurial policies but within centrally managed financial structures. These characteristics have enabled the Hitachi Group to become one of Japan's most effective in addition to being the largest of Japan's industrial groups. The three main companies also belong to the **Sanwa Group** of 43 major corporations, all financed by the former **Sanwa Bank**, now merged and known as the **UFJ Bank** and later the Mitsubishi UFJ Bank. *See also* BANKING HISTORY; KIGYO SHUDAN; ZAIBATSU.

HITACHI SHIPBUILDING. Hitachi Zosen is a first tier **shipbuilding corporation** that grew out of Osaka Iron Works, a company founded by a British trader in 1881. Along with Ishikwajima-Harima Heavy Industries, **Mistubishi Heavy Industries**, and **Mitsui Zosen**, it is one of the major shipbuilders in Japan. In 1975, its peak year, it produced almost 1.5 million gross tons of shipping, representing 10 percent of Japan's total production. The company has engaged in technology transfer with Westinghouse Electric Co. in the United States and companies in Denmark, Germany, and Switzerland. With the decline in shipbuilding, the corporation moved into the areas of chemical manufacturing, ocean development, and industrial plants. It also set up a trading company in Panama. Its head office is in Osaka.

HOKKAIDO DEVELOPMENT AGENCY. Hokkaido Kaihatsucho is an agency established by the Hokkaido Development Law in 1950 to plan and implement strategies for the overall socioeconomic development of the northern island of Hokkaido.

HOKKAIDO TAKUSHOKU BANK. Hokkaido Takshoku Ginko is the smallest of the former 13 **city banks** and the only one to fail. It was founded in 1900 to assist in the development of the island of Hokkaido. In 1950, it became a commercial **bank** as part of the strategy of the Hokkaido Development Law. It collapsed on 17 November 1997 because of massive nonperforming loans, creating one of the events that signaled the banking crisis of the closing years of the 20th century. This was followed by the collapse of **Yamaichi Securities** one week later.

HOKURIKU ELECTRIC POWER COMPANY. Hokuriku Denryoku is a power company serving Toyama, Inshikawa, and Fukui prefectures that were grouped under the postwar restructuring of the energy industry. It provides supply primarily from hydroelectric power. It runs over 100 plants and has its headquarters in Toyama City, Toyama prefecture.

HOLDING COMPANIES. *Mochikabu Gaisha* were banned after World War II by the **Supreme Commander Allied Powers (SCAP)** as a provision of the **Antimonopoly Law of 1947**. A revision of the Antimonopoly Law enacted by the National Diet in 1997 lifted the prohibition and permitted the formation of holding companies. While the law required that any groups having total assets in excess of ¥300 billion that wished to form a holding company should inform the **Fair Trade Commission**, no other restrictions were specified. **Daiei**, a large but financially troubled supermarket operator, was the first company to take advantage of the change in the law, forming Daiei Holding Company in December 1997. *See also* KEIRETSU; ZAIBATSU.

HONDA MOTOR COMPANY. Honda Giken Kogyo is the largest manufacturer of motorcycles in the world and manufacturer of cars, trucks, sport-utility vehicles (SUVs), and industrial engines. Founded by **Honda Soichiro** (1906–1991) as Honda Gijutsu Kenkyujo, primarily a research center, based in Hammamatsu in Shizuoka prefecture, it became a company in 1948. From motorbikes, Honda moved to cars, ushering in the era of low-pollution engines with the Compound Vortex Controlled Combustion (CDVCC) engine and automatic transmissions. Living up to its motto "Adopt a World Perspective," Honda Motors has over 44 international tie-ups of various kinds in 30 countries. Honda was also the first Japanese **automobile** manufacturer in the United States, having set up in Marysville, Ohio, in 1982. Its headquarters are in Tokyo.

HONDA SOICHIRO (1906–1991). Founder of **Honda Motor Company**, he was born in Shizuoka and educated at Hammamatsu Technical Higher School (now known as Shizuoka University), where he studied engineering. Before World War II, he opened his own **automobile** repair shop in Hammamatsu, where he began making racing cars in his spare time. His models had many innovative features, and they won numerous races. In 1936, he entered the All-Japan speed rally, where he had a bad crash that ended his racing career. He then began making piston rings, which he tried, unsuccessfully, to sell to **Toyota**. By effort and perseverance, he became a supplier to Toyota in 1940.

In 1945, he sold his company to Toyota and took a year's sabbatical. He set up his Honda Giken (Honda Technical Research) in 1946 and produced his first motorcycle in 1948. He was joined by **Fujisawa Takeo** in 1949, and together they created Honda Motors, with Honda supervising technical development and Fujisawa managing the business. By 1961, Honda motorcycles had won every prize in the British Isle of Man motorbike rally, against the then famous British Raleigh and BSA machines. Automobiles came next, and the subsequent development of the company is a major part of postwar Japanese business expansion. Both he and Fujisawa retired from the company in 1973, but not before seeing it grow into a worldwide brand name.

HOTOKU. Repayment and indebtedness, a moral ideal put forward by **Ninomiya Sontoku** (1787–1856), an **Edo period** (1615–1868) farmer-philosopher who taught the importance of four important virtues: sincerity of mind (*shisei*), industrious labor (*kinro*), a planned economy (*bundo*), and yielding to others (*suijo*). These values were strongly lauded by the Ministry of Home Affairs in the early 20th century as part of the national cultivation of moral virtue. They were linked into the virtues of thrift and diligence as well as the virtue of perseverance against adversity, taught as the foundation of moral **education** in schools.

The entire concept was symbolized by the presence of a statue of Ninomiya Kinjiro, a little boy reading a book and carrying firewood on his back, placed in every elementary school playground nationwide. He was praised as a model of endeavor, someone who overcame adversity and suffering to achieve success. The ideas of Ninomiya Sontoku still command the respect of many Japanese intellectuals. *See also* BOSHIN SHOSHO.

HOTTA SHOZO (1899–). He was a banker born in Aichi prefecture who joined the **Sumitomo Bank** after graduating from Kyoto University. He became president of the **bank** in 1952 and chairman in 1970. Under his leadership the bank grew to become the third largest in terms of deposits, by means of which it was able to help in the development of the powerful postwar **Sumitomo Group**.

HOUSE FOOD INDUSTRIAL (Haus Shokohin Kogyo). Formed in 1947, the company is famous for its techniques for the production of processed foods, curry sauces, spices, and instant foods. It is a large importer of ingredients from India and China as well as Western countries. Its headquarters are in Osaka.

HOUSE PRINCIPLE. *See* EDO PERIOD MANAGEMENT; IE GENSOKU.

HUMAN NATURE IN CONFUCIAN THOUGHT. In Chinese Confucian thought, there are two antithetical concepts relating to human nature. These are expressed in Japanese by the doctrines of *sei-zen-setsu*, which states that human nature is thought to have a potential for good, and its opposite, *sei-aku-setsu*, which recognizes in human nature a propensity to evil. Under the influence of **Shinto**, which teaches the power of purification, the potential for good came to be stressed. In its essence, human nature is not evil. As the Japanese proverb states it, "Honshin ni oite wa, akunin wa inai" (In their heart of hearts, no one is evil). This squares with the Confucian dictum that "learning should make a man a saint," also an implicit recognition of human potential for good. Consequently, in the event of a serious mistake caused by human error, the emphasis is not so much on punishing the guilty, as Western management might judge, as on how to prevent a recurrence.

HYOGO SHIPYARDS. Dating back to 1870 and built by the *daimyo* (lord) of Kanazawa (now Ishikawa prefecture), the yard was located in

Kobe's Kyogo area. The government took control in 1872, but it was sold to Kawasaki Shozo (1837–1912), a **Meiji period** (1868–1912) entrepreneur who merged it with his own yards in Kobe and Tokyo under the name Kawasaki Zensho, Kawasaki Shipyards, now a part of **Kawasaki Heavy Industries**. *See also* SHIPBUILDING INDUSTRY.

HYOROMAI. This was a **rice** tax imposed when need arose by the Kamakura period (1192–1333) government and continued into the Muromachi period (1338–1573). It was raised to pay for military expenditure in the event of war. Minamoto Yoritomo, founder of the Kamakura shogunate, formally instituted it in 1185. The tax amounted to approximately 2 percent of the average annual yield. Under the Ashikaga Shogunate, a number of ***shoen*** (estates) were given to his officers who levied, in some cases, up to 50 percent of yield. During the period of the Northern and Southern Courts (1336–1392), the Southern Court depended on it as a source of revenue. It fell into disuse during the period of civil war and was replaced eventually by a new system of rice taxation imposed by the **Tokugawa government** in the 17th century.

– I –

IBM JAPAN. Founded in 1937 as the Watson Business Machines Co. of Japan to market IBM's punch-card system, IBM Japan was reincorporated in 1949 under its present name. It is now the Japan subsidiary of International Business Machines Corporation, known worldwide as IBM. In 1950, the Japanese government used the IBM punch-card system for the national census, and in 1958, the Japanese government's Atomic Research Institute bought one of the earliest of IBM's computers. From 1960, IBM began manufacturing computers in Japan and exported them widely. Its most successful business has been in the area of mainframe superlarge systems. As a brand name, it continues to remain prestigious in Japan, and, with its unique rental and leasing system of both hardware and "software, it generates substantial income for IBM World Trade Co. Its head office is in Tokyo.

ICHI. This is the old Japanese word for a market, the origin of which is unknown. It features still in the names of places, usually in combination with a day of the month, such as Yokkaichi, a city in Mei prefecture. Yokkaichi means that a market was set up on all days bearing the number 4, namely, the 4th, 14th, and 24th days of the month. Itsukaichi is in the west of Tokyo and held markets on days that carried the number 5.

Ichi seems to have meant a place where people assembled for various purposes. The oldest known locations almost always bear the name of trees, such as *Tsubaki-ichi* (camellia) or *Ega-ichi* (wild orange). Markets were also cash events, with records showing wagonloads of money being transported at the end of the day.

IDEMITSU KOSAN. Founded by **Idemitsu Sazo** (1885–1981) in 1911 as Idemitsu Shokai, an oil dealership, it was reorganized in 1940 as Idemitsu Kosan. At its peak, it had a refining capacity of 860,000 barrels a day between its refineries in Hokkkaido, Chiba, Yamaguchi, Hyogo, and Aichi prefectures and maintained a tanker fleet of 2.1 million tons to ensure supply, managed by Idemitsu Tanker Company. Idemitsu Oil Development was created in 1976 to expand operations. This led the company to venture into the alternative energy field in order to become a comprehensive energy corporation. It retailed through a network of almost 9,000 filling stations nationwide. The head office in Tokyo supervised its 49 sales offices. It has overseas representation in New York, Los Angeles, Denver, London, Kuwait, Teherana, Royadh, Abu Dhabi, Singapore, Sydney, and Rio de Janeiro. *See also* PETROLEUM INDUSTRY.

IDEMITSU SAZO (1885–1981). He was a **Meiji period** (1868–1912) entrepreneur and founder of **Idemitsu Kosan**, the leading company in the Idemitsu oil enterprise. He began importing high-octane gasoline from the United States as well as crude oil from Iran in a 130,000-ton tanker custom-built in 1951. In his lifetime, he gathered a large collection of Asian art that he housed in the Idemitsu Art Gallery, opened in 1966.

IE GENSOKU. The "house principle" embodies most of Japan's central traditional social values and is one of the important concepts needed to understand the dynamics of the social and business culture of the country. The older House Constitutions date mostly from the 18th century, such as that of the House of **Mitsui**, and call on members to revere the ***kami*** and the Buddha and to follow the teachings of Confucius, in other words, to show deference and respect to the ancestors of the House. In this way, the power of **Confucianism** remains a silent influence that continues to permeate the culture in spite of modernization.

The influence of the *ie gensoku* may be seen in numerous ways. One is that generations are counted meticulously. The Imperial Household claims 125 generations, Izumo Taisha claims 95, Tsubaki Grand Shrine claims 97, Kikkoman Shoyu claims 16, and so on. The House of Tokugawa, although out of power after 15 generations, still continues to count. The present incumbent, Yoshinobu, is listed as the 24th Tokugawa. The Sumitomo family, while no longer in absolute control of the **Sumitomo group**, still has a considerable interest in its welfare. While this kind of aspiration may not seem realistic, in fact many new businesses do aspire to the same style of corporate longevity.

A second consequence of the house principle is seen in the attitude of employees toward the **corporation**. They perceive themselves as guardians of its survival. They feel they have part ownership in the organization, a fact that influences the behavior of shareholders. In the modern setting, the relation of the employee to the company has been characterized as a "kin–tract" system, a combination of "kinship" and "contract." While family-owned businesses still exist in Europe and the United States, they are the exception rather than the rule. In Japan, the kin–tract system functions to strengthen the sense of loyalty throughout the corporate ranks, a value that has served Japanese business well over the centuries. *See also* EDO PERIOD MANAGEMENT; ENTERPRISE UNIONS; LABOR RELATIONS.

IKEDA HAYATO (1899–1965). He was a **Meiji period** (1868–1912) bureaucrat and post–World War II prime minister who proposed the Double Income Policy (Shotoku-Baizo Keikaku) of 1960, which formed the basis of Japan's amazing economic expansion of the succeeding period. Under his leadership, Japan joined the Organization for Economic Cooperation and Development (OECD) in 1964 shortly before his death.

IKUNO SILVER MINE. Ikuno Ginzan is recorded as having been worked as early as the year 807. Taking its name from Ikuno (in what is now Hyogo prefecture), it gained prominence as it was developed by the local *daimyo* (lord) who mined it for income. By the end of the 16th century, it was taken over by the feudal lords **Oda Nobunaga** (1534–1598) and **Toyotomi Hideyoshi** (1536–1595), after which it passed to the **Tokugawa government** of the **Edo period** (1615–1868). The **Meiji period** (1868–1912) government developed it using French engineering methods but sold it to the **Mitsubishi** company in 1896. After the silver had been completely exhausted, the mine produced copper and zinc and had the largest tin refinery in the country. It was finally closed in 1973 after a remarkable history in which it had served successive government interests for over 1,000 years. *See also* MINING.

IMPERIAL RESCRIPTS OF THE MEIJI PERIOD (1868–1912). Just as the **Meiji Restoration of 1868** was carried out in the name of the emperor, so too major ordinances and social directives were issued in his name. The most famous was the Imperial Rescript on Education, which every school pupil was required to memorize and recite. One that had a major impact on the economy was the Imperial Rescript on Thrift and Diligence (**Boshin Shosho**), issued in 1908 with the objective of enjoining the people to frugal ways and to save money, which of course gave the government working capital needed for various purposes to compensate for the great expenses of the wars with Russia and China.

INAMORI KAZUO (1932–). Postwar industrialist and founder of **Kyocera Corporation** and DDI Corporation, he is ranked alongside **Morita Akio** of **Sony Corporation** and **Honda Soichiro** of **Honda Motors** as an entrepreneur. Having been unsuccessful in attempts to enter a prestigious college, he graduated in the field of chemical engineering from Kagoshima University in 1955 and entered Shofu Industries, an electronics manufacturer located in Kyoto. He left in 1959 when the management refused to support his interest in ceramics research and with seven colleagues founded Kyocera. Like many other Japanese business leaders, he placed core values at the center of his business, declaring "reverence for the divine and for other human beings" as part of the corporate mission and goal.

INAYAMA YOSHIHIRO (1904–1987). He was a **Showa period** (1926–1989) business leader born into the family of the Ginza Inayama Bank, which collapsed as a result of the **Financial Crisis of 1927**. After graduating from the University of Tokyo in 1927, he joined the Ministry of Commerce and was assigned to the government-managed **Yawata Iron and Steel Works**. In 1934, the firm merged, and from this the Nippon Steel Co. was created. Inayama remained at Yawata, which was in the private sector. The merged corporations that constituted Yawata split in 1950, and Inayama eventually became president of Yawata in 1970. In 1970, he worked with **Nagano Shigeo**, then president of Fuji Steel, to combine resources and thus avoid unnecessary conflict in the sector, and out of this came the **Nippon Steel Corporation**. He eventually became president and chairman of the board in 1973.

Inayama is remembered for his views that cartels were not necessarily evil and that in some cases they guaranteed market and price stability. He was critical of any rigid application of the **Antimonopoly Law of 1947**. He was also a powerful advocate of increased trade with the People's Republic of China, visiting China as a representative of the Japanese steel industry. He is remembered also for becoming the fifth chairman of **Keidanren** in 1980. *See also* IRON AND STEEL INDUSTRY.

INDUSTRIAL BANK OF JAPAN (IBJ). Nippon Kogyo Ginko was founded in 1902 as a private **bank** specializing in long-term loans to Japanese businesses. It was instrumental in bringing substantial foreign investment to Japan through a variety of strategies, including underwriting corporate debentures and municipal bonds as well as arranging for the overseas issuance of these financial instruments. It was active in promoting the development of Korea and the Japanese-controlled parts of China. After 1945, it became a normal bank, but after the 1952 Long-Term Credit Bank Law, it joined the **Long-Term Credit Bank of Japan** and the **Nippon Credit Bank** as one of the three principal banks specializing in loans for industrial purposes.

During the period of high economic growth from the early 1960s to the late 1970s, the bank supported heavy industry and the chemical industry by underwriting domestic and foreign loans. As Japan's foreign currency reserves grew during the 1970s, the bank began issuing yen-based bonds through the Asian Development Bank and the World Bank. It also created a network of subsidiaries, such as the Industry-Bank von Japan in Germany and the IBJ Finance Co. in Hong Kong. Later branches were formed in New York, London, Saudi Arabia, and other important international centers. Its headquarters are in Tokyo. The IBJ merged with the **Dai-ichi Kangyo** and the **Fuji Bank** in September 2000 to form the **Mizuho Financial Group**.

INDUSTRIAL ORGANIZATION. The manner and degree to which markets and capital are concentrated and controlled within Japan's **industrial structure** shows both similarities and differences with those of Western nations. While the evolution of industrial structure paralleled that of other developed nations, the manner and degree of change are different. Indeed, one key to understanding the key differences is to identify how traditional patterns of business interact with the impact of industrial and economic growth.

With regard to market control, the role of the prewar ***zaibatsu*** and their continued existence as **enterprise groups** (*kigyo shudan*) in the postwar period has preserved the preference for industrial development to be financed by **banks** rather than from public shareholding, ensuring that the **cross holding** of shares continues. This preference led to the revision in 1997 of the **Antimonopoly Law of 1947**, which had abolished holding companies. *See also* KEIRETSU.

INDUSTRIAL POLICY. Unlike Western terms such as "economic policy" or "monetary policy," industrial policy (Sangyo Seisaku) is original to Japan and was developed as part of the postwar restructuring of the virtually nonexistent industrial base of the nation. Government ministries, particularly the **Ministry of International Trade and Industry (MITI),** with the cooperation of business organizations, set various agendas for the development and organization of industry to meet Japan's social and economic needs. While academically less defined than a concept such as fiscal policy, the concept of industrial policy suited the socioeconomic structure of Japan and was most effective in promoting postwar growth and development.

It covers three broad areas: **industrial organization**, the development of measures to keep order in the market; **industrial structure**, the creation of policies to develop key industries and to gradually phase out declining ones; and income policy and international **trade** issues that affect industry as a whole. Unlike Europe and the United States, where industrial policy focuses on industrial organization, Japanese industrial policy centers on industrial structure based on the premise that free-market mechanisms cannot produce the optimal distribution of resources.

The devices used to achieve these ends were severe import restrictions, foreign exchange control, and administrative guidance (***gyosei shido***) along with fiscal and **tax** policies to generate loans and competitive advantages. These measures were spectacularly successful in the 1950s and 1960s and offered protection to fledgling sectors of the period, such as the chemical industry and the heavy industries. These protective devices remained in place and became a source of friction between Japan and particularly the United States in the field of **semiconductors**. While Japan moved to eliminate many restrictions as befitting a developed economy, strong allegations continued to be made about **nontariff barriers**, some of which were genuine but others of which were derived from the structures of Japan's closed culture.

INDUSTRIAL REVITALIZATION CORPORATION OF JAPAN (IRCJ). This is a government-created corporation set up in 2003 to provide discretionary assistance in the rehabilitation of **corporations** struggling with high levels of debt.

INDUSTRIAL STRUCTURE. Normally explained in terms of how power is concentrated in terms of monopolies or oligopolies that control markets and how capital is owned, Japan presents a picture that does not appear to vary widely from Western norms with regard to development but that nevertheless retains several distinctive features of its own.

In terms of the division of the economy into primary (**agriculture**, forestry, and **fisheries**), secondary (mining, manufacturing, **construction**, transport, and communications), and tertiary (**banking**, finance, real estate, services, and public administration) industry, there has been gradual movement of capital and labor from primary to secondary and then from secondary to tertiary as the economy grew and matured since the **Meiji Restoration of 1868**, which began the process of modernization. In this regard, Japan appears to have followed the normally accepted Western model.

National development can be gauged by the composition and balance of exports and imports. In the early **Meiji Period** (1868–1912), Japan's main exports were tea and especially raw silk, which remained a principal export product until 1929. Silk was followed by cotton textiles, which continued into the period after 1945. The postwar expansion of manufacturing industries resulted in textiles being replaced by **electronic** goods, **shipbuilding**, and other heavy industry products. Like other countries entering the postindustrial phase, Japan has experienced a growth in tertiary industries, along with a corresponding decline in the secondary industries. However, the complete "service revolution" as welcomed by the government of Margaret Thatcher in the United Kingdom during the 1980s, accompanied by the **big bang** caused by financial liberalization, has not been seen in Japan in a way that was expected, although some similar reforms were implemented.

Suspicions about unguided free-market mechanisms and a preference to finance new industrial projects and sectors by special banks that raise finance through government-issued bonds rather than through shareholder investment (something deemed too capricious to be reliable) have maintained strong support for secondary industries represented by giants such as **Nissan** and **Toyota**.

In 1964, the government created an Industrial Structure Council (Sangyo Kozo Shingikai, or Sankoshin for short) to make recommendations to the **Ministry of International Trade and Industry (MITI)** on the industrial structure of the economy, which is one reason why change is regulated in a manner that keeps order and balance. The Council was an amalgamation of two earlier bodies, the Industrial Structure Study Commission and the Industrial Rationalization Council, and consists of a mixture of representatives of commerce and industry (over 50 percent), several academics, bankers, and **labor union** officials. The council is weighted heavily toward manufacturing and, not unsurprisingly, mapped out a course for the future that identified knowledge-intensive industries such as computers, **electronics**, aircraft, and satellites as future targets. The introduction of satellite navigation systems into new **automobiles** is one example of how the manufacturing sector has upgraded itself. The council has always stressed consumer satisfaction as well as the need to develop domestic sources of energy. *See also* CAPITAL MARKETS; MONEY MARKETS.

INSTANT FOODS. The oldest recorded "instant food" in Japan is *hoshi-ii*, dried boiled **rice**, the staple diet of travelers and soldiers in earlier periods of Japanese history. In the 1920s, *shiruko* (*adzuki* bean–based thick soup) appeared alongside instant curry sauce, the beginning of the ever-popular dish curry rice. Powdered *misoshiru* (soup made from soybean paste) was developed along with dried vegetables to provide convenient provisions for the military. The postwar period has seen enormous growth in the industry as it has expanded both domestically and internationally. The most famous product worldwide has been the "instant noodles" of **Nissin Food Products**.

INSURANCE INDUSTRY. The insurance industry in its present form traces its roots to the formation of ***mujin*** (mutual financing associations), which vaguely resembled insurance companies in the West. When foreign shipping entered Japan more freely from 1859 on, insurance systems of various types began to appear, especially in seaports such as Nagasaki, Yokohama, and Kobe. Tokyo Marine Insurance (now Tokyo Marine & Fire Insurance) opened for business in 1879. **Meiji Mutual Life Insurance** became the first life insurance company in 1881. Tokyo Fire Insurance (now **Yasuda Fire & Marine Insurance**) opened in 1888. In 1916, the government introduced a basic national insurance program that led to the introduction in 1927 of a system of social insurance, beginning with health insurance, part of a total policy of socioeconomic management. World War II severely damaged the industry, but it was able to recover because of postwar development.

The modern structure of the insurance industry classifies all insurance other than life insurance (*seimei hoken*) as nonlife or accident insurance (*songai hoken*). Private insurers cover fire, accident, and compensation insurance intended to provide a basic minimum income for victims. The government provides cover for nonprofitable insurances, such as forest insurance, shipowners' insurance, and export credit insurance. Most of the nonlife types of insurance in the West can be found in Japan, which has several unique types of insurance, including savings plans and earthquake cover.

Government regulation of the sector has been traditionally quite strict, although the so-called **big bang** of the late 20th century was intended to loosen regulatory controls. The government licenses all companies selling insurance. Insurance for private companies is divided into property insurance and accident insurance. Companies may elect to work in only one or the other category. Nonlife insurance companies conduct business through over 250,000 agents, while life insurance companies employ around 300,000 sales representatives, most of whom are **women**. Insurance brokerages were not permitted by the government, which was one of the many issues that lay behind the arguments for reform of **banking** and insurance.

The protracted **recession of the 1990s** culminated in parallel crises in both banking and insurance, resulting in collapses and amalgamations in what had become overregulated and inefficiently managed sectors of the economy.

INTERNATIONALIZATION. The term *kokusaika*, or "internationalization," which did not exist in English until it was translated from Japanese, was invented in Japan during the 1970s to refer to the process of the yen becoming an international currency. It did not refer to any changes in Japanese society but referred exclusively to the currency. It later came to take on a broader meaning and by the end of the century had become closely linked with the term **globalization**.

INTERNET. The slow development of the Internet was the result of enormous restrictions placed on the already highly regulated **telecommunications system** under control of the Ministry of Posts and Telecommunications. Licenses issued were for limited use of the Internet, hindering its development and its business application. Forced change came about because of three factors. One was a strong-minded individual, Murai Jura, who led a group in 1992 in a movement called "Internet Initiative Japan" in defiance of government regulation. He demonstrated that his system was more efficient than that being promoted by the government. In view of the fact that monitoring the Internet is virtually impossible, he effectively ended the government monopoly.

A second factor that strengthened Murai's position further was the occurrence of the Kobe earthquake in 1955. The Internet facilitated communication at a time when conventional systems had collapsed. In spite of such advances, high charges, low density of personal computers, and the growing global dominance of English still continued to impede growth. However, through slow and steady expansion, around 20 percent of the population became Internet linked by 1999. Slow and expensive access remained an ongoing problem, with individuals paying Internet service providers (ISPs) as well as online time charges to **Nippon Telephone and Telegraph (NTT)**. This made access to the Internet in Japan very expensive by international standards.

On top of these two came a third factor, namely, that of the rapid development of related technology, particularly that of mobile phones. The most important development was the creation of Asymmetric Digital Subscriber Lines (ASLD), a broadband system that enabled large volumes of data to travel the Internet at high speed. Utilizing this, DoCoMo, Inc., the largest mobile phone service provider in the country, launched i-mode, an Internet connection service for mobile phones. By the middle of 2000, 10 million subscribers were using i-mode, and large numbers of websites were being created for mobile phones designed with small screens for e-commerce, known also as "m-commerce." The subsequent explosion of the mobile phone market from business professionals to junior high school students sending each other e-mails with graphics on their mobile phones meant that government control had been rendered impossible. Many technical difficulties still remain as a result of earlier government intervention. While broadband systems exist, in practice they are, in the case of universities, routed through a limited number of suppliers, resulting in congestion at peak hours and consequent delays. Lack of dedicated specialists in software troubleshooting has exacerbated the overall problem, and many organizations in Japan remain relatively disadvantaged when compared to their North American or European counterparts in terms of nationwide service access.

INVESTMENT, INWARD. Japanese aggregate investment in various sectors of the economy, principally housing, plant and equipment, inventory, and government investment in infrastructure and other related development projects, such as highways and airports, has been consistently around or over 30 percent of gross domestic product (GDP). This is one of the highest in the world and is often cited as a reason for overall economic growth. Of particular significance is plant and equipment, which alone accounts for an average of 15 to 20 percent of GDP. Some critics argue that this causes overproduction and generates the need for dumping. The opponents of this position claim that the economy is "export led" and that success in this area generates the capital for investment and growth.

Traditionally, when consumer spending becomes sluggish, the government invests in public works. This leads to a third position that postwar growth has been "investment led" because capital formation has made possible a high level of investment, which has in turn raised the capital-to-labor ratio and consequently labor productivity. In normal cycles, consumption, the other side of domestic demand, maintains manufacturing levels.

INVESTMENT, OUTWARD. Japan is a massive exporter of capital for investment in service and manufacturing industries around the world. Statistics for 2003 showed a massive U.S.$12 billion invested in the United Kingdom, with just over half of that amount invested in the United States. The Netherlands comes third, and the People's Republic of China, although still fourth, has been steadily climbing in the table. The total for all European Union countries was U.S.$17 billion in contrast to just over U.S.$7 billion in Asia. However, that figure should be set beside Japan's regional contribution to Overseas Development Aid (ODA). Sixty percent of all ODA in Asia is Japanese (the grand total being U.S.$11 billion). Added up on a world scale, Japan is the single-largest contributor of ODA, which should be placed alongside investment figures since Japanese ODA is invariably in the form of managed investment projects.

Japan's outward investment has a number of objectives to achieve. A vital one is the procurement of natural resources for manufacturing and for fuels. Access to local markets, **globalization** of business interests, the need for cheap labor, and the expansion of foreign trade are all on the agenda. While Japan is frequently viewed as a predator in foreign markets, the fact is that Japan also makes a major contribution to development of the world economy.

INVESTMENT TRUSTS. Toshi Shintaku are companies that collect money from the general public to invest in stocks, bonds, and other financial instruments, including short-term interbank money markets. Dividends are paid to investors at rates determined according to time and circumstance. By law, monies must be deposited with one of the seven **trust banks**. One key point of difference from mutual and other types of funds is that no stock is issued in the name of the trust.

IRON AND STEEL INDUSTRY. Japan is the world's second-largest but probably most efficient producer of the world's highest-quality steel. It is also the world's largest exporter of steel, which is in great demand and which was a vital element in the postwar economic growth of the country. Although a modern industry, Japanese acquaintance with and ability to produce high-quality steel has a long history, reaching back far beyond the modern period.

Iron was in use in Japan as early as 300 C.E., when both ironware and a manufacturing process were imported, via the Korean peninsula, from China. By the 15th century, a process known as *tatara-buki* had been developed. The first *tatara* furnace is thought to have been built in Izumo no Kuni (now Shimane prefecture) in the 13th century. By the end of the 16th century, lumps of iron known as *nambanbetsu* were imported on Portuguese ships. These were similar to the *tatara* products but contained higher levels of phosphorus and carbon. The *tatara* process was used to produce iron and steel for swords until the introduction of the blast furnace in the early years of the **Meiji period** (1868–1912).

During the latter part of the **Edo period** (1615–1868), in response to an increasing need for iron and steel, **Oshima Takato**, an engineer from Morioka, pioneered Western-style furnaces at Kamaishi (in present-day Iwate prefecture). Although limited in capacity, his furnaces were the first commercial producers of iron for steel manufacture. The Kamaishi Iron Mine was taken over by the government in 1873. The government also built two furnaces with a capacity of

9,000 metric tons imported from the United Kingdom. It was not, however, until **Tanaka Chobei** (1858–1924) took control that the furnaces were successfully operated.

The government took the initiative and created the Yawata Iron and Steel Works in Kyushu in 1896, an integrated facility that began production in 1901 of 60,000 metric tons a year. Steelmaking and rolling equipment were also installed. By 1912, private enterprise had joined the government in the form of **Sumitomo Metal Industries**, **Kobe Steel**, **Kawasaki Steel Corporation**, and **Nippon Kokan**. In 1934, the government created Nippon Steel. After 1945, it was divided into Yawata Steel and Fuji Steel, but in 1970, the two companies merged to form the **Nippon Steel Corporation**.

Japan's ranking as a steel producer grew in terms of both quality and quantity in the postwar high-growth period. Eleven major integrated plants have been built since 1960, bringing the total to 21. These are among the most modern and efficient in the world and have developed new technologies in the field that remain world class. However, while between the early 1970s and 1986, Japan continued to export an average of over 30 million tons per year, the peak was reached, and after 1987, exports began to decline. Production again peaked in the late 1990s but in 2004 was down yet again, as was the case with most major steel producers. A number of factors were responsible. Foremost was competition from South Korea, followed closely by the rise in the yen's value, and trade restrictions imposed by the U.S. government as a result of accusations of dumping. The outcome of this situation that has grown exponentially is that the big five—Nippon Steel, Sumitomo Metal Industries, Kobe Steel, Kawasaki Steel Corporation, and Nippon Kokan—have all created tie-ups with U.S. producers through **joint ventures** or by shareholding. The U.S. government imposed heavy tariffs in 1993, forcing the creation of new strategies, diversification being one. New areas of business include communications, electronics, engineering projects, machinery, and the development of new materials. The process of restructuring the industry will take years to complete as large integrated steel mills search for ways to cut costs and develop new technologies.

ISEKI. Iseki Noki was formed in 1936 to help mechanize the **rice** industry. The company continues to manufacture machinery for rice and fruit farming. It created equipment that mechanizes the entire process of rice cultivation, from planting to harvesting. It also produced small tractors and combines that it exports to about 50 countries. Its head office is in Tokyo.

ISETAN. Founded as Iseya Tanji Dry Goods in 1886 and taking the name Isetan in 1930, it became a leading and comprehensive **department store** headquartered in Shinjuku, Tokyo, with five other branches in the greater Tokyo area. Its business plan anticipated the growth of Shinjuku, now headquarters of the Tokyo Metropolitan government, and was very sensitive to customer profile and tastes, enabling it to survive the protracted **recession of the 1990s**.

ISHIBASHI SHOJIRO (1889–1976). He was the founder of **Bridgestone Tire** who was born in Fukuoka prefecture in Kyushu and who inherited the family business as makers of traditional Japanese footwear known as *tabi*. After 1918, he had the idea of rubber-soling *tabi* so that construction workers could use them. These may still be seen in use. Ishibashi next moved into rubber boots, and in 1931, into automobile tires. Through a 1950 technical agreement with the Goodyear Tire and Rubber of the United States, he was able to produce high-quality tires in time for the expansion of the Japanese **automobile industry**. He is remembered also for creating the Bridgestone Museum of Art.

ISHIDA TAIZO (1888–1979). He was a business leader who contributed to the successful development of **Toyota Motor Corporation** in its early postwar days. Born in Aichi prefecture, he joined Toyoda Spinning & Weaving on leaving school in 1927. He rose to become president of the **Toyota Automatic Loom Works** in 1948. In 1950, he assumed the presidency of Toyota Motor Corporation, where he devised a new production system and began the development of the Crown passenger car. This marked the start of the rise of Toyota to international prominence. Ishida served on the board of several members of the Toyota group, exerting great influence on its business development.

ISHIKAWAJIMA-HARIMA HEAVY INDUSTRIES (IHI). This is a large-scale maker of heavy machinery, ships, planes, and aircraft jet engines, formed in 1960 through the merger of Ishakwajima Heavy Industries and Harima Zosenjo (**Shipbuilding**). Ishikawajima itself dates back to 1853, when the Mito domain government built a shipyard on Ishikawa island at the mouth of the Sumida River in Edo (Tokyo). It also produced various types of machinery, an activity that continued into the **Meiji period** (1868–1912).

Harima Zosenjo was founded in 1907 in **Hyogo** prefecture. It developed its own technology for manufacturing ships and became an affiliate of **Suzuki Shoten**. It had a temporary affiliation with **Kobe Steel** that lasted from 1921 to 1929. The 1960 merger was more appropriate and successful, resulting in a world-class producer of industrial machinery and ships.

IHI has numerous overseas ventures and is actively involved in overseas technical assistance in various areas. It also is involved in training, both dispatching technical experts as well as offering training programs in Japan. It is exceeded in scale only by **Mitsubishi Heavy Industries**. The head office is in Tokyo.

ISUZU MOTORS. Isuzu Jidosha is one of Japan's oldest **automobile** manufacturers. It was founded in 1916, incorporated in 1937, and adopted its present name in 1949. It formed an affiliation with General Motors Corporation of the United States in 1971. It became famous for its diesel engines, and, although a manufacturer of passenger cars, it is the largest producer of trucks in Japan. It has a **joint venture** with Subaru Jidosha (Motors) in Indianapolis in the United States. Its head office is in Tokyo.

C. ITOH & Co. Ito-chu Shoji is a major trading house that traces a common origin with **Marubeni** to a company founded in 1858 by Ito Chubei, who began the business of selling hemp to the outlying provinces. During the **Meiji period** (1868–1912), he expanded into cotton and textile trading and in 1884 moved into international trade. After the war, the company was divided into C. Itoh & Co. and Marubeni Corporation. Thus, it was not until 1949 that their modern identity was established following the breakup of a wartime merger of corporations known as Taiken Industries. C. Itoh & Co. ranked third in size among the top 10 houses in the 1940s and diversified into machinery and chemicals in support of postwar reconstruction.

It expanded to 70 overseas branches and 43 overseas affiliates. Its headquarters are in Osaka and Tokyo. *See also* SOGO SHOSHA.

ITO HAM EIYO SHOKUHIN. Ito Ham Provisions Co., Ltd, was founded in 1928 in Osaka by Ito Denzo. It grew to become the largest producer of ham, sausage, and processed meats. It also owns a baseball franchise. After 1945, it grew into a leading meatpacker and developed **joint ventures** in the United States and Brazil. Its head office is in Nishinomiya in Hyogo prefecture.

ITO-YOKADO. Founded in 1913, the business has grown into a large supermarket chain store retailing clothing, foodstuffs, domestic products, and housing with over 100 stores, mostly in the Kanto region. Its basic policy is high turnover of low-priced goods. It has several affiliates in the United States, including **convenience stores** (*konbini*) such as Seven-Eleven, which it acquired and operates with Southland Inc., and restaurants in Japan operated with Denny's of the United States. Ito-Yokado is unusual for a Japanese business in that it raises capital internationally. It issued continental depository receipts (CDRs) in Europe as early as 1976, and it floated unsecured debentures in the United States in 1978. Its headquarters are in Tokyo.

IWANAMI GINZAN. A 14th-century silver **mine** that was an important source of silver during the **Edo period** (1615–1868). During the 15th and 16th centuries, new technology from Korea made possible the extraction of greater volumes of silver, leading to armed conflict between rival families, among which the Mori became the most successful. The **Tokugawa shogunate** took control in the 17th century, after which the mine provided as much as 14.88 tons of silver each year. A new high-quality vein was found in 1726 that initially yielded 2.19 tons per year. However, by 1814, because of its exhaustion, it was abandoned. Fujita-Gumi, founded by **Fujita Denzaburo** (1841–1912), acquired it to mine copper during the early **Meiji period** (1868–1912), after which it was finally closed. The name "Iwanami Ginzan" was also the name of an arsenious by-product of the mining process, sold during the Edo period as a rat poison.

IWASAKI KOYOTA (1879–1945). He was a nephew of **Iwasaki Yataro** (1838–1885), founder of the **Mitsubishi zaibatsu** and leader of the group in prewar years. Born in Tokyo, he was educated at the University of Tokyo and Cambridge University. He became vice president of Mitsubishi Goshi in 1906 and president in 1916. He restructured the various divisions of Mitsubishi Goshi and created Mitsubishi Shipbuilding (now **Mitsubishi Heavy Industries**), Mitsubishi Mining (now Mitsubishi Mining & Cement), **Mitsubishi Corporation** in 1918, and **Mitsubishi Bank** in 1919. He created other companies, including **Mitsubishi Electric Corporation** in 1921, and in so doing made possible the development of the heavy industry base of the ***zaibatsu***. He was also interested in technology exchange and overseas investment and concluded an agreement with Westinghouse Electric of the United States. In 1931, he created **Mitsubishi Oil** as a **joint venture** with a U.S. oil company. In the development of the Mistubishi *zaibatsu* from its early days under the founder, Iwasaki Koyota was a pivotal visionary figure who linked the 19th and the 20th centuries by providing leadership and direction.

IWASAKI YATARO (1838–1885). Founder of the **Mitsubishi *zaibatsu***, he was born in the Tosa family fiefdom (now Kochi prefecture), the first son of a family that claimed **samurai** status. He was educated by a samurai who saw him as a boy with a future and, at age 20, acquired the lowest samurai rank of *goshi*, a prerequisite for employment by the fiefdom government. He worked in various positions until 1867, but at the age of 33, he quit and began to look for opportunities to advance himself. He discovered that the Nagasaki office of the Industrial Promotion Agency (Kaiseikan), for which he had worked, was actively buying arms and military supplies but by so doing was going heavily into debt. By recommendation of a former supervisor, Iwasaki was offered the opportunity to manage the office, a task that no one of experience appeared interested in attempting. He accepted the challenge and thereafter never looked back.

He was immensely successful in both reducing the debt and in raising funds. The Tosa government appointed him as director of finance, and in this capacity he demonstrated his imaginative talents by counterfeiting the debased shogunate coinage and issuing *hansatsu*, or promissory notes, in order to continue buying military supplies.

He became known for his dexterity in negotiating deals by using a combination of tactics, including persuasion, fabricating stories of fictitious rivals, using veiled threats, and, the hallmark of Japanese business ever since, lavishly entertaining guests.

In 1871, the fiefdoms were abolished by the new government of the **Meiji Restoration of 1868**, and the Tosa clan withdrew from all business activities. Iwasaki proved himself to be creative and capable of thinking on his feet in the unstable environment that appeared to bring out the best in him. When the Meiji government elected to assume responsibility for the "currencies" of the former fiefdoms, the successful efforts of Iwasaki in acquiring the assets of former fiefdoms by his unique methods of negotiation resulted in the government buying Tosa *hansatu* at face value for conversion to Dajokan-*satsu* (Council of State promissory notes). Iwasaki also managed to make a personal fortune at this time by buying a large quantity of notes himself by means of what would now probably be considered insider trading.

With the profits and connections he had made, he founded the Mitsubishi Trading Company in 1873 along the lines of the great **shipping**/trading houses of Hong Kong. Shipping in Japan operated on a coastal basis and was highly competitive. Iwasaki had little difficulty in disposing of smaller rivals by his usual methods, but his greatest success was over the Yubin Jokisen Kaisha (Steam Packet Company), which was financed by several rich merchant houses and supported by government subsidy. By 1874, through a price war, Iwasaki bankrupted his major rival and thereby gained control of the majority of shipping routes.

The Japanese government embarked on the invasion of Taiwan in 1874, and Iwasaki was hired to transport troops and supplies to Taiwan. The profits enabled him to develop his company, and by 1874 he was sailing the Shanghai-to-Japan route. By another price-cutting war, he forced the American Pacific Mail Steamship Company out of business and acquired its entire fleet in 1875. The same strategy was employed against the massive Peninsular and Oriental Navigation Company (P&O) in 1876, gaining him the upper hand in the Shanghai-to-Yokohama route.

By 1877, Iwasaki owned 80 percent of all shipping in and around Japan, controlling its coastal trade. He survived an assault from the

Mitsui trading house in 1882 and with equal success survived public criticism for his incursions into various other businesses. Testimony to his status is the fact that over 50,000 mourners gathered for his funeral rites. He remains a symbol not only of Meiji period entrepreneurship but also of the highly controversial iron-triangle relationship between business, bureaucracy, and government, according to some scholars, one unique contributing factor to Japan's successful growth in the postwar period. *See also* SOGO SHOSHA.

– J –

JAPAN AIR LINES (JAL). The nation's premier international **airline** formed in 1951, initially to serve domestic routes but that began international services in 1954. The airline expanded successfully in its early years in areas of general passenger travel, freight, and tourist packages, expanding its business into JAL shops, outlets at airports, and duty-free sales, most of which were handled by subsidiaries such as JAL Trading or its international freight handler, Kokusai Kamotsu. It also created low-cost subsidiaries such as JAL Express and JALways for some domestic and regional international routes. In the late 1970s and early 1980s, JAL's image was badly tarnished by a number of accidents and mishaps, culminating in the crash in the Japan Alps of Flight 123 from Tokyo to Osaka in 1985. Among causes cited, the issue of management was raised several times and, in particular, the structure and management of **labor unions** in the airline, where, as one report pointed out, three labor unions with competing interests were represented on the flight deck.

There was also a reckless attitude toward expansion and spending at a time when other airlines worldwide were cutting costs and streamlining, thus affected JAL's global competitiveness. Domestic revelations of bad management, combined with the external changes, led to drastic reform inside the airline, principally in the area of corporate governance and overall management. In 1998, Kaneko Isao became the first president of JAL to come from the division of labor management, a fact that emphasized a clear change in policy emphasis, former presidents having been drawn normally from sales or corporate planning. JAL, however, still continued to drag its feet in other areas such as code sharing and international alliances, strategies that most other airlines had agreed were indispensable for survival, let alone profitability, at a difficult time. While JAL clearly wished to set its house in order, airline industry analysts generally held the view that it still had a long list of issues to address before it would really be able to feel secure. As part of industry realignment, JAL merged with **Japan Air System** in October 2002.

JAPAN AIR SYSTEM. Originally founded in 1964 as Japan Domestic Airlines, it merged in 1971 with Toa Airways and became Toa Domestic Airlines. In addition to being the third-largest carrier after **Japan Airlines** and **All Nippon Airways**, it not only handled passenger and freight business but also was engaged in leasing helicopters. At its peak, it ran a fleet of almost 60 aircraft and 16 helicopters and flew 72 routes in Japan and in Southeast Asia. The protracted recession in the 1990s resulted in its forming a close association with Japan Airlines through code sharing as a step toward further integration in the future. It merged with JAL in October 2002.

JAPAN ASSOCIATION OF CORPORATE EXECUTIVES. *See* KEIZAI DOYUKAI.

JAPAN AUTOMOBILE MANUFACTURERS ASSOCIATION (JAMA). Established in 1967 with the stated objective of promoting the growth of the **automobile industry** in Japan and the well-being of society, it resulted from the merger of the Automotive Industry Association and the Small Car Manufacturers' Association. The founding 15 members were Aiichi Kikai, **Isuzu**, Kawasaki, **Suzuki**, **Daihatsu**, **Toyota**, **Toyo Kogyo**, **Nissan**, Nissal Diesel, **Hino**, **Fuji Heavy Industries**, **Bridgestone** Cycle, **Honda**, **Mitsubishi Heavy Industries**, and **Yamaha**. The founding chairman of the JAMA was Kawamata Katsuji, then president of Nissan. To fulfill its mission, the organization worked for the development and internationalization of the industry by opening overseas offices that were intended to facilitate exports and overseas expansion. Paris in 1969 was followed by New York in 1970, Washington, D.C., in 1976, Canada in 1986, Brussels in 1995, and Singapore in 1996.

The JAMA represents the automotive industry's interests in many ways, such as issuing public statements, promoting joint research projects, and working to achieve international consensus on many controversial issues such as global environmental problems or issues relating to taxes and tariffs. It is also concerned with safety devices, international standards, seat belts, safety helmets, and educational programs to improve all aspects of passenger protection.

The JAMA has been active since 1987 in consultation with its counterpart, the U.S. Motor and Equipment Manufacturers' Association, on a range of issues, including the supply of parts to Japanese car manufacturers in the United States. Similar consultative meetings have been held in Canada, Asia, Australia, and Europe with the European Automotive Components and Equipment Industries Association to enhance global cooperation.

JAPAN BUSINESS FEDERATION. New business organization formed by the merger of **Keidanren** (Keizai Dantai Rengo, the Federation of Economic Organizations) and **Nikkeiren** (Nippon Keieisha Dantai Rengo, the Japan Federation of Employers Associations) in 2002, now known as Nippon Keidanren.

JAPAN CHAMBER OF COMMERCE AND INDUSTRY (JCCI). The leading organization of the association of all local Chambers of Commerce nationwide numbering over 500, with registered corporate members totaling around 1.65 million, all small and medium-sized companies (*chu-sho kigyo*). In contrast to **Keidanren**, which represents large **corporations**' interests, the JCCI works regionally with small enterprises by explaining government policies, assisting with management training programs, and engaging in international cooperation where possible.

The oldest chambers of commerce date to the **Meiji period** (1868–1912). The **Tokyo Chamber of Commerce** was formed in 1872 out of the **Edo Chokaisho**, founded in 1791. Kobe and Osaka chambers followed, with other regional ones being formed as commerce and industry expanded. An act passed by the National Diet in 1890 designated them as corporate bodies with special status. All chambers function independently but cooperate extensively in many areas, including finding overseas partners, trade inquiries from overseas, new business trends, and innovations in manufacturing practices. The JCCI controls a network of over 5,000 consultants located in regional chambers. It also provides tests and certification in areas such as bookkeeping and accounting in English, word processing, and use of the ***soroban*** for around 2 million people every year. It also publishes the quarterly *JCCI Japanese Business Guide* to develop its international business activities. *See also* NAGANO SHIGEO.

JAPAN DEVELOPMENT BANK (JDB). A government **bank** founded in 1951 to be responsible for financing regional development projects. It grew out of the Reconstruction Finance Bank, which functioned between 1947 and 1949 to revive key industries destroyed during World War II. The JDB was followed in 1952 by the creation of the **Long-Term Credit Bank of Japan** and other banks permitted to issue five-year debentures that would enable fiscally sound industrial reconstruction. Most of the JDB debentures were acquired by the Ministry of Finance's Fiscal Investment Loan Program, which in turn was funded by the **postal savings system**. The JDB has performed various roles at different times according to the needs of the Japanese economy. From its initial concern with postwar reconstruction, its agenda was switched from industrial catch-up to concerns about social welfare and environmental questions in the 1970s. The agenda from the 1970s to the 1980s was energy conservation, which changed in the 1990s to the restructuring of industry. In 1997, the bank acquired the remains of the collapsed **Hokkaido Takushoku Bank** and was able to survive the collapse of the **bubble economy** because it had less than 10 percent of the level of nonperforming loans of the rest of the banking sector.

JAPANESE-STYLE MANAGEMENT. Known in Japanese as *Nihonteki keiei*, the term refers to various features of Japanese management that are considered unique. Three are usually listed. One is the **lifetime employment system** (*shushin koyo seido*), which refers to the virtual guarantee of a job until age 55. A second is the seniority system, known as ***nenko joretsu***, and a third is the **enterprise union**. The unique character of Japanese management is best seen in an organogram of its vertical structure. It should be noted that the English is presented as a rough equivalent to the Japanese. A term such as *torishimariyaku* (translated as director) is of considerable antiquity, as a cursory examination of 16th- and 17th-century Japanese house constitutions will demonstrate. While other terms were developed in the late 19th century (such as *kaisha*) to identify **joint-stock companies** were indeed linguistic innovations, the terminology for management was derived from older sources. More important, they came from a totally different history of social experience and a different understanding of social order than that in the West. Grasping the significance of this point is essential for anyone trying to understand the Japanese approach:

Management Hierarchy

Japanese	**English Equivalent**
Kaicho	Chairman
Shacho	President
Fuku Shacho	Vice president (only one or two)
Semmu Torishimariyaku	Senior executive managing director
Jomu Torishimariyaku	Executive managing director
Torishimariyaku	Director (board member)
Jicho	Assistant director
Bucho	Divisional (general) manager
Bucho Dairi	Deputy divisional manager
Kacho	Section chief
Kacho Dairi	Deputy section chief
Kakaricho	Chief clerk
Shunin	Supervisor
Shain	Employee

This diagram helps to highlight three features of the Japanese system that distinguish it from its Western counterpart. First, it is directly hierarchical and vertical. For example, there is no horizontal structure of vice presidents as there is in corporations in the United States. There is a personnel division or section, a finance section, and so forth, but all these fit within the overall hierarchy, just as the government ministries in Japan, although theoretically equal, stand in a hierarchy with the Ministry of Finance and the Ministry of Foreign Affairs at the apex.

Second, the line of demarcation, in terms of rights and responsibilities, between board and top management is not clearly defined.

Decision-making functions are almost completely integrated. This applies also further down the hierarchy. Since all company staff, including management, are *shain*, or company members, the line defined most clearly in the West, namely, that between management and labor, is equally unclear. Decision making therefore involves many people, and it means that total support is a necessary condition for the successful implementation of any proposal or plan. Hence, Japanese companies have, like sumo wrestlers, a low center of gravity, centered on the lower ranks, such as *kacho* and *kakricho*.

Finally, as a general rule, no one reaches the rank of *bucho* or higher unless that person has entered as a *shin shain*, a new employee, fresh from college, at the lowest rank. While various corporate consolidations have created boards in which members of the former organizations join, generally outside members are not solicited and are not welcome on boards that are, almost invariably, totally in-house. This practice has undergone review as a result of numerous scandals and collapses that might have been avoided if a more objective eye had examined corporate finances. Corporate governance has become more important as a result of these circumstances.

A number of observations may be made on this system. First, it should be obvious that for Japanese corporations, management evolved as a function of culture and as such is related to the social value system. Second, since this assumption is obviously so alien to modern Western styles of management, it is hardly surprising that interfacing in international contexts with Western organizations can present serious difficulties that have the potential for conflict. Third, however, while some aspects of Japanese management have created interest in the West, along with a range of opinions on the possible applicability of them in non-Japanese contexts, they are taking deep root in Asia because many features have grown out of Asian soil. Japanese practices have become benchmarks for Asia, and in that regard, problems arising from major differences in perception between the West and Asia are liable to increase rather than decrease in the future to the degree that Japan's Asian presence and influence as a model are underestimated.

JAPAN EXTERNAL TRADE ORGANIZATION (JETRO). The Nippon Boeki Shinkokai is located in Toranomon, central Tokyo. A subsidiary of the **Ministry of International Trade and Industry (MITI)**, it has been considered instrumental the postwar Japanese economic miracle. It was first set up in 1951 as the Japan Export Research Trade Organization to provide resources and information for manufacturers about foreign markets. In 1954, its name and role were changed to become the External Trade Recovery Organization, which would provide exhibitions and samples of Japanese products designed for overseas markets. In July 1958, its status and functions as a public corporation were confirmed in law, and the acronym by which it became known, JETRO, was created. During the 1980s, it began to assist in the task of encouraging imports and overseas investment in Japan. It created various centers and fairs to display foreign products and formed the Manufactured Imports Promotional Organization (MIPRO) to encourage imports.

JETRO publishes many materials in English and provides data and information to assist foreign entrants to the Japanese market. It has 76 regional offices in 56 countries around the world, particularly in the United States. It has 37 offices in Japan, including its Tokyo and Osaka headquarters. In 1998, the Institute of Developing Economies (IDE) merged with JETRO, bringing together the IDE expertise on Asia with JETRO's global business experience.

JAPAN FEDERATION OF ECONOMIC ORGANIZATIONS. *See* KEIDANREN.

JAPAN FEDERATION OF EMPLOYERS ASSOCIATIONS. *See* NIKKEIREN.

JAPAN HIGHWAY PUBLIC CORPORATION. The Nihon Doro Kodan builds, maintains, and manages all of Japan's expressways, highways, and toll roads. Capitalized 100 percent by the government, it was founded in 1956, taking over all existing prefectural and national toll roads. Its first major project was the Meishin Expressway between Nagoya and Kobe; this has been followed by another 30 expressways that provide almost 6,000 kilometers of road throughout the country. Over 1.5 million vehicles use the network every day, paying often expensive tolls even for short distances. The income finances new roads, proper maintenance of existing roads, and environmental and safety measures for both users and residents who live near the expressways.

JAPAN METALS AND CHEMICALS (Nihon Jukagaku Kogyo). Founded in 1917 as a carbide manufacturer, it became the largest producer of ferroalloys, also introducing fertilizers and constructing geothermal power plants. It is affiliated with the **Nippon Steel Corporation** and is linked to the **Mizuho Financial Group**. Its head office is in Tokyo.

JAPAN NATIONAL RAILWAYS (JNR). The former state-owned railway system that was privatized in 1987 and broken into six regional **Japan Railways (JR)** companies and one national freight company.

JAPAN PRODUCTIVITY CENTER FOR SOCIOECONOMIC DEVELOPMENT (JPC). Founded as the Japan Productivity Center in 1955 to spearhead the long-term growth of **productivity** and composed of **labor**, management, and academia, it has worked vigorously for the development and sustainment of a national productivity movement that covers every sector of Japanese society. The Government Economic White Paper of 1956 carried the subtitle "No Longer Postwar" because by then productivity had returned to prewar levels. The nation was in the process of making the transition from reconstruction to development. Under the inspiration of the productivity movement, Japan's economy began to grow at an annual real rate in excess of 10 percent, resulting in the Japanese economy becoming second only to the United States by 1968.

The JPC's activities range from corporate education and development to research into ways and means of increasing productivity through conferences, seminars, workshops, and on-site consulting. Its work has been studied by many nations and its advice sought by many developing countries, including Russia following the collapse of the Soviet Union. To further highlight its ideal to maintain the vitality and the relevance of corporate culture, it stresses that equal consideration be given to social profitability as well as to corporate profits. The JPC changed its name in 1994 from *Seisansei Honbu* in Japanese to *Shakai-Keizai Seisansei Honbu*, the Japan Productivity

Center for Socioeconomic Development, when it merged with the Social and Economic Congress of Japan (SECJ). The new organization has three principal tasks: the reform of social systems that have become outmoded, the improvement of productivity combined with structural economic reform, and the development of the international economy, taking into account the need to conserve the global environment. It has the support of over 9,000 sustaining members and has 20 regional offices from northern Honshu to Okinawa. Its headquarters are in the Shibuya district of Tokyo.

JAPAN RAILWAY GROUP (JR). The group comprising the six former **Japan National Railways** companies that were privatized in 1987. *See also* RAILWAY SYSTEM.

JAPAN TOBACCO AND SALT CORPORATION. The Nihon Sembai Kosha was set up in 1904 to make the sale of tobacco a government monopoly. The company remains in control of the sector. It was established in its present form in 1949 and is involved in the purchase and processing of raw tobacco and salt and the import and export of manufactured products. It pays part of its revenue to the government but has suffered considerably from the late 20th-century move away from cigarette smoking, although Japan, like China, still has a higher proportion of smokers than may be found now in most Western nations.

JAPAN TRAVEL BUREAU (JTB). Nihon Kotsu Kosha was founded in 1912 to attract foreign **tourists** to visit Japan. It was reconstituted as a nonprofit organization (*zaidan hojin*) in 1945. In 1963, its business department was made into an independent private corporation. Since then, it has become the nation's largest travel agent for both tourists to Japan and Japanese heading for overseas destinations, for example, on honeymoon package tours. It sells tickets for **Japan Railways**, **Japan Airlines**, and other transport companies. It has over 300 offices in Japan and more than 10 overseas and works with 40 affiliated firms. Its headquarters are in Tokyo.

JIGYO-KIKAKUBU. A division found in large corporations and dedicated to the conceptualization, creation, and development of new business projects. These grew in number in the 1980s, when Japan first began to feel the weight of international competition and the yen began to rise after the **Plaza Accord of 1985**.

JOINT-STOCK COMPANIES. *See* CORPORATION.

JOINT VENTURES ABROAD. Japanese **corporations** have made use of **joint ventures** both inside Japan and abroad for three principal reasons. In the **Meiji period** (1868–1912), a lack of expertise and a need for new technology required that they set up offices or plants in cooperation with local companies, a pattern that was followed again in the early postwar period, when the industrial base of the nation was being rebuilt. Not infrequently, these were related to the procurement of natural resources. A brief survey of regions and countries in which Japanese business has a significant presence clarifies this point.

A second reason for overseas joint ventures has been the need for market access by Japanese companies with little experience. During the mid-1980s, most Japanese companies judged the risk of entering the U.S. market too great and therefore looked for American partners to form joint ventures. Sometimes these were even undertaken with rival companies. **Toyota** and General Motors created a 50-50 joint venture for the purpose of producing small cars for the North American market. The driving need from Toyota's perspective was the know-how to operate a manufacturing facility in the United States. General Motors in return was able to inspect Toyota's production system firsthand. Honda, by way of contrast, has a 26 percent share in Hero Honda of India, which produces around 50 percent of India's motorcycles.

A third reason comes from the fact that Japanese corporations are well known for their ability to work abroad with other Japanese companies that may even be domestic rivals. The Subaru-**Isuzu** manufacturing alliance in Indianapolis in the United States is a case in point. It was formed with the support of the state government of Indiana because it provided a large number of jobs. Joint ventures with other Japanese companies are to be found in China, where the complexities of the business environment have encouraged this kind of cooperation to ensure some security and stability.

JOINT VENTURES IN JAPAN. While most foreign companies prefer to go it alone in other countries, a large percentage of the **foreign companies** exist in the form of joint enterprises (*gonben kaisha*) with a Japanese partner. The general merits for foreign companies are that they facilitate entry into the Japanese market with the minimum of risk, affording speedy access to market information and structure as well as to **distribution** networks, assistance in hiring, and the prestige of being linked with a big name. The same benefits appealed to Japanese companies that entered the markets of Southeast Asia, while the preferred strategy in Europe and North America was a 100-percent-owned subsidiary.

Depending on the kind of strategies being employed, three types of joint ventures can be distinguished. Complementary joint ventures result from the exchange of skills possessed by each partner but absent from the other. **Jusco**'s alliance with Red Lobster of the United States is a simple example of this type. A Western company might contribute a piece of technology or some other type of know-how in return for market entry. This is the normal starting point for most joint ventures whose character may alter with time. Learning-style joint ventures develop where improved shared skills are the goal of both partners. **Bridgestone**'s alliance with Goodyear of the United States would come under this heading. A lot of trust and goodwill is required, as is management interaction between the partners. Market-access joint ventures arise when competitive pressures force companies otherwise in competition to work together. **Yamatake-Honeywell** includes elements of that kind of relationship. Sometimes joint ventures can be unique liaisons between outright rivals who may be willing to trade favors for subsections of a market.

Joint ventures in Japan have a notorious history of failure or collapse. Many factors are responsible, not least of which is a lack of knowledge regarding Japan's business culture and unique market features on the part of foreign enterprises. Most of the 1970s and 1980s joint ventures were gone by the 1990s. Many underestimated the levels of investment and effort required to maintain a relationship that was always fluid and subject to external influences over which it had no control, such as changing market tastes. As many discovered, setting up a joint venture may not be difficult, but maintaining it is a different matter. Regardless of initial good intentions, there is very rarely a "happy ever after" ending. One fact that is true of all joint ventures is the way in which each one evolves in a distinct manner, sometimes resulting in a shift in the balance of power between the partners. There is an inescapable dimension of competition within joint ventures that may lie dormant while cooperation remains mutually beneficial. However, once one company has outgrown the need for the other to the same extent as at the beginning of their agreement, the end may be in sight. Some exceptions do exist. Rover and Honda worked well together until BMW acquired Rover along with Honda's technology, underlining another risk factor that has made the joint venture less attractive. *See also* FOREIGN BUSINESSES; JOINT VENTURES ABROAD.

JUSCO (JAPAN UNITED STORES COMPANY). Japan's third-largest supermarket operator and main company of the Aeon Group of 153 corporations. The company grew out of the merger of three chain stores in 1969, one of which, Okadaya, dates its foundation to the **Edo period** (1615–1868) in 1758. JUSCO is also involved in developing shopping malls, and in addition to its own supermarkets and stores, it has a number of interests in Japan, including Talbot's, the U.S. women's fashion chain, and **joint ventures** with Red Lobster, Laura Ashley, and the Body Shop. The Aeon Group owns or franchises over 3,200 stores worldwide, 450 JUSCO stores, and 2,300 Ministop **convenience stores** (*konbini*), which employ over 44,000 staff. The headquarters are in the Aeon Building in Chiba.

JUST-IN-TIME. A manufacturing concept developed by **Ono Taiichi** when he worked for **Toyota Motor Corporation**. It initially meant producing only what was strictly necessary, thus eliminating waste in time, materials, labor, and costs. Manufacturing was geared to move in time with customer demand in order to eliminate unnecessary inventory. It came to be linked with concepts such as ***kanban*** (labeling of parts, components, and inventory), ***kaizen*** (continuous improvement), and ***heijunka*** (making the manufacturing process proceed smoothly). Ono developed the system in the 1950s and implemented it throughout the Toyota organization in the 1960s, including its suppliers and subsidiaries. By the late 1970s, interest had grown, and during the early 1980s, industrial study missions from around the world, particularly from North America, came to see the concept in action.

– K –

KACHO. Normally translated section chief, a *kacho* is a pivotal position in any organization because it stands roughly midway between the division managers (***bucho***), who often function in a zone that blurs the distinction between upper management and the board, and those in the lower levels of management, who are more hands-on in their activities. The *kacho* can initiate proposals, carry them up from below, or work with other managers on current matters. In government circles, a *kacho* has very considerable prestige both inside and outside the organization.

KADOYA SHICHIROBEI (1610–1672). An international trader of the early **Edo period** (1615–1868) who was permitted by the government to trade with Vietnam. He was born in Matsuzaka in the old province of Ise in a family of successful shipping merchants. In 1631, at age 21, he sailed to Annam (Vietnam) and joined a community of Japanese in Turane (now Da Nang). In 1633, the **Tokugawa government** declared the country closed, initiating a policy of national seclusion (***Sakoku Jidai***) that in effect was ended when Commodore Matthew Perry and his famous black ships (***kurofune***) arrived in Tokyo Bay in 1853. The policy was rigidly enforced for 300 years, but during the Kambun period (1661–1673), letters from abroad were permitted, and Shichirobei was able to communicate with his relatives, informing them that he was married to a lady of rank and that they had a son. Shichirobei had become a leading member of the Japanese community, and he restarted trading with Japan. His son succeeded him in the business, after which nothing is known apart from a few letters dispatched by his widow. Thereafter, with the exception of pirates, Japan had no connections with Southeast Asia until after the **Meiji Restoration of 1868** and the growth of the Japanese Empire.

KAIGI. The core of Japanese corporate life is the system of meetings by means of which information is circulated and decisions are made. The frequency and length of meetings in Japan far exceeds that of Western countries. One reason is that Japanese corporate decision making does not favor the majority vote system used in the West. Unanimity and consensus are considered so fundamental to corporate policy that as much time as is needed can be expended in order to achieve the total agreement of all concerned, hence the reputation of Japanese companies for being slow to reach a decision. The decision, however, once reached, draws the organization into line, and the resultant project moves forward at a relentless pace.

KAIZEN. The concept means continuous improvement and refinement in manufacturing and management that is characteristic of the Japanese approach to production systems. It is a practical idea by means of which many small improvements and modifications made on a daily basis can accumulate into major reforms. Unlike science-led revolutionary breakthroughs in the West, especially in the United States, Japanese **corporations** work at problems in a highly empirical way through group participative activities in factories and on work sites. *See also* JUST-IN-TIME; KAMBAN.

KAMI. The term refers to the object of reverence in Shinto culture, translated into English in a variety of ways. None of these is completely adequate, but the most inappropriate of all is “god.” Divinity, the divine, or the mysterious are better candidates because they are less specific in the imagery they generate, particularly to Western observers.

The etymology of the Japanese is unclear, but the term certainly came to refer to a unique force or power in nature, animals, or people that engendered attitudes of reverence, fear, or gratitude in those who perceived it. Motoori Norinaga (1730–1801), the Kokugaku (National Learning) scholar, made the statement that anything that filled a human being with wonder and awe might be referred to as a *kami*.

It can only be assumed that the ancient Japanese, living in a fascinating world of vast live volcanoes, surging rivers, powerful waterfalls, and other mysteries, felt that they lived in an environment inhabited by *kami*. This too is probably the origin of the expression, which opens the *Jinno Shotoki* of Kitabatake Chikafusa (1293–1354), that Japan was the "*kami no kuni*," the land of the *kami*, namely, a land filled with mysterious wonders.

To most Japanese, *kami* are local in their status and identity and derive their meaning from historical community rites. **Construction** companies frequently hold groundbreaking ceremonies before the commencement of a project to ask for the understanding and cooperation of the *kami* of the ground where the work is to take place.

KAMI-DANA. An altar (shelf) for reverencing tutelary and family ***kami***. The offerings placed on it are normally changed daily, bring water, **sake**, **rice**, and salt. These, however, may also be found in restaurants that serve traditional Japanese food and companies or businesses that have a tutelary shrine to which they make regular offerings. They are frequently found in businesses, restaurants, and even railway stations.

KAMIGUMI COMPANY. A harbor transport and warehousing corporation located in Kobe, Tokyo, Yokohama, and Osaka. It dates to the organization of a cooperative of stevedores when Kobe was opened to foreign trade in 1867. It has consistently tried to streamline and modernize systems at ports it serves. Its headquarters remains in Kobe. *See also* SHIPPING INDUSTRY.

KANBAN. A traditional business **advertising** board that continues to exist in various modern forms. It also refers to a feature of the **just-in-time** manufacturing system of the **Toyota Motor Corporation**, whereby production of new components is initiated only when the existing stock has been completely exhausted. The use of *kanban* to label components between stages of production is the origin of the name.

KANDAKA SYSTEM OF TAX. An old system of **tax** computation that was replaced by the ***Kokudaka*** system, according to which productivity was measured in kind rather than cash. New currency was also issued to facilitate transactions. This happened under the rule of the feudal lord **Oda Nobunaga** (1534–1582).

KANEBO. Founded under the name Kanegafuchi Boseki (Spinning) Company in Tokyo in 1887, it expanded into the spinning, weaving, and finishing of cotton, wool, silk, and rayon. It developed a reputation for high-quality fabrics in various creative designs. It subsequently expanded further into new types of fabrics, pharmaceuticals, industrial and housing materials, and for what it is best known in the media, cosmetics. Its flame-resistant fabrics are especially popular in Japan, although it sells through its over 100 subsidiaries in Japan and overseas locations such as the United States, Brazil, and Indonesia. The cosmetics business represents only about 30 percent of its total turnover, but its popular image is well established. The company is also famous because it was the first Japanese corporation to introduce a **suggestion** system for employees to express opinions. It started the program in 1905. Its headquarters are in Osaka. *See also* TEXTILE INDUSTRY.

KANEGAFUCHI CHEMICAL INDUSTRY. Kanegafuchi Kagaku Kogyo was established in 1949 from the seven chemical manufacturing plants of Kanegafuchi Boseki. Now known as **Kanebo**, it is a general chemical manufacturer whose main products are vinyl chloride and soda. This was expanded into butanol and electrolytic soda. It produced an acryl fabric Kanekalon in 1957 and entered the synthetic-fiber business in the 1960s. It also began processing oils and fats and moved into the food industry, presently handled by Kanebo Shokuhin, now a general food producer of foodstuffs alongside **Kagome** and **Ajinomoto**. It has subsidiaries in Belgium, the Philippines, and Indonesia. The head office is in Osaka.

KANEMATSU GOSHO. A major trading house formed by the merger in 1967 of Kanematsu and Gosho, also a trading house, founded originally in 1905 as a cotton importer and textile exporter. *See also* SOGO SHOSHA.

KANRI KAKAKU (ADMINISTERED PRICES). While to all appearances Japan has a market economy, in reality, there was—and continues to be—a high degree of price fixing, going back in recent times to the 1960s period of mergers involving heavy industries. Price cartels have seldom been prosecuted because the resultant market price usually seems responsive to the needs of supply and demand and is therefore not considered exploitive. Sometimes prices are "agreed" within an industrial sector, usually to stabilize prices, and sometimes they are regulated by the government to control competition, as in the case of taxi fares.

In the early 1970s, there was a major controversy over imported beef prices that resulted in the exposure of what came to be called the Meat Mafia. Public reaction gradually forced prices down to the extent that imported beef from Australia and the United States became cheaper than local varieties. The prices of many imported products subsequently decreased in tandem with the price of beef, notably wines and spirits, which were restricted by heavy **taxation**.

The government still tries to regulate competition in order to protect small and medium-sized business as well as the farmers. Ironically, the elimination of administered prices, often a major concern of importers, has not always been a benefit, as European spirits exporters found out when the import duties that had artificially kept up the prices of imported products was removed. As the price of brandy and Scotch whisky steadily went down, so too did their sales because cheaper prices resulted in loss of prestige and consequently altered public perception of these products.

In 1993, an Osaka court ruled against the Transport Ministry's principle of maintaining the same taxi fares in certain defined areas as illegal. Five **Mitsubishi group** taxi companies applied to delay an increase in fares. The district transport bureau, through administrative guidance (***gyosei shido***), ordered them to make their fares uniform. The court ordered ¥50 million to be paid in compensation for their losses. While the principle has worked in some sectors, it has clearly not popular in others.

KANSAYAKU. These are mandatorily appointed auditors of ***kabushiki kaisha*** under the provisions of the **Commercial Code** that also prevents them from being board members. They have powers to investigate all aspects of a **corporation**'s activities and summon board members to explain or clarify any aspect of the business about which they may be dissatisfied.

KAO CORPORATION. Kao Sekk is one of Japan's oldest soap manufacturers, founded in 1887 by Nagase Tomiro. The company is renowned for the fact that it has constantly tried to adapt to changing tastes and needs in society by changing its name nine times and its corporate logo seven times. As well as soap, it produces a total of over 600 domestic products ranging from shampoos and detergents to computer disks. It has expanded abroad over the years and operates in Asia, Europe, and North America. Another unique feature of the company is that around 1,500 of its 6,000 employees worldwide are engaged in research-and-development projects.

Kao is sensitive to the use of technology and is well known for its marketing information system (MIS) that permits anyone in the company to access data about sales and marketing, production, and **distribution**. Its distribution system is particularly efficient and has been rated one of the nation's best organized. It can deliver orders from its Tokyo Distribution Center to any one of 6,000 retailers in the greater Tokyo area within 24 hours of receipt of an order. It prides itself in its attainment of global standards in the industry and has declared its policy as providing its global customers with superior products and services. Its headquarters are in Tokyo.

KAROSHI. "Death from overwork" has long occurred in Japan, but only since some highly publicized legal claims were processed through the courts during the 1990s has the concept been accepted. The term was coined to refer to forced overtime and general stress that resulted in the premature death of an individual. Fukoku Seimei (Life Insurance) Company in the early 1990s highlighted the fact in a survey in which 80 percent of workers polled felt that they were unable to sleep enough, 70 percent felt continually stressed, and 42 percent were afraid of death from overwork. The Ministry of Labor has been hesitant to give *karoshi* formal recognition, although some government sources admit that up to 10,000 cases occur each year. It has tended to blame workers for being overweight, drinking too much and eating poorly (which contribute to high blood pressure or high blood sugar), or ignoring the stress factors that can prompt intemperate habits.

A revision of the labor laws in 1995, while stating the standards for death from overwork, excluded **suicide**, although numerous cases of suicide because of overwork came to light when the phenomenon of death from overwork was formally recognized. The second case to ever come to court (and the first on which a judgment was handed down in favor of the plaintiff, a widow who blamed Kawasaki Steel for the stress-related suicide of her husband) took place when a branch of Okayama court ordered the company to pay ¥52 million to the family on 23 February 1998. Since it has been recognized in law and since the courts have opened a route for redress of grievances, the numerous cases where compensation has had to be paid have made corporations more sensitive about their employees' working conditions. Nevertheless, the surviving ingrained feudalism within the social system still inhibits thousands of families from seeking legal advice.

KATA KYOSO. Meaning "excessive competition," the term refers to competition in the Japanese market, something that is perceived quite differently from the way it is understood in Western economies. "Excessive competition" refers to a market situation in which supply substantially exceeds demand and prices are far below costs to the extent that the livelihood of producers is threatened. The concept is by no means universally agreed, but those who stress its role argue that investment in plants and equipment can become a liability if its use cannot be conveniently transferred to other production projects. When this is the case, the manufacturer must keep on manufacturing in order to meet interest payments, even if they are running at a loss.

Fundamentally, the Japanese concern about *kata kyoso* conceals the premise that business failure, far from being what it is understood as in the West (a natural phenomenon in market economies), is viewed as an abnormality or even a failure in the market mechanism. This has been used to justify Japan's highly regulated economy and regular government intervention to place limits on competition and to protect businesses that are experiencing difficulties.

The problem of "excessive competition" in relation to **the recession of the 1990s** has led some Western observers to argue that Japan needs more vigorous competition to rid the economy of inefficiency and waste. The issue for the Japanese is looked on in the wider context of the **lifelong employment system**, the idea of the ***ie gensoku***, the obligation to keep the business of the house surviving, and the relationship of these and other aspects of **Japanese-style manage-**

ment to social stability. Rather than see one weak performer forced out of business, Japanese industrial sectors would prefer to realign market share accordingly. To this, one rider must be added, namely, that entry by a new player into the market can be resisted, as **Yamaha** discovered to its great cost in the 1970s when it tried to oust Honda from its top spot in the motorcycle market. Honda's response through redeployment of staff to design and produce new models that undercut Yamaha was as swift and ruthless as in any Western economy.

KAWAMUMRA ZUIKEN (1617–1699). A merchant of the early **Edo period** (1615–1868) born in Ise province (now Mie prefecture) into a poor family who went to Edo (modern Tokyo) at the age of 12 and established himself in the lumber business. The Meireki Fire, which destroyed much of Edo in 1657, provided him with not only wealth during the rebuilding but also an opportunity to contribute to the development of the city. He pioneered water routes for the rice trade between the northeastern mainland and Edo. He also successfully implemented a flood control system on the Yodogawa River in Osaka. He was awarded the rank of *hatamoto* by the shogun, giving him status as a direct vassal.

KAWASAKI HEAVY INDUSTRIES. Kawasaki Jukogyo was founded in 1878 by Kawasaki Shozo as the Kawasaki Shipyard and followed by the Kawasaki Hyogo Shipyard in Kobe in 1886, then merged into Kawasaki Shipyard in 1896. The company built ships and manufactured industrial machinery, engines, aircraft, and industrial plants. World War I enabled the company to expand, and diversify. It took its present name in 1939. After 1945, it began developing original technologies by creating liquefied natural gas (LNG) tankers. In 1989, it absorbed its various affiliates, Kawasaki Car Manufacturing (in 1928) and Kawasaki Aircraft (in 1937), to return to being a comprehensive heavy machinery manufacturer on the same scale as **Mitsubishi Heavy Industries** and **Ishikawajima-Harima Heavy Industries**. Its headquarters are in Kobe. *See also* SHIPBUILDING INDUSTRY.

KAWSASAKI KISEN KAISHA. A leading ocean freight carrier founded in 1919 and affiliated with **Kawasaki Heavy Industries** and

Kawasaki Steel Corporation. It was separated from the old Kawasaki Shipbuilding in 1919 and set up to provide sea freight service, container ships, tankers, and regular tramp steamer services. It has a fleet of almost 60 ships and uses around a further 140 other ships that cover eight international container routes and 10 conventional routes. Its headquarters are in Tokyo. *See also* SHIPPING INDUSTRY.

KAWASAKI STEEL CORPORATION. One of the five major steel manufacturers established in 1906 by Kawasaki Shipbuilding (now **Kawasaki Heavy Industries**). It was separated from the parent company in 1950 as a result of postwar industrial reorganization, after which it expanded dramatically both domestically, with new state-of-the-art plants, and internationally, with offices in New York, Los Angeles, London, Dusseldorf, Bangkok, Singapore, Brazil, and the Philippines. Its headquarters are in Kobe. It is also affiliated with the **Mizuho Financial Group**. *See also* IRON AND STEEL INDUSTRY.

KAWASE KAISHA. These were money-changing companies organized in 1869 during the early **Meiji period** (1868–1912) as forerunners of the modern **banks**. They replaced the earlier **Edo period** (1615–1868) ***ryogaesha***, or money changers for the merchants of Osaka.

KAWASHO CORPORATION. Kawasho Shoji was founded in 1954 from the trading division of **Kawasaki Steel** and was made into an independent trading corporation to sell iron and steel products and import raw materials. It works with the parent company in many of its overseas markets and has been able to move into new and affiliated fields as opportunity arose. Its headquarters are in Osaka.

KAYABA INDUSTRY. Kabaya Kogyo, founded in 1935, is Japan's largest producer of shock absorbers under the brand name KYB. Its hydraulic technology is used for **automobiles**, motorcycles, special-purpose vehicles such as cement mixers, aircraft, and ships. It has five overseas operations including four factories. Its head office is in Tokyo.

KEIDANREN. Keizi Dantai Rengo, the Federation of Economic Organizations, was the most powerful body of industrial Japan and represented the interest of big business. Its influence on government policy has been enormous, and it has functioned almost as a shadow government during its history. Keidanren was established in 1946 as part of a general restructuring of Japanese business organizations to cope with the situation created by the dissolution of the ***zaibatsu*** by the **Supreme Commander of the Allied Powers (SCAP)**. In 1952, it absorbed the Nippon Sangyo Kyogikai (Japan Industrial Council), increasing both its size and its influence. Its role was initially to mediate among the different opinions of the various business groups and to make representation to the government on measures to stimulate the economy. It functions through 32 standing committees covering all areas of economic and business activity. It also engages in commercial diplomacy involving North American and European business leaders on global trends and regional cooperation.

The creation of the Liberal Democratic Party (LDP) by the amalgamation of the Japan Democratic Party (Nihon Minshuto) and the Liberal Party (Jiyuto) was at the behest of Keidanren in 1955, indicating the degree of its influence, frequently imposing its policies on the LDP.

The changing economic climate of the 1990s, combined with other factors, such as the declining population and the aging of society, resulted in the need to streamline and modernize the major business organizations. The other major ones are **Nikkeiren** (Japan Federation of Employers' Associations, which deals mostly with labor relations issues), the **Keizei Doyukai** (the Japan Association of Corporate Executives), and the **Japan Chamber of Commerce and Industry**. Keidanren and **Nikkeiren** began negotiations that were announced in 2000 as a prelude to a 2002 merger of the two groups into the **Japan Business Federation**. *See also* DOKO TOSHIO; NAKAUCHI ISAO.

KEIHAN ELECTRIC RAILWAY. Keihan Denki Tetsudo is a private **railway** company founded in 1906 to cover the Osaka-to-Kyoto route. It merged with the Hankyu Electric Railway Co. (**Hankyu Corporation**) but became independent in 1949. It expanded into housing, **department stores**, and the leisure business. Although it has only 89.5 kilometers of track, its income has grown steadily with the economic expansion of the region. Its headquarters are in Osaka.

KEIHIN ELECTRIC EXPRESS RAILWAY. Keihin Kyuko was founded in 1898 as the Daichi Electric **Railway**, serving passengers between Tokyo, Kawasaki, and Yokohama. It merged with the **Tokyu Corporation** during World War II but regained its independence in 1948. It has almost 40 affiliated companies covering various activities, such as real estate, bus lines, hotels, and leisure facilities. It has only 83 kilometers of track, but because of the population density, it is a profitable operation. Its headquarters are in Tokyo.

KEIRETSU. These are industrial groupings that were created to fill the vacuum left by the abolition of the ***zaibatsu*** after 1945. The major ones are the **Mitsui** *keiretsu*, the **Mitsubishi** *keiretsu*, and the **Sumitomo** *keiretsu*. Other forms of *keiretsu* include *kin'yu keiretsu* (finance groupings, usually named after the principal supporting bank) and *shihon keiretsu* (capital groupings that are based on one parent company), such as **Matsushita Electric** or **Japan Airlines**. In such groups, the parent company holds from 20 to 50 percent of the subsidiary companies. *Kigyo keiretsu* are formed by companies that undertake subcontracted work for the same major enterprise. **Holding companies** were banned by the **Antimonopoly Law**, but the formation of new ones was approved by a change in the law enacted in 1997, early among which was the stores group Daiei when it was undergoing restructuring.

Shihon keiretsu tend to have stronger ownerships ties than a former *zaibatsu keikretsu* because the companies tend to be small to medium-sized companies with closer links than the older groups, which consist of large **corporations**. It is difficult to give a consistent definition of a *keiretsu* because the factors that brought them into being are so varied and the nature of the relationship of members with each other is not always similar. Shared business interest and sometimes a common background may be grounds for an affiliation. It is this fact that frustrates foreign observers who find the relational structures far from transparent. Like many organizational systems in Japan that evolved organically and to meet specific needs at various times and that in turn developed new goals and activities, *keiretsu* should be viewed as groupings that demand not absolute loyalty from members but rather preferential treatment or cooperation from each other while recognizing that, from time to time, members will do business with companies that are not in the group or that are even rivals in some sectors, for perfectly justifiable reasons. *See also* ENTERPRISE GROUPS.

KEIZAI DOYUKAI. The Japan Association of Corporate Executives began as an organization of young businessmen formed after World War II to revive and modernize Japanese industry. Leading figures included the **Tsutsumi** brothers, who ran the **Seibu Group** of department stores and **railways**. Its stated corporate philosophy in 1956 read as follows:

"The function of management in a modern corporation goes far beyond that of a search for profit. From the moral as well as the practical point of view, it is vital that modern corporate managers strive to supply products of the highest quality at the lowest possible prices through the most effective utilization of product resources consistent with the welfare of the whole economy and the society at large. It is indeed the social responsibility of modern executives to serve as an effective instrument to develop a managerial system capable of accomplishing this mission."

The Keizai Doyukai holds seminars and workshops to stimulate discussion of themes it considers important. *See also* KIKAWADA KAZUTAKA.

KENTUCKY FRIED CHICKEN JAPAN. An American fast-food chain that opened in Japan in 1974. After initially struggling because of lack of identity, the company began placing a life-sized statue of the founder, Colonel Sanders, outside each outlet, a strategy that proved quite successful. Japan is the only market where these statues may be seen. The head office is in Tokyo.

KIKAWADA KAZUTAKA (1899–1977). An influential business leader and former president of the **Tokyo Electric Power Company (TEPCO)** and of the **Keizai Doyukai** (Japan Association Corporate Executives) who published a book titled *A Social Economy Based* *on Humanism* (*Ningenshugi no Keizai Shakai*) in 1971, outlining the nature of the social responsibility of corporate executives toward the welfare of the nation.

KIKKOMAN CORPORATION. A well-established soy sauce manufacturer founded in the **Edo period** (1615–1868) that started production in the city of Noda north of Tokyo on the Edo River. Two families, Mogi and Takanashi, were the founders. After the process of **modernization** had begun with the **Meiji Restoration of 1868**, the company expanded rapidly and won a prize at the 1873 World's Fair in Vienna. In keeping with trends, the company was incorporated as Noda Shoyu Co., Ltd, in 1917, and changed to Kikkoman Shoyu in 1964 and finally to Kikkoman Corporation in 1980. The company now produces other types of sauces, tomato ketchup, and many types of food seasonings. In addition, it produces **pharmaceuticals**, medical reagents, industrial enzymes, various chemicals, juices, *shochu*, and Japanese rice wine (sake). It has expanded worldwide to the United States, Europe, and Taiwan. In addition to the Noda City head office, there is also a head office in Tokyo. Unlike many family businesses that outgrew their family leadership, Kikkoman Corporation is still headed by a member of the founding Mogi family.

KINKI NIPPON RAILWAY. Kinki Nippon Tetsudo, or Kintetsu, as it is known for short, is the largest of the older private **railway corporations** founded in 1912 as the Nara Railway Co. It began serving passengers between Osaka and Nara. In 1938, it extended its line to Nagoya. Its present name was adopted in 1944, and it is the central business of the **Kintetsu Group**. Its head office is in Osaka.

KINOKUKNIYA BUNZAEMON (ca. 1660–1734). A mid-**Edo period** (1615–1868) merchant, possibly from Kii province (now Wakayama prefecture) who, like **Kawamura Zuiken** before him, was successful in the lumber business in the old Hatchobori district of Edo (now Tokyo). He successfully obtained several large government contracts, enabling him to amass enormous wealth. Since he was also the subject of literary narrative, history and legend are intertwined. Three simple facts about him seem to be credible. One is that he was well connected and another that he engaged in lavish hospitality, often on the Sumida River in Edo, consorting with celebrities of the day from the world of entertainment. In addition, the death of his major patron in the government led to a reversal of fortune, and as a result he died in comparatively austere surroundings at Fukugawa in Edo.

KINROKU KOKUSAI. These are government bonds issued to members of the former **samurai** class in the early **Meiji period** (1868–1912) to replace the stipends formerly paid by the **Edo period** (1615–1868) **Tokugawa government**. The facilities established to permit the trade of these bonds was the foundation of the Japanese **stock exchange**.

KINTETSU GROUP. A Kinki regional business group centered on the **Kinki Nippon Railway** (or Kintetsu, as it is usually known, the Kinki Regional Railway), the largest private railway company in Japan in terms of track, passengers, capital, and employees. It has 160 subsidiary companies, including Kintetsu Real Estate, Kinki Nippon **Tourist**, Mie Kotsu, and Kintetesu Department Stores. Isao Saeki, who died in 1989, led the company for 21 years as president and 13 as chairman, during which the entire railway system was upgraded. He also acquired a baseball team, the Kintetsu Buffaloes, that plays from the headquarters city of Osaka. It announced a merger with the Orix Blue Waves in 2004. The group presidents formed a *kinyu-kai*, or regular meetings to discuss policy and plans for the future. The group remains a core enterprise structure of the Kansai regional economy and is active in urban development in Osaka.

KIRIN BEER. Founded in 1870 by an American in Yokohama as Spring Valley Brewery, it became Japan Brewery Co., Ltd, in 1885 with the financial support of **Iwasaki Yataro** of **Mitsubishi** and others. The popular "Kirin" image was introduced, a Chinese dragon figure on the label, which has remained the well-known logo of the German-style Kirin Lager brand. By 1948, only two breweries remained, Kirin and Dai Nippon. According to the requirements of the 1947 **Antimonopoly Law**, Dai Nippon was split in 1949 into Asahi Breweries (western Japan) and Sapporo Breweries (eastern Japan). The market share then was Kirin 25.3 percent, Asahi 36.1 percent, and Sapporo 38.6 percent. In the postwar period, Kirin quickly pulled ahead of its rivals to become Japan's leading beer until it was briefly deposed by the introduction of Asahi Super Dry in 1992. By introducing a new brand, Ichiban Shibori, with a very strong taste, Kirin had regained 40 percent of the market within a few years.

The postwar growth of Kirin Beer has been the subject of research and speculation. One reason normally given is that Kirin had created a nationwide image that it used effectively. Perhaps more important was the anticipation of increased demand for beer as the farming community shrunk and the consumption of Japanese sake declined. Beer had no history in agricultural communities because of a lack of cooling facilities. In this connection, with the introduction of home refrigerators in the 1950s and 1960s, the home market began to grow. The flavor of Kirin was also highly suited to the rather bland diet of postwar Japan and made itself popular with salaried workers. Its long links with the Mitsubishi group gave it **distribution** routes and access to thousands of outlets frequented by Mitsubishi staff.

KOBAYASHI ICHIZO (1873–1957). An early **Showa period** (1926–1989) business leader who guided the **Tokyo Electric Light Company**, later the **Tokyo Electric Power Company (TEPCO)**, out of a management crisis. He is also remembered as the founder of the **Hankyu Business Group** and Takarazuka Revue Company.

KOBE STEEL. Kobe Seiko was founded in 1905 as a division of **Suzuki Shoten** and became a subsidiary in 1911. The heavy involvement of the Imperial Navy in World War I was a major stimulus to growth, allowing the company to prosper and expand. In 1921, it acquired Harima Shipbuilding from Teikoku Steamships. Harima became independent in 1929, becoming the basis for **Ishikawajima-Harima Heavy Industries**. Suzuki Shoten became a victim of the **Great Depression**. However, because of new products and rising militarism in the 1930s, steel was in demand, enabling Kobe Steel to regain substantial market share.

After World War II, it began to diversify, forming Shinko Electric (from its former heavy electric machinery division), Shinko Shoji (from its iron and steel sales division), Shinko Engineering (from its engineering division), and Shinko Wire (from its steel wire division). Kobe Steel's own manufacturing system was restructured around four principal products: steel, welding rods, heavy machinery, and aluminum and copper. Its first blast furnace was started at the Kakogawa plant in Hyogo prefecture, giving it a capacity for the manufacture of pig iron for steel manufacture and enabling it to become an integrated steel manufacturer.

Kobe Steel's overseas expansion has resulted in 22 factories in various parts of the world and **joint-venture** companies in Brazil, Canada, India, Nigeria, Quatar, Venezuela, and Southeast Asia. It also has subsidiaries in both the United States and Europe. In the late 1990s, the company also developed an interest in China, for which it formed a joint venture. Its head office is registered in Kobe, but, as with many companies, the Tokyo office is of greater importance in policymaking and general administration. *See also* IRON AND STEEL INDUSTRY.

KOGYO IKEN. Literally "opinions on industry," it was a collection of reports and data on industrial production during the first 17 years of the **Meiji period** (1868–1912), commissioned by the then Ministry of Agriculture and Commerce and compiled by Maeda Masana (1850–1921). Around 40 percent of the reports consisted of policy suggestions for developing industry, while the rest was made up of regional reports that were circulated among prefectural governors. It remains an important research resource on the early period of Japan's **modernization**.

KOITO CORPORATION. Auto parts maker and member of the **Toyota Group**. *See also* PICKENS, T. BOONE.

KOKU. The unit in which **rice** was measured for purposes of calculating domain income and **tax** liability. It was adopted from China and was included in the Ritsuryo Seido (Ritsuryo System), dating to the seventh century. The system was later overhauled by Toyotomi Hideyoshi (1536–1598), the second of Japan's three great unifying warlords. He increased the *koku* to almost twice its size. Under the **Tokugawa government**, in 1690, one *koku* was equal to 5.12 U.S. bushels. As a measurement unit for timber or ship capacity, one *koku* was equal to 10 cubic *shaku*, about 0.28 cubic meter. The Tokugawa House domain produced 6 million *koku* of rice each year for the central government in Edo, an amount that could feed 6 million people per year. This was the key to national stability. However, the system was dramatically affected by the failure of several rice crops in the early 19th century, one of the factors leading up to the **Meiji Restoration of 1868**. *See also* KOKUDAKA.

KOKUDAKA. A **tax** system instituted by **Oda Nubunaga** (1534–1582), the first of Japan's three great unifying warlords, that assessed tax base in terms of ***koku*** of **rice**. It replaced the older ***Kandaka*** system and was employed nationwide by Toyotomi Hideyoshi (1536–1598). Wealth was measured in *koku* of unpolished rice rather than in any other form of assets. New **currency** was also issued at the introduction of the *kokudaka* to facilitate commercial transactions. The system remained in force until the Land Tax was reformed between1873 and 1881.

KOKUGA. Provincial administration offices established during the **Nara period** (710–794) and the **Heian period** (794–1185). Provincial governments usually positioned themselves near the largest local center of population in order to manage **agriculture** and commerce, collect **taxes**, and oversee social life.

KOKURITSU GINKO JOREI. The National Bank Ordinance that was issued in December 1872 to introduce a new **banking system** modeled on that of the United States. *See also* BANKING HISTORY.

KOKUSAI DENSHIN DENWA (KDD). Founded in 1952, it is the country's largest international communications company. As a government monopoly corporation, it was heavily criticized for holding charges at artificially high levels during the 1970s and early 1980s until the beginning of the deregulation of the industry, which permitted a number of new companies to enter the sector. The criticisms were exacerbated by the uncovering of a scandal involving the president that resulted in the controversial suicide of the financial director in the mid-1970s. KDD's headquarters are in the Shinjuku district of Tokyo. *See also* TELECOMMUNICATIONS INDUSTRY.

KOKUSAIKA. *See* INTERNATIONALIZATION.

KONBINI. *See* CONVENIENCE STORES.

KONOIKE FAMILY. An **Edo period** (1615–1868) merchant **house** that survived to 10 generations before being eclipsed by the new entrepreneurs of the **Meiji period** (1868–1912). The son of a proud **samurai** family and loyal retainer of **Tokugawa Ieyasu**, Shinemon Shinroku of Konoike village forsook that heritage and became a sake brewer by inventing a refining process that yielded high-grade wine. He opened his business in 1600, and very quickly it expanded. His first son was designated to manage the brewery, and his second and third sons moved to Osaka as sake retailers. He himself set up a new brewery in Osaka along with a retail outlet. Although concealing his samurai roots, he knew well the preferences of samurai who were soon clamoring for his sake. He sold some in Edo (now Tokyo) and found it more than ready for his brand. Since horseback consignments were small and slow to arrive, he received permission to transport his sake to Edo by sea. He could deliver sake to the various *han* (feudal domains) en route and carried goods from Osaka for which he was paid commission, all of which made him remarkably rich. The youngest son took the name Zenemon, thereafter reserved for the head of the House of Konoike, and by 1656, he had entered the business of the *ryogae*, in which he was very successful.

House rules were created during the time of the third head. The House continued its various business activities, and the branch houses were encouraged to maintain great solidarity. The House was also able to lend to impoverished *daimyo* (lords), adding to its prestige. Lack of sound management in the later years of the Tokugawa period and heavy loans to the government weakened the House. When the **Tokugawa government** collapsed, the House was unable to retrieve its losses from the new Meiji government. Although he supported the new government, the head of the House did not display the kind of imagination needed to work successfully and effectively in the new business environment. Such was the fate of numerous Osaka merchant houses that did not fully comprehend the nature of the changes that were taking place or the implications for institutions that could not adapt to them.

KURABO INDUSTRIES. Founded as a cotton spinning company in Kurashiki, Okawayama prefecture, in 1888, it gradually expanded into wool and took over several small local businesses. In 1926, it formed a subsidiary, Kurashiki Kenshoku (now **Kuraray**) to specialize in silk thread. For a time, because of wartime demands, it was in the machinery business, from which it withdrew in 1945, returning to its field of expertise. From the 1970s it became interested in environmental issues. It has **joint ventures** in Brazil, Indonesia, and Thailand. The head office is in Osaka. *See also* TEXTILE INDUSTRY.

KURARAY. Founded initially as Kurashiki Kenshoku in 1926, a subsidiary of **Kurabo Industries**, it became Kuraray in 1970. It was the first company in the world to manufacture polyvinyl alcohol fiber on a commercial scale by developing an integrated production process. It formed a group of subsidiaries to source and produce raw materials. It has exported its technology to numerous countries and, during the 1960s, set up three production plants in China. Its subsidiaries include seven overseas operations in the United States, the Middle East, and Southeast Asia. Using the technology it developed in the field of polymer chemistry, it moved into fine chemicals, principally isoprene derivatives, as well as medical equipment for kidney dialysis. The head office is in Tokyo. *See also* TEXTILE INDUSTRY.

KUROFUNE. The famous Black Ships (as the Japanese referred to them) that formed the small fleet under the command of Commodore Matthew Perry sent as emissaries by U.S. President Millard Fillmore to request the establishment of diplomatic and commercial relations with Japan. Although they arrived in 1853 and the **Tokugawa government** managed to survive until 1868, the technological threat that the ships symbolized had a profound effect on many of Japan's more visionary young people and was one of the important factors that led to the **Meiji Restoration of 1868** and to Japan's subsequent modernization, bringing to an end almost 300 years of international isolation. *See also* SAKOKU JIDAI.

KYOCERA CORPORATION. Founded as Kyocera Ceramics in 1959 by **Inamori Kazuo** (1932–), the company grew to become the world leader in ceramic casings for **semiconductors**, producing also circuit boards, liquid crystal displays, printers, mobile phones, and single-lens reflecting optical equipment. Through effective strategies involving mergers and acquisitions, it has expanded into the United States, Europe, Korea, and China. It now employees almost 14,000 people worldwide. Its activities are now largely in **electronic** equipment, telecommunications equipment, and semiconductor components. Its head office is still in Kyoto.

– L –

LABOR LAWS. In the early postwar years, from 1945 to 1948, the **Supreme Commander Allies Powers (SCAP)** instituted numerous regulations to improve working conditions and to contribute to the demilitarization and democratization of Japanese society as a whole. The three most important were the Trade Union Law of 1945, the Labor Relations Adjustment Law of 1946, and the Labor Standards Law of 1947. The Ministry of Labor was established in 1947 to implement the new laws, which in their fundamentals followed the conventions of the International Labor Organization. Workers **in public corporations** were governed and protected by the Public Corporation and National Enterprises Labor Relations Law of 1948.

These laws remained unchanged until a wave of foreign criticism attacked the long working hours of Japanese labor, claiming that they encouraged saving over consumption, a structural impediment to importing. True or false, the Labor Standards Law was amended to shorten the working week to 40 hours and to require staff to take holidays. An **Equal Employment Opportunity Law** was approved in the Diet in 1985, taking effect from April 1986, giving **women** equal rights in order to end discrimination. It had to be amended in 1997 and took effect in 1999. Penalties were specified, such as the publication of the names of companies that engaged in discriminatory practices. **Sexual harassment** was also banned in the workplace, and corporations were required to take adequate preventive measures. In addition, a 1995 Family-Leave Law was introduced to permit family assistance to sick members. Up to three months is stipulated in the law, and some corporations began urging staff to take advantage of the law. Nevertheless, old habits die hard, and a mid-1990s survey showed that less than 20 percent of all companies and barely 50 percent of major corporations permit staff to benefit from the law. The increased number of law suits relating to ***karoshi***, death from overwork, may force companies that refuse to comply with the law to reconsider the implications of their policies. *See also* LABOR–MANAGEMENT RELATIONS; LABOR UNIONS.

LABOR–MANAGEMENT RELATIONS. One of the distinguishing marks of Japanese labor–management relations is the relative absence of extremely confrontational behavior and action that is typical of British or American labor relations. There are a number of reasons for this. One is that the majority of unions do not belong to any national federation or organization. There are a total of over 36,000 unions composed of **enterprise unions** (95 percent), craft unions (2 percent), and industrial unions (1.6 percent). All members of a **corporation** are included in the union with the exception of temporary workers or subcontracted staff.

A second reason derives from an important fact of postwar history. During the early period of reconstruction, labor relations were marred by radical actions that affected a number of major corporations such as **Nissan Motor**, **Oji Paper**, and **Japan Steel**. By the end of the 1960s, both sides had realized that confrontation was unproductive and that cooperation was the way forward. This became the pattern thereafter with what has been described as an institutionalized bargaining process known as ***shunto*** taking place annually in spring until the **recession of the 1990s** started.

A third reason lies within the character of Japanese corporate culture itself. In the absence of a reinforcing class system (as in England) where corporate ranks and class background are linked or a wide disparity in wealth (as in the United States), labor and management are not clearly distinguished. Indeed, at the level of upper management and the board, the distinction is equally vague. It is open to question whether the Western differentiation between labor and management is applicable at all or, if it is, the degree to which it must be modified or qualified to have any explanatory value in describing Japanese practices. It has actually been argued by some of the most experienced and reliable researchers that the Anglo-Saxon neoclassical model of corporate culture does not apply in two important respects. One is that members of the company are not treated as hired labor to be bought and sold according to the needs of the labor market. The other is that the company is not the property of stockholders who may dispose of it as they wish.

Many corporate activities conducted for the improvement of the company, such as **quality control**, ***kaizen***, or **just-in-time**, involve the cooperation of all ranks within the organization. This reinforces the spirit of cooperation that is the hallmark of many Japanese corporations. In principle, morale is lifted and **productivity** increased. Workers are consulted and their comments and **suggestions** taken seriously. In this regard, labor–management relations are marked by the absence of the kind of cynicism that is widespread in the Anglo-Saxon model. Workers in the public sector have the right to bargain but not to take industrial action. In reality, the **Ministry of Finance** was in complete control of budgets and, de facto, also of wages and salaries to some extent, removing the feeling of arbitrariness. However, some public sector strikes have taken place, such as in the case of **Japan Railways** when they were owned by the state. *See also* LABOR LAWS; LABOR UNIONS.

LABOR UNIONS. Prior to 1987, the over 70,000 union units of all three kinds of unions—**enterprise unions**, craft unions, and industrial unions—were organized into four major federations. The largest was the General Council of Trades Unions of Japan (**Sohyo**), which included government workers. The three others were the association of private sector unions (Rengo), the Japanese Confederation of Labor (Domei), and the Federation of Independent Unions (Churitsu Roren). The Japan Trade Union Confederation (JTUC-Rengo) was created in November 1987 by the private sector unions. It quickly became the largest in the country, claiming over 5.5 million members. This development led to Domei and Churitsu Roren voluntarily dissolving. In 1989, Sohyo followed them into extinction with its members joining JTUC-Rengo, giving it a total strength of over 8 million, at the time around 65 percent of organized labor. While negotiations with management at the ***shunto***, the spring offensive, are handled by the enterprise unions, JTUC-Rengo's role lies in informing the public of needs and demands. It also presents these to both government and business organizations.

One trend of the 1990s, due in part to the recession but also to shifts within the structure of the economy, has been the decline in union support. While numerically reaching over 12 million members, the actual percentage of unionized people has steadily declined from around 35 percent in the mid-1960s to just over 23 percent in the late 1990s. All sectors of the economy have shown a decline, the worst being **agriculture**, forestry, **fishing**, and mining (over 22 percent), while only **construction** showed a modest increase of around 3 percent.

Many other factors may be cited, including the serious decline in steel, **shipbuilding**, heavy machinery, and related traditional sectors. New areas of growth, such as retail and service industries, are difficult to unionize and use part-time and temporary workers. To this may be added the general belt-tightening strategies forced by the appreciation of the yen (***endaka***), mechanization, and the hollowing out of some sectors of manufacturing to cheaper labor markets. JTUC-Rengo, in the face of these changes, announced a new agenda including quality-of-life issues, such as working hours, child care, housing conditions, and social security. How successful the federation will be in changing ingrained habits and practices remains to be seen. *See also* LABOR LAWS; LABOR–MANAGEMENT RELATIONS.

LAND POLICY. The prewar **agricultural** landlord system was abolished in 1945 in a major land reform by which tenant farmers became owners of small farms in their own right. The Owners-Farmers' Establishment Law of 1946 implemented this as part of a total program intended to decentralize and democratize Japanese society in as many areas as possible. It was followed by the Agricultural Land Act of 1952, which restricted land transfers, tenure, and tenant rents in order to protect tenants from abuses and to restrict landownership. Joint-stock companies were prohibited from owning land, and even agricultural **cooperatives** were prohibited from owning land unless they were using it for agricultural purposes. The net result of the reform was that the average farm size was reduced to 1.65 acres, smaller than the prewar size. However well intended, this, like many of the **Supreme Commander Allied Powers (SCAP)** reforms, was based on a lack of understanding of Japan in general and of how aspects of the society and government actually functioned.

One negative consequence of the policy was that it contributed to the increase in land prices, in turn making home ownership for most Japanese an unrealizable dream. Protection of **rice** farmers, a political priority, enabled subsidized farmers to justify working tiny parcels of land, however small, even in the capital city, Tokyo. This further aggravated land prices to the point that one square meter under the famous Takano Fruits Parlor in Shinjuku, Tokyo, came to be worth over ¥55 million at the time (1985), equivalent to around U.S.$600,000. Thus it remained until the burst of the **bubble economy**.

Subsequent attempts to implement a policy have been hampered by the protracted **recession of the 1990s** and the conflict of interests in business and politics that prevented any effective measure from being implemented. One other factor aggravating the problem is the massive concentration of business and government offices in Tokyo. In response to this, proposals have been made to move the nation's capital. But such is the Japanese penchant for close contact that moving the nation's capital would simply be to transfer the problem to another city. The most effective solution would be to disperse the organs of government to different parts of the country, which has been attempted on a modest scale but is equally unlikely to be the herald of a major move.

LARGE RETAIL STORE LAW. The Daitenho is a 1974 law revising the **Department Store** Law of 1956 that was designed to protect small retailers by restricting the growth of large-scale stores and supermarkets. The opening of stores with floor space of 3,000 square meters in the 10 largest cities and 1,500 square meters in the rest of the country was placed under the supervision of the **Ministry of International Trade and Industry (MITI)** to permit consultation with local government and business associations. MITI had power to reduce floor space, shorten opening hours, require closed days, or even order postponement of opening if it was thought beneficial to local interests. When medium-sized stores seemed a threat, the law was changed to cover floor spaces of 500 square meters. MITI used administrative guidance (***gyosei shido***) to slow down the process of development.

American negotiators brought this up in the **Structural Impediment Initiative (SII)** talks as a **nontariff barrier** to market access.

Nevertheless, the U.S. toy retailer, Toys "R" Us opened in 1991 and rapidly expanded to over 60 stores by 1998. Others, such as Warner Bros. Studio Stores, The Gap, Pier 1 Imports Inc., and Tower Records, have followed. Wal-Mart took a sizable share in the **Seiyu** supermarket group. How successful these will be remains to be seen if proposed further changes in the law were to delegate more power to regional authorities.

LIBERAL DEMOCRATIC PARTY (LDP). *Jiminto*, as it is known in Japanese, has been popularly described as being "not liberal, not democratic, and not a party." This refers to the fact that in essence it has very conservative leanings and dictates through one-party rule and that it is not a unified party in the Western sense but rather a cobbling together of various interests, such as big business and **agriculture**.

Founded in 1955 at the request of **Keidanren**, it is made up of a group of factions all seeking power. The leader of the strongest faction has traditionally become prime minister, normally for an average of two years. It has traditionally survived by having not merely a majority in the house but also a majority over all the other parties combined. The architect of the postwar period when the party came into being was Yoshida Shigeru (1878–1967), who replaced part founder Hatoyama Ichiro (1883–1959) as prime minister in 1946, retiring in 1954.

The LDP worked with government agencies to plan and implement policies that benefited a broad range of interest groups. Its policy on agriculture protected the domestic industry, banning **rice** imports until 1993, while on trade it worked to expand exports while limiting imports. After nearly 40 years of one-party rule, the LDP became weakened initially through several scandals (principally the **Lockheed Scandal** and the **Recruit Scandal**) and because of the introduction of the **consumption tax** in 1989. The upper-house majority was lost in 1989, and the lower-house majority was lost for the first time in 1993. Various coalition combinations came into being. Hashimoto Ryutaro was elected LDP president 1996, and to counter the protracted **recession of the 1990s**, he began **deregulation** of the financial system through major reforms referred to as the **big bang** and restructuring government to reduce costs and improve efficiency. The reforms were continued under the leadership of Koizumi Junichiro, who became prime minister in 2001, although the general revitalization of the Japanese economy has continued to be stalled by various interest groups that prefer the status quo.

LIFETIME EMPLOYMENT SYSTEM. *Shushin koyo seido* implies a "stable employment system" intended to provide employment from university or high school graduation until age 55 or whatever is the retirement age of an individual company. It is sometimes mistakenly regarded as a system of "lifetime employment." Its modern form originated in the late **Meiji period** (1868–1912) when skilled labor was at a premium and talented staff were given numerous fringe benefits in order to remain with the company. The objective was to encourage longer service in return for which welfare programs, work councils, and industrial relations sections were instituted in large **corporations** where the system still primarily prevails rather than in **small and medium-sized enterprises**. The government supported these initiatives because it considered roaming gangs of laborers a threat to political and social stability. Accordingly, ***oyakata*** (labor gang headmen) were encouraged to become part of the system with their workers.

The **Factory Acts** of 1911 modernized the concept of the house principle (***ie gensoku***), which became the moral basis of workers' loyalties. Eventually, along the same lines as the **Edo period** (1615–1868) **apprentice system**, corporations preferred people who had recently graduated from college or high school and who could be trained in the culture of the organization. The whole concept implied an implicit contract that the employee would loyally remain in the organization in return for security and stability of employment and other benefits. Dismissal in rare cases could be effected if an employee committed a crime or an error of such proportions that the company itself was at risk. In reality, provided an employee showed an appropriate degree of abject humility and sincere remorse, he or she would probably be retained.

One of the demerits of the system from the viewpoint of Western-style functional management is that it is difficult to manage poor performers out of the system. This led to the development of the *madogiwa-zoku*, the "window sill tribe," people who literally sat beside windows, indicating that they had been marginalized into performing menial or trivial tasks. The economic decline of Japan from the death of Emperor Showa in 1989 through the collapse of land prices to the **recession of the 1990s** resulted in the first major layoffs since the close of World War II in 1945. These were achieved through a combination of various methods, including golden handshakes, corporate amalgamations, early retirement of executives, and other devices designed to avoid drastic rises in unemployment figures.

Faced with the option of inefficient corporate performance or the threat of social instability through a large body of unemployed, social stability will always be preferred. While Western critics and observers argue that the system should or will disappear, it has shown remarkable resilience, probably because it has served Japan so well in the past. It is natural for a system to be modified to suit changing times, but it is unlikely to disappear entirely. Outsourcing showed increases during the early years of the 21st century, but it is highly likely, once economic stability has been achieved, that a modified version of the old system will survive, at least for people designated for the management track or for future leadership roles. *See also* KASEI; NENKO-JORETSU.

LOCKHEED SCANDAL. A major scandal o f the early 1970s involving leading business and political figures who were alleged to have received bribes from the Lockheed Corporation of the United States in order to favor Lockheed aircraft for government procurement. The broker was identified as Kodama Yoshio, a former military leader credited in part with the creation of the kamikaze concept. His involvement angered one rightist who rented a plane and crashed it kamikaze style into his house in the Tokyo suburb of Chofu. Osano Kenji, president of Kokusai Kogyo, was implicated and was hospitalized to evade questioning. The Lockheed scandal brought down the government of **Tanaka Kakuei**, who subsequently faced a trial that lasted 10 years. In the public inquiry, it was revealed that payments were referred to as "peanuts," one "peanut" being a unit of U.S.$1 million. Tanaka was accused of receiving six peanuts. While the sum of U.S.$6 million was enough to create outrage at the time, it was modest compared to the financial irregularities of subsequent prime ministers, such as Nakasone Yasuhiro and Takeshita Noboru, both of whom were severely damaged by the **Recruit Scandal** of 1989. *See also* MARUBENI CORPORATION.

LONG-TERM CREDIT BANK OF JAPAN (LTCB). This was a major investment **bank** that was established in 1952 as a semi-governmental financial institution. It took over the business of the Nihon Kangyo Bank and the Hokkaikdo Takshoku Bank. The LTCB became a private financial institution in 1961 and concentrated on the chemical industry as well as the development of small and medium-sized businesses. From 1970, it expanded into Europe and the United States with offices in London, New York, and Los Angeles. In the 1980s, it entered the Asian market through offices in Singapore and Hong Kong and became involved in mergers and acquisitions and some high-risk business, including derivatives trading. The LTCB formed an alliance with Swiss Bank in the field of investment banking. In October 1998, under the massive burden of ¥5 trillion in nonperforming loans, the bank was taken over by the government under an emergency provision passed in the National Diet. In February 1999, it was sold to a consortium headed by the U.S.-based Ripplewood Holdings and relaunched as the Shinsei (new life, or newborn) bank in June 2000.

LOYALTY. Identified as a characteristic virtue of Japanese culture and made its central theme by Royce in his famous work *The Philosophy of Loyalty*. Loyalty, while an integral part of Japan's family system, was strengthened by **Confucian** influences, particularly in the early **Edo period** (1615–1868), when the shogun demanded it of his *daimyo* (domain lords) and who in turn demanded it as their retainers. All levels of course owed absolute loyalty to the emperor as apex of the hierarchy. The **Meiji period** (1868–1912) of modernization benefited enormously from the virtue of loyalty as people worked tirelessly for the development of the nation. The same virtue, however, reached the level of fanaticism in Japan's early 20th-century military culture. It was again harnessed in the postwar reconstruction of the country when the nation's industrial base had to be rebuilt, and it can be seen surviving in the **Lifetime Employment System**, which still functions in major **corporations**. One aspect of the Japanese understanding of the virtue of loyalty is that it is a two-way street in the sense that while the individual owes unequivocal loyalty to the organization, the organization in turn has a categorical moral obligation to look after its loyal workers. This is one of the reasons why the government prefers to rehabilitate ailing corporations than allow them to collapse and why there is so much resistance to **mergers and acquisitions**, especially by **foreign companies**. *See also* INDUSTRIAL REVITALIZATION CORPORATION OF JAPAN (IRCJ).

– M –

MACHINE TOOL INDUSTRY. Among Japan's 2,000 **small and medium-sized enterprises** (***chu-sho kigyo***), the machine tool industry ranks fourth in the world production of machine tools behind the United States, the former Soviet Union, and Germany.

MADOGUCHI SHIDO. Literally meaning "window guidance," it was a device used by the **Bank of Japan** (Nippon Ginko) to impose controls on the **banking** system during the postwar period until the burst of the **bubble economy**. The Bank of Japan indicated what it considered appropriate levels of lending, thereby controlling the nation's monetary base. Although the **Ministry of Finance** exerted some influence on the Bank of Japan on fixing the discount rate, the bank was relatively free in its ability to "guide" banks. Japanese industry was and is heavily dependent on **bank** finance because the **capital markets in Japan** do not function as they do in the Western world. The system came to an end in 1991 and was replaced by controlling credit flow through manipulating interest rates.

MARUBENI CORPORATION. A major trading house (***sogo shosha***) that traces its roots to a company founded in 1858 by Ito Chubei to sell hemp to outlying areas. In 1872, he opened a dry-goods store in Osaka called Benichu, using Beni as the business logo. By the early 20th century, Benichu had expanded into Kobe and Kyoto. In 1914, the company was reorganized into **C. Itoh & Co.**, which was further divided in 1918 into Itochu Shoten, consisting of the Osaka and Kyoto stores and C. Itoh & Co., having the Kobe store as its main business. The post–World War I business decline weakened the commodity markets, in turn creating the need to consolidate.

In 1921, Itochu Shoten merged with Ito-chubei Shoten, taking the name Marubeni Shoten. From its single office in Kyoto, it expanded in 1931 to Osaka and began the transformation to a trading house. Branches were opened in India and China. As the business expanded, the desire grew to reunite the various branches of the Ito family business. In September 1941, three companies—Kishimoto Shoten (a steel trader), Marubeni Shoten, and C. Itoh & Co.—merged to form Sanko Kabushiki Kaisha. Although Japan's involvement in World War II limited the company's business, it still traded in China and in Southwest Asia. Sanko KK merged in 1944 with Daido Trading and Kureha Cotton Spinning (also founded in Ito Chubei) to create Daiken Industries. By 1945, the group comprised 103 companies in Japan and was internationally involved in a range of businesses, including **shipping**, **textiles**, heavy industry and chemical products, grains, fertilizers, and various kinds of military procurement.

When the **Supreme Commander Allied Powers** (**SCAP**) implemented its policy of breaking up the prewar ***zaibatsu***, Daiken was broken into Marubeni, C. Itoh & Co., Kureha Cotton Spinning, and Amagasaki Nail Works. Marubeni was established in 1949, and by 1951 it had opened an office in New York. By 1954, it had expanded to 22 overseas offices. In keeping with the government policy of trade expansion, Marubeni was partnered with another trading company, Iida & Co. (subsequently Takashimaya Department Store), which had incurred massive losses in the soybean market, under the tutelage of the **Fuji Bank** to form Marubeni-Iida in 1955. Marubeni-Iida expanded into polyethylene production and in 1958 began **automobile** exports to the United States for **Nissan Motor Corporation**. Totsuka Company, a smaller metal trading company that was also a sales agent of Nippon Kokan (NKK), was absorbed in 1966, effectively making heavy and chemical industry products over 50 percent of Marubeni-Iida's business and making Tokyo the corporate headquarters. Also in 1966, the **Fuyo Group** was constituted around the Fuji Bank, and the largest postwar ***keiretsu*** of companies was formed. Marubeni-Iida changed its name to Marubeni Corporation in 1972.

By the late 1970s, the large trading companies came under heavy criticism for their monopolistic practices that were forcing former manufacturers to enter markets by more direct routes. In the case of Marubeni, its involvement in the **Lockheed Scandal** and its influence in the rice business did not help its reputation. Marubeni made up for its losses by exporting power systems and steel pipe for oil producers during the 1980s. From the early 1990s, Marubeni began a long process of restructuring through consolidation, liquidation of nonprofitable activities, and a narrower focusing of corporate energy on a smaller number of key areas of business, principally retail, information and **telecommunications**, electric power infrastructure, high-value-added materials, resource development, and trading. In spite of its efforts, it posted large losses in 1997, the first time in 46 years. This forced further economies, including a reduction of staff through early retirement, layoffs, and other strategies. With many observers predicting the demise of the large trading companies, the fate of Marubeni will be significant for the Japanese business world as well as for the corporation itself.

MARUZEN. An importer, retailer, and publisher of books, particularly Western, founded as Maruya Shosha in Yokohama by Hayashi Yuteki, a disciple of **Meiji period** (1868–1912) intellectual leader **Fukuzawa Yukichi**. It moved to Tokyo in 1893 and became Maruzen. It is still a highly reputed publisher and retailer of books.

MARUZEN OIL. Maruzen Sekiyu is an oil refining manufacturer and retailer of petrochemical products, founded in 1933 to produce industrial lubricants and various oil products. In cooperation with **Daikyo Oil**, it formed the Abu Dhabi Oil Company in 1968. It has been active in pursuing sources of crude oil and has worked to increase its supply of liquefied petroleum gas (LPG) used especially in taxis. It is also engaged in researching new energy sources. It is considered one of the major all-Japanese (*minzoku-kei*) corporations. Its head office is in Tokyo. *See also* PETROLEUM INDUSTRY.

MATSUNAGA YASUZAEMON (1875–1971). An industrialist and business leader whose life spanned the **Meiji** (1868–1912), **Taisho** (1912–1926), and **Showa** (1926–1989) **periods**, during which he helped to create and manage the entire **electric power industry** in Japan. Born in Nagasaki, he graduated from what is now Keio University and founded the Fukuhaku Railways (later Kyushu Electric Railways) in 1909. He worked tirelessly in the industry and became president of the Japan Electric Association in 1924.

After World War II, Matsunaga returned to the industry, fighting for the privatization of the power companies, and as a result the modern structure of nine regional companies was created. His last major task was the establishment in 1953 of the Central Research Institute of the Electric Power Industry, of which he became director.

MATSUSHITA ELECTRIC INDUSTRIAL. Matsushita Denki is a manufacturer of commercial and consumer **electronics** products and components. Matsushita Electric Appliance Factory (MEAF) was set up in Osaka in 1918 by **Matsushitua Konosuke** (1894–1989) and incorporated under its present name in 1935. Its first product was the double-ended electric socket, which made it famous. This was followed by a battery-powered bicycle lamp. By the 1930s, the company was selling irons, radios, fans, lightbulbs, and other useful daily appliances. Early evidence of Matsushita's innovative approach to management was demonstrated during the **Great Depression** of 1929. All workers were given full pay for only a half day at the company, and holiday pay was canceled. Workers were asked to go out and sell outstanding inventory. By 1930, all staff were back to full-time work. Radio production, at first unsuccessful, commenced in 1931, but by 1942, Matsushita was the largest radio manufacturer in Japan.

In 1933, Matsushita adopted a radical style of organization through divisions, each with fiscal responsibility for itself. This gave great solidarity and power to each division with the net result that, by 1945, Matsushita had 49 subsidiaries beneath its divisions. The company was ordered to be broken up by the **Supreme Commander Allied Powers (SCAP)** as a ***zaibatsu***, but a combination of lobbying the occupation, as well as clear evidence that Matsushita could not be compared with military procurement suppliers, resulted in gentler treatment. By 1950, it had regained its autonomy, after which it moved quickly into black-and-white television sets, transistor radios, tape recorders, air conditioners, washing machines, and general domestic appliances. In 1954, it acquired majority ownership of **Japan Victor Corporation**, although JVC continues as a separate enterprise.

Matsushita also has a long history of international business, using Japan's overseas markets from the time of the formation of Matsushita Electrical Trading Company in 1935. Post-1945, Matsushitua lost 39 of its overseas facilities. Philips, the Dutch electronics corporation, approached Matsushita in 1948 to reestablish its business links. Masushita Konosuke himself visited the United States and Philips in the Netherlands in 1951. In 1952, Matsushita and Philips had established a **joint-venture** company that began operating in Osaka in 1954, manufacturing picture tubes, vacuum tubes, transistors, and various electrical components. An office was opened in New York in 1953, followed by Matsushita Electric Corporation of America in 1959. National Thai was opened in Thailand in the same year. This led to global expansion of production, marketing, and sales.

In 1974, Matsushita bought out Motorola's **electronics** division, whose products used the brand name Quasar. The last Motorola television factory was closed in 1995. More controversial was the unsuccessful acquisition of the U.S. entertainment and movie corporation MIA in 1990 for U.S.$6 billion. After numerous problems that suggested that it was a complete mismatch, Matsushita sold MIA to Michael Bronfman in 1995 at a loss of around U.S.$300 million. By the turn of the century, Matsushita had over 233 manufacturing and sales subsidiaries in 160 countries worldwide and a network of 25,000 retail outlets nationwide. Much of Matsushita's strategy was through merger and acquisition of smaller companies to acquire technology and market entry. To develop its own technology, Matsushitua established a research and development facility in Osaka in 1953 that over the years has registered some 27,000 product **patents**.

MATSUSHITA KONOSUKE (1894–1989). The founder and, until his death, guide of **Matsushita Electrical Industrial**. The Matsushita Rekishikan (historical museum) of the corporation displays a large range of artifacts that were part of the life of Matsushita Konosuke, including a large picture of the fields in which he grew up as the eighth child of a wealthy farmer who lived in Wakayama prefecture, south of Osaka. When he was only four, his father lost everything he owned while speculating on **rice** futures. Growing up in an atmosphere where adversity had to be faced and overcome, Matsushita went through the "school of hard knocks." All his brothers and sisters died, and even his own son died when he was young. These experiences made him a prime candidate for cult status, endowing him with almost a spiritual aura, as a brief visit to the Rekshikan will confirm.

Many of the founders of new religions in Japan were people who were able to say that their extensive sufferings were a school of character and belief. For Matsushita, who was an entrepreneur, industrialist, and management philosopher, it was a powerful addition to his personal qualifications to lead his company both commercially and morally. He is perhaps the best example of how the corporate and the cultic can overlap in the Japanese business world.

Matsushita worked from the age of nine in a bicycle shop and found a job at age 16 at the Osaka Electric Light Company. His outstanding ability led to his speedy promotion, which made him responsible for major projects, such as wiring houses and businesses. He was further promoted to the rank of inspector but complained that there was not enough hands-on work. He used his free hours to develop his light socket, which he offered to the company. As is often the case with new ideas, it was rejected, and he decided to set up in business for himself. He started up his company with ¥100 of capital and five staff, including himself and his wife. This was in 1917, and Matsushita was 22 years old. The double-outlet adaptor that screwed into the light socket, providing light plus capacity for one appliance, was his first successful product, after which the company never looked back. In 1922, he developed a bicycle lamp that could run for 50 hours on one set of batteries. He had prospective retailers place them in their window, with one lit, and asked to be paid only for what was sold. The quality of the product commended it, and, like the socket, it was successful. By 1931, Matsushita had 140 registered patents and over 200 products. In 1935, he registered a corporation that grew steadily over the years.

Matsushita did not even have a high school education, yet he wrote 46 books between 1953 and 1990, principally on aspects of management, for which he is perhaps best remembered and most respected in Japan, particularly his philosophy of human resource management. He developed his famous seven principles that defined the company's goals and values. He believed that educating staff in these was the first priority, or, as it stated in the company philosophy, Matsushita placed people before products and thus, in his own words, could achieve extraordinary results from ordinary people.

Matsushita continued as president until 1961, after which he served as chairman and adviser, although he moved back into a leadership role whenever the company was in difficulty. His last major involvement was around 1984, after which he became less and less active. After his death in 1989, he was enshrined as the guardian ***kami*** of management within the grounds of Tsubaki Grand Shrine in Mie prefecture.

McDONALD'S JAPAN. Opening its first outlet in 1972, McDonald's is the oldest of the foreign fast-food chains to enter the Japanese market. Led for most of its life by Fujita Den, who retired in 2003, it fought local and international competition and by the turn of the century had over 3,000 outlets. A combination of shrewd marketing and well-chosen sites created a national identity. Like many of the fast-food businesses, it has been the object of criticism from animal rights activists, environmentalists, and health critics. It remains to be seen at an international level how the company will deal with these issues. Its founding president in Japan, Den Fujita, who is also known as the "founding father" of hamburger chains, retired in 2003 after 32 years as chief executive officer. Headquarters are in Shinjuku in Tokyo.

MEIDENSHA ELECTRIC MANUFACTURING. Founded in 1897 as a pioneer in the manufacture of electric motors and generators, it graduated to heavy electrical machinery and electrical work in major construction projects. It joined the **Sumitomo *keiretsu*** in 1966 and further developed into an integrated manufacturer of electrical machinery. Meidensha further showed its versatility by developing water treatment machinery and devices for identifying gas leaks and by expanding its operations to Singapore. The head office is in Tokyo.

MEIJI MILK PRODUCTS. Meiji Nyugyo was established in 1917 to produce milk-related products, such as ice cream, cheese, butter, margarine, powdered milk for babies, and various frozen foods, all marketed under the Meiji brand name. It experimented with various **joint ventures**, not all of which were successful. It also branched into other food areas, such as chocolate, cookies, and snack foods. It is affiliated with Meiji Seika, both of which grew out of **Meiji Sugar**. Through a tie-up with Borden Inc. of the United States, the company introduced the Lady Borden ice cream brand in the 1970s. Its headquarters are in Tokyo.

MEIJI MUTUAL LIFE INSURANCE. Japan's first modern life **insurance** company was founded in 1881 and became a mutual life insurance company in 1947. It expanded through developing new insurance products that served the needs of various groups in society, particularly the elderly. In 1976 it bought into Pacific Guardian Life Insurance (Hawaii) and in 1981 formed Meiji Realty Inc. of America (New York). It is active in Brazil, Europe, and Southeast Asia. It is a member of the **Mitsubishi Group**, and its headquarters are in Tokyo.

MEIJI PERIOD (1868–1912). Following the feudal **Edo period** (1615–1868), the **Meiji Restoration** government launched a program to modernize and develop the country to become strong enough to resist Western pressure and to ensure autonomous development. The objective was the creation of a modern economy that was able to survive in the world of the day, and from the beginnings of **modernization**, Japan grew rapidly until the pinnacle of recognition was achieved in the Anglo-Japan Alliance (Nichi-Ei Domei) of 1902. Emperor Meiji reigned from 1868 until his death in 1912, which evoked the emotions of the nation, including the ritual **suicide** of General Nogi Maresuke (1849–1912) and his wife, who committed suicide with him on the day of the late emperor's funeral. *See also* INTRODUCTION.

MEIJI RESTORATION OF 1868. Following the arrival of the American black ships (***kurofune***) in 1853, carrying implications of a foreign threat, a succession of bad harvests, and a steadily collapsing economy, the last shogun of the Tokugawa regime, Yoshinobu, was forced to resign in 1868 to make way for new leadership. A group of young **samurai** from the Kyushu fiefdoms of Choshu and Satsuma, *daimyo* (referred to in Edo as *tozama*), the outer clans, presented themselves as restoring imperial rule to Japan in order to strengthen the country against the foreign danger. No emperor in history had ever actually ruled, but they used this as a device to pretend that they were taking society back to an ideal imperial past while in fact they were about to destroy any piece of tradition that posed a threat to change. They successfully caught the nation's imagination and were able, within the space of 30 years, to effect the speediest and most comprehensive **modernization** program in the history of the world.

In 1867, the Japanese were under the **Tokugawa feudal system**, carrying swords and wearing the distinctive top-knot hairstyle (*chon-mage*). By 1902, the most recent member of the community of advanced nations had forged an alliance with the United Kingdom (the Nichi-Ei Domei) and from 1914 was an active participant in World War I, providing logistical support to the British Royal Navy. The amount of fighting in Japan of 1868 was remarkably small if considered alongside other similar civil upheavals and revolutions, such as those in England or the American Civil War.

Two important factors that helped speed the process were the fact that Japan had developed a powerful social structure and had also evolved an effective business culture of its own. In addition, various **tax** revenues that had been collected toward the end of the **Edo period** (1615–1868) provided capital for a large amount of basic infrastructure and construction expenditure needed to create the new Japan of the early **Meiji period** (1868–1912). While the Meiji government had some natural resources that were necessary to begin industrial development, many of these were exhausted in a short space of time, and Japan was forced thereafter to import almost all the raw materials needed for manufacturing. Nevertheless, within a little over 100 years after Emperor Meiji ascended the throne, in spite of being disastrously defeated in 1945, Japan had created the world's second-largest economy after the United States. *See also* INTRODUCTION.

MEIJI SEIKA. This is the largest confectionery company in Japan, founded in 1916 to produce and export Western confections. The dairy division became independent as **Meiji Milk Products** in 1940. Postwar recovery was delayed because of economic weakness and lack of raw materials, but by 1952 production had been resumed. It expanded into new products, such as snack foods, instant foods, and health foods. It also created a successful **pharmaceuticals** division, particularly in the field of antibiotics. It has **joint-venture** manufacturing companies in Indonesia, Singapore, and South Korea. The head office is in Tokyo.

MERCHANT HOUSES OF THE EDO PERIOD. Houses involved in different kinds of business during the **Edo period** (1615–1868), whose management structures prefigured many modern aspects of modern **Japanese-style management** and whose business itself was in many cases the foundation of a modern enterprise. The **Mitsui House** and the **Sumitomo House** are two of the best examples, each with a history of over 300 years. The original Mitsui store at Nihombashi in Tokyo is depicted in *ukiyoe* (woodblock prints) of the period.

MERGERS AND ACQUISITIONS. Because of the relatively closed nature of Japanese corporate culture, Western-style mergers and acquisitions are much less common than elsewhere, making it difficult for **foreign companies** to acquire Japanese enterprises. The resistance of **Koito Corporation** to the advances of **T. Boone Pickens**, the notorious corporate raider of the 1980s, is a good illustration of how Japanese corporations traditionally viewed themselves and behaved when they felt threatened. However, the protracted **recession of the 1990s** plus the collapse of several large banks and corporations, such as **Yamaichi Securities**, the **Long-Term Credit Bank of Japan**, and the restructuring of **Daiei** and **Nissan Motor Corporation**, permitted foreign intrusions on a scale hitherto unseen. It remains to be seen how successful these will be, but, as always, it will depend very much on how newcomers can adjust to the distinctive character of the Japanese market. *See also* INTRODUCTION.

MINAMATA DISEASE. *See* ENVIRONMENTAL PROBLEMS.

MINING. Digging for minerals and natural resources is one of Japan's oldest local industrial skills. Several major enterprises started as mining operations. **Sumitomo** began with the **Besshi Copper Mine**, while names such as the **Ikuno Silver Mine**, the **Ashio Copper Mine**, and the **Iwanami Ginzan** are a central part of Japan's early commercial and economic history. Undersea drilling for **petroleum** also started in Japan long before Western technology had arrived. All the major ***zaibatsu*** had a mining and smelting **corporation** within the group, and while these have long since exhausted all domestic resources, their skills have been put to good use in **joint-venture** operations overseas to procure natural resources or for offshore production of various products ranging from **automobiles** to home **electronics** appliances. *See also* SOGO SHOSHA.

MINISTRY OF FINANCE. The Okurasho, or MOF as it is also known, was formed in the second year of Meiji (1869) as one of the first steps toward **modernization** in the area of **banking** and finance. Its role was confirmed by the **Supreme Commander Allied Powers** (**SCAP**) after World War II by the Ministry of Finance Establishment Law, which left it untouched as the premier government agency entrusted with the task of maintaining banking and financial stability. Other ministries, such as the Ministry of Home Affairs (Naimusho), were restructured or abolished, but the MOF continued to draw up the national budget, collect **taxes**, oversee monetary policy, regulate private sector finance, manage the national assets, and supervise the liquor and tobacco industries. This range of responsibilities was much wider than those of corresponding ministries in other countries.

The problems of the **bubble economy** and the general crisis in the banking world caused by massive nonperforming loans resulted in severe criticism of the ministry and its inability to clean its own house. This became a political issue, and in 1997, legislation was introduced in the National Diet that devolved control of monetary policy to the **Bank of Japan**, and the Bank of Japan Law was amended accordingly. In 1998, the regulation of private sector financial institutions was delegated to an independent Financial Services Agency. This brought the powers of the MOF into line with those of most other major nations, thus rationalizing national financial governance. The ministry's Japanese name was changed from the traditional title of Okurasho (a term derived from the idea of a comprehensive asset storage facility) to the narrower term Zaimusho (*zaimu* referring to finance). The English translation remains Ministry of Finance.

MINISTRY OF INTERNATIONAL TRADE AND INDUSTRY (MITI). The major government ministry concerned with **trade** and **investment** and the powerful instrument of Japan's postwar economic expansion. It was established to replace the Ministry of Commerce and Industry, which was abolished 1949. MITI's early role, particularly from 1951, was to provide leadership and support for the rebuilding of Japan's ruined economy in the postwar period, a task that it went about with determination and vigor. Its remit covered most of the private sector industries, such as wholesale, retail, manufacturing, service industries, transportation, **construction**, and **telecommunications**. It provides technical support, performs an advisory role, and mediates in trade conflicts and disputes both domestic and international. In 1958, the **Japan External Trade Organization** (**JETRO**) was established to research and provide information about the economies of foreign nations with a view to doing business abroad.

During the late 1950s and early 1960s, MITI focused on economic development. It was successful, but at the price of serious **environmental problems**, such as **Minamata disease** (perhaps one of the most internationally publicized pollution cases) and rural depopulation. To address these concerns, the Basic Law for Environmental Pollution was enacted in 1967 and an Industrial Relocation Promotion Law in 1973.

MITI was active in resolving the U.S.–Japan trade friction over cheap **textile** exports to the United States and negotiated the U.S.-Japan Textile Agreement of 1972 while encouraging the reduction of excessive domestic textile capacity. It followed a similar policy when numerous industries were affected by a general slump in the late 1970s. By implementing various laws to deal with changes in the economy, MITI successfully maintained national competitiveness through guiding corporations into new areas and improving efficiency. U.S.–Japan trade issues dominated the 1980s, and as a result the **Structural Impediment Initiative** (**SII**) talks began to deal with **nontariff barriers** to imports. The **Plaza Accord of 1985**, which led to the sudden appreciation of the yen, created considerable hardship for small and medium-sized enterprises (***chusho kigyo***) for which the government had to provide temporary relief.

MITI's functions have changed with changes in the economy. After it became clear that **deregulation** and liberalization were necessary for the economy to develop more in keeping with market mechanisms, various steps were taken, such as the abolition of the **Large Retail Stores Law of 1974** to reform the retail industry and the deregulation of electric power prices. Generally, MITI's stance on the economy has changed little by little, reflecting changes in the perceived needs of the economy, particularly in the process of liberalization.

The name of the ministry was changed in 2001 as part of an overhaul of the organs of government to the Ministry of Economy, Trade, and Industry (METI) to enable it to help the nation deal with new challenges in the world economy, such as the dramatic expansion of China and the emergence of new economic forces in Europe.

MINISTRY OF THE ECONOMY, TRADE, AND INDUSTRY (METI). *See* MINISTRY OF INTERNATIONAL TRADE AND INDUSTRY (MITI).

MINOLTA CAMERA. Founded in 1937 as a manufacturer of optical products, the name Minolta was adopted in 1962, quickly becoming a well-known international brand name for high-quality cameras and copy machines. It moved successfully into the field of mechatronics and office automation. It has subsidiaries in the United States, Europe, and Southeast Asia. Its head office is in Osaka.

MINOMURA RIZAEMON (1821–1877). Business leader born in the **Edo period** (1615–1868) who became an adopted member of the Minomura family, chief managers of the **House of Mitsui**. He persuaded Mitsui to support the imperial cause in return for which the house benefited through various contracts after the **Meiji Restoration of 1868**. He was instrumental in establishing the **Mitsui Bank** and the Mitsui Trading Company, both leading members of the **Mitsui *zaibatsu***.

MITSUBISHI BANK. The Mitsubishi Ginko was the **bank** of the pre–World War II Mitsubishi ***zaibatsu*** that was formed in 1880 by **Iwasaki Yataro**. It was established as Mitsubishi Exchange Office, becoming the banking division of **Mitsubishi Corporation**. It became Mitsubishi Bank in 1919 but changed its name to the Chiyoda Bank after World War II when the ***zaibatsu*** were being broken up. It has always been a major source of finance for industrial development.

Its corporate client base benefited from the bank's international support in overseas financing. At its peak, it had 21 operational centers abroad, including a **joint-venture** bank and five subsidiaries, including the Mitsubishi Bank of California. It merged in 1996 with the **Bank of Tokyo**, which, while strong in international business, needed the benefit of Mitsubishi's 200-plus domestic branches. The Tokyo-Mitsubishi Bank was part of a major restructuring of the Japanese banking sector during the 1990s. It merged with the **UFJ Bank** in 2006. *See also* MITSUBISHI GROUP.

MITSUBISHI CHEMICAL INDUSTRIES. Mitsubishi Kasei Kogyo is one of the major members of the **Mitsubishi Group** and the largest chemical company in Japan. It was capitalized in 1934 as Nihon Tasu Kogyo by **Asahi Glass** and **Mitsubishi Mining & Cement**. From a solid base in chemicals, producing coke, tar products, and fertilizers, it expanded during the mid-1960s into **petrochemicals**. Its main plant is in Kurosaki City, Kita-Kyushu. It also set up a Life Sciences Institute in Yokohama. The company has international business operations around the world and several **joint ventures** in Brazil, Malaysia, Norway, and the United States. Its head office is in Tokyo.

MITSUBISHI CORPORATION. Mitsubishi Shoji Kabushiki Kaisha, or MSK as it is known, is a major trading house (***sogo shosha***) that traces its origins to Tosa Kaisai Shosha, founded by **Iwasaki Yataro** (1838–1885) in 1870. It was renamed Mitsubishi Shokai in 1873, when it began **shipping** and trading. It gained its modern identity when the **Mitsubishi** ***zaibatsu*** separated its general commerce activities from other specialized sectors. As part of the postwar reforms of 1945, it was broken up into 139 separate corporations and forbidden to use either its name or its famous "three diamonds" (*mitsu-bishi*) logo.

The Korean War forced a reconsideration of policy, and MSK was reconstituted in 1954, after which it opened a worldwide network of offices. During the 1980s and early 1990s, *Fortune* magazine listed it as the world's largest business as defined by volume and value of transactions. Like other large trading houses, because of the challenge of a different business environment, **e-commerce**, and the hollowing out of the Japanese economy, MSK has been forced to restructure to meet these needs. Some analysts argue that the goliath trading house age is over. However, MSK's role in the procurement of natural resources remains a key feature of the nation's economic strategy.

MITSUBISHI ELECTRIC. Mitsubishi Denki is a manufacturer of heavy electrical and industrial machinery as well as household goods transmission transformers. The company was created in 1921 from the electric equipment division of Mitsubishi Engineering & Shipbuilding (now **Mitsubishi Heavy Industries**). It was particularly successful in the early postwar years between 1950 and 1970, when the domestic household electric goods market was developing. After 1970, it began to export production plants and to develop high-efficiency solar batteries. It has several **joint-venture** companies in India, Taiwan, Thailand, and South Korea as well as over 60 manufacturing and sales subsidiaries Asia, Australia, Europe, and the United States. It ranks third in the **electronics industry** behind **Hitachi** and **Toshiba**. The head office is in Tokyo. *See also* ELECTRONICS INDUSTRY.

MITSUBISHI REAL ESTATE. Mitsubishi Jisho is a real estate company engaged principally in the leasing of land and buildings as well as the sale of land. It is the largest owner of buildings in the central Tokyo district of Marunouchi, known as **Mitsubishi Mura** (village), which dates back to 1887. It owns over 75 buildings nationwide and has interests in the United States through its subsidiary, Mitsubishi Estate New York, Inc. Along with **Mitsui Real Estate Development** and the **Tokyu Land Corporation**, it is one of the big three in the industry.

MITSUBISHI GROUP. A major group of corporations belonging to the Mitsubishi "family" that became successor to the prewar Mitsubishi ***zaibatsu*** that was broken up in 1945. The word *mitsubishi* means "three diamonds," and its famous logo is found on many products ranging from **automobiles** to household **electronic** goods.

MITSUBISHI HEAVY INDUSTRIES. Mitsubishi Jukogyo is the nation's largest manufacturer of heavy machinery and is also engaged in **shipbuilding**, air-conditioning equipment, machine tools, and aircraft manufacturing. It dates to 1875, when the Mitsubishi Mail Steamship Company was formed. In 1887, the government transferred its Nagasaki Shipyards to the Mitsubishi Company. The shipbuilding company was made independent of the main company and assumed its present name in 1934. It became the nation's largest defense contractor and was responsible for building the giant battleship *Musashi* and for the development of the Zero fighter aircraft. By 1945, it had over 400,000 employees and was a target for the **Supreme Commander Allied Powers (SCAP)** order relating to the dissolution of the ***zaibatsu***. It was broken up but by 1964 had reformed. Only the **automobile** division separated completely, becoming **Mitsubishi Motor Corporation**. In addition to the head office in Tokyo, it has six branch offices and seven subsidiaries and **joint ventures**. It also uses the worldwide sales network of **Mitsubishi Corporation**, the trading house (***soga shosha***).

MITSUBISHI METAL CORPORATION. Mitsubishi Kinzoku was created in 1873 to meet the national demand for metals such as copper, zinc, lead, gold, and silver and to operate the Yoshioka Copper **Mine** in Okayama prefecture. It was split from the parent company in 1918 to become Mitsubishi Metal Mining. Domestically, it is concerned more with smelting than with mining, but it has invested in mines in Australia, the Philippines, Peru, and Venezuela. Through its subsidiary, Mitsubishi Aluminum, it processes aluminum, and through Mitsubishi Nuclear Fuels, it processes reactor fuel. Corporate headquarters are in Tokyo.

MITSUBISHI MOTOR CORPORATION. Mitsubishi Jidosha Kogyo was founded in 1970 when the motor division of **Mitsubishi Heavy Industries** separated from the parent company. In the following year, a **joint venture** was formed between Mitsubishi Heavy Industries and Chrysler Corporation of the United States.

Although not the largest manufacturer, its quality is widely recognized particularly in the field of emission control. Because of the small range of its products and the severe competition, it experienced various problems in the early 2000s, resulting in major losses. It has subsidiaries in the United States, Europe, Australia, and Southeast Asia, particularly in Malaysia. Its headquarters are in Tokyo. *See also* AUTOMOBILE INDUSTRY.

MITSUBISHI MURA. "Mitsubishi Village" is the name given to a large group of buildings in Marunouchi on the south side of Tokyo Station that house the headquarters of 22 of the 45 members of the **Mitsubishi Group** of companies. The area was originally a military barracks that was moved to Azabu by the Ministry of War in 1890. The minister of finance, Masukata Masuyoshi, invited **Iwaski Yataro** (1838–1885) to buy the vacant 350,000-square-meter site, which he did for the sum of ¥1.28 million. He began erecting red brick buildings in the style of London, and from that time around 30 percent of the buildings have been owned by **Mitsubishi Real Estate**. The protracted recession of the 1990s resulted in increasing overhead, and, with rents averaging ¥50,000 per 3.3 square meters of space on every floor, many of the companies in the group felt that the time had come to move. Most of the **Meiji period** (1868–1912) buildings in the area have stone floors, which are not convenient for laying underfloor information technology lines. Consequently, removal to modern custom-made premises at lower rent became attractive.

The breakup of the village began from 26 April 2003, during the **Golden Week** holiday period. The headquarters of **Mitsubishi Corporation** remained, although its sales department moved to a new location in Shinagawa. The Bank of Mitsubishi-Tokyo was scheduled to remain as was **Meiji Life Insurance** and **Mitsubishi Electric**. The **Mitsubishi Trust and Banking Corporation** was also scheduled to return from its temporary location in Nagatacho to a new building in Marunouchi. However, with a large number of the major corporations, such as **Mitsubishi Heavy Industries**, **Mitsubishi Chemical Corporation**, and **Mitsubishi Motor Corporation**, leaving, the breakup of the village brought to an end a long tradition in the Japanese business world that dates to the last decade of the 19th century.

The village still plays host to over 4,000 corporations housed in 100 buildings occupied by 240,000 staff who commute there every day.

MITSUBISHI TRUST & BANKING CORPORATION (Mitsubishi Shintaku Ginko). Founded in 1927 as the Mitsubishi Trust, it was set up as one of the central financial institutions of the **Mitsubishi *zaibatsu***. In 1948, in line with the **Supreme Commander Allied Powers** (**SCAP**) directive on the breakup of monopolies, the company assumed the name Asahi Trust Bank, engaging in trust and regular banking activities. It reverted to the Mitsubishi name in 1952. It works with the **Mitsubishi Bank** (now the Tokyo-Mitsubishi Bank), **Meiji Mutual Life Insurance Co.**, and the **Tokio Marine & Fire Insurance Co., Ltd**, to provide financial support and services for the **Mitsubishi Group**. *See also* TRUST BANKS.

MITSUI & CO. Mitsui Bussan is a major trading house (***soga shosha***) set up in 1876 as a successor to Senshu Kaisha, a corporation founded in the early years of the **Meiji period** (1868–1912) to break the foreign monopoly over Japan's international trade. It grew extensively during the pre–World War II years into a massive conglomerate (***zaibatsu***) employing almost 3 million people. It was broken up in 1945, and the present-day Mitsui & Co. was formed in July 1947. Daiichi Co. merged with Mitsui in 1959, giving the company greater breadth and much of the character it developed over the ensuing years. In 2000, in keeping with its information technology development policy, it launched a **joint venture** involving eight corporations, including **Sony Corporation**, 7-11 Japan Co. (**Ito Yokado**), and **Nippon Denki**, called 7dream.com. This was an early attempt to employ **e-commerce** in general retailing and became the pattern for adding many new functions to the business of convenience stores (***konbini***).

MITSUI BANK. Mitsui Ginko was the first private **bank** established in Japan in 1876 by the **House of Mitsui**, becoming one of the core companies of the **Mitsui *zaibatsu*** and subsequently of the postwar **Mitsui Group**. It became a **joint-stock company** in 1909 and merged with the Dai-Ichi Bank (later the **Dai-ichi Kangyo Bank**) in 1943. The merger ended in 1948. At its peak in the 1980s, it was the sixth ranked among the 13 **city banks** (*toshi ginko*) in terms of deposits. Its specialized skills were in securities and foreign exchange, which it handled for numerous second- and third-tier banks. In 1965, Mitsui became the first Japanese bank to introduce an online computer system. By that time, its e-global network included 10 overseas branches, one agency, 13 representative offices, four Mitsui-owned ventures, 18 **joint ventures**, and 878 correspondence banks. In April 1990, the already merged Taiyo and Kobe Banks joined the Mitsui Bank to form the Sakura Bank. The banking crisis of the late 1990s, as well as requirements by the Bank for International Settlements (BIS), forced further mergers. Mitsui joined with **Sumitomo** in 2002 to form the Sumitomo-Mitsui Bank. The head office is in Tokyo.

MITSUI BUNKO. The Mitsui Research Institute for Social and Economic History consisting of records and documents that were created by the founding family of the **House of Mitsui**. It is considered to be of the same quality as the Yomei Bunko of the Konoe House and the Seikado Bunko of the Iwasaki House. The collection includes books and family records, genealogical records, and financial and accounting records dating from the closing years of the **Genroku period** (1688–1704).

MITSUI ENGINEERING & SHIPBUILDING. Mitsui Zosen, a comprehensive heavy industry company in the field of **shipbuilding**, ocean development, **steel** structures, chemical plants, and industrial machinery, was established as the shipbuilding division of **Mitsui & Co.** in 1917, becoming a separate company in 1937. It took its present name in 1976. It was the inventor of the triple-engine, triple-screw, high-speed diesel container ship. It went into a phase of overseas links in Hong Kong and Brazil and has also been moving into the production of desalinization plants and **electric power** plants. Its head office is in Tokyo.

MITSUI, HOUSE OF. This was the earliest of the great entrepreneurial houses of the **Edo period** (1615–1868), founded by **Hachirobe Takatoshi** (1622–1694). He opened his first store in Edo (now Tokyo) in 1672, and he opened his famous Echigoya dry-goods store in 1683 on the site of what is now **Mitsukoshi Department Store**. On his death, he bequeathed the house to his sons, with the proviso that the house should never be divided and must always be united. The headquarters (***omotokata***) was moved to Kyoto, from which the business of the entire organization was managed. A House Constitution was formally drawn up in 1722 and remained unchanged until it was revised in 1900. The house grew in wealth and influence, employing a record 1,000 staff in the three stores in Edo.

The eighth head of the house acceded in 1835, and after steering the house through the difficult economic conditions of the late Edo period, from 1841 on, he successfully navigated the house into the **Meiji period** (1868–1912). By astute negotiation, the chief manager, **Minomura Rizaemon** (1821–1877), avoided paying the sum of 500,000 *ryo* to the impoverished shogunate in 1865. Hachiroemon successfully received government appointment as financial agent for customs collection after the 1859 opening of Kobe and Yoyohama to foreign ships. In 1860, at the request of the government, the house opened an import–export shop in Yokohama and in 1866 founded the **Mitsui Bank** to advance loans to other houses that wished to engage in foreign trade.

Once into the Meiji period, the House of Mitsui entered a new and even more illustrious phase of its history. The survival of the house was due to good management and farsightedness and its being located in both Edo and Kyoto. This fact alone provided it with knowledge of contemporary and coming trends long before the **Osaka merchants** could sense the winds of change. After the **Meiji Restoration of 1868**, the House of Mitsui was appointed banker for the new government. Mitsui was also one the few merchant houses to survive into the modern period, becoming eventually the great ***zaibatsu***. Sound strategies and a sense of the times kept it alive when others, like the houses of **Ono** and **Shimada**, were unable to make the transition to the new age and collapsed.

MITSUI MINING. Mitsui Kozan was founded in 1911 to administer the Miike Coal Mine in Fukuoka. The company produced coal and was involved in environmental business activities. After the mine closed in 1997, the company began selling portions of real estate that did not realize the anticipated returns because of the deflationary spiral in land prices. The **Industrial Revitalization Corporation**

(IRC), formed in May 2003 to deal with corporate bankruptcies, decided in September 2003 to provide government finance to save the company. This became the first major nonbank case to be dealt with by the IRC.

MITSUI O.S.K. LINES. Osaka Shosan Mitsui Sempaku, the second-largest liner operator in Japan, was created in 1964 through the merger of Osaka Shosen (founded in 1884) and the Mitsui Steamship Co. (freight handler for **Mitsui & Co.** founded in 1876). It started containerization on its California route in 1968, after which it introduced containerization into its northern Pacific, Europe, U.S. East Coast, and Mediterranean trunk routes. It developed a freighter in 1965 exclusively for transporting **automobiles** and introduced the first computerized tanker to go into service. It has numerous **joint ventures** as far apart as Southeast Asia and Saudi Arabia and engages in terminal management in several ports, including Oakland, Los Angeles, and Australia. It has a total fleet of over 300 ships. Its headquarters are in Osaka. *See also* SHIPPING INDUSTRY.

MITSUI PETROCHEMICAL INDUSTRIES. Mitsui Seiyu Kagaku was founded in 1953 by seven affiliates of the **Mitsui Group** plus Koa Oil. The company became an integrated petrochemical manufacturer of high-density polyethylene. It has a major facility at Iwakuni in Yamaguchi prefecture and a second one in Chiba, where it produces ethylene and polyethylene. In cooperation with the Nippon Petrochemical Company, it created the Ukishima Petrochemical Company to produce ethylene. It has operations in South Korea and Belgium. The head office is in Tokyo.

MITSUI REAL ESTATE. Mitsui Fudosan is a real estate company that deals primarily in sales of land and houses. It began as the real estate division within the **Mitsui Zaibatsu** but became independent in 1941. From 1957, it became interested in dredging and land reclamation projects and moved to housing in 1961. In 1967, it initiated the new era of high-rise buildings with the completion of the Kasumigaseki Building in 1968. As it moved into home sales, it set up Mitsui Real Estate Sales in 1969 and Mitsui Homes in 1974. In this process, it evolved into a comprehensive land and housing development company. Subsequently, it became involved in building warehouses in Los Angeles and Seattle, townhouses in Saudi Arabia, and, perhaps most famous of all, Tokyo Disneyland. Its head office is in Tokyo.

MITSUI RESEARCH INSTITUTE FOR SOCIAL AND ECONOMIC HISTORY. *See* MITSUI BUNKO.

MITSUI SUGAR REFINING. Mitsui Seito is the largest sugar refiner in Japan. It was established in 1970 by the merger of **Mitsui Group** affiliate Osaka Sugar Refining, Shibaura Sugar, and Yokohama Sugar Refining to rationalize production to match actual needs. **Mitsui & Co.** actively supported the new company, on which it relies quite heavily. It has **joint-venture** companies in Singapore and Thailand. The head office is in Tokyo.

MITSUI TAKATOSHI (1622–1694). *See* HACHIROBE TAKATOSHI.

MITSUI TRUST AND BANKING. Mitsui Shintaku Ginko is Japan's oldest trust and banking company. It was established up in 1924, growing to become the third-largest trust company in deposits during the 1980s. It has almost 50 offices in Japan, plus a presence in New York, Los Angeles, London, Singapore, São Paolo, and Sydney. It established two subsidiaries, Mitsui Trust Finance (Hong Kong) Ltd and Mitsui Trust (Europe), S.A., located in Brussels. The head office is in Tokyo. *See also* TRUST BANKS.

MITSUI ZAIBATSU. This was the vast financial combine that evolved around the **Mitsui House** during the **Meiji period** (1868–1912). At its peak, it was second in size only to the **Mitsubishi *zaibatsu*** but held the largest amount of overseas investments. By order of the **Supreme Commander Allied Powers** (**SCAP**), the combine was broken into 223 separate companies. By 1959, Mitsui & Co. had been formed, and the Mitsui Group had begun to be built as a replacement for the *zaibatsu*.

MITSUKOSHI, LTD. Famous as one of the largest **department stores** operator in Japan, it traces its history to **Hachirobe Takatoshi**

(1622–1694). It was the origin of the fortunes of the **House of Mitsui** and helped to create the **Mitsui *zaibatsu***. The original store with the corporate logo is depicted in woodblock prints (*ukiyoe*) of the **Edo period** (1615–1868). The modern store in Nihonbashi was first constructed along Western lines as a three-story building in 1908, and it began its characteristic emphasis on high-quality luxury goods.

The introduction of the Mitsukoshi brand name dates to 1928, after which it expanded internationally, making it the largest store in Asia. The postwar period was not initially conducive to the purchase of expensive goods, consequently putting pressure on the store's finances. By good management and careful planning, it slowly returned to its former status as an expensive value-added store at the top end of the retail market. Mitsukoshi has branches and sales offices in Paris, Rome, London, Dusseldorf, Singapore, and the United States. The company remains a central institution of the **Mitsui Group**, and a gift wrapped in Mitsukoshi paper remains a prestigious and prized present. The corporate headquarters are in Tokyo.

MIZUHO FINANCIAL GROUP. The name of a group of **city banks** formed in 2000 by the merger of the **Daiichi Kangyo Ginko**, the **Fuji Bank**, and the **Industrial Bank of Japan** (**IBJ**). Since the Fuji Bank was formerly the principal bank of the **Yasuda *zaibatsu***, it became more closely linked to the **Fuyo *keiretsu***. With over 33,000 staff and almost 750 offices, given its assets, it became the world's largest bank as of 2000. The merger itself, although designed to assist the three banks with their problems of nonperforming loans, proved costly, and initially all 540 branches had to remain open because of different computer and operational systems, resulting in a 62 percent ratio of personnel and supply costs to gross profit, the highest of any commercial bank in Japan. Plans were adopted in early 2003 to reduce this ratio to 40 percent by closing 100 outlets by fiscal 2005.

MOCHIAI. Short for ***kabushiki mochiai***, it is the system of **cross shareholding** that enables companies to have a financial interest in each other and that is considered in Japan to contribute to economic and fiscal stability, although **foreign companies** tend to view it as an exclusivist defense mechanism and a barrier to **merger and ac-**

quisition activities. *Mochiai* is one feature of the ***keiretsu*** industrial groupings.

MODERNIZATION. A general term used by sociologists during the 1960s and 1970s to describe the process by which agricultural and nonindustrialized nations transformed themselves, frequently on Western models, to become industrially, economically, and politically developed nations. Many terms were used loosely to refer to this process before the term "modernization" was used, such as "Europeanization," "westernization," or "industrialization," the last implying that modernization was essentially an economic process. Discussion of the concept was accompanied by the idea of cultural convergence, the tacit assumption that as nations modernized, the core values of Western civilization would automatically replace local traditional values and the standardization of the norms of human civilization would be realized. Both of these assumptions led to an inadequate understanding of what modernization meant in reality because it was a much more encompassing process than was at first realized and one that affected all aspects of premodern life.

The modernization of Japan in the eyes of the government of the day was primarily a process of industrialization designed to keep potential Western predators at bay. However, in order to industrialize, a variety of new institutions had to be introduced, including a **banking** and financial system, an effective military machine, a representative system of government to ensure a national basis for policymaking, and an educational system to create citizens of the new regime. All of these were created within a short space of time. Compulsory **education** was introduced in 1871. The Hong Kong and Shanghai Banking Corporation assisted in the process of creating a **currency**. The shipyards of Glasgow and the naval architecture department of the University of Glasgow helped to build a navy, while the military prowess of Prussia became the model for the newly formed Imperial Army.

A factor that is often overlooked by Western observers is that Japan's modernization was contemporaneous with that of the United States, whose Civil War of 1861–1865 corresponds to the **Meiji Restoration of 1868** and with that of Germany and Italy. As the first Asian nation to break with tradition and respond to Western norms, by adopting and adapting them, Japan was well placed to become an economic superpower of the future.

A further point of importance is that Japan is not, as often misrepresented, a mere copier. Historically, Japan has vied with and adapted any and all models that would appear to offer comparative advantage. Tang dynasty China was the first well-known example of such a model, which resulted in the creation of the cities of Nara and Kyoto on the Chinese model of cities built on a grid system. But Japan's cultural acquisitions have been eclectic, and modern Japan can boast of Tokyo Tower, taller by a meter than the Eiffel Tower and the largest Disneyland in the world, having created in Nara, in 674, the largest bronze-cast Buddha in the world of that time and housed it in a temple that was also the largest wooden building in the world.

MONEY HISTORY. The earliest coins, Chinese in origin, have been found in burial sites of the Yayoi period (ca. 300 B.C.E.–300 C.E.). They are also referred to in the classical text, the *Nihon Shoki* (720). Japan's first minting of coins dates to the Wado period (around 708) made in silver and in copper. They were modeled on the coinage of the Chinese T'ang dynasty (618–697). Eleven further mintings took place between 760 and 958, but the local preference for barter trade hampered the development of currency transactions. Cash markets did appear in Nara and Kyoto, but by the ninth century, the quality of coins became debased because of a lack of copper. The working of the Chuenshi (government mint) was suspended, and by 987 government-minted coins were no longer legal tender. Thereafter, Chinese, Korean, and Southeast Asian coins were used. Legitimate trade, as well as the activities of pirates and smugglers, added to the volume of the monetary economy in existence.

During the *Sengoku Jidai*, the civil war period from the middle of the 15th century to the establishment of a central government under the **Tokugawa feudal system**, precious metals were mined by the great warlords to fund their war chests. The metals were melted into bars of gold and silver. **Oda Nobunaga** (1534–1582) was the first to use such gold and silver to import Western weapons, enabling him to achieve military superiority over his rivals. His successor, **Toyotomi Hideyoshi** (1536–1598), built Osaka Castle and, to finance his projects, took control of all metal mines in the country. He introduced the production of gold coinage of fixed quality. He minted the *oban-kin*, one of the largest gold coins ever created in 1588. It was an oval-shaped gold and silver alloy weighing 165 grams and measuring 145 by 86 millimeters. These are considered now to be collector's items and works of art rather than simply coins. Under the direction of **Tokugawa Ieyasu** (1543–1616), a monetary system was created using five types of coins: *oban*, *koban*, *ichibu-kin*, *cho-gin*, and *ma-meita-gin*. The mints for gold (*kinza*), silver (*ginza*), and copper or base coins (*zeniza*) were established in separate locations. During the **Edo period** (1616–1868), the value of specie currency, the *ryo*, did not remain stable because of various devaluations. During the **Genroku period** (1688–1703), the gold percentage was reduced by 30 percent. The *ryo* was considered initially to have the purchasing power of one ***koku*** of **rice**, the amount needed to sustain one human life for a complete year. So sensitive was the government to the reality of debasement that in the latter half of the Edo period, one of the few strange crimes that carried the death penalty was ownership at home of any kind of balance for weighing metals.

Deposit receipts of silver as payment began to appear in Ise Kuni (now Mie prefecture) as early as 1620, and from 1661, various feudal lords began issuing paper money as currency, valid only within their own domains. Thereafter, private issues of paper money grew and expanded into the 19th century and were in circulation until the creation of the modern currency system in the **Meiji period** (1868–1912). There was a total of five completely domestic currency systems spanning the period from 1601 to 1853. As a result of the visit of Commodore Matthew Perry and the black ships (***kukrofune***), the currency system of the final period (1854–1868) was forced into accepting an exchange rate of one-fourth of one *ryo* to one U.S. dollar. Under the terms of a treaty of commerce and navigation signed between Japan and the United States in 1858, the rate was to become three-fourths of one *ryo* to a dollar. Foreign currency was to be circulated in Japan and Japanese currency abroad. Similar agreements were made with the United Kingdom, France, Russia, and the Netherlands.

Japan's gold–silver parity was between 1 to 5 and 1 to 10 in contrast to the world parity level of 1 to 15. This led to Japanese coins being exchanged for lower-value foreign coins, with the obvious negative result of the flight of gold out of the country. Measures taken to deal with the situation failed because the differential gold–silver parity remained unchanged. For a time, Mexican silver dollars with a stamp of approval were circulated, a unique event in Japanese history. In 1860, U.S. Consul-General Townsend Harris recommended to the shogunate a change in the gold–silver parity that stemmed the flow of gold abroad. Nevertheless, chaos continued, and regional feudal lords continued issuing paper money until, finally, the bankrupted system collapsed in 1868.

The Meiji government immediately decided to create a new currency, and after the purchase of the British Mint in Hong Kong in 1870, the yen as the official currency of the new Japan was born and confirmed in the New Coinage Act of May 1871. Inadequate supplies of coins forced the printing of paper money, which was estimated at around ¥100 million in 1876. The **Bank of Japan** was set up in 1882. However, it was not until 1885 that Bank of Japan notes were issued, and thereafter government paper money and National Bank notes were withdrawn from circulation and finally prohibited in 1899. Japan briefly joined the gold standard in 1930 but was forced to leave in 1931 because of unexpectedly large outflows of gold. During the war with China and World War II, various kinds of notes were printed and circulated in Japan and its colonies. The postwar period experienced rampant inflation that could not be checked until the 1949 yen–dollar rate was set at ¥360 for U.S.$1. The *sen* (100 to 1 yen) ceased circulating in 1953, and the modern range of ¥10,000, ¥5,000, ¥1,000, ¥500, and ¥100 notes was introduced. A further revision was made in the late 1970s when the ¥10,000 note was reduced in size, and the face of **Shotoku Taishi** was replaced by that of **Fukuzawa Yukichi**. The ¥500 and ¥100 notes were replaced by coins, and in the late 1990s, ¥1,000 and ¥2,000 coins were introduced. These did not prove popular, and for a number of other reasons, such as their inability to be used in ticket and vending machines, their circulated gradually stopped.

The yen remained at the level of ¥360 to U.S.$1 for several decades, boosting Japan's exports and undermining other currencies that were unable to price exports attractively to market in Japan. This situation was rectified in 1985 by the **Plaza Accord**, through which the yen was allowed to rise freely, creating a situation that the Japanese referred to as *endaka*, the rising yen. While it did help exporters to Japan, it also enabled Japanese **corporations** to buy raw materials less expensively because of the strong currency. At its weakest, the dollar dipped to just below ¥70 and the pound sterling to ¥145.

The problem of counterfeit yen became serious in the late 1990s because computer technology had made reproduction of fake notes easier and the fake notes themselves very difficult to detect. The Bank of Japan began to design new notes in 2001, planning to have them in circulation by 1 November 2004. The new ¥500 bill carries the image of Higichu Ichiyo (1872–1896), a novelist. The ¥1,000 bill features the scientist Nogushi Hideyo (1876–1928), and the ¥10,000 bill retains **Fukuzawa Yukichi** (835–1901), the founder of Keio University. The new bills are protected by a color-changing hologram, distinctive watermark patterns, luminescent ink on the seal, and latent imaging of the currency value. Apart from the cost to the BOJ, at the microlevel, costs to banks will be enormous. It was estimated that one new automated teller machine (ATM) costs ¥5 million and the upgrade of an old one ¥1 million. Both **Sumitomo Bank** and **Mitsui Bank** have 5,600 machines each. Nationwide, 135,000 ATMs would require replacement or upgrade.

MONEY MARKETS. Japan has several markets in which financial assets of less than one year are traded by their owners (even at less than their value) in order to raise capital. These can be subsumed under two headings: the interbank market and the open market. The interbank market functions among financial institutions and covers the call-money market (the traditional borrowing mechanism to cover temporary deficits with loans from overnight to three weeks at rates not heavily regulated by the **Bank of Japan**), the bill market (selling of unmatured bills of various kinds at discounted rates), and the dollar-call market (trading and lending of foreign currencies for loan periods of overnight to four weeks).

The Bank of Japan deregulated the bill market in 1985. The dollar-call market was opened in 1972. Under the heading of open market, there are included the ***gensaki* market** (the bond repo market for trading bonds with a repurchase date and price determined by market mechanisms), the certificate of deposit (CD) market (trade in CDs, issued by banks to compete with the *gensaki* market's business), the bankers' acceptance (BA) market (the BA market for trading in yen-denominated fixed-term bills of exchange issued by importers or exporters guaranteed by foreign-exchange banks), the treasury bill market (started in 1986 to create a short-term government bond market), the commercial paper market (started in 1987 to trade in unsecured promissory notes among corporations only with top credit ratings), and the Tokyo offshore market (established in 1986 to enable foreign exchange banks to conduct business with nonresidents).

The entire business is controlled by six large *tanshi* companies that function as Japan's money market dealers. In addition to working in these markets, they work with the Bank of Japan (from which most of the presidents of the companies are hired), to regulate the flow of money in these markets on a day-to-day basis. *See also* CAPITAL MARKETS; DAIMYO BONDS; SAMURAI BONDS; SHOGUN BONDS.

MONZEN-MACHI. This is the name given to markets established within the precincts of or in front of **Shinto** shrines and **Buddhist** temples, particularly during the **Kamakura period** (1185–1333).

MORINAGA & CO. Morinaga Seika was started in 1899 in Tokyo as a Western-style confectionery maker. The name dates to 1912. It became a very successful manufacturer of confectionery and packaged groceries. To have an adequate supply of raw materials, it created a company that became **Morinaga Milk Industry** in 1917. Its chain of retail outlets was created before World War I, providing it with a nationwide **distribution** network. Morinaga formed an alliance with the Sunkist Co. of the United States to sell its soft drinks in Japan. The head office is in Tokyo.

MORINAGA MILK INDUSTRY. Morinaga Nyugyo was established originally to supply **Morinaga & Co.** with raw materials as its milk division. It became independent in 1949 and expanded into butter and cheese products and is a leading member of the Japanese dairy industry. It has three **joint ventures** and offices in the United States, Europe, and Taiwan. The head office is in Tokyo.

The company was embroiled in a serious case of food poisoning in 1955. Some 12,000 infants were poisoned, of whom 130 died because of arsenic in cans of powdered milk. The company used sodium disulfate as a stabilizer to make their powdered milk more soluble in water. It appeared that an inferior grade of sodium disulfate, intended for industrial rather than human consumption, was used, with no safety test being implemented. A 1955 Ministry of Health and Welfare committee report declared that there were no aftereffects and that the families of children who died should be compensated by a solatium of ¥250,000 and any parents of victims of poisoning by ¥10,000. However, subsequent research in 1969 showed that not only were there side effects, but cerebral palsy was frequent among victims who survived. This led to a retrial. The verdict resulted in the production manager being sentenced to three years in prison. The company agreed thereafter to provide support for the victims for the rest of their lives.

MORI NOBUTERU (1884–1941). He was the founder of the Mori Konzern, a pre–World War II financial and industrial group that now is associated with the modern **Fuyo Group** of companies. He started by forming Sobo Suisan Co., an iodine manufacturer, in 1908 and Showa Fertilizer Co., in 1928, which eventually merged with Nippon Electric Industries to become **Showa Denko** in 1939.

MORITA AKIO (1921–1999). The founder of **Sony** Corporation was born into a business family that owned a sake brewery and that created the Pasco brand name for bread. He refused, however, to take over the family business, the first son to do so in 15 generations. He married the daughter of an old former **samurai** family that had moved into publishing after the **Meiji Restoration of 1868**, founding the Sanseido publishing company. After what became the Sony Corporation had been founded and after its early struggles, Morita began to implement his three principles of creativity: creative ideas in technology, product development, and marketing. This philosophy drove him to set specific targets. When he developed the famous "Walkman" against the judgment of his sales staff, he threatened to resign if he had not sold 100,000 by the end of the first year. For his entire life, he drove the company forward through sharing new ideas and not by suppressing them in the interests of consensus. Morita continued to work with his longtime colleague Ibuka Masaru (1908–1997) until he stepped down to the position of adviser in 1976, a role he kept until his death.

MUJIN. These are mutual financing associations, the precursors of modern insurance systems in **Edo period** (1615–1868) Japan.

– N –

NAGANO SHIGEO (1900–). Born in Shimane prefecture and a graduate of Tokyo Imperial University, he became manager of Fuji Iron in 1925, at the time bankrupt, which he rehabilitated. He became director of the purchasing division when Fuji Iron merged with the Nippon Steel Co. (now **Nippon Steel Corporation**) in 1934. After World War II, he returned to Nippon Steel, which was split in 1950 into Fuji Iron and Steel and **Yamato Iron and Steel Works**. He became president of Fuji and subsequently chairman of Nippon Steel when the two companies merged to their original form in 1970. Nagano became chairman of the **Japan Chamber of Commerce and Industry** in 1969 and is considered one of Japan's most influential postwar business leaders. *See also* IRON AND STEEL INDUSTRY.

NAGASAKI SHIPYARDS. Located at the only port permitted to have links with the outside world during the **Edo period** (1615–1868) policy of seclusion (***sakoku jidai***), the first naval academy was established there in 1855 followed by shipyards in the early **Meiji period** (1868–1912). *See also* HYOGO SHIPYARDS; SHIPBUILDING INDUSTRY; YOKOSUKA SHIPYARDS.

NAKAJIMA CHIKUHEI (1884–1949). Born in Gunma prefecture and a graduate of the Imperial Naval Engineering School, he was one of the first people to see the potential of **aircraft** in warfare and resigned in 1917 to establish an Airplane Research Institute. This later became the Nakajima Aircraft Co., the manufacturer of various fighter plans, including the Nakajima Model 5, and the engine of the famous Zero fighter. In 1950, under direction of the **Supreme Commander Allied Powers (SCAP)**, the company was broken into 12 separate companies. Five of these joined to form **Fuji Heavy Industries, Ltd**, the manufacturer of the Subaru car brand.

NAKAUCHI ISAO (1922–). An entrepreneurial figure of the postwar period who founded the **Daiei** supermarket chain. Born in Osaka, he graduated from Kobe Commercial High School (now Kobe University of Commerce) in 1941. He then entered but did not graduate from Kobe Economics University (now the Faculty of Economics of Kobe University). After World War II, during which he served in Manchuria, in 1945 he joined the family business, Daiei Yakuhin Kogyo (Daiei Pharmaceutical Company), but left to join **Nichimen** in 1950.

His *Shufu-no-mise* (Housewives' Store) was Japan's first supermarket, opened in Osaka in 1957. A second followed in Fukukoka in 1963, after which Daiei, the name taken in 1970, spread nationwide. Nakauchi became chairman of the Japan Chain Store Association in 1967 and became president in 1970 and (in 1982) chairman of Daiei. He received numerous accolades, including a decoration from the emperor, an economics prize in 1980, and the Pegasus-Club Diamond Award for business excellence in 1987. Daiei also acquired the Hawks baseball team of the Japan Pacific League, later to become the Daiei Hawks. In 1990, Nakauchi became the vice chairman of the Federation of Economic Organizations (**Keidanren**) in 1990 and acquired the **Recruit Company** in 1992 and subsequently several rival supermarkets. Although an adviser to Daiei, his son's unexpected resignation as vice president in 1999 cast a cloud of uncertainty over the future of the Daiei chain, which had already been affected by the **recession of the 1990s** as well as overextension during the **bubble economy**. His rise and fall is matched by several similar cases of failed family-controlled businesses of the period.

NARA PERIOD (646–794). The early Nara period, Hakuho, is usually dated 646–710 and the later from 710 to 794, the preceding era of Asuka (552–645) being an era of extensive borrowing from China. Nara was Japan's first recorded capital city, built on a Chinese grid model, and symbolizes the first documented phase of the history of Yamato, the oldest name of the country. **Buddhism** expanded in both presence and influence, and Buddhist monks tried to interfere with government and the imperial line to the extent that the government elected to move to Heian, modern Kyoto, toward the end of the eighth century. The basis of law, the social system, and the regulation of trade and commerce all date to this period. *See also* SHOTOKU TAISHI; TAIKA NO KAISHIN.

NAYOSECHO. A premodern land register used in the Kamakura (1185–1333) and Muromachi (1333–1568) periods as a basis for **tax** collection by ***shoen*** (estates) supervisors. They listed fields by size and type and the appropriate taxes for each. Landowners were listed who were responsible for the payment of taxes. By the **Edo period** (1615–1868), the *Nayosecho* had become simply village ledgers that listed taxes due from each villager. Village officials prepared these on the basis of land survey ledgers (*kenicho*) that recorded details of all arable land within the bounds.

NCR JAPAN (NIPPON NCR). Founded in 1920 and 70 percent owned by National Cash Registers of the United States to manufacture and sell cash registers and various business machines, the company imports and sells **computers** made by the parent company. It continues to produce a range of business products, including electronic cash registers, which it began selling in the 1970s. Its head office is in Tokyo.

NEC. Nippon Electric Corporation, or Nippon Denki, is a leading producer of **computers**, **telecommunications** systems, and **semiconductor** devices. It was founded in Tokyo in 1899 as a **joint venture** with the Western Electric Company (later Lucent Technologies) of the United States. After 1923, it moved into the developing radio market and expanded research-and-development facilities. From 1946 to the mid-1960s, it began producing computers and electronic switching systems. Transistor technology research led to the registering of **patents** and with these the subsequent global expansion of the company between 1964 and 1978, involving listings on the London, Swiss, and Dutch stock exchanges. Advanced satellite systems came next along with NEC's B&C strategy, namely, computer and communications technologies brought together for more effective use. NEC unveiled its first supercomputer in 1979, followed in 1986 by Dynamic Random Access Memory (DRAM). In 1990, it entered the semiconductor market and expanded aggressively into the United States and Europe.

NEC is structured into three operations: NEC Solutions (**Internet**-related solutions through creating software applications to create integrated Internet services such as the access system Biglobe), NEC Networks (ranging from automated teller machines [ATMs] to digital broadcasting systems), and NEC Electronic Devices (such as semiconductors and ion rechargeable batteries).

NEC is now an influential member of the **Sumitomo Group** and ranks worldwide among the top 10 in its field, particularly in semiconductors. NEC America was set up in 1963 as Nippon Electric New York, Inc., after which NEC established overseas facilities in over 30 countries with over 80 offices in the world's principal business centers. In Japan it has 56 subsidiaries and 20 affiliated companies. Its headquarters are in Tokyo.

NEMAWASHI. The term is a metaphor taken from the Japanese gardening practice of digging around the roots of a tree to prepare it for transplant. In **Japanese-style management** practices, it refers to the consultation process by which support is built up for a project prior to the meeting at which the decision will be made.

NENGU. Annual rents from ***shoen*** (estates) paid to feudal lords during the **Edo period** (1615–1868).

NENKO-JORETSU. The seniority system by which rank in **Japanese-style management** is determined according to years of service. Traditionally, it meant that promotions and salary increases occurred according to a schedule that fixed the number of years of service for a promotion. **Loyalty** and lengthy service were rewarded under the old system, which was designed to maintain corporate solidity. The downside to this system was the automatic promotion of poor performers, something frequently criticized by younger staff. ***Kibo-taishoku*** is one device companies have used to thin the ranks of middle-aged and older employees who are only average performers. The future of the *nenko-joretsu* system is under review, especially at times when the economy is performing poorly. However, with an improved business climate, the system is unlikely to disappear.

NEWS AGENCIES. Dating to the early **Meiji period** (1868–1912), the first telegraphic line (linking Shanghai and Nagasaki) was completed in 1871 by the Great Northern Telegraph of Denmark. An English-language paper in Yokohama, the *Japan Mail*, contracted with Reuters and began publishing news stories from around the world. These were then translated into Japanese until the Naigai Tsushisha (Domestic and International News Agency) contracted directly with Reuters in 1893. In 1888, **Mitsui & Co.** established the Jiji Tsushisha (no relation to the modern agency of that name) at the behest of the government, which hoped to control news flows. By 1926, there were 33 agencies in Tokyo. The Nihon Dempo Tsushisha (Japan Telegraphic News Agency), founded in 1907 by **Mitsunaga Hoshio**, was also an advertising agency. It had agreements with the Wolff Agency of Germany and United Press International. In 1926, the Japan Telegraphic News Agency was formed through cooperation of eight major newspapers, modeled on the Associated Press, with which, along with Reuters, it had an agreement. In 1936, the government united all agencies to form the Domei Tsushisha (Domei News Agency). The Telegraphic News advertising business remained separate and in due course evolved into **Dentsu**, Japan's largest advertising agency. The Domei Agency after 1945 was transformed into the Kyodo News Service (Kyodo Tsushinsha) and the modern Jiji Press.

NEWSPAPER BUSINESS. From the beginning of the **Edo period** (1615–1868), printed broadsheets existed known as "*yomi-uri*" (literally "read and sell" because of the way they were sold while being read by the salesman). There were also known as *kawaraban* (literally tile-block printing) because of the way they were produced by means of clay printing blocks.

The first modern-style newspaper was the *Nagasaki Shipping List and Advertiser*, a twice-weekly paper produced in 1861 by an English resident, A. W. Hansard. He moved it to Yokohama in November of the same year, renaming it the *Japan Herald*. In 1862, the Tokugawa shogunate started the *Kampan Batabuya Shimbun*, a translated and edited version of the *Javasch Courant*, the Dutch government paper in Batavia (modern Djakarta). Both papers reported only international news. In 1868, domestic newspapers were started in Edo (renamed Tokyo), Osaka, Kyoto, and Nagasaki. The first national daily, the *Yokohama Mainichi Shimbun*, was launched in 1871, followed in 1872 by the *Tokyo Mainichi Shimbun* (now the *Mainichi*

Shimbun), the *Yubin Hochi Shimbun* (later the *Hochi Shimbun*), and the *Kochu Shimbun* (later the *Yamanashi Nichinichi Shimbun*), the oldest of all local papers.

After the great Kanto earthquake of 1923, the ***Asahi Shimbun***, which had been started in Osaka in 1879, and the *Mainichi* in Tokyo became the two major papers nationwide. The ***Yomiuri Shimbun***, originally launched as a popular and sensationalist paper in 1874, survived bankruptcy with the help of Shoriki Matsutaro in 1924 and became the third great national daily. Between 1939 and 1942, because of paper rationing, the number of newspapers fell from 848 to 54. After 1945, restrictions on the press were eased, although newsprint was in short supply. After 1951, when controls on newsprint were lifted, competition became fierce, with small papers suffering as a result. The three major national dailies continued to dominate, with 2004 circulation figures reporting the *Asahi Shimbun* at 8 million copies per day, the *Mainichi Shimbun* at 4 million, and the *Yomiuri Shimbun* topping these at 10 million. Subsequently, each of the three newspapers produced its own English-language edition for the growing foreign communities in Japan's major cities. *See also* NEWS AGENCIES; NIHON KEIZAI SHIMBUN.

NICHIMEN. Nichimen Jitsugyo is a major trading house (***soga shosha***) founded in 1892 as a cotton importer and textile exporter. It diversified after World War II and expanded dramatically in the 1960s. It traces its roots to Nippon Menka Kaisha (Japan Cotton Trading Company), founded in 1892.

The present name was adopted in 1957 when the country was moving away from textiles into heavy industry with the purpose of giving the company a new identity as a general trading house. It grew to become one of the major trading houses with 80 overseas offices linked by a computerized communications system. It is also involved in over 100 **joint-venture** companies. It was originally a principal member of the enterprise group (***keiretsu***) headed by the **Sanwa Bank**, which merged with the **Tokai Bank** to form the **UFJ Bank** in 2002. It has central offices in both Osaka and Tokyo.

NIHON CEMENT. A major cement manufacturer that started from a government-built factory bought over by **Asano Soichiro** (1848–

1930) in 1884. It became a central company in the prewar **Asano *zaibatsu***, which included many large corporations, now independent but still maintaining corporate links. Formerly known as Asano Cement, the company changed its name after World War II. Besides cement, the company has a reputation for building and construction materials, industrial equipment, and Asano Clean Set, an agricultural chemical for softening hard soil. Its headquarters are in Tokyo.

NIHON KEIZAI SHIMBUN. The *Nikkei*, as it is colloquially known, is Japan's leading business and economics newspaper, founded originally in 1876 as a business weekly that became a daily **newspaper** in 1885. It became the *Chugai shogyo shimpo* in 1889. It was separated from its **Mitsui** roots, and in 1911 a company was set up to manage it. During World War II, in 1942, it merged with the *Nikkan kogyo shimbun* and *the Keizai jiji shimpo* and became the *Nihon sangyo keizai Shimbun*. The *Nikkan kogyo* became independent after 1945, and the name *Nihon keizei shimbun* was born.

The *Nikkei* became a quality paper similar to the *Wall Street Journal* or the London *Financial Times*, both of which have international reputations of considerable standing. Its influence in Japan is enormous in both its news coverage, nationally and internationally, and its opinions in leader columns. It has offices in Tokyo, Osaka, Nagoya, and Sapporo and has 20 overseas bureaus. Its daily circulation is around 3 million.

NIKKEIREN. *See* JAPAN FEDERATION OF EMPLOYERS ASSOCIATION.

NIKON. Nippon Kogaku is a manufacturer of cameras and optical equipment under the brand name Nikon. It remains one of the largest makers of single-lens reflex cameras, although it has moved into the general field of mechatronics, like others in the field. It was founded in 1917 through the merger of the optical division of Tokyo Keiki Seisakukjo and the reflex mirror division of Iwaki Garasu Seizojo. **Iwasaki Koyata** (1876–1945) of the **Mitsubushi *zaibatsu*** provided the necessary capital. Before World War II, it was primarily a supplier to the military, but after 1945, it turned to domestic and international commercial markets. Its first postwar product, the Nikon-I camera, had achieved considerable popularity by the 1950s.

Nikon began forming subsidiaries as early as 1953, beginning with Nippon Kogaku, Inc., in New York followed by the Netherlands in 1968, Germany in 1971, Canada in 1979, and the United Kingdom in the same year. The next highly successful product was the Nikon F, which was widely used by professional photographers as well as by the general population, a fact that helped enormously in raising the company's profile. From 1975, it began selling spectacle frames and eyeglasses along with other ocular instruments, such as microscopes, telescopes, and surveying equipment. Like others in the field, Nikon is now working to find a place in the newly expanding markets in digitalized and **computer** products. The head office is in Tokyo.

NINOMIYA SONTOKU (1787–1856). A peasant sage of the **Edo period** (1615–1868) who was an outstanding leader in the field of agricultural science and philosophy. He created the concept of ***hotoku***, repayment of virtue, meaning by this that by repayment of benefits received from heaven and earth and other people, society would be peaceful and prosperous. Sincerity, diligence, thrift, and cooperation were the key values he preached, and these accorded well with both the Tokugawa government's thinking and that of the Meiji government after 1868.

Ninomiya's ideas were furthered by his disciple Fukuzuki Masae (1824–1892), who was one of the founders of the *Hotokusha* (Society for the Repayment of Virtue). One of the physical remains of his thinking was in the statues of a mythical figure, Ninomiya Kinjiro, a little boy who is depicted carrying a sack of wood on his back and who is, at the same time, reading a book. This became a symbol of the virtue of hard work to overcome hardship that became popular during the **Meiji period** (1868–1912). Statues were placed in all elementary school playgrounds to encourage children to emulate the efforts of Ninomiya Kinjiro. They were removed by a **Supreme Commander Allied Powers** (**SCAP**) order in 1945, presumably because they were considered to be part of prewar moral **education**. The confusion of this with militarism was an illustration of how little the occupation understood Japanese culture. Many were removed to local shrine grounds, others vanished, but some remain as they were.

Suggestions arose within the Ministry of Education during the early 1990s that the statues might be replaced, itself an interesting idea, demonstrating the importance of the role of symbols in Asian moral education.

NINTENDO. This is a video console hardware and software manufacturer founded in 1983 and best known for its GameCube console, which had sold 25 million units by 2003. Nintendo ranks behind **Sony**, whose PlayStation holds the world's number one spot but ranks alongside Microsoft Xbox. Its game software, however, is dominant in the market. The company employs almost 3,000 staff, placing it in the group of largest **corporations**. Its head office is in Kyoto.

NIPPON COLUMBIA. An **electronics** manufacturer specializing in sound systems that was founded in 1910 by an American, F. W. Horn, under the name Nipponophone. Initially producing only gramophones and records, it grew to become the largest of its kind in Japan. The Columbia companies of the United States and the United Kingdom put money into Nipponophone in 1927 but withdrew their interest in the 1930s as relations began to cool. The Columbia name was adopted in 1946 when it began to manufacture again and by 1956 was producing tape recorders, television sets, and sound systems, which it exported under the brand name Denon. In 1969, it came under the control of **Hitachi**. Its head office is in Tokyo.

NIPPON CREDIT BANK. The Nippon Saiken Shin'yo Ginko is a long-term credit bank, set up in 1957 under the Long-Term Credit Bank Law. Its first name was Nippon Fudosan Bank, which was changed in 1977 to Nippon Credit Bank. Its funding comes from the issue of five-year interest-bearing debentures and one-year discount debentures. It is also active in housing loans and in the financing of small enterprises. It has also issued foreign currency debentures in Europe and has worked in the field of international development in partnership with foreign enterprises, the **Bank of Japan**, and the Japanese government. It has 16 domestic branches and several overseas, including in New York, London, Paris, and Frankfurt. The head office is in Tokyo. *See also* INDUSTRIAL BANK OF JAPAN; LONG-TERM CREDIT BANK OF JAPAN.

NIPPONDENSO. Formed in 1949 as an independent company from the electrical and radiator departments of the **Toyota Motor Corporation**, it remains a member of the **Toyota Group**. It has a network of overseas operations that include production, distribution, maintenance, and servicing functions. Its principal products include car heaters, air conditioners, meters and gauges, and emission controls. It has business links with most European **automobile** makers as well with the big three in the United States. It also produces corrosion-resistant chemical equipment as well as new ceramics and environmental control equipment. Its headquarters are located in Kariya City, Aiichi prefecture, the heartland of the Toyota Group. The head office is in Nagoya.

NIPPON GAKKI. *See* YAMAHA.

NIPPON HOSO KYOKAI (NHK). The Japan Broadcasting Corporation dates back to the beginning of broadcasting in Japan in 1925 and the amalgamation of the three stations that served Tokyo, Osaka, and Nagoya in 1926. The Broadcasting Law of 1950 opened the way for commercial broadcasting. Telecasts started in 1953, and both public (NHK) and private channels began to appear, linked to other media companies such as **newspapers**.

NHK is still funded by income from license fees collected from all families owning a television set. The chairman of NHK is appointed by the government. The company has two main channels and broadcasts on radio through three channels and internationally in 21 languages to 18 zones worldwide. The head office is in Tokyo.

NIPPON KOKAN. A major integrated **steel**maker and **shipbuilder** founded in 1912 by Shiraishi Motojiro as a maker of seamless steel tubing. It moved into shaped steel, steel plates, and steel alloys during World War I. In spite of the 1934 government program to create the Japan Iron & Steel Co. to consolidate production, Nippon Kokan remained independent. It entered the shipbuilding field, but because of wartime damage, it was unable to resume production until 1948, after which it began to regain its former status. As of 1961, it built a modern steel mill in Fukuyama City in Hiroshima prefecture. Nippon Kokan has been a powerful innovator in Japan's steel technology development through use of the basic oxygen process and the continuous casting process as well as through the development of large-diameter pipes and a continuous rolling mill for thin plates. It expanded internationally into Indonesia, Nigeria, and Saudi Arabia. Its headquarters are in Tokyo.

NIPPON LIFE INSURANCE. Nippon Seimei Hoken is a **life insurance** and reinsurance sales company, founded in 1899, that became a **joint-stock company** in 1891. It was the first insurance company to use data about mortality in calculating premiums and the first to pay out dividends to the insured. It has numerous international tie-ups and owns hospitals and real estate. It is not only Japan's largest insurer but also one of the largest insurance companies in the world. Its head office is in Osaka.

NIPPON LIGHT METAL. Nippon Kei Kinzoku is an aluminum products manufacturer that handles an integrated process from smelting and processing to the finished item. The company started in 1939 as an aluminum refiner with the help of Tokyo Dento (now **Tokyo Electric**) and **Furukawa Electric**. It entered a capital tie-up with Aluminium Ltd, which became Alcan Aluminium in 1952. In 1974, it absorbed Nikkei Aluminum, a processing subsidiary, and in 1978, it absorbed another subsidiary, Nikkei Aluminum Rolling, to complete its integrated processes. The 50 companies that make up the Nikkei Group produce every kind of aluminum for industrial products, housing, and household products. The company began to move into China and Brazil in the 1980s. The head office is in Tokyo. *See also* FURUKAWA ZAIBATSU.

NIPPON MINING. Nippon Kogyo is a major **petroleum** refiner as well as smelter and refiner of nonferrous metal that began with the development of underground mineral resources in 1905, taking its present name in 1929. It has a leading position in the production of copper, brass, zinc, ferronickel, gold, silver, and sulfuric acid. Along with its affiliates, it engages in exploration, extraction, mining, smelting, and the production of nonferrous metals in addition to petroleum exploration, drilling, and **petrochemical** production. Radical restructuring within the petroleum industry led to the merger in 1992 of Nippon Oil with Kyodo Oil in 1992. Its headquarters are in Tokyo.

NIPPON OIL. Nippon Sekiyu is the oldest and largest oil and **petroleum** company in Japan, dating to 1888. Its role is to produce oil, while its subsidiaries and affiliates engage in oil exploration. It began its drilling history in Niigata prefecture in 1890, using imported equipment from the United States, and was the first to find an oil field in Japan. The Takarada Oil Company was its major rival, and after a merger in 1921, Nippon Oil began refining imported crude oil. In 1941, it merged with Kokura Oil, further increasing its capacity. In 1951, it formed an oil refining **joint venture** with Caltex Petroleum known as Nippon Petroleum Refining. Nippon Oil began to sell the products of the refinery as well as those of Koa Oil. It then moved into the oil transportation business by forming the Tokyo Tanker Company in the same year.

Nihon Sekiyu formed Nippon Petroleum Chemicals in 1955 along with Nippon Petroleum Gas. Next was the Nippon Oil Terminal Company in 1967, created to construct the world's largest crude oil transshipment facility able to hold over 5,550 million barrels. In 1968, it formed Nippon Oil Exploration and began work in the South China Sea in collaboration with Texaco, Inc., and the Standard Oil Company of California. Although the oil business underwent radical restructuring in Japan, Nihon Sekiyu has remained a powerful force in the field with a controlling interest in more than 20 large **corporations**. Its headquarters are in Tokyo.

NIPPON SEIKO. Manufacturer of steel ball and roller bearings sold under the NSK brand name. It is the largest bearings maker in Japan, dating to 1916. It has two manufacturing plants in the United States, one in Brazil, and one in the United Kingdom. It belongs to the **Fuyo Group**. The head office is in Tokyo.

NIPPON SHINPAN. A major consumer credit finance organization, popularly known as Nicos, that was founded in 1951. The firm became engulfed in a major scandal when a senior managing director and seven senior officials were arrested on 16 November 2002 on suspicion of violation of the **Commercial Code** by paying ¥28 million to a corporate racketeer (***sokaiya***) who was also arrested. On 17 November, police raided the head office in Bunkyo Ward in Tokyo and 10 other Tokyo branch offices to collect information and evidence relating to a total estimated figure of ¥80 million between 1991 and 2002. At the time, the company was undergoing restructuring, due to be completed by fiscal year 2004.

NIPPON STEEL. Shin Nippon Seitetsu, or Shin Nittetsu, with a history stretching back to 1967, has been consistently the industry leader. It has played an important role in every era since **modernization** started. The name Nippon Steel dates to 1934, when Yawata Iron and Steel Works, a state-owned company, acquired several private steelmakers. The company was broken up into Yawata Steel and Fuji Steel to make the industry more competitive. However, Yawata and Fuji became the two largest steelmakers and merged in 1970 to form the present corporation. With the decline in demand for steel, other members of the big five, **Nippon Kokan**, **Kawasaki Steel**, **Sumitomo Metal Industries**, and **Kobe Steel**, began to diversify. Nippon Steel elected to remain with its core business and to develop new technologies based on **iron**. In 1991, it opened its Comprehensive Technology Center near Chiba City, the largest private sector research facility in the country. The main objective of the ongoing research is new basic studies of iron with a view to developing technologies that combine iron with new materials.

The Nippon Steel group consists of 200 companies employing 110,000 staff. Annual turnover is in the 7 trillion range, bringing it into the company of **Toyota**, **Hitachi**, and **Matsushita**. It employs the world's most advanced technology and exports steel plants and engineering projects. It is providing technical assistance in 35 countries worldwide. It has overseas offices in New York, Los Angeles, Houston, Rio de Janeiro, Dusseldorf, London, Rome, Singapore, and Sydney. The head office is in Tokyo.

NIPPON SUISAN KAISHA. The largest fishery company in Japan dating back to Nippon Suisan, a **fishing** conglomerate that covered fishing as far north as the Bering Straits, trawling in the South Seas, **whaling**, and marine food processing. The company was broken up by the government as a wartime measure to control food production. In 1942, the fishing division was separated and became the company as it now is. It resumed whaling in the Antarctic in 1952, but after the 200-mile territorial waters agreement came into force and the ban on whaling became an international issue, the company began to examine new fishing prospects. It formed subsidiaries in the South Pacific, Australia, the Indian Ocean, the Canary Islands, Ireland, and Seattle in the United States to diversify its areas of interest. Nippon Suisan is financed by the **Mizuho Group** because it was formerly under the wing of the **Industrial Bank of Japan**. Its head office is in Tokyo. *See also* TSUKIJI SHIJO.

NIPPON TELEGRAPH AND TELEPHONE PUBLIC CORPORATION. NTT, or Denden Kosha, as it is known, was set up in 1952 as a **public corporation** with a monopoly on all domestic **electronic** communications. Its business covers telephone, telegraph, and data communication. Its domestic monopoly was threatened by the development of the mobile phone industry in the 1990s. To deal with this, it created NTT DoCoMo, a company that provides mobile phone service. The main rival company, J-phone, was strengthened in 2003 by the tie-up with Vodafone of the United Kingdom, although the market rivalry remained very fierce. *See also* E-COMMERCE; TELECOMMUNICATIONS INDUSTRY.

NIPPON TSUUN. NITTSU, as it is known, is Japan's largest transport and freight company, founded in 1937 as a semigovernmental corporation. It played a central role in both areas during World War II, after which it was made private and was required to reorganize. By concluding agency agreements in the expanding area of civil aviation, with airlines such as Northwest and the former British Overseas Airways Corporation (BOAC), in 1949, it quickly regained pole position in the industry. In 1953, it formed an agreement with the International Air Transportation Association (IATA) and established Nippon Express USA, Inc., in 1962, the first of several overseas subsidiaries. The corporate headquarters are located in Tokyo.

NIPPON UNIVAC. This is a company established in 1958 to sell, lease, and maintain **computer** services as a **joint venture** between **Mitsui & Co.** and the Sperry Rand Co. of the United States. It distributes Sperry Rand's Univac electronic equipment and computers manufactured by Oki-Univac Co., a joint venture of Sperry Rand and **Oki Electric Industry**. The head office is in Tokyo.

NIPPON YUSEN. NYK is a major **shipping** company started in 1870 by **Iwasaki Yataro**, founder of the **Mitsubishi *zaibatsu***, as part of the Mitsubishi Company. The shipping division was separated in 1885 to merge with Kyodo Un'yu to become Nippon Yusen. NYK has a fleet of 80 carrier ships that can handle oil, ore, **automobiles**, and a range of special cargoes. It has 22 advanced technology carrier ships but also offers conventional services on 16 routes. It has a worldwide network of 45 offices in major cities and seaports. To supplement its business, it entered the air cargo field with a consortium of several Japanese companies. Its head office is in Tokyo.

NISSAN MOTOR CORPORATION. Founded by **Aikawa Yoshisuke** (1880–1967) as the Tobata Foundry in Kyushu, the company eventually began to manufacture vehicles in the Hiro district of Tokyo. In 1928, Aikawa took over Kuhara Mining, which was run by his brother-in-law Kuhara Fusanosuke, turning it into a holding company with the name Nihon Sangyo, which was shortened to Nissan. In 1931, as the stock market boomed, Aikawa took over 148 of Nissan's subsidiaries and created the Nissan ***zaibatsu***, making it the largest after **Mitsui** and **Mitsubishi**. In 1933, it moved to Yokohama, and in the postwar years, it grew alongside rivals **Toyota** and **Honda**. The protracted **recession of the 1990s** stunted the growth of many parts of the economy, including the **automobile** industry. A tie-up with Renault of France saw Carlos Ghosn, the Lebanese-born director of Renault, become president of Nissan in 2002. The company's performance was improved by radical restructuring that included various strategies to cut costs. It was also decided that all international communication within the Nissan group should be conducted exclusively in English. The company survived the traumas of restructuring and began to make a comeback. Its head office remains in Yokohama.

NISSHO-IWAI. This is a major trading house (***soga shosha***) formed by a merger of two established houses. Iwai Shoten was formed originally in 1862, later becoming Iwai Sangyo. Iwai Sangyo merged with Nissho Company in 1968. Nissho had emerged as one of the successors of the failed **Suzuki Shoten** of the prewar period and had become the 12th-largest trading house by the 1960s. It was a merger of two established trading houses, similar to the merger that produced

Kanematsu Gosho. Until then, growing houses had acquired small trading businesses and integrated their operations as a means to expand. The merger of two sets of established houses suggested that a realignment or a rationalization within the trading house business had started.

Both Nissho-Iwai and Kanematsu Gosho were part of the 43-strong **Sanwa Bank** group of Kansai-based corporations that included other major names such as **Kyocera**, **Suntory**, **Kobe Steel**, and **Hitachi**. The major trading houses of the group have diversified further into what they hope will be the businesses of the 21st century, such as satellite communications. This, however, is all part of the general problem of the future of the *soga shosha* in modern global business.

NISSIN FOOD PRODUCTS. The famous Nisshin brand name was founded by Ando Momofuku in 1952 as a producer of an experimental food, the instant noodle, the first of which was Chicken Ramen, which appeared in 1958. The company, whose name means "daily purity," produces 4 billion packs per year. It also introduced Cup Noodle in 1971. Nissin occupies 40 percent of the Japanese market and 10 percent of the world market, with 25 plants in eight countries. Its head office is in Tokyo.

NOKYO. *See* AGRICULTURAL COOPERATIVES.

NOMURA SECURITIES. Nomura Shoken is the largest of the big three (the big four until **Yamaiichi Securities** collapsed in 1997). It was founded in 1925 when the **securities** division of the Osaka Nomura Bank (subsequently the **Daiwa Bank**) was turned into an independent company. Initially engaged in bond trading, it began stock trading in 1938 and started investment trust operations in 1941. After World War II, Nomura moved into underwriting newly issued stocks and bonds and engaged in a major policy change, moving from margin profit to percentage commissions. It was very active in underwriting the American depositary receipts (ADRs) of numerous Japanese corporations functioning in the United States. It formed Nomura Securities International, Inc., in the United States in 1969, followed by Nomura Europe, N.V., in Amsterdam in 1972. It actively raised foreign capital for Japanese enterprises through listings in stock exchanges in the United States and Europe through the 1970s and 1980s.

However, the bursting of the **bubble economy** and the **deregulation** of financial institutions cut billions of yen from the paper value of stocks, and Nomura headed into rough waters. The company did survive and worked to reestablish the financial stability of the most affected of its major clients. Nomura has been the object of criticism for its methods, particularly because it paid substantial compensation to large **corporations** while allowing smaller but perhaps equally deserving ones to languish or go under. It has around 105 branches in Japan and 27 in major world financial centers. It created the Nomura Research Institute in 1965, the biggest think tank in Japan. The head office is in Tokyo.

NONFERROUS METALS INDUSTRY. This is a key industrial sector that divides into aluminum and copper (including lead and zinc). The aluminum industry's major corporations, **Nippon Light Metal** and **Sumitomo Light Metal Industries**, were affected in the late 1970s and 1980s by the strong yen, which made imported metal cheaper than domestic products. Much of their capacity is unused, while smelting projects were developed in Brazil, Indonesia, and Australia. With the final closure of the **Sumitomo Group**'s historical **Besshi Copper Mine**, Japan's domestic supply of crude ore ended, and the industrial leaders **Mitsubishi Metal Corporation**, **Nippon Mining**, and **Mitsui Mining and Smelting**, along with the copper wire and cable producers **Sumitomo Electric Industries**, **Furukawa Electric**, and **Hitachi Cable**, were forced to depend on imported ore for production.

NONPERFORMING LOANS. The term is used to refer to the excessive bad debts that **banks** incurred by excessive lending to corporate customers that precipitated a bank crisis in the mid-1990s. The deflation of real estate assets, combined with the protracted **recession of the 1990s**, among other factors, led to the dramatic restructuring of the **banking industry** between the late 1990s and the early 2000s. *See also* TOBASHI.

NONTARIFF BARRIERS (NTBs). Recited like a mantra by frustrated foreign exporters, the term includes policy provisions, commercial structures, and business practices that have the effect of obstructing imports. While there is no doubt that these exist, less attention is paid by foreign exporters than they should to cultural differences, market preferences, and the complex Japanese **distribution system** that has its roots in the **Edo period** (1615–1868). The Japanese argument is that foreign corporations should take into account these crucial differences when preparing products they wish to sell in Japan. Most foreign exporters reject this position. The **Structural Impediments Initiative** (**SII**) talks from 1989 to 1990 between Tokyo and Washington were intended to tackle these issues systematically, particularly the politically sensitive matter of U.S. agricultural products, especially **rice**. Views range from dismissing NTBs as fictions to claiming that they are part of a vast conspiracy to maintain an imbalance of trade in Japan's favor.

– O –

OCCUPATION OF JAPAN. *See* SUPREME COMMANDER ALLIED POWERS (SCAP).

ODAIRA NAMIHEI (1874–1951). He was the founder of **Hitachi**, born in Tochigi prefecture. After graduating from the University of Tokyo, he joined Tokyo Dento. He left there in 1906 to join the Hitachi mine of Kuhara Kogyosho, where he developed electric machinery production in order to help the company become more profitable and self-sufficient. In 1920, he founded Hitachi by separating the mine's manufacturing and repair divisions. He was president from 1929 to 1947, during which time he transformed Hitachi into one of the leading corporations in the field of general electric machinery manufacturing.

ODA NOBUNAGA (1534–1582). He was the first of the three warrior lords who played key roles in the unification of Japan during the period following the *Sengoku Jidai* (1467–1568), the century of civil war and political instability. *See also* HIDEYOSHI TOYOTOMI; TOKUGAWA IEYASU.

OIL. *See* PETROLEUM INDUSTRY.

OJI PAPER COMPANY. Oji Seishi was founded in 1873 by the famous **Meiji period** (1868–1912) entrepreneur and business leader **Shibusawa Eichi** (1840–1931), the first ever **joint-stock company** created in Japan. After 1945, it was broken into Oji Jujo Paper and Honshu Paper. It thereafter merged with Kita Nihon Paper Manufacturing in 1970 and with Nippon Pulp Industry in 1979. Its products include newsprint, packaging, and specialty papers. It imports half of its needs from North America and has set up **joint ventures** for pulp production in New Zealand and Brazil, where it is also involved in reforestation projects. It is closely affiliated with the **Mitsui Group**. The head office is in Tokyo.

OKAMURA CORPORATION. Okamura Gumi was founded in 1938 as a civil engineering enterprise. The company gained a reputation for the **construction** of **railways**, highways, draining and irrigation systems, and dams for hydroelectric power. Initially it relied heavily on government contracts but eventually became successful in the private sector and overseas. It won the contract for the subway system in Hong Kong and has worked in the Philippines and Nepal. The head office is in Osaka.

OKI ELECTRIC INDUSTRY. Oki Denki Kogyo is an **electronic** communications manufacturer founded in 1949 that is a member of the **Fuyo Group**. Originally it depended on public works and government contracts, but it began to move more into the private sector, especially with its overseas manufacturing subsidiaries in North America and in Europe. Like its major competitors, **Nippon Electric** and **Fujitsu**, it is active in the field of mechatronics and office automation. The head office is in Tokyo.

OKURA & CO. Okura Shoji was founded in 1873 by **Okura Kihachiro** (1837–1928) as Okura-Gumi Shokai and in 1874 was the first Japanese company to establish a London office. Along with Okura Public Works (now **Taisei Corporation**) and Okura Mining, Okura Shoji formed the core of the Okura ***zaibatsu***, one of the second-tier pre–World War II conglomerates. After 1945, it concentrated on general trading and made plans with U.S. Steel to set up an iron-mine project in China. The company ranks as a second-tier trading company (***sogo shosha***), and its head office is in Tokyo.

OKURA HOTEL. The Okura is a world-famous five-star hotel, opened in 1962 in the Toranomon district of central Tokyo. Hotel Okura Co, Ltd, is the **holding company** of the group and includes Hotel Okura Space Solutions Co., Ltd (HOSS), working in reconstruction projects of Okura Hotels and Resorts members and the British P & O cruise line; Hotel Okura Enterprise Ltd, seller of Okura brand gourmet products; and Continental Foods Co, Ltd, which provides restaurant and banquet services in Nagoya. The Hotel Okura has 17 affiliated properties in Japan and seven overseas, including offices and hotels in New York, Los Angeles, Amsterdam, and Hong Kong.

OKURA KIHACHIRO (1837–1928). He was a late **Edo period** (1615–1868) and **Meiji period** (1868–1912) entrepreneur, born in Niigata, who founded the **Okura *zaibatsu***. Following the **Meiji Restoration of 1868**, he opened a gun store that provided him with sufficient profits to form Okura-Gumi Shoji (later **Okura & Co.**) in 1873 and engage in international **trade**. In 1874, he became the first business leader to set up a London office, which was extremely successful. Out of his accumulated wealth, he created Tokyo Dento (later **Tokyo Electric Power Company**) and the Imperial Hotel in Tokyo, Okura Public Works Co. (later **Taisei Corporation**), and Okura Kogyo. A philanthropist as well as a businessman, he founded the Okura Commercial School (later Tokyo University of Economics) and the Okura Museum.

OMRON TATEISHI ELECTRONICS. Omron Tateishi Denki is a manufacturer of **electronic** control components and medical equipment founded in 1938 by Tateishi Kazuma. It markets its products under the name Omron. In the postwar period, Omron made numerous contributions to the **automation** of Japanese industry. The company's own cybernetic technology has been applied to information systems and its medical appliances. Overseas sales companies were set up in Chicago, São Paulo, Amsterdam, Hamburg, and Singapore. Manufacturing facilities were set up in Malaysia and in Hong Kong.

Much of Omron's capital comes from European and Hong Kong depository receipts and German mark convertible bonds. The headquarters are located in Kyoto.

ONODA CEMENT. The company was a cement manufacturer founded in 1881 that grew to have 27 plants in Japan and in Japan's overseas possessions. Defeat in World War II cost the company all of its 18 overseas facilities. However, it made a remarkable recovery, and its famous dragon brand is exported to over 50 countries. Its head office is in Onoda City, Yamaguchi prefecture. In October 1994, Onoda Cement merged with **Chichibu Cement** to form **Chichibu Onoda Cement**, the largest cement maker in Japan.

ONO, HOUSE OF. One of the great merchant houses of the **Edo period** (1615–1868) that failed to make the transition to the modern post-1868 period. The great houses of Ono, **Mitsui**, and **Shimada** were courted by the **Meiji period** (1868–1912) government, which tried to use their functions as commission merchants of the **Tokugawa feudal system** to finance projects. They were given roles as managers of government finances, selling **tax rice** for the government, and holding government money interest free. Ono became the commission banker and supplier to the army and navy along with various offices in the treasury. The government's Banking Act of 1972, promoted by Ito Hirobumi, a key political figure, was to create a system of national **banks** on the American model. The largest of the four initially formed was the First National Bank, with Mitsui and Ono as principal shareholders.

The House of Ono, however, went bankrupt, largely because its management was not capable of functioning in the fluid situation of Japan's fledgling modern economy. The bank survived, but the government realized that while some aspects of the Tokugawa tradition might serve the needs of the new regime, much would not. In 1873, the government ended the special roles they performed and called in deposits. Mitsui had sufficient resources to pay, but Ono collapsed, in effect bringing to an end the long economic role of the merchant houses. While some survived and prospered, the future lay with the entrepreneurs who created the foundations of the modern industrial nation. *See also* BANKING HISTORY; IE

GENSOKU (HOUSE PRINCIPLE); OSAKA MERCHANTS; ZAIBATSU.

ONO TAIICHI (1920–). Engineer and executive officer who developed the postwar production system of **Toyota Motor Corporation**. After graduating from Nagoya Higher Industrial School (now Nagoya Industrial University), he worked for the Toyoda Spinning Company before joining the **automobile** manufacturer in 1943. Under the influence of the Taylor theory of scientific management, he began to eliminate waste within the production system, not simply waste in materials but also in time and in space. This in turn help to improve **productivity** in the production line and in so doing increased cost-effectiveness in all areas. Ono's developments included the **just-in-time** and the ***kanban*** system, both of which found their way not only into other Japanese **corporations** but also into companies around the world, including the United States, from where the inspiration had originally been drawn.

OSAKA GAS. Founded in 1897 to supply gas to the Osaka area, it commenced supply in 1905 once its infrastructure had been completed. It subsequently acquired several smaller local companies and steadily built its market. By the 1980s, it was supplying almost 4.5 million consumers, ranging from domestic households to offices and factories in Osaka, Kyoto, Nara, Shiga, Wakayama, and Hyogo prefectures. It went into the liquefied natural gas (LNG) business by importing it from 1972 and supplying it after 1975. The company has been innovative in developing various technologies to improve and stabilize service as well as conserving energy and resources. It has been researching in the field of substitute natural gas (SNG), and its technology and products are being introduced abroad through its subsidiaries in Japan and overseas. The head office is in Osaka.

OSAKA MERCHANTS. The *Osaka Shonin*, as they were known, were the business houses that evolved during the **Edo period** (1615–1868), principal among which were the families of **Mitsui**, **Ono**, and **Shimada**. The Osaka merchants themselves were concerned primarily about the survival of the wealth of the house and the behavior of its members, which was strictly regulated by the rules each house prescribed. Members of the house were required to revere the ancestors, for whose sake the house must be preserved, and be upstanding model citizens who practiced the virtues of honesty, hard work, perseverance, and, above all, **loyalty**. By way of contrast, the merchants of Edo (now Tokyo) were more like pork-barrel traders who, in addition to being such, aspired to public office. The Kyoto merchants, because they had grown out of landowning families, were conservative in the concern over maintaining their property.

One interesting question of Japanese economic history concerns the reasons why the Osaka merchants became gradually more conservative and why some of the great houses failed after the **Meiji Restoration of 1868**. Many reasons have been adduced, not least of all their isolation from the dynamic events happening in Tokyo, but unlike the bourgeoisie of Europe, it has been argued that they did not develop the progressive, individualistic, and utilitarian mentality needed to cope with change. It was the early **Meiji period** (1868–1912) and 20th-century entrepreneurs like **Matsushita Konosuke** (1894–1989) who displayed that type of thinking, perhaps because of the greater freedom of thought and action they possessed in comparison with those who lived under the rigid structures of the **Tokugawa feudal system**. *See also* IE GENSOKU (HOUSE PRINCIPLE).

OSAKA SPINNING MILL. Osaka Boseki Kaisha was formed in 1882 under the leadership of **Meiji period** (1868–1912) entrepreneur **Shibusawa Eiichi** (1840–1931) with technology imported from England and capital from former *daimyo* (lord) and new businessmen. The factory began with 10,500 spindles but eventually had over 70,000. It was very successful and laid the foundations of the cotton industry of the late 1880s, becoming the model for future enterprises. In 1914, it merged with the Mie Spinning Mill (Mie Boseki Kaisha) to become **Toyobo**, which is still active in the **textile industry**.

OSHIMA TAKATO (1826–1901). He was a mining engineer who studied gunnery and mining in Nagasaki and who helped modernize mining in Japan. In 1858, he built the first Western-style blast furnace at Kamaishi, Iwate prefecture, producing pig iron for a reverberatory furnace he had built at Mito (now in Ibaraki prefecture). At Mito, he produced the first-ever Japanese-made rifle. After the **Meiji Restora-**

tion of 1868, he led in the mining and refining of copper, **iron**, and other metal ore deposits through the country.

OTSUKA HISAO (1907–). Internationally famous University of Tokyo and latterly International Christian University professor of economic history who tried to apply aspects of the theory of **Max Weber** (1864–1920) about the link between the Protestant work ethic and economic development to Japan and Asia. By noting its absence and the absence of the concept of saving, he tried to explain why some societies find economic development extremely difficult. He was decorated with the Order of Culture for his original work by **Emperor** Heisei.

OYATOI-GAIKOKUJIN. This was the name given to foreign nationals employed by the Japanese government during the late **Edo period** (1615–1868) and early **Meiji period** (1912–1926). It first appeared officially as a heading for a list of hired foreign nationals in 1872. They ranged from Chinese laborers to professors hired for the emerging Japanese higher **education** system. The list also included engineers needed to teach machine technology and other necessary skills for the **modernization** process. These foreign residents often faced hostility and prejudice because they were linked with the image of unfair treaties, Western territorial acquisition in Asia, and unfavorable trade arrangements. Consequently, in their various settlements, such as Yokohama and Kobe, special police forces were appointed to protect them.

One famous incident involved a young officer who ordered his men to open fire on the foreign settlement in Kobe, resulting in his being condemned to commit ***seppuku***. The act was the first ever seen by non-Japanese and was recorded in the memoirs of Lord Redesdale, an eyewitness to the event. Some of the early figures were highly colorful as well as controversial, but as Japanese acquired the skills that the *yatoi* were hired to teach, they steadily decreased in number.

– P –

PACHINKO. This is a popular pinball machine game developed in Nagoya in 1948 that is played in large, gaudily decked-out parlors with loud music playing outside to attract customers. Pachinko is big business, with an estimate that more than 10 percent of the population plays on a regular basis. The 17,000 parlors generate an estimated turnover of U.S.$15 billion. The industry is strictly supervised by the National Police Agency, Prefectural Police, Prefectural Gaming Business Associations, and Prefectural Wholesale Associations for Pachinko Prizes. Suppliers of machines, steel balls, and other facets of the business include most of the major trading houses (***sogo shosha***), a large number of **semiconductor** manufacturers, and other **corporations** producing, for example, steel balls or machine parts.

PART-TIME WORK. Two terms describe part-time work in Japan. One is *arubeito*, which comes from the German word *arbeit* (meaning "work"), and the other is *pa-to* (from "part-time"). They refer to temporary moonlighting activities, most frequently by students who are in need of money to pay for university fees, books, or apartment rent. Corporations can employ workers as *arbeito* on what is a virtually full-time basis, although they are paid usually by the day or by the hour and receive no fringe benefits.

Pa-to is usually distinguished from *arubeito* in advertising for new employees. Viewed in terms of hours worked and method of payment, it seems like a distinction without a difference. Both are paid hourly or daily rates, neither receives any benefits, and neither offers a guarantee of continuity. However, the term "part-time" is more likely to appeal to housewives wishing to begin to reenter the labor market or simply to make some extra money. *Arubeito*, by contrast, has a long association with students. Part-time is typically a limited, defined role, such as sales and service in a shop, and is part-time as against full-time. *Arubeito* for many students is teaching in a cram school (*juku*), which may be for a specific number of weeks or for a set number of classes.

Because of the protracted **recession of the 1990s**, new categories of employment began to appear and develop. Outsourcing was one, creating a class of workers known as *hakken* (implying "picked up" or "found" from outside). The company can dispense with the *hakken* at short notice because it pays the outsourcing organization and not the *hakken*. There are also *shokutaku*, short-term contracted workers on a full- or part-time basis but with none of the benefits of regular employees. The majority of **women** workers fall into one of these categories.

PATENT SYSTEM. The system was created during the **Meiji period** (1868–1912) in 1885. Compared to England (1623) and the United States (1790), it is relatively new but has developed very rapidly because of the nation's economic growth. From 1990, the Patent Office began accepting applications online. Over 300,000 patent applications are filed annually, about 15 percent of which come from overseas applicants. The average rate of success in application is about 30 percent. Japanese corporations also file applications in other countries. In the closing years of the 20th century, the U.S. Department of Commerce's Patent and Trademark Office approved over 100,000 applications each year, approximately 21 percent of which were from Japanese companies. In Japan as in Europe, it is the first applicant who receives the patent. In the United States, it goes to the inventor.

Applications are made public after 18 months, preventing inventors from exploiting their secret. If a patent is granted, the receiver may claim compensation from any imitators. The process in Japan takes almost twice the length of time (average 33 months) required in the United States. The record is the 29 years (applied in 1960, approved in 1989) it took for Texas Instruments to receive approval for its integrated circuit.

Criticisms of the system are that it deliberately slows down foreign applications to allow Japanese corporations to produce competing products while preventing those **foreign companies** from selling in Japan. The nature of patent definition is rather specific in Japan, meaning that to cover a complex product, several applications, all costly, must be filed at the same time. Japanese law also permits challenges to be filed while an application is still in process. Small corporations were frequently unable to face the cost of defending themselves in court against large numbers of applications. These and other issues came under review during the **Strategic Impediments Initiative (SII)** talks of 1989–1990. The Japanese Patent Office conceded on several issues, but because of the vast documentation required for any application, the length of time remains around 22 months. One further contentious issue is the registration of trademarks. Japanese companies have frequently registered foreign brand trademarks either to prevent their use in Japan or to "sell" them back to the owner.

Finally, one factor that exacerbates the entire system is the drastic shortage of patent law specialists. An increase in the number of law schools may help in the long run. In the short term, though, the problems will remain.

PETROCHEMICAL INDUSTRY. The growth of the industry from the 1950s was promoted by a number of circumstances. The shift of energy production from hydroelectric power and coal distillation to oil resulted in the production of a large surplus of naphtha in the **petroleum** refining process, thus creating the raw materials for the development of the petrochemical industry. Added to this was the Foreign Investment Law of 1950, which permitted foreign technology to be imported. As a result, four of the major corporations in the field built large petrochemical complexes. **Mitsui Petrochemical Industries** built a plant at Iwakuni in Yamagichi prefecture in the latter half of the 1950s; **Sumitomo Chemicals** began producing ethylene at its Niihama plant in Ehime prefecture, Shikoku Island; Nippon Petrochemical, established by Nippon Oil Refining, began production in Kawasaki in 1959; and **Mitsubishi Petrochemicals** began production at Yokkaichi in Mie prefecture, also in 1959.

The industry grew rapidly, reaching a peak production of 5.3 million metric tons of ethylene in 1977. The 1980s witnessed a steady decline, partly because of the increase in crude oil prices and partly because of the parallel development of the industry in developing nations, where labor and materials costs were lower. This has also reduced the market for Japanese exports. Since then, the industry has been researching and developing its own original processes and products. Some progress has been made in the field of specialty chemicals with high profit margins, but none of the Japanese corporations has the stature yet of Hoechst, Dupont, or the Imperial Chemical Industries (ICI), raising serious and unanswered questions about their global competitiveness.

PETROLEUM INDUSTRY. The earliest recorded oil strike in Japan dates to 1875 and took place at Kurokawa in Akita prefecture.

The method used stunned Western observers who saw workers digging inside one-square-meter holes whose sides they shored up with wood as they dug deeper into the ground. They kept on digging down in the same hole until they found oil. This was the same method that was traditionally used for finding water. The total yield was about 7.5 million barrels, sufficient to assist in the early process of **modernization**. An entrepreneur named Hisakida Nanto had the idea of looking for oil below the seabed. To attempt this, he created an artificial offshore island that he began digging in the traditional way. In spite of enormous technical problems, he succeeded in making Japan the first country to retrieve oil from beneath the seabed. All this was accomplished without any Western technology.

Boring has continued to the present, with finds in the Japan Sea off northern Honshu and on the Pacific Ocean side, but even at its best, the number of barrels per day remained between 4,000 and 8,000. The mining law in 1975 extended drilling rights to the edge of the continental shelf, producing modest oil and gas fields. The area off west Kyushu remains to be explored thoroughly, something that has not happened because of border disputes with Korea and China. Hence, Japan has had to rely almost entirely on imports.

The serious implications of this situation were demonstrated by the oil crisis of 1973, when it became known that Japan's supply could not last more than 90 days. Government strategy therefore turned to a proposed stockpiling of 30 million kiloliters of strategic reserves. At the same time, transformation of the social and industrial structure was given priority to move from high-energy consumption to alternative sources, such as wind, tidal energy, solar, and geothermal sources. Because of oil's strategic importance, no oil refiners may have more than 50 percent foreign capital. Sales and marketing companies are not restricted. Several of the major **corporations** have foreign affiliations. In the 1980s, during a realignment in the industry, Shell absorbed Showa Oil, and in 1992, Nippon Mining and Kyodo Oil merged. With the creation of Exxon Mobil in the United States, further changes became necessary in Japan. Given Japan's enormous dependence on Middle East exporters, the 21st century should see continued streamlining and integration within the industry.

PHARMACEUTICALS INDUSTRY. Heavily protected during the postwar period, with government setting prices and condoning the modified copying of Western products, the industry did little **research and development** in its early years. Since the import of foreign products was severely restricted, the Japanese companies had no impetus to develop. The pharmaceutical makers sold their products to physicians in private practice at a discount, and these were passed on to the patients at government-fixed prices, giving the doctor additional income. The negative side has been the profusion of medicines produced, particularly antibiotics, many of which are becoming less effective through overuse, resulting in strains of bacteria emerging that resist conventional treatment. As a result of all these factors, pharmaceuticals is one area where, in international terms, Japan has no significant world ranking and lags far behind the United States and Europe.

From the mid-1970s, however, the comfortable arrangements of the previous quarter of a century began to fall apart. In 1975, Japanese intellectual property laws were brought into line with those of developed nations, preventing the copying of products. The oil shock of 1973 put heavy pressure on the economy, and cost cutting began in earnest. Since almost one-third of medical costs was attributed to pharmaceuticals, it was clear that prices had to be lowered, which indeed happened. A final factor came as a result of **foreign companies** being permitted to enter the market in the 1980s. Within a decade, one-quarter of all pharmaceuticals sold in Japan were foreign. A further, large symbolic wall collapsed when the drug Viagra was licensed in a few months, effectively refuting complaints about required safety testing time and other excuses offered for the unreasonable time taken to license foreign products.

With such changes taking effect, new domestic entrants to the industry were able to compete with established firms that relied on networks of private clinics they hitherto supplied. Various alliances with foreign firms became possible, and the once-stable industry became an international battleground. Although there has been progress, Japan does not have a single company in the global top 10, indicating just how far behind it is.

PICKENS, T. BOONE. Chairman of Boone Co. of Dallas, Texas, he was a well-known corporate raider of the 1980s and 1990s who ventured into Japan by acquiring 20 percent of the stock of Koito Corporation, a member of the **Toyota Group**. Even with his shareholding weight, he was unable to procure a seat on the board in spite of using every resource he had available. He finally gave up, but in a bitter good-bye letter to the *Fortune International* edition of 31 December 1990, he claimed that an article in the previous month's magazine extolling the virtues of Toyota failed to mention the plain truth that Toyota was head of a ***keiretsu*** that it manipulated for price advantage against competitors in a manner that would be in violation of U.S. antitrust laws. Other commentators on the Pickens–Koito episode pointed out that the culture of Japanese business puts less emphasis on the rights of transitory shareholders than on the obligation of the company to its employees and to the well-being of society as a whole.

PLAZA ACCORD OF 1985. This is an agreement reached by the finance ministers of five major industrial nations at meetings held in the New York Plaza Hotel in September 1985 to cooperate in bringing down the exchange value of the U.S. dollar. This in turn had the effect of forcing the Japanese yen to appreciate very rapidly. *See also* ENDAKA.

POLLUTION. *See* ENVIRONMENTAL PROBLEMS.

POPULATION. Like other advanced industrial nations, such as the United Kingdom, and other European nations, Japan began to show signs of an aging population in the last quarter of the 20th century. With almost 1,000 people becoming 65 every day, it has been estimated that by 2020, one-quarter of the population will be over 65 years of age, placing enormous pressure on the national pension system. Government policymaking has set this as a priority issue. Proposals have come from various sources to promote immigration to make up the shortfall in **labor**.

POSTAL SAVINGS SYSTEM. The *yubin chokkin* system in Japan dates to the **Meiji period** (1868–1912) and to the work of Mejima Hisoka, who founded the national postal system in 1871, modeled on the British postal savings system. It was a bold and imaginative step for a country just emerging from three centuries of feudalism and economic isolation. However, the example of the Chinese being forced into foreign indebtedness acted as a powerful stimulant to the Japanese government, whose famous slogan of the period "*fu-koku-kyohei*" (strong economy and powerful army) was a response to that concern. Japan was thus able to proceed with the program of **modernization** without foreign borrowing for the ensuing 30 years. Compared with the general debt levels of many developing nations, most of which possess more resources than Japan did in 1868, the achievement is all the more remarkable.

Postal savings advertisements of the Meiji period and the subsequent **Taisho period** (1912–1926) praised the virtue of savings for its own sake (to be a help in the future) and for the sake of the nation. This was in tandem with the **Boshin Shosho** (Imperial Rescript on Thrift and Diligence) of 1908, issued after the two costly wars with Russia and China. The Post Office was willing to accept as little as one-half of a single sen (at the time, 100 sen was 1 yen). **Banks**, in contrast, were more interested in corporate funding and remained so until the 1990s. Between 1945 and the end of the century, the postal savings system, which had been brought under control of the **Ministry of Finance** around 1885, received preferential treatment, such as exemption from national and local **taxes** on interest as well as a better rate of return than the current interest rate. A long-running controversy since the 1970s has centered on the fairness of the system.

Given the traditional preference of Japanese banks for lending to business rather than individuals as well as charging expensive commissions for even small transactions, it is hardly surprising that the Post Office remains popular. The system is also very convenient, with over 24,000 offices nationwide, including rural areas, as against the decreasing number of bank branches, less than 16,000 in total at the end of the century. The average citizen lives within just over a kilometer from the nearest post office. Moreover, the charges for various operations at Post Office banks are lower than at **city banks**. The serious crisis of the **banking industry** during the **recession of the 1990s** showed the government's wisdom in not eliminating the postal savings system, estimated in 2000 to be worth the equivalent of U.S.$260 billion, one-third of all personal savings in the country.

However, proposals to **privatize** the system have been extremely controversial. *See also* INTRODUCTION.

POSTRETIREMENT EMPLOYMENT. On retirement from a **corporation** at the normal mandatory age of 55, there are normally three options. One is to look for a job in a related sector or where the individual's skills can be utilized. A second may be to move to a subsidiary in a new role or to another company in the group if the group is large enough. For those on the ladder upward, a place on the board may beckon. In government sectors, postretirement jobs are usually in the industry that the retirees have been regulating. This is the notorious and much-criticized system of the ***amakudari***, those who receive the golden parachute from heaven to the private sector. Many retirees take on quite unrelated jobs in start-up companies or new sectors. These usually end at 65 years of age, although in some private organizations, such as Shinto shrines, priests may function well into their 70s or early 80s if they are fit. Japanese have not warmly embraced the American dream of the relaxed life "on golden pond," enjoying fishing and other retirement activities. Some retired professors have even gone as volunteer teachers of the Japanese language in Southeast Asian countries. In short, postretirement activities may also be said to be "for life."

PRIVATIZATION. Between 1985 and 1987, three public **corporations** underwent privatization: **Nippon Telegraph and Telephone (NTT)**, **Japan National Railways (JNR)**, and **Japan Tobacco and Salt Corporation**. The objective was to make them profitable through streamlined management and enhanced efficiency. NTT remains Japan's largest employer and second worldwide to America's AT&T in size. The government sold 1.95 million shares in 1986 and 1987 and a further 1.15 million shares in 1988, but it still remains the majority shareholder. Telephone charges did decrease, and further restructuring was planned on the basis of the **Antimonopoly Law of 1997**.

JNR was broken into six regional **railway** companies and one freight company in 1987 under the general **Japan Railways (JR)** banner. This also was successful, and the new system became profitable and offered improved services. Japan Tobacco and Salt Corporation became Japan Tobacco in 1985, but it still retains a monopoly on domestic production, meaning that it is not totally free of government regulation.

The concept of privatization employed in these cases differs from its Western counterpart. It is privatization within the context of an economy where private and public ownership of the same company is possible. Less dramatic have been the instances of complete Western-style privatization in the cases of **Japan Airlines**, the Tohoku Development Corporation, and the Okinawa Electric Power Co., to name but three.

Prime Minister Koizumi Junichiro brought bills to the Japanese Diet in early 2005 for the privatization of the public postal services (including the **postal savings** and insurance business) to take effect in 2007. This move remains controversial, and observers question if the full plan will actually be implemented and, if so, how much of the bill will require to be sacrificed in order to have it passed.

PRODUCTIVITY. Two aspects of the productivity movement summarize its postwar development. At the national level was the formation of the **Japan Productivity Center** (JPC; *Nihon seisan seihonbu*) in 1955 to spearhead leadership, training, and expertise in developing effective production systems that would promote growth in all sectors of the economy. It became the Japan Center for Socioeconomic Development in 1995 after merging with the Social and Economic Congress of Japan (SECJ), suggesting that after 40 successful years, its remit had become broader and more closely related to questions of social development.

At the level of individual **corporations**, productivity as a means to competitiveness became a dominant theme nationwide from the early 1960s. Total productivity maintenance, along with **just-in-time (JIT)** and **total quality control (TQC)**, became the three-pronged assault on the productivity problem. In the late 1960s, Denso, a member of the **Toyota Group**, developed a productivity maintenance system. This was further developed by **Shino Shigeo**, who created the concept of zero quality control (ZQC), a means of controlling productivity by detecting, preventing, and eliminating errors in production systems. Simultaneously, the Japan Institute of Plant Management (JIPM) began a program of education on total productivity management (TPM). This culminated in the 1988 publication of an English version of a book written by a former official of the JIPM, Nakajima Seiichi, on TPM. This stimulated the growth of the movement, particularly in the United States.

The JIPM redefined and expanded its philosophy in 1989 through laying down principles, guidelines, and methods of achieving TPM as an integrated approach to manufacturing management. Its approach is empirical in the extreme and pays attention to microaspects of production management in concepts such as overall equipment effectiveness (OEE) with an achievement target of 85 percent based on an achievement calculus that links time availability of plant equipment, output compared to standard, and conformance quality of output. Highly technical steps are defined, and these are implemented by corporations in different ways according to their needs. While there is some similarity and overlap with the TQC movement, these should be clearly distinguished.

PROMISSORY NOTES. *See* TEGATA.

PUBLIC CORPORATIONS. There are over 80 special corporations (*tokushu hojin*) of which 42 are 100 percent government owned, a dozen are partly private and partly government funded, and the remainder are receivers of public funds. All are subject to government regulation in proportion to their size. Their staff are government employees but do not count as full-fledged civil servants. In the peak year of 1976, there were 113 such corporations, a number that has declined because of **privatization**, **deregulation**, and general changes in the economic structure. The corporations can be classified in various ways, but the principal categories are fairly clear according to roles.

The largest service companies in the group date to the immediate post-1945 period, when basic public services had to be restored. The **Japan National Railway Corporation**, the **Nippon Telegraph and Telephone Corporation**, and the Japan Monopoly Corporation were the leading members of the group, which was privatized between 1985 and 1987. Their stock went public, but the government still has majority holdings, a fact what merely changed the nature of government ownership.

A second group is concerned with public works–related projects and services, such as the **Japan Highway Public Corporation**, the

Japan Housing Corporation, the Japan National Oil Corporation, and the various regional development agencies.

A third group comprises small foundations with specific economic or social roles, such as the Small Business Promotion Corporation and the Japan International Cooperation Fund. These might be grouped along with the public financial corporations such as the People's Finance Corporation, the Housing Loan Corporation, and the Small Business Finance Corporation, which also have quite specific remits. The **Japan Development Bank** and the **Export-Import Bank of Japan** are in a special category of government-owned banks set up with special responsibilities.

There are numerous other types of government-owned or -controlled corporate legal persons, such as the Japan Broadcasting Corporation (**Nippon Hoso Kyokai**) and the well-known **Japan External Trade Organization** (**JETRO**), set up as a company under the control of the then **Ministry of International Trade and Industry**.

The structure of government-owned corporations is a labyrinth of complex and sometimes interrelated roles and relationships that is administratively often difficult to define but that was created to relieve pressure on certain departments of national and local government by identifying a need and creating an organization to deal with it. Because they are not part of the permanent structure, these corporations may be created or dissolved as needs dictate. The tendency of the government in the last decade of the 20th century has been to move away from all but those that fulfill a function that could not otherwise be handled.

– Q –

QUALITY CONTROL CIRCLES. Quality control circles are a feature of the **total quality control** (**TQC**) movement. They are small groups of employees who have a hands-on role in production and who meet regularly to discover and implement ways of improving processes, products, and services on an ongoing basis. They apply a variety of techniques and use staff talents to develop ability overall, to make the factory floor and the workplace in general more vital and satisfying, to improve customer satisfaction, and to make a contribution to the well-being of the **corporation** and society as a whole.

Quality control (QC) first appeared in postwar Japan as part of the overall **productivity movement**. A magazine, *Genba to QC* (the Workplace and QC), was published in 1962 to promote the formation of QC circles in the workplace. The movement spread quickly from 36 circles registered with the QC headquarters in 1963 to the huge total of 30,000 in 1984. **Lockheed** was the first American corporation to institute QC circles. By 2000, QC circle activities were to be found in over 70 countries worldwide.

QC circles are distinguished from other groups in several defining ways. Their overall goal is to develop a scientific approach to problem solving through the rational analysis of quality control principles and techniques. They aim to build teamwork through encouraging the discussion and sharing of knowledge and experience. There are numerous techniques for the implementation of these goals. The overall result is the creation of a highly motivated workforce that can raise quality and productivity, results that benefit both the corporation and society.

QC circles started in the manufacturing sector but have spread to engineering, sales, and service industries. Hospitals, banks, hotels, and department stores have their own versions of QC circles. These are less formally structured and are not built into the corporate structure in the way in which **total productivity management (TPM)** groups are formalized.

– R –

RAILWAY SYSTEM. The Japanese government laid great stress on the development of an effective passenger and freight railway system from the very start of the **modernization** process that began with the **Meiji Restoration of 1868**. The first section of track dates to 1872 and was laid under direction of engineers from Scotland, between Shimbashi (now a station in the Tokyo area on the modern Yamanote line) and Yokohama. In 1874, a similar railway link between Osaka (like Tokyo, a center of commerce) and Kobe (like Yokohama, a seaport) was established. In 1887, the link extended to the ancient capital city of Kyoto. By 1880, a railway line had been laid in the largest of the northern islands, Hokkaido, which was becoming steadily populated.

In 1882, Shimbashi was linked with Nihombashi, the first station of the old Tokkaido road traveled by merchants from Edo (the old name of Tokyo) to Osaka. Following that original route, the Tokkaido line from Shimbashi to Kobe was opened in 1889, the same year in which the Kyushu Railway Company opened its first line between Hakata and Chitosegawa. Moji and Kumamoto in Kyushu were linked in 1891. Also, 1891 saw the Nippon Railway Company open a line between Ueno, a major junction station in Tokyo, and Aomori in north Honshu. The nation's first domestically manufactured steam locomotive was built in Kobe in 1893. The Kyoto Electric Railway began running in 1895, and by 1900 the Kansai Railway Company linked Nagoya and Osaka. The Sanyo Railway Company linked Kobe and Shimononseki in 1901, and the Kobu Railway Company opened lines between Iidamachi and Nakano in 1904.

A National Railways Law was passed in 1906, and private railways were nationalized in 1907. Under government supervision, the railway system expanded and developed until the intense damaged inflicted during the bombings of World War II. The **Japan National Railway** (**JNR**) was created in 1949, and a new era of development was started. The Tokkaido line between Tokyo and Kobe was electrified in 1956, and a new high-speed train line, the Tokkaido Shinkansen, was opened between Tokyo and Osaka to mark the Olympic Games in Tokyo. Other lines followed, such as Osaka to Okayama in 1962, Okayama to Hakata in 1975, and Niigata to Omiya in 1982. The Joetsu Shinkansen from Ueno to Omiya was opened in 1989 and was expanded to link Tokyo to Ueno and Omiya to Maebashi in Gunma prefecture.

The management of such a large network was becoming exceedingly difficult, labor relations were becoming strained, and operating costs were creating heavy debts because economies could not be effected. Privatization was introduced to create six regional companies and one freight company. At the time of **privatization**, JNR owned 27,600 kilometers of track, with 345 billion passengers per kilometer and 21 billion tons of freight per kilometer. Debts were canceled, and the new **Japan Railways (JR)** system began operating. In the late 1990s, new generations of Shinkansen trains, the Nozomi, were introduced, capable of speeds up to 300 kilometers per hour. The time from Tokyo to Nagoya was reduced from two hours to one hour and 35 minutes.

JR has also been experimenting with mag-lev (magnetic levitation) technology, which would reduce the time between Nagoya and Tokyo to just over 40 minutes. Whether use and efficiency could justify the capital outlay, time alone can tell. *See also* HANKYU CORPORATION; SEIBU TETSUDO; TOBU TETSUDO; TOKYU CORPORATION.

RECESSION OF THE 1990s. This is the collective name given to a number of problems that simultaneously engulfed the Japanese economy after the bursting of the **bubble economy** in 1990. The economy began to slow down in the months leading up to the death of Emperor Showa (Hirohito) in 1989. The government and the **Liberal Democratic Party (LDP)** were somewhat overzealous in calling for a period of self-restraint (*jishoku*) during the months prior to his passing. Celebratory events were canceled, such as end-of year parties (*bonen-kai*), New Year's parties (*shinen-kai*), weddings, national days of foreign embassies, and, in general, any event that was of a lighthearted nature. Red, the color of celebration, was withdrawn from the market, including red beans. It was estimated that over 200,000 weddings were canceled and perhaps a million parties, a fact that hurt hotels, restaurants, and bars. While the immediate effects were obvious, the long-term ones were more serious. Consumer spending patterns, once changed, are difficult to reverse. Added to the drop in land prices engineered by the **Bank of Japan** to prevent further inflation, this ensured that the economy became stagnant virtually overnight. The stock market dropped from its peak of around 39,000 to a low of 14,000. While this figure grossly undervalued the economy, it shook international confidence in the yen.

The financial sector began undergoing some drastic restructuring in preparation for the deregulatory **big bang** that started in 1997. But it had also undergone numerous crises during the previous years. Major **banks** and **securities** companies failed, largely because of **nonperforming loans** that had been extended during the bubble economy. The Hyogo Bank (August 1995) was the first major bank collapse in the postwar period. In 1997, the Hokkaido Takshoku, a **city bank**, collapsed, followed by the **Long-Term Credit Bank of Japan** in 1998 and the Nippon Credit Bank. Both Sanyo Securities and **Yamaichi Securities** collapsed in 1997.

Any one of these individually could have triggered a recession. Cumulatively, they locked Japan into a long period of recession that proved resistant to normal methods of dealing with economic stagnation. While the *tankan* monitor of business sentiment displayed more positive signs in the early 21st century, the longest recession in modern Japanese history proved the most difficult to bring under control, underlining the point that while the Japanese economy has enormous resilience, it also has great areas of vulnerability.

RECRUIT SCANDAL. A 1989 insider trading scandal in which former prime ministers Nakasone Yasuhiro and Takeshita Noboru were deeply implicated through receiving under-the-counter shares in the Recruit Corporation before the issue was made public. It led to the effective end of their holding public office, and while they continued as Diet members, they were finally forced into resignation at the turn of the century by Prime Minister Koizumi Junichiro as part of a house-cleaning exercise.

RESEARCH AND DEVELOPMENT (R&D). R&D can be divided into the public and the private sector. The public sector is covered by the science and technology policy of the government, while the private is covered by **corporations**. Public expenditure is relatively small, divided between government institutes and universities, while the public sector spends much more. The total amount spent on R&D between the two sectors has been typically approximately 3 percent of gross national product.

The smallest group of researchers is the university community, in which a few prestigious universities are considered leaders in research. National Universities such as Tokyo, Kyoto, and Osaka, along with private schools such as Keio, Waseda, and Aoyama, are the main centers along with a handful of others in various fields. Compared to American universities, Japanese universities are not even ranked in R&D activities. Even the University of Tokyo Press is modest in its output alongside the presses of Harvard, Princeton, or Columbia. However, professors from top institutions often sit on government advisory panels.

Government ministries and agencies all have their own R&D programs and facilities. They generate white papers (annual reports) and vast amounts of statistical data. The **Bank of Japan** produces annual and monthly statistics (in English as well as Japanese) and the extremely important quarterly economic outlook, the Tankan. The **Economic Planning Agency** (**EPA**) produces extensive reports and analyses of various aspects of the economy, as does the **Ministry of Finance** and the former **Ministry of International Trade and Industry** (**MITI**). These organizations produce annually the most authoritative data on the economy. They are supplemented by a raft of smaller government-affiliated research institutes that have legal status and are subsidized by the government.

Private research institutes vastly outnumber the first two groups. All major banks, securities houses, industrial corporations, and trading houses have their own in-house research institutes, and many have more flexible attached think tanks (*shinku tanku*) all of which belong to an association of independent research institutes. These form a long and prestigious list, including names such as **Daiwa**, **Mitsubishi**, Nikko, **Nomura**, and ***Nikkei Shimbun***, all of which publish various kinds of reports.

The field of technology was traditionally the first to be developed dating back to the **Meiji period** (1868–1912), when the objective was to adapt foreign technology in the interest of national defense. This was the basis of the science and technology policy that was formulated during the postwar period. Once the catch-up period was over, by the 1970s, basic research became a priority. The Council for Science and Technology, formed in 1959, was the beginning of a coherent forward-looking policy on R&D, although the emphasis on acquiring foreign technology did not totally disappear.

Overviewing Japan's R&D compared with that of the United States, for example, there is less emphasis on innovative military technology as such and consequently fewer offers of government procurement orders. However, as a balancing statistic, **Matsushita** has registered 27,000 patents worldwide for new products. The most successful and effective R&D clearly belongs to the major manufacturers, whose product development is a basic part of their global strategy. Organizations such as **Toyota**, **Sony**, and **Matsushita**, to name but three, depend for success on R&D and how it can be directed to serve the needs of market research.

RESCRIPT ON EDUCATION. *See* IMPERIAL RESCRIPTS.

RESONA HOLDINGS. This is a **bank holding company** formed when the former **Daiwa Bank** underwent restructuring and merged with the **Asahi Bank** and several regional banks. Even after radical reform, the Resona Bank required in 2002 substantial and, at the time, controversial injections of public funds to maintain its viability.

REVISED BANKING ACT (1876). This was the third attempt of the **Meiji period** (1868–1912) government to set up a national **banking** system, the first two having failed for various reasons. The first was in 1863, and the second was in 1972, when the guiding concept was national banks on the U.S. model. The 1876 act was successful because capital was more readily available, principally bonds issued to **samurai** in lieu of their feudal period stipends. Banks were permitted to issue their own notes (up to 80 percent of their capital), and the notes could be converted to government paper money. For the first time, banking became profitable, and by 1879, 153 banks had been successfully capitalized.

RICE. This is traditionally the staple diet of the Japanese nation, thought to have been introduced from China, according to some agricultural scientists, possibly the Shanghai region, at least 2,000 years ago. Its introduction transformed Japan from a hunting/gathering tribal society into an agricultural one. In addition to providing a basic diet, rice came to acquire enormous religious significance, becoming central to all **Shinto** rituals, with its growth and harvesting being protected by them. Rice, salt, and water are the three universal elements found on all Shinto altars.

Much of the character of Japanese society comes from the culture of rice, which requires cooperation with others to both plant and harvest. The modern Japanese open-plan office is often likened to the rice paddy. For all these reasons, rice came to occupy a unique position in Japanese culture. It was therefore hardly surprising that the Americans encountered strong resistance to the **Structural Impediments Initiative (SII)** of the early 1990s when the question of importing California rice was raised. The enormous pressure exerted on Japan to import rice took no account of the central place of rice in Japanese religious culture. The U.S. negotiators also forgot that if Japan opened its doors to California rice, every rice-exporting country had to be treated similarly. When importing commenced, the results were barely short of chaotic. Different kinds of rice from different countries were imported and mixed in varying combinations, most of which proved unpopular with consumers. Those who put pressure on Japan failed also to recognize the distinctive character and taste of Japanese rice when compared to the drier rices of East Asia. This finally doomed the proposal because of a lack of cultural sensitivity and ignorance. The last nail in the coffin was consumer taste, which expressed a clear preference for Japanese rice. *See also* SAKE.

RINGI-SEIDO. This is a central part of the internal communications system of organizations and **corporations** that functions as a consensus-building device. *Ringi-sho* are memoranda containing proposals that normally start at a lower level and are gradually circulated upward, finally reaching the president via the various levels of **Japanese-style management** where each section head places his or her seal (*hanko*) in the box designated for it. They may also circulate horizontally among managers before moving up to the president's office. Corporate decisions are not made without this process taking place, which is one reason why responses to proposals from outside the company appear to require undue lengths of time to take shape. Prior to the actual circulation of a written document, ***nemawashi*** takes place, which is consensus building through meetings, both formal and informal after work.

The system has two great merits. One is that everyone becomes involved in the decision-making process. The other is that, if anything should go amiss, responsibility is diffused throughout the organization. Reports about domestic and international travel, special leaves of absence, promotions, transfers, and other relevant business are simultaneously approved as they circulate within the organization.

The absence of a single seal of approval stops the process and sends the proposal back for further consideration.

RITSURYO SEIDO (RITSURYO SYSTEM). This was the great systematic reform of government that was begun in the seventh century and completed in the eighth century. It covers the period when the imperial institution first began to create a rational bureaucratic system that lasted until 967 C.E., when a regency government replaced **bureaucratic** control with prerogatives of status and law based on custom.

The threat of an apparently expansionist Tang dynasty (618–907) in China compelled the Japanese to **modernize** their government. The only way it was thought possible to compete with Chinese power was to emulate it. It was basically a continuation of the implementation of Chinese moral and political values begun by **Shotoku Taishi** (574–622) in the early seventh century. The extension of the power of the central government was achieved through the creation of detailed laws and regulations that reduced local discretionary powers to a minimum.

With regard to business, the *kanshi-ryo* section of the code defined the market system within the imperial capitals. The following provisions were included. An appointed controller was responsible for quality, price, and volume of goods sold in the market. Markets were opened at noon and closed at 3.00 P.M. by three loud beats of a drum. Stalls run by men and those by women were strictly separated. Goods on sale were displayed on the *ichi-no-kura* and their names posted. Stalls were called *machi-ya*. Trading was to be peaceful, with no swords permitted in the market, even if carried by highly ranked guards.

The Sutra-Copying Office (*Shakyoji*) accounts book kept lists of goods for sale. These included textiles (silk, linen, cotton, thread, and hemp), foodstuffs, (**rice**, wheat, soybeans, red beans, salt, *miso* [soybean paste], **sake**, vegetables, seaweed, and fruits), and other miscellaneous items (firewood, charcoal, medicines, paper, brushes, and pottery).

Overarching was the **emperor system** and the court, which were expected to be moral exemplars to the people; the laws, issued as an expression of the imperial will, were to be morally educative. The basic moral stance survived the death of the system and, indeed, was continued through the **Edo period** (1615–1868), revived in the **Meiji period** (1868–1812), and still has a clear presence in the **educational** and corporate philosophy of modern Japan. *See also* CONFUCIANISM.

ROBOTICS INDUSTRY. Japan boasts the largest number of industrial robots in use in any one country, 389,442 in 2003, slightly down on the listed 402,212 in 1999. The comparative figure for the United States was 89,880. Germany had 91,184 and the United Kingdom a mere 12,344. The Japan Robot Association was formed in March 1971 under the name Industrial Robot Coversazione. It became the Japan Industrial Robot Association in October 1972 and changed its name to its present one in 1994 to cover both industrial and nonindustrial robots, such as "personal robots."

In keeping with Japanese corporate culture, the association states its goals as to encourage the **research and development** of robots and associated system products and to promote the use of robot technology. This is part of a wider remit to promote the use of advanced technology in industry and to enhance the welfare of the nation, contributing to healthy economic growth and improved living standards.

While the language employed may sound frivolous to some, a brief inspection of the leading member companies will confirm the seriousness of the Association. These include, along with new robotics corporations, formidable organizations, such as **Denso**, **Fuji Electric**, **Fuji Heavy Industries**, **Fujitsu**, **Hitachi**, **Ishikawajima-Harima Heavy Industries**, **Kawasaki Heavy Industries**, **Kawasaki Steel**, **Kobe Steel**, **Matsushita Electric**, **Mitsibishu Electric**, **Mitsubishi Heavy Industries**, **Omron**, **Sony**, **Toshiba**, **Toyota**, and **Yamaha**.

The automation of Japanese industry has a long history, and the development of industrial robots is equally long, with Omron being a notable early pioneer. The **automobile industry** was probably one of the first to introduce them on a large scale in manufacturing, as a visit to any production line will quickly confirm. Some Japanese corporations have become fascinated by the idea of robot technology for nonindustrial purposes, and leading manufacturers such as Sony regularly introduce robots of various kinds, ranging from ones that perform household functions to ones that entertain. This has led them further into the field of artificial intelligence, which also seems to hold great fascination.

One question that observers have raised is the definition of an industrial robot. Japanese have tended to classify any kind of automation as a robot, which could include automated ticket vendors. This broader definition would slightly increase the number in use in other countries, but there is no doubt that even automated technology by itself, robotic or not, is more widely in use in Japan than elsewhere and that the robotics industry in Japan is set for even more imaginative applications.

RONIN. Traditionally the term referred to masterless **samurai**, a warrior whose master had been killed or who had himself been disgraced. He was therefore a wanderer either for life or until he could find someone to serve. Modern society uses the name for high school students who fail to enter a university and will try again a year later or for either people who are selective in their occupational preference and therefore may choose to remain unemployed or college graduates who miss the April hiring for their graduating year and will attempt the corporate examinations the following year.

– S –

SADO MINES. Gold and precious metals mine near Aikawa village on the island of Sado, dating to the 16th century and currently managed by **Mitsubishi Kinzoku**. Intensive mining started in 1601, with production rising to between almost 70 to 100 tons of gold and silver per year between 1618 and 1627, making a major contribution to the **Tokugawa government** in the 17th and again for a period in the 18th century. After the **Meiji Restoration of 1868**, it was taken over by the new government but eventually handed over to the Mitsubishi organization in 1896.

SAKE. Japanese **rice** wine, the nation's traditional alcoholic beverage used not only when dining but also in **Shinto** rituals, making rice itself a religious and culturally sensitive commodity. According to the Sake Brewer's Association, it has a history of 2,000 years, a long time within which to develop a mature industry. There are over 10,000 brands on sale in Japan, all coming from different regions where differences in soil and water and subtleties in manufacturing technique are reflected in taste and texture. While popular brand names such as Ozeki exist, the higher-graded varieties tend to be produced in smaller amounts, and some makers sell sake by the barrel (*taru*). *Taru-zake*, as it is called, is less refined but rich in taste when drunk from a small square wooden cup called a *masu*, made of *hinoki* (Japanese cypress) with its distinctive fragrance. The unique character of sake culture can be experienced at New Year or some celebratory event such as an anniversary or the completion of a construction project. The **Strategic Impediments Initiative** (**SII**) also failed to recognize the role of rice in sake brewing and the hostility of the 2,000 sake brewers that lay in the background of the rice question.

SAKOKU JIDAI. Period of the closed country from 1633 to the mid-1850s when Japanese were not permitted to leave and foreigners were not permitted to enter the country. It was severely enforced in a 1635 document that placed an absolute prohibition on any voyage abroad (*Kaigai toko kinshi rei*). However, the government eventually became lax in the enforcement of the law, permitting castaways to return within five years and permitting travel to the Ryukyu islands (now Okinawa), which had come under the jurisdiction of the *daimyo* (lord) of Kagoshima after 1609 and Pusan in Korea. Some **Dutch trade** was permitted in Nagasaki, which became a source of Dutch learning known as Rangaku. These exceptions aside, Japan remained remarkably isolated from the rest of the world and free from foreign influence until the collapse of the Tokugawa shogunate in 1867. *See also* KUROFUNE.

SAKUMA SHOZAN (1811–1864). He was a distinguished and farseeing late **Edo period** (1615–1868) intellectual of the **samurai** class who took the threat of the Western powers seriously long before Commodore Matthew Perry and the black ships (***kurofune***) had appeared. After study and reflection, he concluded that the Japanese had to see the West at firsthand, a policy not implemented until after the **Meiji Restoration of 1868**, when the Iwakura Mission was dispatched with precisely that objective. Sakukma was appointed adviser to the shogunate and was sent to Kyoto, where he was assassinated by radicals of the *Sonno joi* ("Revere the Emperor, Expel the Barbarians") movement. He is remembered for his criticism of the shortsightedness of the government and his attempts to prepare it for the changes that were to come.

SAKURA BANK. Founded as the **Mitsui Bank** in 1876, it merged in 1990 with the Taiyo-Kobe Bank, itself a merger of the Taiyo Bank and the Kobe Bank dating to 1973. The name Sakura (cherry blossom) was adopted in 1992. It remained, as it began, the principal **bank** of the **Mitsui Group**, until it merged with the **Sumitomo Bank** in 2001 to become the **Sumitomo Mitsui Banking Corporation**.

SAMURAI. Formally referred to as ***bushi***, they were the warrior class of the **Edo period** (1616–1876) **Tokugawa feudal system**. Initially powerful supporters of the regime, their status eroded over the years as the merchant class, the lowest of the four ranks (***shi-no-ko-sho***) of warriors, farmers, artisans, and merchants, gradually became the most influential. The warrior code, *bushido*, governed their conduct until its social relevance and that of the laws governing the warrior houses (***Bukeho***) ceased to exist.

After the **Meiji Restoration of 1868** signaled the beginning of the **Meiji period** (1868–1912), many samurai joined the newly formed imperial army, while others continued to fight for the regional domains until they were finally crushed. Once the struggles had ended, some remained as soldiers, while others took up civilian occupations, including opening barber shops or similar businesses.

SAMURAI BONDS. Yen-denominated debentures issued in Japan by nonresident organizations. The Asian Development Bank began issuing them in 1970 and the World Bank in 1971. During the 1970s, the market was restricted to **foreign corporations** and other nongovernmental organizations that had credit ratings of single-A. After August 1992, market access was eased to cover institutions with BB-plus or BBB ratings. Some European governments, such as that of Hungary, began issuing bonds, and many of these were bought by Japanese investors because of the low interest rates in Japan. Euroyen bonds are the principal competitor in debt financing, exceeding the ***daimyo* bonds** eight times in volume. *See also* SHOGUN BONDS.

SANKIN-KOTAI. The required alternate-year residence system of *daimyo* (domainal lord) during the **Edo period** (1615–1868) by order of the **shogun**. While they were back in their domain, their families remained in the family's Edo residence, in effect as hostages, guaranteeing the good behavior of the *daimyo*. Their trips to Edo, actually vast processions, did much to encourage trade and commerce en route.

SANKO STEAMSHIP. Sanko Kiksen is a major maritime transport company founded in 1934 that eventually developed into one of the world's largest tanker operators. When the government issued a plan to consolidate the **shipping industry** in 1964, Sanko Kisen plotted its own course and, in defiance of trends, expanded its operations. The company also buys and sells securities and ships and has affiliates in Hong Kong, Singapore, Amsterdam, and New York. The head office is in Osaka.

SANWA BANK. Founded in 1933 as a merger of the Konoike Bank, the Yamaguchi Bank, and the Sanushi Bank, it became the central **bank** of the Sanwa Group (***keiretsu***). Its headquarters are in Tokyo. It joined with the **Tokai Bank** and the **Toyo Trust** to form a joint **holding company** on 2 April 2001, called the **UFJ Holding Company**. It merged with the Tokai Bank to form the **UFJ Bank** on 15 January 2002.

SAN'YO ELECTRIC. Founded by Inoue Toshio in 1947 as San'yo Denki Seisakusho to manufacture bicycle lamps, the company became San'yo Electric Co, Ltd, in 1950. It was the first Japanese **electronics** manufacturer to produce radios in plastic casings. In 1953, the company introduced the whirlpool-action washing machine, an innovation that sparked the household appliance boom symbolized by the washing machine, the refrigerator, and eventually the air conditioner. When the company began making television sets, it had become a comprehensive manufacturer of household electronic goods.

It expanded overseas and created 28 facilities in 19 countries, and with the decrease in sales due to a saturated market, San'yo started research in the field of information processing and energy-linked technologies. It also started working in several new fields, including Hi-Vision technology. It began to experience difficulties caused by massive losses during fiscal years 2004–2005; as a result, the board appointed, in April 2005, a 50-year-old former woman journalist as president on the grounds that she had a better grasp of the consumer mind than the board members. The head office is in Moriguchi City, Osaka prefecture.

SAN YO-KOKUSAKU PULP. A manufacturer of paper, pulp, construction materials, and chemical products formed in 1970 by the merger of the San'yo Pulp and Kokusaku Pulp. It became the largest manufacturer of printing and writing paper in the country with several international tie-ups in various parts of the world. The head office is in Tokyo.

SAPPORO BEER. This is Japan's oldest beer, famous for its red Polaris star logo, which first appeared in 1876. It is brewed by Nakagawa Seibi on the Bavarian beer model. **Shibusawa Eiichi** and **Okura Kihachiro** acquired the brewery and formed the Sapporo Beer Company, which merged in 1906 with Osaka Breweries to form Dainihon Beer Ltd. This was broken up in 1949 into **Asahi Breweries Ltd** and Nihon Breweries Ltd. In 1956, Sapporo Beer was revived, and in 1964, Nihon Breweries became Sapporo Breweries Ltd. The company is now known as Sapporo Holdings Ltd and has third spot in the Japanese market.

SARAKIN. Meaning cash for salaried workers from the combination of "*sara*" from "salaryman" and "*kin*" from the Chinese character for gold or money. *Sarakin*, usually referred to as loan sharks, were consumer finance companies that grew up in the late 1970s, in the very early days of **consumer credit finance**. Their activities were highly publicized, principally because of their exorbitant interest rates and the number of incidents of violence and even **suicide** that resulted from their dubious debt-collection methods. Links with ***yakuza*** groups added to their image as underworld-linked corporations. The protracted **recession of the 1990s** and the consequent low interest rates weakened their business on top of more strict government regulation of their activities.

SECURITIES EXCHANGE LAW. The Shoken torihiki ho was passed in 1948 to protect investors by legal regulation of the issuance and trading of securities. It was modeled on the U.S. Securities Act of 1933 and the Securities Exchange Act of 1934. The Japanese law covers only stocks, convertible bonds, and unsecured bonds. Until 1952, a Securities Exchange Commission supervised the process, after which the role was transferred to the **Ministry of Finance**, which has a Securities Bureau that actually conducts the supervision. The procedures to be observed when a **corporation** issues stocks or bonds are stated in the **Commercial Code**, which is under the Ministry of Justice. *See also* CAPITAL MARKETS IN JAPAN; DAIMYO BONDS; MONEY MARKETS; SAMURAI BONDS; SHOGUN BONDS.

SECURITIES INDUSTRY. The industry can be divided into three broad sectors. The two principal ones are, first, the stock business, of which over 65 percent is conducted through brokerages, with the rest being handled by investors themselves. There is also the bond business, in which securities companies underwrite and distribute new issues of bonds as well as trading in already existing issues. Around 60 percent of all bond trading is in the ***gensaki*** market, or the sale of bonds with a buy-back agreement. There was an enormous issue of government bonds in 1975 that had the effect of increasing the bond market on a huge scale. **Internationalization** of the securities market also resulted in the increase of the underwriting of Japanese corporate bonds issued on foreign markets. Finally, there are other lines of business that include transactions involving a variety of instruments, such as domestic certificates of deposit (CDs), yen-denominated banker's acceptance, commercial papers (CPs) issued on the domestic market, land- and mortgage-backed securities, and both CDs and CPs issues on foreign markets. This sector also includes investment trust business.

The business was dominated by the big four, **Nomura**, **Daiwa**, Nikko, and **Yamaichi**, which collapsed in 1997, leaving only three major players. The 10 second-tier companies were Kokusai, Wako, Okasan, New Japan, Kankaku, Cosmo, Tokyo, Yamatane, Dai-ichi, and Sanyo, which collapsed in 1997, reducing the 10 to nine.

While the **Securities Exchange Law** exists, it has never prevented practices that would be considered elsewhere as at least unethical, if not illegal. One of these is compensating large corporate investors for losses at the expense of small investors through the manipulation of funds held in *eigyo tokkin* (special sales capital), or accounts held by securities accounts on behalf of big investors. Some of the funds handled were traced back to ***yakuza***, or organized criminal gangs. Insider trading is also against the law, but the first prosecutions did not take place until 1990.

Financial deregulation from 1993 began to break down the strict separation of **banking** and **securities** business. This also permitted some **foreign companies** to become more active in Japan's markets. When Yamaichi collapsed, Merrill Lynch Capital International Management took over 30 percent of the Yamaichi branches and 2,000 former staff to run them. In 1998, Travelers Group took a 25 percent stake in Nikko Securities. The **Daiwa** scandal in New York indicated just how loosely Japanese financial sector corporations were managed. *See also* CAPITAL MARKETS; CROSS SHAREHOLDING; MONEY MARKETS; SECURITIES EXCHANGE LAW; STOCK EXCHANGES.

SEIBO. Formally referred to as *oseibo*, these are end-of-year gifts exchanged between people and organizations. *See also* GIFT-GIVING CULTURE.

SEIBU DEPARTMENT STORES. Seibu Hyakkaten is a major **department store** chain whose flagship is located in Ikebukuro, Tokyo. It has nine branch stores in the Kanto district. The Musashino Railway Company opened the store in 1940. It was originally named after the **railway**, but when the railway became Seibu Tetsudo, the store name was changed in 1949. In 1956, a chain of supermarkets was created, originally Seibu Stores, Ltd, but later renamed **Seiyu Stores**. It expanded further into shopping precincts, working through its subsidiary Parco Com. It has six overseas subsidiaries and has affiliations with 45 foreign corporations. See also SEIBU-SAISON GROUP; SEIBU TETSUDO.

SEIBU RAILWAY. Seibu Tetsudo was founded originally as Musashino Tetsudo in 1912. It began services from 1915 on a 43.8-kilometer route through the northwest of Tokyo, from Ikebukuro to Hanno City in Saitama prefecture. After World War II, it began to acquire other lines and became Seibu Tetsudo in 1946. It electrified its lines, and by 1982 it had two main lines (from Ikebukuro Station and from Shinjuku Station), 10 branch lines, and 178.2 kilometers of track. The **railway** transports around 2 million passengers per day. It became the center of a scandal involving the **Tsutsumi** Yoshiaki, leading to his downfall in 2004. Its headquarters are in Tokyo.

SEIBU-SAISON GROUP. Founded by Tsutsumi Yasujiro (1964), the enterprise comprises **departments stores**, a **railway** system (**Seibu Railway**), and a wide range of consumer services that divided between his two sons, Seiji and Yoshiaki. There are around 100 companies in the group. Seiji's main interest was the department store and retail businesses, which he expanded to include Family Mart, Loft, and Parco sales outlets. Yoshiaki managed the railroad and subsequently ventured into sports, making the Lions Baseball team a Seibu member. Saison provided consumer credit in the late 1970s, at a time when credit cards were still a novelty in Japan. In a famous poster advertisement of the mid-1970s, the Seibu Group depicted a nuclear family, with one child, declaring that Japanese consumers wished to protect their livelihood through material and spiritual satisfaction. In this respect, it can be considered a key **corporation** whose influence helped to serve as well as define consumer needs in the last quarter of the 20th century.

Like many retail organizations, the **bubble economy** affected Seibu Department Stores, which were forced to undergo corporate rehabilitation. Its capital dropped to ¥1.7 billion after the collapse of Seiyo Kankyo Kaihatsu, a Saison Group real estate company, in February 2002. Early in 2003, the company issued a proposal to ask shareholders, including Seiyu and Credit Saison as well as the Saison Group, to reduce its capital by over 50 percent. This was to permit the company to liquidate without court protection according to rules drawn up by the Japan Bankers Association. The restructuring was to be supervised by the **Mizuho** Corporate Bank. *See also* TSUTSUMI FAMILY.

SEISHIN SHUYO. This is a distinctively Japanese character-building process that is intended to cultivate group harmony. It teaches self-discipline that accepts the deferment of gratification, physical hardship even when sick, **loyalty** to the group (organization or **corporation**) above all else, self-sacrifice when necessary, and unlimited commitment to work. New employees have this instilled into them by being taught when they join as well as seeing it in their managers' behavior. The main point of contrast with Western styles of management is that the basis of **group dynamics** is derived from the belief that the fate of the corporation is the direct result of staff and worker effort rather than by examining external factors. The employees, however, if the company is successful, expect to share in the benefits of success. Loyalty, benevolence, and self-interest are not mutually exclusive. *See also* AMAE; GIRI-JINJO; JAPANESE-STYLE MANAGEMENT; SEMPAI/KOHAI.

SEIYU STORES. Originally part of the **Seibu Department Stores**, Seiyu became independent in 1956 and functions as part of the Seibu **distribution** network, particularly in Tokyo, although the Seiyu Supermarket chain exists nationwide. It established business links with companies in the United States, Hong Kong, Beijing, London, and Paris. At its peak, Seiyu operated 226 stores. Management problems in the late 1990s imposed the need for drastic restructuring. Wal-Mart of the United States bought a controlling interest in the group with a view to applying its own formula of mass buying on a global scale to keep prices lower than all other competitors. Whether or not Wal-Mart's methods will work remains to be seen. At the time, Seiyu's labor and administration costs absorbed 26 percent of income from sales as against Wal-Mart's 16 percent. Wal-Mart, however, was simultaneously under attack in the United States for dubious labor practices that almost certainly could not be implemented in Japan. Some analysts have argued that Wal-Mart's pricing policy and profitability cannot be sustained in the long run, raising the intriguing question of whether the world's largest retailer could be successful in Japan. *See also* FOREIGN BUSINESSES; MERGERS AND ACQUISITIONS.

SEKISEN. These were tolls collected at ***sekisho*** in the form of **rice** to provide payment for the guards or for the upkeep of state-supported temples from the **Heian period** (794–1185) on.

SEKISHO. These were checkpoint toll gates for the inspection of goods and travelers. By the mid-**Heian period** (794–1185), the earlier system of military checkpoints had all but collapsed. The estate owners of the **Muromachi period** (ca. 1333–1568) established these in order to collect **taxes** or goods in lieu thereof to compensate for deficits in estate finances. Although they were abolished by **Oda Nobunaga** and **Toyotomi Hideyoshi**, they were restored by **Tokugawa Ieyasu** during the **Edo period** (1615–1868) in order to restrict freedom of movement and to keep the population under rigid controls. *See also* SEKISEN.

SEKISUI CHEMICALS. Sekisui Kagaku Kogyo was founded in 1947 by seven employees of Nippon Chisso Fertilizer. It started the production of plastic goods using the nation's first automatic injection molding machine. In 1949, it opened a factory in Osaka that concentrated on industrial components and consumer products made of vinyl-related resins, from which the company grew into the nation's top-ranked producer of synthetic resins and unit prefabricated homes. It then expanded through a nationwide network of production subsidiaries—Sekisui Rein, Sekisui Kasehin Industries, and eventually **Sekisui House**—in 1960. The company has a close affiliation with the **Asahi Chemical Industry**, which grew out of the same corporation as Sekisui. It has 20 overseas affiliates and **joint ventures** supervised from Hong Kong. The head office remains in Osaka.

SEMICONDUCTOR INDUSTRY. The manufacture of electronic devices and components, including semiconductors, liquid crystal displays (LCDs), and related parts, is the largest segment of the **electronics industry** in Japan. The various projects undertaken during the 1960s and 1970s within the **computer industry** were designed to help Japanese makers catch up with the United States and **IBM** in particular. Central to this was the development of a successful semiconductor industry. Japanese makers focused on memory semiconductors for use in calculators and watches. Government policies were set in place to obstruct foreign firms and enable Japanese makers to develop new products.

The industry became a source of international dispute, and it required an agreement between the governments of Japan and the

United States, signed first in 1986 and again in 1991, to deal with the problem. Japan agreed that as from 1 August for five years, the government would promote the foreign share of the Japanese market to more than 20 percent by December 1992. In order to prevent dumping, which started the dispute in the first place, all semiconductor makers would collect cost and price information and give them to U.S. officials if an antidumping investigation was required. It was further agreed that to prevent dumping in third markets, both governments would cooperate with the **General Agreement on Tariffs and Trade** (**GATT**) if allegations were made.

There was a great deal of argument in the early 1990s about the capacity of foreign firms to supply 20 percent of the Japanese market, leaving to one side the question of their adaptability to Japanese needs. The growing European Union was next to complain, insisting that the Japan–U.S. agreement was discriminatory against European manufacturers. By 1996, the year in which the agreement was due for renewal, foreign products accounted for 27.5 percent of the Japanese market. Consequently, when the 1991 agreement was updated in 1996, the Japanese argued that numerical targets were no longer necessary. The agreement had two main provisions. One was the formation of a Global Government Forum of countries with semiconductor industries to look at the global semiconductor market with reference to market access and intellectual property rights. A Japanese Semiconductor Council was created to monitor the industry as a whole and would invite other countries to join if they abolished tariffs on semiconductors.

SENIORITY SYSTEM. *See* NENKO JORETSU.

SENJU WOOLEN MILL. This was Japan's first woolen mill established by the government of the early **Meiji period** (1868–1912) in the Senju district of Tokyo in 1879. Using imported German technology, it was intended to serve as a model for the expanding private sector. In 1881, its administration was transferred from the Ministry of Home Affairs to the Ministry of Agriculture and Commerce and later to the Army Ministry in 1888 for the production of military uniforms and other woolen goods. It survived as the major manufacturer of woolen textiles until the early 20th century. *See also* MODERNIZATION; TEXTILE INDUSTRY.

SEVEN-ELEVEN. *See* KONBINI (CONVENIENCE STORES).

SEXUAL HARASSMENT. *Seku-hara*, as it is referred to in Japanese, is one form of discrimination against **women** that is addressed in the **Equal Opportunity Employment Law** of 1986 in its revised form of 1997. That the problem appears so widespread is due in part to the traditions of a male-dominated society in which roles and behavior are determined. Surveys have shown that up to 60 percent of groups of women polled have experienced harassment. The academic world was the first to experience public exposure of the problem when a professor from Aoyama Gakuin University was imprisoned in the early 1970s for forcing sexual favors from a student in return for a passing grade. The publicity the case received brought other instances to light where the traditional lines of relationship between professor and student had been transgressed.

The corporate world was slower, but problems with Japanese corporations abroad that were dealt with according to local law made the whole subject of Japanese behavior abroad controversial. Congressional hearings in 1991 in the United States marked the beginning of the challenge. While welcoming Japanese **investment** in the United States, the chairman of the hearings stated that no violation of the law would be tolerated. The notorious case of the lawsuit brought against the **Mitsubishi Motor Corporation** in 1996 was a timely reminder that the kind of male-chauvinist outlook that was tolerated in Japan was quite unacceptable outside of Japan. While the Ministry of Education has issued strict guidelines to schools and colleges, the corporate world has still a long way to go before its response can be called satisfactory.

SHARP CORPORATION. The company was founded as the Hayakawa Electric Industry Co. in 1915 by **Hayakawa Tokuji** (1895–1981). The entire facility was destroyed in the Kanto earthquake of 1923, after which he moved to Osaka and established Hayakawa Metal Works. He built a crystal radio set in 1925, launching the company as an **electronics** manufacturer. He remained president until 1970. The board decided to rename the company Sharp Corporation in honor of his first invention, the mechanical "ever-sharp" propelling pencil.

SHIBUSAWA EIICHI (1840–1931). He was a **Meiji period** (1868–1912) entrepreneur, financier, and business leader, born in a district of what is now Saitama prefecture, north of Tokyo. Although coming from a long line of small farmers, his father became wealthy through dealing in indigo, which enabled him to give his son a good education. Shibusawa's early teenage years were lived during the traumatic period when Commodore Matthew Perry and the black ships (***kurofune***) arrived in 1853, an event that helped to bring about the end of the **Edo period** (1615–1868), ushering in the era of **modernization**. Shibusawa was ambitious and was critical of the rigidity of the **Tokugawa feudal system**. However, he took up a post in the Hitotsubashi family, which was related to the House of Tokugawa. In 1867, he was delegated to assist the shogun's younger brother, who was leader of the Japanese delegation to the Paris International Exhibition of that year. Shibusawa was stunned by what he saw and returned home full of ideas about transplanting Western industry into Japan. Although a member of a discredited and failed regime, his experience in France translated into expertise in Western civilization, giving him perceived value to the new Meiji government. He received financial support from the government to form a trading company, Shoho Kaisho, one of Japan's first **joint-stock companies**. In 1869, he was appointed an official in the **Ministry of Finance**. He was instrumental in forming the **Tomioka Silk-Reeling Mill** in 1872.

Shibusawa left the Ministry of Finance at the rank of assistant to the vice minister in 1873 to devote more time to his work as the first president of the Dai-ichi Bank (which later became the **Dai-ichi Kangyo Bank** and subsequently the **Mizuho Bank**), created with the cooperation of the **Mitsui** house. He was also president of **Oji Paper**.

His next major venture was the formation in 1882 of the **Osaka Spinning Mill**, which he capitalized through the help of leading businessmen and the former *daimyo* (lord). The company was remarkably successful, actually turning a profit in its first year of operation. Between 1886 and 1890, Shibusawa's enterprise became a model for many new companies being established nationwide. At that time, he himself became involved in 36 new ventures, one of which was another "first," namely, the Tokyo Chemical Fertilizer Company. Between 1895 and 1897, he was involved in the creation of a further 23, and by the end of this life, this number had risen to over 300.

Shibusawa as a man was charitable, motivated by a deep sense of values derived from **Confucianism** but influenced also by Christianity. His ultimate desire was to serve the well-being of the nation and its people, and while he was successful to a remarkable degree, his moral values did not deteriorate in the process. He also founded schools and homes for the needy and the aged.

He was also international in outlook and sensed the growing importance of Japan–U.S. relations, which he tried to foster in the early years of the 20th century. He lived through the **Taisho period** (1912–1926) and died in the early years of the **Showa period** (1926–1989) as one of the great servants, benefactors, and nation makers of modern Japan. *See also* JITSUGYOKA.

SHIBUSAWA KEIZO (1896–1963). He was a grandson of **Shibusawa Eiichi** (1840–1931) who was born in Tokyo and who graduated from the University of Tokyo. His business career began in the Yokohama Specie Bank (later the **Bank of Tokyo**) and the Dai-Ichi Bank (later the **Dai-ichi Kangyo Bank**), of which his grandfather had been the first president. He became head of the **Bank of Japan** in 1944 and served as minister of finance from 1945 to 1946. Initially, he was debarred from public office by the **Supreme Commander Allied Powers (SCAP)**, but once the restriction had been limited, he became president of **Kokusai Denshin Denwa** and chairman of Nippon Cultural Broadcasting.

SHICHI. This is a traditional term used to refer to various kinds of collateral used to secure loans. Provisions in the **Ritsuryo Seido** of the seventh century, unrepaid loans resulted in the forfeit of the *shichi*, which was then sold to cover the debt. During the **Kamakura period** (1185–1333) and **Muromachi period** (1333–1568), the concept was refined into *irejichi* (pawned security, referring to movable property) and *kenjichi* (mortgaged security, referring to estates or lands). The use of a *hitojichi* (a hostage) as collateral was common practice.

During the **Edo period** (1615–1868), similar usage continued with pawnshops (*doso*, or *kuramoto*) as in the two previous periods, handling all transactions. *Shichiboko* (labor as collateral), in effect using people as security, was common, with houses and farmlands also being offered. In keeping with the aspirations of Japan's **modernization** drive of the **Meiji period** (1868–1912), human collateral was banned, and regulations covering such matters were built into the 1898 civil code. The term *shichi* remains in use to refer to pawnbroking. More commonly, **banks** use the term *tampo* to refer to collateral needed to secure a loan.

SHICHIBUKIN TSUMITATE. Meaning literally "seven tenths of total cash reserves," the term was invented by a senior government official of Edo (modern Tokyo) in 1791, Matsudaira Sadanobu, as an emergency reserve fund to cover income shortfalls. After careful study of public finances between 1785 and 1789, he implemented a policy to reduce annual expenses by 10 percent. One-tenth was designated for unallocated expenses, and two-tenths were refunded to merchants and landlords. The remaining seven-tenths were in the hands of the Edo Machikaisho (office of town affairs) for emergency use, usually the purchase of rice. Some of the money was lent to low-income borrowers at nominal rates of interest. The business acumen behind the plan resulted in growing surpluses. The people of Edo were actually fed from this fund during the Tempo Famine of 1833 to 1836. After 1868, in the early **Meiji period** (1868–1912), the accumulated reserves were almost 1.5 million *ryo*, which permitted the erection of new public buildings and welfare facilities, initially supervised by **Shibusawa Eiichi** (1840–1931), one of the leading entrepreneurs of the period. This is one of many examples of the ways in which institutions, technologies, and even business practices of the **Edo period** (1615–1868) provided foundations for the modernization process following the **Meiji Restoration of 1868**.

SHIMADA-KE. The house of Shimada, one of the great **Edo period** (1615–1868) merchant houses, along with **Ono**, that failed to make the transition to the modern age, unlike **Mitsui** or **Sumitomo**, which were able to become key institutions in modern Japan. *See also* OSAKA MERCHANT HOUSES.

SHIMIZU CORPORATION. Shimizu Kensetsu was founded in 1804 during the **Edo period** (1615–1868) and is one of the big five

construction companies in Japan. It built the Tsukiji Hotel, one of Tokyo's first Western-style buildings, in 1868. It works in the field of high-rise buildings and has constructed atomic power facilities and other energy-related projects. It also became involved in environmental concerns and in forestry as well as entering the space industry along with its major competitors. It has a total of 18 offices, including seven international subsidiaries. The head office is in Tokyo.

SHIMONAKA YASABURO (1878–1961). He was the founder of **Heibonsha**, an academic publishing house set up in 1914. He was also an educator and founded Japan's first teachers union. He was considered by the **Supreme Commander Allied Powers** (**SCAP**) an ultranationalist and could not return to Heibonsha until 1951, thereafter publishing several encyclopedias, confirming the company's reputation as a publisher of authoritative reference works.

SHIN-ETSU CHEMICALS. Shin-Etsu Kagaku Kogyo was formed in Nagano prefecture by the Kosaka family in 1926 to produce nitrolime and carbides. After 1945, it moved into plastics and silicone resins for **semiconductors**. It is known for its advanced technology for the production of synthetic resins and electronics related materials. The company has joint ventures in Europe, South America, and the United States. The headquarters are in Tokyo.

SHINGO SHIGEO (1909–1990). He was the famous production management expert in **Toyota Motor Corporation** and inventor of zero quality control (ZQC), a concept based on preventing errors in the production process or detecting them and eliminating them immediately through source inspection and the *Poka-yoke* system. Various devices were installed to provide blocks or checks that highlight problems before damage can be done. He also developed the single-minute exchange of die (SMED) technique, which enabled faster changes to be made in production lines. He taught his techniques in a seminar in 1986 at Ford's Van Dyke plant, where he helped management reduce die exchange time from five hours to two and a half minutes.

SHINKI-HATTO EDICT. An ordinance issued by Shogun Yoshimune (r. 1716–1745) during the decadence of the **Genroku period**

(1688–1703) in an attempt to recall **Edo period** (1615–1868) society to sterner virtues and higher values. He condemned the unnecessary lavishness, particularly in dress and lifestyle, of the rising merchant class. He judged it as social decline and inappropriate in a society that was expected to embrace the frugal and dutiful disposition of the **samurai** class. In reality it was a reaction to the changes in the economic system that were beginning to show as the merchant class started asserting itself on the basis of its growing wealth. In spite of the edict, society continued to evolve, and by the late 18th century, merchants were carrying swords, a privilege hitherto confined to the warrior class. *See also* SHI-NO-KO-SHO.

SHI-NO-KO-SHO. This term describes the **Edo period** (1615–1868) social structure of warriors, farmers, artisans, and merchants that formed the hierarchy of society with the military houses in a predominant position. By the end of the Edo period, while the hierarchy remained the same, the distribution of wealth had become reversed, with the merchants being rich and the warrior class, by comparison, impoverished and demoralized.

SHINTO. This is the oldest and indigenous religious tradition of Japan based on the culture of **rice** and practicing reverence for nature as a divine source of energy through ***kami*** and belief in the value of purity. Its rituals follow the cycle of the agricultural year and are performed in the nation's 100,00 shrines found all over the country. Most famous are the Grand Shrines of Ise, with their imperial connections, and most controversial is the Yasukuni Jinja in Kudanshita, Tokyo, enshrining almost 3 million war dead. Visits by Japanese prime ministers have provoked angry responses from Asian neighbors who still see it as a symbol of Japanese militarism almost 60 years after the abolition of state Shinto in 1945.

SHIONOGI PHARMACEUTICALS. Shiomnogi Seiyaku was initially founded as a drug wholesaler in 1878 by Shiono Gisaburo in Osaka. The company now manufactures, distributes, exports, and imports **pharmaceuticals**, industrial and agricultural chemicals, veterinary drugs, and cosmetics. The present name dates to 1943. It also manufactures under license a variety of products from internationally well-known pharmaceutical companies, and its own **research-and-development** laboratories have been successful in creating a variety of valuable and innovative drugs, including antibiotics and anti-inflammatory analgesics. It has three overseas subsidiaries. Its headquarters remain where it was founded, in Osaka.

SHIPBUILDING INDUSTRY. From modest beginnings in the **Meiji period** (1868–1912), the industry expanded steadily until, by 1956, Japan had overtaken the then world leader, the United Kingdom, and from there moved up the table in gross tonnage until, by 1980, it was producing half of the world's ships. Before **modernization**, for an island nation, the government of the **Edo period** (1615–1868) had little understanding of the importance of shipbuilding, primarily because of the closed-nation policy (***sakoku***). The year in which Commodore Matthew Perry and the black ships (***kurofune***) arrived, the legal prohibition on building large ships was lifted, and shipyards were created at Uraga and Ishikawajima. Naval engineers were hired from France and the Netherlands, and a naval academy was established in 1855 under Dutch management. The first Western-style ship was built in 1853 and a steamship in 1866.

It was not until the Meiji government took over the shipyards that serious investment in the new industry began in the **Yokosuka Shipyards**, the **Nagasaki Shipyards**, and the **Hyogo Shipyards**. Yokosuka remained under government control, but the others were sold to private enterprise. The government then passed two laws in 1896: the Law to Promote Shipbuilding (*Zosen Shorei Ho*), which offered subsidies for ships of over 700 tons, the amount increasing with size, and the Law to Promote Shipping (*Kokai Shorei Ho*), which offered ships of over 1,000 tons a subsidy measured per mile of voyage. Between 1897 and 1914, three-quarters of all government subsidies went on these two laws, indicating how important the government considered both industries. Thereafter, shipbuilding was affected by world economic conditions, and it was not until after 1945, in the wake of postwar reconstruction, that it began to develop into a world-class industry.

The 1973 oil crisis, appreciation of the yen, and excess capacity worldwide forced the shrinkage of the industry, whose output dropped over 60 percent between 1983 and 1989. In a bid to rationalize the situation, the Ministry of Transport began to intervene with various suggestions. In the end, 44 companies left the industry, and the remainder were organized into an "eight group system," each group centered on one major shipbuilder. **Mitsubishi Heavy Industries**, **Mitsui Zosen**, **Hitachi Zosen**, **Sumitomo Heavy Industries**, **Kawasaki Heavy Industries**, Tokoishi Zosen (now merged with the **Mitsui group**), and Sasebo Heavy Industries remain the leading corporations. Fortunately for Japan, marine transport experienced a revival, many older ships needed replacement, and there was a need for more new-generation deep-draught tankers and containers, faster ships, and liners. This has enabled the streamlined industry to maintain its viability, given that near neighbors China and Korea are beginning to occupy the place that Japan captured between 1956 and 1973. *See also* SHIPPING INDUSTRY.

SHIPPING INDUSTRY. For a nation heavily dependent on international **trade**, a strong maritime transport industry has always been a necessity. However, high labor costs and other government regulations, such as requiring companies to hire only Japanese crew members, have forced several lines to "reflag" ships under different jurisdictions that permitted greater freedom. A policy encouraged by the government reduced the number of major shipping lines to six: **Nippon Yusen** (NYK), Mitsui OS, Kawasaki Kizen, Showa Line, Yamashita Shinnihon Steamship, and Japan Line. In 1989, Yamashita and Japan Line merged to become Navix Line. Nippon Yusen and Mitsui OSK have also moved closer to integration within their groups. New business ventures in the leisure area have been developed to compensate for the loss of freight trade. Nevertheless, while it is generally thought that the nadir of the shipping industry's fortunes was around 1988, the combination of offshore manufacturing, competitive Southeast Asian lines, and general economic uncertainty combine to leave the industry contemplating an uncertain future.

SHISEIDO. This is a leading Japanese cosmetics maker that traces its roots to a Western-style pharmacy opened in Ginza in 1872 that introduced the sale of cosmetics in 1897. After World War II, Shiseido engaged in serious **research and development** and became internationally recognized for the quality of its products. It received the highest award at the Ninth International Conference of the Association of Cosmetic Chemists for its research on the emulsification of amino acids. Shiseido has 25,000 retail outlets supervised by 15 sales companies that have 105 branches. It expanded into the United States in 1965 and Italy in 1968. It has 27 offices overseas. From 1981, Shiseido entered the Chinese market with a plan to expand and open 5,000 retail outlets in China by 2110. The head office is in Tokyo.

SHITAMACHI. The term refers to the downtown areas of **Edo period** (1615–1868) cities that were centers of merchant and artisan activity.

SHODEN JIKEN. This was Japan's first major post–World War II business scandal that erupted in 1948 when members of the government were accused by opposition members of accepting bribes from **Showa Denko** in return for low-interest loans from the U.S.-funded Reconstruction Finance Bank. The entire cabinet of the Ashida Hitoshi government was forced to resign. Two of the originally accused 64 were indicted after protracted hearings that lasted until 1962. *See also* LOCKHEED SCANDAL; RECRUIT SCANDAL.

SHOEN. These were private estates that grew up in the early **Heian period** (794–1185) as a result of the collapse of the land-allotment system of the Nara period. The increase of these private estates threatened the political system, with many attempts being made to regulate them. *Sho* originally meant a warehouse or storage facility but came to include the ground around it. From this, the acquisition of additional wasteland enabled these estates to multiply.

SHOGUN. This was the formal title, granted by the emperor, to the head of military governments during the premodern period. The family of Minamoto Yoritomo in the **Kamakura period** (1185–1333), the Ashikaga family in the **Muromachi period** (1392–1573), and the **Tokugawa** family in the **Edo period** (1615–1868) were the principal bearers of the title.

SHOGUN BONDS. These are foreign currency–based bonds issued by nonresident institutions and sold in Japan. *See also* DAIMYO BONDS; MONEY MARKETS; SAMURAI BONDS.

SHOGYO KAIGISHO. In American English usage, this term translates as "board of trade," while in British English usage, it refers to a chamber of commerce. Tokyo Shogyo Kaigisho calls itself Tokyo Chamber of Commerce in English.

SHOGYO KOTOGAKKO. These are commercial high schools that usually date to the **Meiji period** (1868–1912) in which engineering, **accounting**, and business courses were taught to prepare students for careers in these fields. Although postwar educational reform tried to liberalize and broaden the base of **education**, many of these schools continued to follow their specialized practices while combining them with other studies. Many still have links with colleges and **corporations** that traditionally recruited from them.

SHOHIZEI. The formal title of the consumption **tax** instituted on 1 April 1989 set initially at 3 percent (6 percent for automobiles). Businesses earning less than ¥30 million a year were exempted. It was raised to 5 percent in 1997, and some bureaucrats thereafter began arguing for a further increase to 10 percent. While the tax cannot be held directly responsible for the protracted **recession of the 1990s**, there is no doubt that its imposition and subsequent increase adversely affected consumer spending patterns, which, once changed, were not inclined to recover easily. The controversial status of the tax remains one aspect of the larger problem of tax reform that successive governments have studiously avoided confronting.

SHORIKI MATSUTARO (1885–1969). He was a businessman best remembered as the father figure of professional baseball in Japan. Born in Toyama and a graduate of the University of Tokyo, he joined the Tokyo Metropolitan Police, from which he resigned in 1924. He eventually became president of the ***Yomiuri Shimbun***, making it Japan's most widely circulated **newspaper**. After 1945, he became director of the Science and Technology Agency and chairman of the Japan Atomic Energy Commission. He is also responsible for the link between the *Yomiuri Shimbun* and the Tokyo Giants baseball club, which his son faithfully maintained in his honor.

SHOWA DENKO. This is a chemical company founded in 1939 through the merger of Nippon Electric Industries (Nippon Denki Kogyo) and Showa Fertilizer Company, hence the name Showa Denko. Its main businesses are the manufacture of **petroleum** products and aluminum smelting. The roots of the company go back to Sobo Suisan, an iodine manufacturer founded by **Mori Nobuteru** in 1908. It became part of Toshin Denki and then independent in 1926 under the name Nippon Iodine. Showa Fertilizer was formed in 1928 and successfully produced lime nitrogen and ammonium sulfate. Nippon Iodine began producing potassium chloride, and by 1934 it had developed aluminum-refining technology. Coinciding with this was its change of name to Nippon Electric Industries when it began electrolytic refining of ferrous and nonferrous metals. It was also the central **corporation** of the Mori ***zaibatsu***. After World War II, the company underwent restructuring, developing a concentration on fertilizers. In the late 1950s, it entered the **petrochemical** business. Aluminum-smelting companies were set up in New Zealand, Indonesia, and Venezuela. The head office is in Tokyo.

SHOWA DEPRESSION (1930–1935). *See* GREAT DEPRESSION.

SHOZEI. This was a **tax** payable in the form of **rice** collected under the provisions of the **Ritsuryo Seido** of the seventh century. The collected rice was managed by the *kokushi* (provincial governors), much of which was used to finance loans to farmers in return for substantial volumes of interest when the harvest was over.

SHUNTO. This is the traditional spring labor offensive performed every year to determine levels of basic wage increase. The practice virtually collapsed on account of the **recession of the 1990s** that followed the burst of the **bubble economy**. While it as a form of collective bargaining between **labor unions** and **management**, it was conducted like a ritual, with workers wearing headbands (*hachimaki*), chanting slogans, and carrying banners while negotiations were being conducted. Token one- or two-day strikes were held if agreement was slow, but these were normally announced in advance to minimize inconvenience to the public. *See also* LABOR–MANAGEMENT RELATIONS.

SHUSHIN-KOYO-SEIDO. *See* LIFETIME EMPLOYMENT SYSTEM.

SILVER BUSINESS. This term refers to selling products and services to the growing population of over-65s, estimated to reach 34 million by 2025. Many new businesses sprung up in the late 20th century, some of which were dubious but most of which were in the hands of legitimate concern. These covered welfare-related projects, medication, housing-related problems, asset management, and leisure activities. *See also* TOYODA SHOJI AFFAIR.

SMALL AND MEDIUM-SIZED ENTERPRISES. *See* CHU-SHO KIGYO.

SOGO DEPARTMENT STORES. With roots going back to an Osaka clothing store, opened in 1830, Sogo grew to become one of Japan's largest **department store** groups, headquartered in Osaka. At its peak, it had branches in Osaka, Kobe, and Tokyo and a network of subsidiaries in Matsuyama (Ehime prefecture), Chiba and Kashiwa (Chiba prefecture), Hiroshima and Sapporo, and Hong Kong. It collapsed in the wake of the **bubble economy** because of poor sales performance, high overheads, and inept management. Only the Osaka, Chiba, and Yokohama stores remain, with Chiba Sogo occupying the largest retail space in the world at 90,000 square meters.

SOGO SHOSHA (GENERAL TRADING CORPORATIONS). The collective name given to trading firms established in their present form mostly postwar and that became powerful engines of the Japanese economy after Japanese sovereignty was restored in 1952. Apart from **Mitsubishi Corporation**, **Mitsui Bussan**, and **Sumitomo Corporation**, which have longer histories, the other corporations grew out of the prewar ***zaibatsu*** and were encouraged to grow as leading companies or supply companies for the postwar industrial groupings (***kigyo shudan*** and ***keiretsu***) that replaced the older system in the 1950s.

Characterization of the *sogo shosha* in Western terms is difficult because little exists with which comparisons can be made. The closest would be large, diversified Hong Kong trading corporations, such as John Swire, Caldbeck MacGregor, or Jardine Matheson, but even there, parallels are incomplete.

They are not, in any sense of the word, cartels. First, they are too diversified, and, second, they do not control prices. Indeed, they frequently compete for market share. They are also trading conglomerates rather than manufacturing conglomerates, handling on average 10,000 to 20,000 products each. The bulk of their trade has been with developing nations, either to source raw materials or to gain access to finance for new projects. Trade with Europe and North America is much lower on their priorities, except for the import of grains from North America.

From the 1960s on, the *sogo shosha* became involved in third-country trade, such as exporting U.S. scrap metal to the People's Republic of China. Much of their trading is related to Japan's direct overseas investment activities. They are not oligopolistic, although that is one tendency that exists within the Japanese economy as a whole. In essence they are large-scale facilitators that broker thousands of deals in a single day. The year 1973 was a watershed one in the postwar history of the *sogo shosha*, forcing restructuring and the development of new business strategies. Of the top 10 *sogo shosha* of the economic boom of the 1960s, only nine survive, and several of these, such as **Kanematsu Gosho** and **Toyo Menka**, have had severe problems. The three great groups are usually distinguished by their defining characteristics, Mitsui depending on its people, Mitsubishi on its organization, and Sumitomo on its unity.

SOHYO. Known by its full name in English as the General Council of Trade Unions of Japan, this was Japan's largest federation of labor unions prior to 1987. It merged in 1989 with the Japan Trade Union Confederation (JTUC-Rengo). *See also* LABOR–MANAGEMENT RELATIONS.

SOKAIYA. This is the term used to refer to corporate racketeers who specialize in disrupting shareholders' meetings (*sokai*) in order to extort money from **corporations**. The Commercial Code was amended in 1982 to prohibit corporate payoffs, but the menace of the *sokaiya* continued. Police estimated that there were as many of 1,700 in 1983, but with the law becoming stricter and corporations deliberately holding their annual meetings on the same day to prevent *sokaiya* from attending more than one meeting, the number decreased to 1,200 in 1992. By 1997, the number had been further reduced to 1,000, of whom only around 250 are effectively engaged in the business.

In May 1997, a *sokaiya* named Koike Ryuichi, already involved in a payoff scandal with **Nomura Securities**, was found to have received ¥600 million in questionable loans from **Dai-Ichi Kangyo Bank**. He used the money to buy 300,000 Nomura shares in order to have the right to speak at shareholders' meetings. He was "compensated" for trading losses by Nomura to avoid public disclosure. This incident resulted in several executives of these corporations being arrested for violation of the **Commercial Code** and the **Securities Exchange Law**.

The question remains unanswered as to why Japanese corporations have been so vulnerable to *sokaiya* and so ready to pay extortion money even though it is against the law. Studies have revealed a number of possible reasons. One is that the personnel in charge of dealing with the *sokaiya* usually have close ties with them that grow in influence as the managers rise in the corporate ranks. Senior executives treat such links as a priority. In the case of the Dai-Ichi Kangyo scandal, the chairman, president, and five other senior executives resigned. Sensitivity to corporate image is another top priority. To prevent other *sokaiya* from attending meeting, firms may ask one very powerful one to attend.

Shareholders' criticisms are taken very seriously, and therefore there exists a cultural mind-set that is susceptible to the kind of threats (and apparent benefits) that such links may provide. It is expected that with increased **globalization** and the entry of more **foreign companies** into Japan through various routes, including **mergers** and **acquisitions**, *sokaiya* will find their market shrinking. However, like other corporate practices in Japan that have historical or cultural roots, their elimination often proves more difficult than it would seem.

SONY CORPORATION. A corporation founded originally as Tokyo Tsushin Kogyo (or Totsuka) in 1946 by Ibuka Masaru and **Morita Akio** with 20 employees and a capitalization of ¥190,000 (U.S.$527 at the then rate of ¥360 to U.S.$1) that grew into an

electronics giant employing almost 180,000 staff worldwide, working for over 1,000 subsidiaries. Like its major rival, **Matsushita**, it started with a revolutionary product, in this case a device that could convert medium-wave radios to receive all wavelengths (the superheterodyne receiver). Sony was fortunate in that it found a ready-made market in government procurements and **NHK** (Japan Broadcasting Corporation) contracts. Working with the U.S.-led Occupation Forces further opened Sony's vista to the idea of magnetic sound recorders. The first Japanese-made magnetic tape recorder was produced in 1949, marking the beginning of the engineering inventiveness that has been a hallmark of Sony's products over the years.

A visit by Totsuka to the United States in 1952 led to a 1953 licensing agreement for transistor technology with Western Electric. The deal was almost stillborn because of Japanese government currency export restrictions, but approval was finally forthcoming, and, in 1955, Sony marketed Japan's first transistor radio. This led to the transistorization of numerous consumer products that were well received domestically and internationally. It was at this time that the name Sony was introduced (being a combination of the root word of "sonic" and "sonny") because it was easier to remember. The Trinitron TV tube, produced in 1968, is considered its greatest piece of technology and the Walkman one of its most original products. Sony introduced the Japan's first CDs in 1982 and in the 1990s broke into the computer games market by challenging market leader Nintendo with the PlayStation. Sony's only serious mistake was the introduction of the Betamax cassette recording system as a challenge to Japan Victor's VHS system.

Sony was the first Japanese manufacturer to produce television sets abroad, starting with the United States in 1971 and Europe in 1974. In 1988, it acquired Columbia Broadcasting System, a record company, and Columbia Pictures in 1989. Sony has numerous other "firsts" to its credit in appointing non-Japanese to its boards and in contravening standard Japanese procedure in refusing to select new staff on the basis of the prestige of the university from which they graduated. The key to Sony's success has been the way in which it has combined innovative engineering and imaginative design into sophisticated product development.

SOROBAN. This is the traditional manual calculator made of bamboo rods that carry pierced beads. Each rod bears five beads, with the top row separated by a crossbar. All digits from zero to nine can be indicated on a single rod, and beads can represent multiples of 10. A seven-bead variant was introduced from China in the 16th century, and by the mid-17th century the *soroban* assisted commercial activities in the field of **accounting**.

By 1926, the *soroban* was being taught in arithmetic (*shuzan*), and in 1938, it was introduced into the elementary school curriculum. It is still taught in accounting and business courses in commercial high schools (***shogyo kotogakko***). The soroban is believed to assist students' mental calculation skills, and special schools for the *soroban* exist nationwide. Modern accountants, who use calculators and computers, often use the *soroban* to verify their calculations. It is thought to be instrumental in developing superior mental arithmetical skills. *See also* ABACUS.

STEEL INDUSTRY. *See* IRON AND STEEL INDUSTRY.

STOCK EXCHANGES. Japan's *Shoken Torihikijo* group is made up of eight exchanges: Tokyo (the largest), followed by Osaka, Nagoya, Kyoto, Hiroshima, Fukuoka, Niigata, and Sapporo. The exchanges handle not only stocks but also bonds, bank debentures, and other **securities** instruments. They opened in the late 1870s to facilitate the trading of ***kinroku kokusai***, government bonds issued to former members of the **samurai** class. The markets expanded rapidly during and after World War I but were closed at the end of World War II. They reopened in 1949 under the provisions of a U.S.-style **Securities Exchange Law**.

Generally, Japan's **capital markets** differ significantly from their Western counterparts in several distinctive ways. Primary financing of development after 1945 was, as in the past, through **banks**, effect making the stock market a secondary financial market. However, it produced higher price-to-earnings ratios than elsewhere because of other factors. New share issues prior to the 1970s were affected through granting stock subscription rights to shareholders. This enabled shareholders to purchase below market value, which was determined as the par value of the stock or 50 per share. This in turn put pressure on companies to pay high dividends because of demands from financial institutions engaged in **cross shareholding**. It also meant that, to maintain high returns, continued reinvestment was required of shareholders. Also distinctive to Japan has been the idea of rewarding shareholders with the free distribution of shares (similar in principle to a stock split in Western markets). At its peak during the **bubble economy**, the market climbed to a high of 39,000 but subsequently dropped to a low of below 10,000 during the protracted **recession of the 1990s**. *See also* MONEY MARKETS.

STRUCTURAL IMPEDIMENTS INITIATIVE (SII). This was a strategy proposed during the presidency of George H. W. Bush during the late 1980s to work systematically to modify or eliminate import obstructions that were hindering U.S. exports to Japan. Three areas of agricultural concern were beef, citrus fruits, and **rice**. The SII had moderate success in a few areas, resulting in the Beef-Citrus Agreement of 1988, according to which quotas were to be increased from 1988 to 1990 and replaced by tariffs in 1991. However, talks stalled completely on the highly controversial and symbolic question of rice, one of the fundamental realities underlying Japanese culture. In 1993, a "minimum access" agreement was achieved according to which a small volume of rice would be imported through 2000. The issue was forced by its becoming part of the Uruguay Round of **General Agreement on Tariffs and Trade (GATT)** negotiations of 1993. The amount of U.S. rice that entered Japan was quite small because the rice market was opened in tiny increments to all rice-producing countries, including cheaper Asian suppliers. Imported rice did not prove popular because it did not suit Japanese tastes and blends had to be produced.

Although the concept was theoretically sound by tackling the market piece by piece over a range of taxes and nontariff barriers, it was not as successful as it might have been. According to some critics, both Western and Japanese, the way in which the SII was undertaken betrayed a naive lack of sophistication in understanding the scale of the problem. Little attention was paid to the complex structures that exist below the government level, down through the various commodity associations to local retailers, all of which have some influence on market mechanisms. Around the same time, the British government in the person of Prime Minister Margaret Thatcher, acting on bad advice, successfully pressured the Japanese government to reduce the import tax on Scotch whisky, then a popular product, particularly for the **gift** market. The lack of understanding of market mechanisms and of cultural differences in drinking that lay behind the demand effectively destroyed the Scotch whisky market. When Scotch appeared in discount liquor stores at the same price as local brands, sales went flat because public perception of quality was linked to price and price in turn determined prestige. *See also* AGRICULTURAL POLICY; TRADE.

SUEYOSHI MAGOZAEMON, also YOSHIYASU (1570–1617). He was a merchant and international trader of the early **Edo period** (1615–1868). With his father, he established an office for minting silver coins (the Ginza), in 1601, by government request. Because of other services to the government, he was permitted to engage in foreign trade. His *sueyoshibune* (Sueyoshi ships) sailed annually to Luzon in the Philippines and Tonkin in Vietnam until the country was closed in 1635. *See also* SAKOKU JIDAI; SUMINOKURA RYOI.

SUGGESTION BOX SYSTEM. The concept of a suggestion system is over a century old in Japan, having been initiated by **Kanebo** in 1905. It was modeled on systems already in place in American companies. It was not until the postwar period that the system became widespread in Japan. Japanese workers who had been accustomed to top-down management practices supported by a vertically integrated hierarchical society did not readily respond at first. However, with the expansion of small-group activities such as **quality control circles**, a context was created in which suggestions could be made. By the mid-1970s, **Matsushita** was receiving around 50 suggestions per employee each year, which translates into an average of one per week, a figure far above the national trend. By the 1980s, the Japan Suggestion System Association reported that from a survey of over 500 companies and organizations, the rate of suggestions per employee per year was over 14 percent. Of these, 90 percent were about improving production processes, while the rest related to the work environment, energy savings, or resource conservation.

The idea percolated through different institutions in society, including schools and colleges down to first grade of elementary school classes. The suggestion box became a symbol of the ideal of **Japanese-style management** to utilize all employee skills on the principle that if they are fully informed and properly consulted, they can make a real contribution to the effectiveness of the organization.

SUGI MICHISUKE (1884–1964). He was a business leader born in Yamaguchi prefecture. A graduate of what is now Keio University, he began working for Kuhara Kogyosho, a mining company, after which he moved to the textile business in Osaka, working for several companies in succession. He became president of Yagi Shoten in 1938. His principal contribution to the region was as chairman of the Osaka Chamber of Commerce from 1946 to 1960, in which capacity he worked hard for the development of the Kansai region. He also sought to promote foreign **trade** and was instrumental in the formation of the **Japan External Trade Organization** (JETRO), which he served as its first chairman.

SUICIDE. According to the values of pre–**Meiji period** (1868–1912) Japanese society, derived from the **samurai** code, serious errors of judgment as well as proven crimes required the guilty to commit ritual suicide (*seppuku*, colloquially referred to as *hara-kiri*, literally cutting of the stomach) in accordance with tradition and law. Although formally abolished by the Meiji government, offenders continued to expiate their guilt by taking their own lives even long after the end of World War II in 1945.

The culture of suicide occupies a unique place in Japanese culture, not necessarily in the area of statistics, although the annual deaths are in the higher range of over 20 per 100,000 people, but in terms of the range of ages and the varying motives and methods. In the corporate world, resignation to take responsibility remained standard procedure until the end of the 20th century, although the negative consequences for the guilty became gradually ameliorated by the softening of legal penalties.

While Japan's suicide statistics are not the highest in the world, the variety of reasons for suicide remains complex for cultural reasons, and the concept of "*seppuku mono*," meaning "a situation calling for suicide," remains unique to Japanese culture, although not practiced with the same fervor as half a century before. *See also* KAROSHI.

SUMINOKURA RYOI (1544–1614). An **Azuchi-momoyama** (1568–1615) period merchant and trader who received a license from **Toyotomi Hideyoshi** (1536–1598) to trade with what is now Vietnam. He started a career in moneylending during the 1590s, after which he began international trading. His ships, known as the *suminokurasen*, brought vast income for him and his son Soan (1571–1632) until the implementation of the closed-country policy of the ***Sakoku Jidai*** in 1635. *See also* SUEYOSHI MAGOZAEMON; VERMILION SEAL SHIP TRADE.

SUMITOMO BANK. Sumitomo Ginko originated as a money-changing business (***ryogae***) in Osaka founded by Izumiya Rihei in 1743. It was chartered as a **bank** in 1895 by Sumitomo Kichizaemon VII (Sumitomo Tomoito, 15th head of the **Sumitomo House**). It was the first private bank to open branches abroad, in San Francisco and Hawaii in 1916 and the Sumitomo Bank of California in 1925. It became the central bank of the **Sumitomo *zaibatsu*** in the pre–World War II period and the **Sumitomo Group (*keiretsu*)** in the postwar period. It acquired the regional Heiwa Sogo Bank in 1986 in order to enhance its business in the Tokyo area. At its peak, it had 200 branches in Japan and nine overseas operations, including Brazil, Indonesia, London, and the Cayman Islands. It merged with the **Mitsui Bank** in 2001 to form the **Sumitomo Mitsui Banking Corporation**.

SUMITOMO CHEMICALS. Sumitomo Kagaku Kogyo is a manufacturer of **petrochemicals** and specialized chemicals and one of the core companies of the **Sumitomo Group**. It started in 1925 as Sumitomo Fertilizer Manufacturing to produce fertilizer and sulfur out of by-products from the **Sumitomo Besshi Copper Mine**. It expanded subsequently into the production of ammonia, methanol, formalin, synthetic resins, tars products, and aluminum refining. In 1934, Sumitomo Aluminum Reduction Co. (later Sumitomo Aluminum Smelting) was created because of technological advances in the refining process. The company changed its name to its present one and continued in the chemicals business, moving into the petrochemicals field after World War II. It has joint ventures in Taiwan, Thailand, Singapore, Brazil, and the United States. It has corporate headquarters both in Tokyo and in Osaka.

SUMITOMO CORPORATION. Sumitomo Shoji is a leading member of the **Sumitomo *keiretsu***. It is a major trading house (***sogo shosha***) set up originally as a real estate and construction company in 1919 as Osaka Hokko Kaisha. It became central to the Sumitomo ***zaibatsu*** that was dissolved in 1945. It was reestablished as a trading company to serve the **Sumitomo Group** in 1945 and took the name Sumitomo Shoji in 1952 with Sumitomo Shoji Kaisha, Ltd, as its English name. This was changed to Sumitomo Corporation in 1978. The head offices are in Tokyo and Osaka.

SUMITOMO ELECTRIC. Sumitomo Denko Kogyo is a core company of the **Sumitomo Group** formed in 1897 to produce electric wire and cable. It established a high reputation for these before World War II and had capital tie-ups in the United States. After 1945, it expanded from New York, Los Angeles, and Chicago to London, Singapore, Sydney, São Paolo, and Hong Kong and has **joint ventures** in Thailand, South Korea, Singapore, Nigeria, Australia, Venezuela, and the United States. Its head office is in Osaka. *See also* ELECTRONICS INDUSTRY.

SUMITOMO GROUP. The Sumitomo ***keiretsu***, successor to the former Sumitomo ***zaibatsu***, consists of 20 core corporations and a further 20 affiliates that revolved round the **Sumitomo Corporation**, **Sumitomo Bank**, **Sumitomo Chemicals**, and **Sumitomo Metals Industry** and that grew out of the **Sumitomo House** and its **Besshi Copper Mine**. The presidents of these companies meet regularly to discuss trends and to exchange information.

SUMITOMO, HOUSE OF. This was a great merchant house of the **Edo period** (1615–1868) that grew into the **Sumitomo** *zaibatsu* prior to World War II, third in size behind **Mitsui** and **Mitsubishi**. While the latter two began as merchants and traders, Sumitomo's core activities centered on mining. The historical founder was Sumitomo Masatomo (1585–1652), whose adopted son brought to the family a technique for refining copper in a way that released its silver content.

In 1690, the family acquired the **Besshi Copper Mine** in Shikoku, and from that acquisition the house grew after mining had started in 1691. The house became the official supplier of copper to the **Tokugawa government** and a principal exporter of copper through the Nagasaki route to China and the Netherlands. The house also became *goyo shonin* (accountant/agent) to the three highest-ranked branches of the Tokugawa House.

The politics of the **Meiji Restoration of 1868** created a problem for the houses, which had close ties with the deposed regime. The Tosa (now Kochi prefecture) clan leader impounded the mine in the name of the new government and actually tried to seal it. However, in the absence of mining expertise on the part of the government, the house general manager was successful in receiving government permission to continue operating the mine. The government, for its part, was preoccupied with other developments and returned the mine to the Sumitomo house. The mine was modernized and produced greater yields and facilitated expansion into the production of copper rolling, steel manufacture, and other metallurgical businesses.

During the **Taisho period** (1912–1926), various Sumitomo enterprises were individually transformed into **joint-stock companies**. In 1921, the house became Sumitomo Ltd (Sumitomo Goshi Kaisha), capitalized at 150 million, a large sum for that time. House and corporate finances were finally separated. Sumitomo Ltd acted as a **holding company** for the numerous companies it had spawned. In 1937, the holding company itself became a joint-stock company with paid-up capital of ¥150 million with the House of Sumitomo still in control. The head of the house was 16th in succession, holding 98 percent of the stock. World War II forced expansion, and the number of companies grew from 40 to 135.

In accordance with orders of the **Supreme Commander Allied Powers (SCAP)**, the holding company was dissolved in 1948. The Sumitomo ***keiretsu*** was formed in the early 1950s, but the role of the house was drastically reduced. The group consists of around 80 corporations, of which 20 are members of the presidents' club (*Hakusui-kai*), a meeting that assists corporate activities and promotes cooperation within the group. All the companies' head offices are in central Osaka in a manner similar to the **Mitsubishi Mura** in central Tokyo.

SUMITOMO METAL INDUSTRIES. Sumitomo Kinzoku Kogyo is a leading corporation in the **Sumitomo Group** and the oldest of all Japan's major businesses, dating to 1590 and the mining of copper from the **Besshi Copper Mine** by the Sumitomo family. The Sumitomo Copper Works were established in Osaka in 1897, followed in 1901 by the Sumitomo Steel Works. It merged to become Sumitomo Metal Industries in 1937. After 1945, the company changed its name to Fuso Metal Industries but reverted to its former name in 1952. It is active internationally through affiliates in the United States, Thailand, Saudi Arabia, Brazil, Venezuela, Germany, Australia, Iran, Singapore, and the United Kingdom. The headquarters are in Osaka. *See also* IRON AND STEEL INDUSTRY.

SUMITOMO METAL MINING. Sumitomo Kinzoku Kozan is a mining operation formed in 1590 when Soga Riemon, brother-in-law of Sumitomo Masatomo (1585–1652), founder of the **Sumitomo House**, began copper mining and smelting, first in Kyoto and then in Shikoku island at the **Besshi Copper** Mine. The early 20th-century **Sumitomo *zaibatsu*** grew from this and subsequently the modern **Sumitomo Group**. It is one of the 20 core companies of the Sumitomo ***keiretsu***. *See also* IRON AND STEEL INDUSTRY.

SUMITOMO-MITSUI BANKING CORPORATION. A merger of two **city banks**, the **Mitsui Bank** and the **Sumitomo Bank**, formed in 2001 in response to changes in global financial structures as well as the restructuring of the Japanese **banking industry**.

SUMITOMO MUTUAL LIFE INSURANCE. Sumitomo Seimei Hoken Sogo Kaisha dates to 1907 and became a mutual company in 1947. It became known for its aggressive sales style and highly sophisticated policyholder service. Assets are comprised of loans, securities, real estate, and policy loans. It has various overseas tie-ups and has offices in New York and London. It is one of the 20 core companies of the Sumitomo ***keiretsu***. The headquarters are in Osaka. *See also* INSURANCE INDUSTRY.

SUMITOMO TRUST & BANKING. Sumitomo Shintaku Ginko is a core member of the **Sumitomo Group** that dates back to 1925. It was created initially for basic trust and **banking** services but subsequently branching into real estate, corporate agency, securities, and investment advising. It added commercial banking services in 1948 and was an important source of finance in the reconstruction of postwar Japan, working with companies in the fields of **electric power**, steel, chemicals, and **shipbuilding**. It has overseas branches in New York, London, Los Angeles, and Singapore plus liaison offices in Europe, South America, Australia, and the Middle East. It has two wholly owned subsidiaries in Hong Kong and London. Its head office is in Osaka.

SUNTORY. Founded in 1899 by **Torii Shinjiro** as a wine manufacturer under the brand name Akadama, the company branched into distilling spirits, becoming the third-largest whiskey producer in the world and the leading one in Japan. Its most famous brand, Suntory Old, retails over 10 million cases a year. It produces, in addition to wines and spirits, beer and soft drinks and has developed a worldwide restaurant chain. In the cultural field, the Suntory Foundation provides for cultural exchanges between Japan and other countries. There is also a Suntory Museum of Art and the Suntory Music Foundation, which was instrumental in building Suntory Hall, a venue for orchestral concerts, in the Akasaka district of Tokyo. The head office is in Osaka.

SUPREME COMMANDER ALLIED POWERS (SCAP), DOUGLAS MACARTHUR. Under the direction of the Supreme Commander of the Allied Powers, the occupation, usually referred to as GHQ, supervised the transformation of postwar Japanese society and the economy. Through various means, such as personnel policies, government controls, and reforms, it undertook a large agenda that included the pacification and rehabilitation of the ***zaibatsu***, the radical decentralization and demilitarization of **education**, the reform of civil and criminal law from its 19th-century German principles of duty to the state to a more Anglo-American style of law based on rights, and the rebuilding of Japan's collapsed economy and devastated industrial base. The overarching objective was to guide Japan toward more democratic processes characterized by transparency and accountability. These characteristics of the business world, however, became less important after the restoration of Japanese sovereignty in 1952.

SUZUKI BUNJI (1885–1946). He was an influential labor leader and graduate of the University of Tokyo who developed an interest in social problems. He founded a society, the Yuaikai, in 1912, intended to improve labor conditions and workers' lives. By 1919, it had attracted 30,000 members and was known as the Dai Nippon Rodo Sodomei Yuaikai. He was appointed four times as the Japanese representative to the International Labor Organization (ILO) and was vice chairman of the 14th ILO Assembly in 1932. *See also* LABOR UNIONS.

SUZUKI MOTORS. Suzuki Jidosha Kogyo is a manufacturer of minicars, motorcycles, and outboard motors, third in size after **Honda** and Yamaha. It is affiliated with General Motors and Isuzu Motors. It started as the Suzukishiki Loom Company, formed by Suzuki Michio in Hammamatsu City in Shizuoka prefecture in 1920. With the decline in the **textile** industry after World War II, the company switched its interests to small vehicles, producing its first minicar in 1955. It has motorcycle plants in Thailand, the Philippines, Indonesia, and Pakistan. The head office remains in Hammamatsu City. *See also* AUTOMOBILE INDUSTRY.

SUZUKI TRADING. Suzuki Shoten was a trading house (***sogo shosha***) founded in 1877 by Suzuki Iwajiro that was active during the **Meiji period** (1868–1912) and the **Taisho period** (1912–1926). It collapsed in the financial crisis of 1927. Several companies developed as a result of the collapse, including **Kobe Steel**; Teijin, Ltd; and Harima Shipbuilding, now part of **Ishikawajima-Haraima Heavy Industries Co, Ltd**. *See also* GREAT DEPRESSION.

– T –

TAIKA REFORM. The Taika no Kaishin (645–646) was an early attempt at organizing the emerging Japanese nation into a hierarchical order. A system of provincial districts was created during the work of governmental restructuring known as the Great Reform. The underlying policy was that family-based political structures should be dismantled and that all land should become the property of the state. All individuals became subjects and were assigned parcels of land according to regulations drawn up by a thoroughly centralized **bureaucracy**.

Improvements were introduced in **agriculture**, such as fertilizers, new methods of cultivation, and more varied crops. Overall **productivity** and general economic improvement took place. Courtiers, **Shinto**, and **Buddhist** priests were the first to acquire luxury goods that helped to expand the economy. To make possible the collection of **taxes**, silk weaving was encouraged. Silk came to be the exchange medium in tax collection. Infrastructure, roads, and toll stations were set up for military, administrative, and commercial purposes. This was the first time that the government actively demonstrated its role in economic and social management to a degree that became a precedent for all future legislation up to and including modern times.

TAISEI CONSTRUCTION (TAISEI KENSETSU). Founded in 1873 during the **Meiji period** (1868–1912) by Okura Kihachiro as part of Okura Gumi Shokai, it became independent in 1946 and is one of the five major **construction** companies in Japan. It has several subsidiaries, such as Taisei Road Construction, Taisei Prefab Construction, and Yuraku Real Estate. Its main areas of core business are public works (on bridges, tunnels, water, and sewage projects), office buildings, factories, hotels, and large buildings. Its head office is in Tokyo. *See also* ZAIBATSU.

TAISHO DEMOCRACY. This is the name generally given to the **Taisho period** (1912–1926), during which the social and political atmosphere of the nation was generally perceived as relatively liberal compared to the more rigid and undemocratic period of military rule during the early **Showa period** (1926–1989), which ended with Japan's defeat by the Allied powers in 1945.

TAIYO FISHERY CO., LTD. Taiyo Gyogyo was founded in 1880 by Nakabe Ikujiro as Hayashikane Shoten to buy and sell fish, growing to become one of the leading **fishery** corporations in the world. In the post–World War II period, it diversified into a wide range of food-processing activities and even acquired a baseball team, for a time known as the Taiyo Whales. The head office is in Tokyo.

TAKASHIMA COAL MINE. Takashima Tanko is one of Japan's largest coal mines, located on the island of Takashima, south of Nagasaki. It was under control of the Saga fiefdom, but in 1868, it was put under joint management with Glover & Company led by **Thomas Blake Glover** (1836–1911) and modernized. Glover went bankrupt in 1870, and after a Dutch concern had taken over, the mine came under government control. It was eventually sold to **Mitsubishi** in 1881 and became an important source of finance for the company in its early days. *See also* MINING.

TAKASHIMAYA DEPARTMENT STORE. A highly ranked and prestigious store opened in 1919, dating back to a cotton goods store started in Kyoto in 1831. It has branch stores in Osaka, Tokyo, and Kyoto along with several other branches in international centers such as Hong Kong and London. Like **Mitukoshi**, it specializes in luxury goods and international brand names. Its head office is in Osaka.

TAKATAYA KAHEI (1769–1827). He was an **Edo period** (1615–1868) trader and merchant who pioneered a new trade route to Ezo (now Hokkaido). He also assisted the **Tokugawa government** to plan defenses in the event of Russian aggression in the northern region. He specialized in clothing, tobacco, and salt and won exclusive trading rights that enabled him to amass a large amount of wealth before he retired in 1813.

TAKEN AKA-KE, TAKENAKA KOMUTEN. This is an **Edo period** (1615–1868) family business founded in 1610, still unlisted, but one of the big five **construction** companies in Japan. It specializes in individual contracts rather than on general bidding. Its most famous piece of technology is the Takenaka Aquareactive Chemical Soil Stabilization process for strengthening foundations (TACSS) developed jointly with **Dai Nippon Ink & Chemicals**. It has overseas subsidiaries and offices and is active in developing new kinds of building technology. The head office is in Osaka.

TAKEOVERS. *See* MERGERS AND ACQUISITIONS.

TANAKA KAKUEI (1907–1985). Born in Niigata prefecture, Tanaka was a powerful and dynamic prime minister from 1972 to 1974 who was forced to resign because of the **Lockheed Scandal**. He is best remembered for his efforts to successfully restore full diplomatic relations with China and for his book *Nihon retto kaizo ron* (*Remodeling the Japanese Archipelago*) published one month before he became prime minister. His term in office marked a major change in the development of the Japanese economy from postwar reconstruction to global industrial strength. Tanaka remains the sole politician who became prime minister with only an elementary school education.

TANKAN. This is a quarterly report issued by the **Bank of Japan** to assess business sentiment. The tankan diffusion index measures the percentage of companies that judge business conditions to be favorable compared to the percentage that consider them unfavorable. If the resultant percentage is minus, it means that the overall mood is pessimistic. The survey also breaks down statistics by industrial sector, providing a picture of conditions in any sector or for manufacturing compared to nonmanufacturing corporations or small and medium-sized corporations (***chu-sho kigyo***) compared to heavy machinery or **shipbuilding** corporations.

TAN-SEN. This was a **tax** of the **Muromachi period** (1333–1392) levied on tan units of **rice** fields, paid in coin. It represented an important source of income for the authorities. It was extended during the **Sengoku period** (1467–1568) to being an annual levy on all rice fields and dry fields.

TAXATION. Aside from corporate taxes, individual taxes in Japan are levied on income and paid to the national government, and local taxes are paid to the prefectural or city government where the individual resides. Taxes paid to the central government are approximately twice the amount paid to local authorities.

Besides these direct forms of taxation, there are a number of indirect taxes, including **consumption tax** (*shohizei*), liquor tax, cigarette tax, gasoline tax, excise taxes, and various fees for services and documents. The income tax is the largest source of revenue (over one-third), and corporate tax accounts for around 25 percent of revenue. In a series of reforms in 1988, individual and corporate tax rates were cut and eight excise-related taxes eliminated to compensate, for which a consumption tax was introduced. It became the third-largest source of revenue after the top two.

While local governments receive support from the national government, they have a range of taxes from which they draw revenue. Resident tax, based on income, is levied on individuals and **corporations** that live or trade within the municipality. Prefectures levy a business tax from individuals and corporations that is calculated on the basis of income. Property tax on land, buildings, and other similar assets is calculated on only a small percentage of the market value, leading to different rates being applied to different communities. There is also a list of minor taxes that resemble fees for specific situations, such as when buying a car.

The major problem with the Japanese tax structure is its inherent inequality. Medical doctors were traditionally given large allowances, while the farming community also pays very little. One calculation, based on the data that only 10 percent of the population earns over ¥10 million, suggests that with there being no tax on income of less than ¥3 million, 10 percent of the nation's individuals tax payers end up paying 90 percent of all income tax. This imbalance reflects something of the complexity of the **Liberal Democratic Party (LDP)** largesse to various groups in society. While the national tax agency is strict and impartial in its management, it displays much more understanding of the problems of some sectors of the economy than others. Adjustments are usually made through consultations with individual companies and sometimes with individual taxpayers that take place from time to time or as the need arises. Tax policy is formulated by the Tax Bureau of the **Ministry of Finance** on the basis of recommendations that come from the Tax Commission.

TEGATA. These were promissory notes issued from the end of the first century of the **Edo period** (1615–1868) that were abolished from 1882 with the establishment of the **Bank of Japan**, which replaced these with legal currency notes. *See also* BANKING SYSTEM; CURRENCY.

TELECOMMUNICATIONS INDUSTRY. The modern industry dates to the postwar period and until 1985 was a government monopoly in the form of the **Nippon Telegraph and Telephone Public Corporation**, Denden Kosha (NTT). As part of the **privatization** initiatives of the period, the company was privatized in 1985, although the government retained 65 percent of its shares, and it remains the largest company in the sector. The domestic long-distance market is controlled by NTT and several small rivals, including Daini Denden (DDI) and Japan Telecom Co. Local services are also dominated by NTT, but again there are some smaller corporations, the principal of which is Tokyo Telecommunications Network (TTNet).

The international market is dominated by **Kokusai Denshin Denwa** (KDD) and two smaller companies, International Digital Communications (IDC) and International Telecom Japan (ITJ). The Ministry of Posts and Telecommunications proposed the breakup of NTT as early as 1982, but stiff resistance kept prices high and service poor. As with other government-controlled sectors of the economy, the threat of international competition forced change on an unwilling industry.

NTT was broken into one long-distance and two local companies under a **holding company** formed after the law was changed in 1997. Up to that point, Japan had been defying the global trend toward **deregulation** in the industry and toward the **globalization** of procurement. Even the division of the industry into local, long distance, and international is based on outmoded technology, which made regulation and control simple.

Radical restructuring began when Japan Telecom and International Telecom discussed a merger and an alliance with AT&T of the United States. These developments promise change, but as with any other "radical" restructuring in Japan, much less is delivered than seems to be promised. As with the **Internet**, only consumer- or technology-driven developments can truly force change. *See also* E-COMMERCE.

TENKA TAIHEI. The concept of a "Great Peace Under Heaven" was the social ideal of peace and tranquillity throughout the land that was the goal of the **Tokugawa feudal system**. It was implemented through an elaborate **bureaucracy** supported by the **samurai** class and one of the most elaborate spy networks in human history. The concept of *tenka* in particular and service to the *tenka*, the whole nation, became a powerful moral sanction on human behavior that bequeathed to the Japanese the principle that collective, national, or house goals take precedence over personal or family considerations. *See also* BAKU-HAN SYSTEM; CONFUCIANISM.

TERAKOYA. This was an **Edo period** (1615–1868) system of basic **education** given in "under temple roof" schools. It was not a formalized government-sponsored system, but it provided the foundation for the national education system instituted after the **modernization** process started with the **Meiji Restoration of 1868.**

TEXTILE INDUSTRY. This was the first major modern industry developed in the late 19th century after the **Meiji Restoration of 1868**, which that signaled the beginning of Japan's **modernization**. It remained the largest industry until World War II. The names of many famous companies still reflect that period, such as the trading house (***sogo shosha***) **Toyo Menka**, which refers primarily to the cotton trade, or **Kanebo**, the short form of Kanegafuchi Boseki (spinning mill). Even **Toyota Motor Corporation** began life as a manufacturer of mechanized looms under the name Toyoda Automatic Loom Works in 1926. In 1937, almost 40 percent of all industrial workers were engaged in textile production, at the time representing 56 percent of all Japanese exports.

World War II saw the loss of overseas assets and reduced demand with the disbanding of the Imperial Army. However, persistence paid off, and by 1956 production had exceeded prewar levels. This helped greatly in the rehabilitation of national finances. The loss of the Chinese market and the emergence of Southeast Asian textile manufacturers forced a contraction in the industry, and by the 1970s, China was exporting textile goods to Japan. The chemical fiber industry and the synthetic fiber industry began to expand as a consequence, and manufacturers began inventing new types of fabrics. These are being developed for the Southeast Asian market as well as for Europe and North America, although Japan became a net importer of textiles after 1973.

To match the prices of North American goods, Japanese textile companies developed two main strategies. One was to move more to the production of fashion goods but not to flood the market with single lines. Renown, the largest clothing manufacturer in the world, never produces more than five pieces of any line in the same color and size. A second strategy has been to transfer manufacturing to China, offering a cost advantage. The protracted **recession of the 1990s** hurt the brand-name sector of the market but made room for lesser-known but good-quality products to find a market.

TOA DOMESTIC AIRLINES. *See* JAPAN AIR SYSTEMS.

TOA NENRYO KOGYO. A **petroleum** refining company formed in 1939. It began refining in Wakayama in 1941, in Shimizu (Shizuoka prefecture) in 1943, and in Kawasaki in 1962. It began as association with what became Esso Eastern and Mobil Petroleum and thereafter confined itself to refining, leaving sales to **Esso Standard Oil** and **Mobil Sekiyu** and processing to Tonon Sekiyu Kagaku. In 1972, it formed Kygnus Sekiyu in partnership with Nichimo Corporation. The company is now the leading member of the Tonen group. The head office is in Tokyo.

TOBACCO. *See* JAPAN TOBACCO AND SALT PUBLIC CORPORATION.

TOBASHI. This is a controversial **practice** among **securities** firms by which brokerages transfer devalued securities from one company to another to avoid having to declare losses. They normally agree to purchase these back at a higher price before the purchasing company is forced to record any losses. It is also considered to be one contributing factor to the **nonperforming loans** problems of the banking sector that surfaced in the mid-1990s.

Tobashi is another example of dubious corporate practice that has destroyed several major **corporations**, including the **Long-Term Credit Bank (LTCB)** and **Yamaichi Securities**, both of which collapsed, at least in part, because of *tobashi*.

TOBU GROUP. A conglomerate of 80 companies lead by **Tobu Railway**. Formerly a member of the Nezu ***zaibatsu*** prior to World War II, the group remains affiliated to the Fuyo ***keiretsu*** headed by the Fuji Bank, now part of the **Mizuho** Banking Group.

TOBU RAILWAY. The Tobu Tetsudo is a Kanto-based **railway** company formed in 1897 during the **Meiji period** (1868–1912). The company has 483 kilometers of track, which ranks it third among the private railways according to size. It is the leading member of the **Tobu Group**, which also includes a number of **department stores**. Its headquarters are in Tokyo.

TOKAI BANK. The Tokai Ginko is the only **city bank** whose main business is in the Chubu region and which is headquartered in Nagoya. It dates back to the Eleventh National Bank (later the Aichi Bank) founded in the early **Meiji period** (1868–1912) in 1877. A merger in 1941 of the Aichi Bank, the Ito Bank, and the Nagoya Bank resulted in the present Tokai Bank. At its peak it had 230 domestic branches and 26 overseas offices. It joined with the **Sanwa Bank** and the Toyo Trust to form the **UFJ Holding Company** on 2 April 2001 and subsequently merged with the Sanwa Bank on 15 January 2002.

TOKIO MARINE & FIRE INSURANCE. Tokyo Kaijo Kasai Hoken was founded in 1879 by the **Meiji period** (1868–1912) entrepreneur **Shibusawa Eiichi**. The company was and still is the largest of the 23 non–life insurers in the country. It began as a marine insurer with offices in Paris, London, and New York in 1890 under the name of Tokio Marine. The old romanized form of the capital's name, "Tokio," remains in its English title. In 1944, it merged with Mitsubishi Marine & Fire Insurance and Meiji Fire and Marine Insurance under its present name. With marine **insurance** in decline, it built up new markets in fire and automobile insurance. It has 27 main offices, 284 branches, 1,121 service centers, and over 30,000 agents. It has 35 offices located in 23 different countries. It is a member of the **Mitsubishi Group**. Its head office is in Tokyo.

TOKUGAWA ECONOMIC POLICY. The Tokugawa House domain financed the central government from **rice**, estimated at 6 million ***koku*** (4.69 bushels); owned all mines of any kind; and issued coins (***ryo***) in gold, silver, and copper. While the government was characterized by its rigidity, economic changes were slowly taking place, the principal of which was the growth of a merchant class that eventually became the dominant economic force that displaced the **samurai**

who were reduced to stipends of diminishing value. The government policy can be considered successful during the first two centuries of the **Edo period** (1615–1868) but was weakened by mismanagement combined with the rise of the great **merchant houses** in Osaka and Edo (modern Tokyo). *See also* TOKUGAWA FEUDAL SYSTEM.

TOKUGAWA FEUDAL SYSTEM. Four social classes—warrior (*shi*), farmers (*no*), artisans (*ko*), and merchants (*sho*)—made up the social order at the peak of which was the shogun, who ruled in the name of the emperor. The value system in force was derived from the Chinese neo-Confucianism of Chu Hsi (Zhu Xi, 1130–1200). One highly important aspect of the system was that it was totally comprehensive and covered all aspects of life, including **agriculture**, commerce, human relations, politics, and religion, all of which reflected the structure and order of society. While it created a rigid society and imprinted many features of Japanese behavior that are still identifiable, it also put in place many structures that survived to support modern business, such as the **House Constitutions** of the 17th century. After the violence of the civil war era (***Sengoku Jidai***), it gave Japan a long period of peace during which commercial and cultural activities flourished.

While many features of the Tokugawa system were positive, there were others that were extremely negative. Agriculture thrived during the first century of Tokugawa rule, but when income declined because of decreased **productivity** in rural areas, the option of **taxing** merchants and commercial enterprises did not fit the narrow and rigid **Confucianism** of the government's policy.

Typical of the government approach was the response of Mizuno Tadakuni between 1841 and 1843 to public rioting caused by poor harvests at the end of the Tempo period (1830–1843). He demanded a return to more frugal ways. Manufacturing was positively discouraged, and organizations such as trade guilds (***za***) were abolished. Mizuno believed that merchants would force prices up, thus causing inflation. In the absence of the guilds, regulatory controls were eliminated, resulting in market instability. Elimination of manufacturing created unemployment, a situation that only exacerbated matters.

Ultimately, the essentially inward-looking nature of the Tokugawa system and its lack of economic sophistication—evidenced by the closed-country (***sakoku***) policy that lasted over 300 years and its rigid controls that placed limits on the development of technology—brought it down. All this was openly exposed when Commodore Matthew Perry arrived in Tokyo Bay in 1853 with the famous black ships (***kurofune***), as the Japanese called them. This prompted radical criticism of the regime, which was further aggravated by an economy on the verge of collapse, a series of bad **rice** harvests, and an inflated **currency**. The outer lords, the **Tozama**, particularly of Kyushu, moved to open rebellion, and by 1868 the shogunate had collapsed, and Japan was free to begin the process of **modernization**. *See also* INTRODUCTION; SHI-NO-KO-SHO.

TOKUGAWA GOVERNMENT. *See* TOKUGAWA FEUDAL SYSTEM.

TOKUGAWA IEYASU (1543–1616). The last of the three warlords who completed the unification of Japan in the early 16th century. A ruthless but efficient administrator, he created a feudal military regime that lasted until 1868, when the last shogun resigned, making way for the **Meiji Restoration of 1868** and the beginning of Japan's **modernization**. *See also* ODA NOBUNAGA; SAKOKU JIDAI; TOKUGAWA FEUDAL SYSTEM; TOYOTOMI HIDEYOSHI.

TOKYO CHAMBER OF COMMERCE AND INDUSTRY. Tokyo Shogyo Kaigisho, the modern Chamber of Commerce, had its origins in the **Edo Chokaisho**, a town assembly that dates to 1791. In 1872, it became known as the **Tokyo Eizen Kaigisho** (Tokyo Chamber of Building and Repair). Its next name was the **Tokyo Kaigisho**, after which **Shibusawa Eiichi** (1840–1931) became chairman. The government ignored this development and created the **Shokokai**, which was a public sector organization. In 1891, the Tokyo Chamber of Commerce emerged from the Regulation of Chambers of Commerce Law of Meiji (1890). Its office is near the headquarters of the former Mitsui Bank, close to the Imperial Palace in central Tokyo.

The work of the Chamber consists of assisting mostly small and medium-sized **corporations** (***chu-sho kigyo***) in various practical ways through organizing seminars and other events covering a wide range of interests, including business expansion, management improvement, business start-ups, information technology, human resource development, and employee welfare as well as information on international business and market trends. *See also* JAPAN CHAMBER OF COMMERCE AND INDUSTRY.

TOKYO ELECTRIC POWER COMPANY (TEPCO). Tokyo Denroku is the largest of the nine regional **electric power** suppliers covering Tokyo, Saitama, Chiba, Yamanashi, Tochigi, Gunma, Kanagawa, and Shizuoka prefectures, east of the Fujikawa River. It is also the largest private power company in the world measured by capital, equipment, facilities, and volume of power produced. It grew out of the **Tokyo Electric Lighting**, founded in 1883, and took its present name in 1951. The head office is in Tokyo. *See also* KIKAWADA KAZUTAKA.

TOKYO GAS. Tokyo Gasu is Japan's largest gas supplier and the world's largest private gas corporation, covering Tokyo and the surrounding prefectures of Saitama, Chiba, Kanagawa, Gunma, Tochigi, Yamanashi, Ibaraki, and Nagano. It was founded in 1885, and its first president was the **Meiji period** (1868–1912) entrepreneur **Shibusawa Eiichi** (1840–1931). Originally used for lighting, gas became used for heating and cooking during World War I. Through developing its technology, it became the first company in Japan to use heavy oil for the production of gas rather than coal. In 1969, in a joint exercise with **Tokyo Electric Power Company (TEPCO)**, it began to import liquefied natural gas (LNG) from Alaska, and its specially designed underground LNG storage tanks are highly regarded internationally. It is also engaged in technology transfer with the United States, the United Kingdom, West Germany, and China. The headquarters are in Tokyo.

TOKYO MITSUBISHI BANK. The Tokyo Mitsubishi Ginko was formed in 1996 by the merger of the **Bank of Tokyo** and the **Mitsubishi Bank** during the period of radical restructuring of the **banking industry** during the last decade of the 20th century. One of the factors that brought about the merger was the complementary nature of each bank's business. The Mitsubishi Bank was very strong domestically, while the Bank of Tokyo was an international specialist with branches in many parts of the world. The Tokyo-Mitsubishi Financial Group merged with the **UFJ Bank** in January 2006.

TOKYO SAN'YO ELECTRIC COMPANY. This is a subsidiary of **San'yo Electric** established in 1959 as a manufacturer of household electrical appliances, **electronic** equipment, office equipment, and **semiconductors**. It manages San'yo Electric's production division. Products, including television sets, refrigerators, air conditioners, and sound equipment, are sold under the brand name Sanyo. It introduced the manufacture of glass vacuum-tube solar collectors in 1978 and works in developing new products and new technologies. Its headquarters and main facilities are in Gunma prefecture, north of Tokyo.

TOKYO STEEL. Tokyo Seitetsu was established in 1934 to produce various products through the open-hearth method. It moved to the use of electric furnaces and from the 1970s began to produce rolled steel products. It acquired the Tosa Steel Works in 1975 and became a major electric furnace steelmaker. Founded by the Iketani family, it has remained a successfully managed family business that resisted steel industry trends to contract. Its head office is in Tokyo. *See also* IRON AND STEEL INDUSTRY.

TOKYU CORPORATION. The company was founded originally in 1922 as a local **railway** in southwest Tokyo. It has expanded to become the largest real estate developer in the region and the leading corporation of the **Tokyu Group**. It now has 100 kilometers of rail track and 521 kilometers of bus routes.

TOKYU DEPARTMENT STORE. Tokyu Hyakkaten was opened in 1919, and from the import business necessary for early sales, it moved to exporting and to restaurants and amusement centers. It functions as a part of the **Tokyu Group** marketing organization. The modern name was adopted in 1958 through a merger with Shirikoya and the original Tokyu company. A Shirikoya **Department Store** was opened in Hawaii in 1959, and Tokyu Feedlot was opened in Australia in 1974. The Saint Germain bakery name was introduced to Hawaii in 1977, and thereafter expansion included Los Angeles, Paris, and other major centers. The head office is in Tokyo.

TOKYU GROUP. A large group of 29 major corporations and 380 affiliates and subsidiaries employing over 100,000 people. The group began with the Tokyu **railway** system, which before World War II included **Odakyu Electric Railway** and **Keio Teito Electric Railway**, making it the largest in the country. The enforced breakup of that group drove **Tokyu Corporation** into other interests. Under the aggressive leadership of **Goto Keita** (?–1989), business expanded into four areas: transportation, property development, **distribution** and retailing, and recreation and leisure. The group is controlled by the Tokyu Summit, a group leadership concept in which the three principal corporation presidents work together. The most important of the 14 listed companies in the group cover a wide area. In transportation is the **Tokyu Corporation**, followed by **Japan Air System** and the Shiroki Corporation. In the leisure field, the Tokyu Hotel Chain (the largest in Japan) and Tokyu Tourist Corporation lead. In development, Tokyu Construction and Tokyu Land Corporation are at the top, and in distribution, **Tokyu Department Stores** and the Tokyu Store chain are leaders. Its advertising business, Tokyu Agency, is very successful although not listed, and equally popular is the all-purpose store Tokyu Hands.

TONYA. These were the wholesalers of the **Edo period** (1615–1868) who exercised powerful controls on the nation's markets. *Tonya* have been described as merchants par excellence of the era, with diversified interests including extending credit to their middlemen (*nakagai*) and their partners and, in effect, functioning as merchant bankers. They worked in groups with a commodity such as **rice**, salt, and tea or in regional specialization. The chief money exchangers (*ryogae*) were also leading *tonya*. While the role of the *tonya* helped to create a stable economy, it also stifled innovative thinking, especially in Osaka, in contrast to the more entrepreneurial **merchant houses** of Edo. *See also* IE GENSOKU.

TOPPAN PRINTING. Founded in 1900 as a relief printer, the company grew into a comprehensive printing firm that has an integrated system covering all stages from design to the finished product. It is second in size nationally after **Dai Nippon Printing** but is highly regarded for its innovative approach to technology, which it exports to overseas customers. It produced an automatic color-correcting system known as the Toppan Image Conductor and is active in the field of TV Shadow Masks and Image Storage systems necessary for Hi-Vision Television (based on the high-definition screen) and its potential application in many other fields, including printing. The head office is located in Tokyo.

TORAY INDUSTRIES. Founded as a subsidiary of **Mitsui & Co.** in 1926 as Toyo Rayon Co. to produce rayon, it grew into the largest manufacturer of synthetic fibers in Japan. It expanded into plastics and chemicals. It imported technology from E. I. duPont de Nemours & Co. of the United States in the early 1950s and acquired (in cooperation with Teijin) the technology for polyester from Imperial Chemical Industries (ICI) of the United Kingdom. By 1964, it had developed its own acrylic fiber, Toraylon. It began producing carbon fibers in 1971. It has 35 **joint ventures** in 15 countries and is active in exporting technology to eastern Europe. It remains a major producer of polyester and is expanding into biotechnology. The head office is in Tokyo. *See also* TEXTILE INDUSTRY.

TORII SHINJIRO (1879–1962). He was the founder of **Suntory Ltd**, Japan's largest distiller of whiskey. Born in Osaka, he founded Torii Shoten in 1899 as a wine producer. His Akadama brand was very successful, and by 1907 it was well established. He thereafter turned to whiskey and began the Suntory brand in 1929. His position as leader of the Japanese industry remained intact until his death. He was also a man of principle, devoting 30 percent of corporate profits to social welfare projects.

TOSHIBA CORPORATION. Prewar member of the **Mitsui *zaibatsu*** that established an independent identity as an **electronics** manufacturer specializing in heavy electrical machinery, household appliances, and **telecommunications** equipment. Originally the Tsurumi plant of Shibaura Engineering Works (formed in 1904), it merged with Tokyo Electric in 1939 and added Tokyo to become Tokyo Shibaura Denki, abbreviated to "Toshiba." Combining the products of both companies, it expanded to become a comprehensive producer of electronic goods and became second only to **Hitachi** in both size and sales. However, by 2004, it dropped down to fourth place in sales with operating profit declining seriously. It retains links with General Electric of the United States and is still associated with the **Mitsui group**.

In the postwar period, Toshiba expanded into atomic power, energy-producing equipment, **semiconductors**, office **automation**, and electronic machines for medical use. Its electricity-generating technology is among the world's most advanced. Toshiba engages in worldwide sales of hydroelectric, thermoelectric, geothermal, and atomic power-generating systems. It manufactures a variety of electronic goods in different countries through its 23 overseas subsidiaries. The modern progressive character of the company was the work of **Doko Toshio**, president of **Ishikawajima-Harima Heavy Industries** and past chairman of **Keidanren**, who was asked in 1965 to become president. His efforts resulted in very successful group restructuring. Toshiba was unfortunately embroiled in a defense scandal when it was found to have sold sensitive submarine technology to the Soviet Union during the 1980s.

The group structure around Toshiba Corporation and the Toshiba Research Center is made up of five heavy electrical companies, nine companies in consumer electronics, six in machinery, eight in materials production, and seven in service industries ranging from **insurance** to **tourism**.

TOSHIN STEEL. This is the major steel manufacturer of the materials manufacturing group affiliated with **Toshiba Corporation**. The materials plant of Toshiba was made independent in 1950, and in 1955 it formed a capital link with **Nippon Kokan**. A 1970 merger with Nisshin Seiko (an affiliate of Nippon Kokan) extended its domestic market, and a further 1973 merger with Harashima Tekko consolidated the Nippon Kokan group of electric furnace steel manufacturers. It has a **joint-venture** manufacturing plant in Indonesia. The head office is located in Tokyo. *See also* IRON AND STEEL INDUSTRY.

TOURISM. According to the Japan National Tourist Organization (JNTO), Japan hosted an average of 6 million tourists per year between 2000 and 2004, when the figure reached 6,137,905. Visitors from Asian countries made up the largest single group. South Korean visitors were the largest number from any single country, with Taiwan in second place and the United States in third. Australia, for its size, was ahead of any European country, even Canada, which is roughly similar in population to Australia. While the national tourist organization has been active, so too has the private sector led by the **Japan Travel Bureau** and other agencies, such as the tourist arm **Japan Airlines (JAL)**, **All Nippon Airways (ANA)**, and a number of foreign carriers selling package tours to Japan.

Figures for tourists from Japan per year reached 16 million in 2004. While many travel abroad on business just as many visitors are businessmen, the fact that departures for 2003 were at around 1.2 million per month, a figure that rose to 1.3 million in 2004, indicates that the traveling public is steadily increasing.

Domestic travel is a mix of tourism and people returning home for New Year's celebrations, when the Shinkansen runs at 120 percent overload, and Obon, the brief summer celebration of **Buddhist** ancestral rites. Junior and senior high schools usually travel once a year to some historical or cultural site, while **corporations**, by sections or other groups, have at least one trip each year for the purpose of building esprit de corps. One other relatively new trend is the increase of people creating their own tour plan as distinct from the traditional package tour or honeymoon trip. Younger people, after graduation from college, frequently travel abroad, in the past in large groups but more recently sometimes in groups of two or three on often quite adventurous journeys. These are all phases in the evolution of the travel industry.

TOYOBO. Toyo Boseki has roots in the early **Meiji period** (1868–1912) but was formally incorporated in 1914 as a spinning company dealing with cotton and woolen goods. It was a merger of Osaka Spinning, set up in 1882 by **Shibusawa Eiichi** (1840–1931) and Mie Spinning, founded in 1886. In 1956, the company ventured into synthetic fabrics such as acrylic fiber. In 1961, it developed polyester fiber, and after a merger with Kurehara Spinning in 1966, it began manufacturing nylon. It produces products from all natural fibers except silk and linen flax and from three kinds of artificial fibers. Its first overseas venture was in Brazil in 1955, but since then it has expanded to eight in Central and North America, one in Australia, and six in Southeast Asia. Toyobo is one of the group of companies in the **textile industry** that diversify through development of new materials. The group includes **Teijin** and **Unitaka Sangyo** (of the **Sanwa Group**). The headquarters are in Osaka.

TOYODA AUTOMATIC LOOM WORKS. Toyoda Jido Shokki Seisakusho was started in 1926 to manufacture the automatic loom invented by **Toyoda Sakichi**. In 1933, an automobile division and a steelmaking division were created. The **automobile** division became **Toyota Motor Company** in 1937, and the steelmaker became independent as **Aichi Steel Works** in 1940. After World War II, the company began producing new products, beginning with automotive gasoline engines in 1952, gasoline-powered forklifts in 1956, car air-conditioning compressors in 1959, and small business cars and battery-powered forklifts in 1967. Also in 1967, in a technology transfer agreement with George Fisher, Ltd, of Switzerland, Toyoda entered the field of metal-casting plants. The company continued to expand in **textile** manufacturing and has been a powerful influence on manufacturing in developing economies as well as on structural reform of reform of the industry in advanced economies. Technology transfer agreements and **joint ventures** in many parts of the world have made the company one of the world's leading textile-machinery makers. It is also a leading member of the **Toyota Group**. The head office is located in Kariya City, Aichi prefecture.

TOYODA SAKICHI (1867–1930). He was an entrepreneur and businessman, born in Shizuoka prefecture in the last year of the **Edo period** (1615–1868). He invented Japan's first power loom in 1897 and created an automated power loom in 1926 that was the world's most advanced at the time. His work revolutionized the **textile industry** and gave Japan comparative advantage that translated into total domination of the world silk industry in the 1920s. He created an industrial research-and-development organization out of which many innovations emerged that assisted Japanese business, not least of all those that became the foundation of the **Toyota Motor Corporation**.

TOYODA TSUSHO CORPORATION. Toyoda Tsyusho Kaisha is a trading company established in 1948 to retail domestically and internationally the spinning and weaving machinery produced by the **Toyoda Automatic Loom Works**. It expanded to handle various products from the **Toyota group** of companies and now handles the export and import business of the **Toyota Motor Corporation**. It is evolving into a ***sogo shosha*** through its 26 overseas offices and 44 overseas subsidiaries. However, around 70 percent of its core business remains with Toyota. The head office is located in Nagoya.

TOYO KOGYO. This is the manufacturer of the Mazda and fifth largest of Japan's **automobile** manufacturers. It dates to 1920, when it was established as Toyo Cork Kogyo, which was changed to Toyo Kogyo in 1927. It produced three-wheeled lightweight trucks in 1931 and moved to automobile production in 1979. The company's reputation for innovation was tied to its production of the world's first twin-rotor engine for the Cosmo Sports/110S model. It was the only manufacturer in the world to produce three kinds of engines: the conventional piston engine, the rotary engine, and the diesel engine. Mazda cars are sold in over 100 countries through 5,000 dealerships. It has a close affiliation with the Ford Corporation of the United States, which has provided it with new leadership since the impact of the **recession of the 1990s** on the industry. Its corporate headquarters are in Hiroshima.

TOYO MENKA (TOMEN). This is one of Japan's general trading houses (***soga shosha***), founded in 1920. Until then it was the cotton department of **Mitsui & Co.** It was set up to serve the **Mitsui *zaibatsu*** as its cotton importer and its **textile** marketing channel for domestic and international business. Facing bankruptcy in April 2000, it entered a three-year reconstruction plan in which it asked the **Tokai Bank** to write off ¥219 billion in bad loans, agreed to reduce its capitalization by 30 percent, and issued ¥30 billion of new shares. It sold its steel Division to Toyota Tsusho, a member of the **Toyota Group**. **Toyota Motor Corporation** announced in early 2003 that it would take a stake in Toyo Menka.

TOYO SEIKAN. The company was founded in 1917 by Takasaki Tatsunosuke to produce containers for canning salmon and sea trout caught of the northern coast of Japan. It grew to become the largest manufacturer of containers for canned foods. A 1941 merger with seven other can makers gave it a virtual monopoly that was ended by the **Supreme Commander Allied Powers** (**SCAP**) in 1945 when it was broken up into several smaller companies. After 1954, it began upgrading its technology by means of a tie-up with Continental Can of the United States and after 1970 began producing soft-drink cans and plastic containers. It has exported its technology to Southeast Asia (Thailand and Indonesia), South Korea, and the United Kingdom. It owns Toyo Kohan, which it established as a supplier. The head office is in Tokyo.

TOYO SODA. This is a chemical manufacturer founded in 1935 to produce soda ash and caustic soda by means of its own ammonia soda process. After its first success, the company began producing bromide in 1942, portland cement in 1953, vinyl chloride monomer, and low-density polyethylene in 1966. Ten percent of all employees are researchers working on development projects. **Joint ventures** exist in Greece, Indonesia, the Netherlands, and Iran and subsidiaries in Amsterdam and Atlanta. The corporate headquarters are in Tokyo.

TOYOTA GROUP. Apart from the six major conglomerates that grew out of the pre–World War II ***zaibatsu***, the Toyota ***keiretsu*** is the largest single corporate grouping in Japan. The Toyota group consists of 18 core companies led by the **Toyota Motor Corporation**, plus the affiliates made up of 234 parts suppliers, known as the *Kyo-kai*, and 77 companies producing equipment and manufacturing related items, a total of 311 companies, all dependent on the Toyota Motor Corporation for their business.

TOYOTA MOTOR CORPORATION. Toyota Jidosha was formed from the **automobile** division of **Toyoda Automatic Loom Works** in 1937. It began production of the A-1 prototype in 1935, and by 1941 it was producing 2,000 units a month. After World War II, it elected to chart its own course without seeking foreign investment or technology. The Toyopet Crown, which first appeared in 1955, was a turning point for both Toyota and the automobile industry in Japan. This was followed by a series of models, the hallmark of all of which was quality and efficiency. Between 1950 and 1982, sales were in the hands of Toyota Motor Sales, which merged with Toyota Motor to form Toyota Motor Corporation. **Toyota Auto Body**, **Kanto Auto Works**, and **Daihatsu Motor Company** all are involved in the manufacture of Toyota cars, while over 200 companies provide car components, including **Nippondenso** and **Aisin Seiki**. Toyota's famous **just-in-time** system helps to eliminate inventory by means of its use of ***kamban***, both ideas being parts of its emphasis on ***kaizen***, continuous improvement in manufacturing and management. Toyota has 27 plants worldwide, including the United States, the United Kingdom, and Australia. It began planning moves to eastern Europe and China at the close of the 20th century. Its corporate headquarters are located in Toyota City, Aichi prefecture.

TRADE. As an island nation, Japan has out of necessity been a trading nation. Some of the earliest artifacts that suggest international trade with China and Korea date to the first century C.E., and samples may be seen in the museum of the Munakata Taisha (an ancient **Shinto** shrine) in Kyushu, which offered protection to travelers between Kyshu and the Asian mainland. Details of the nature and extent of trade with the mainland are not known, but Japan's early military exploits in Korea under the legendary Empress Jingu (r. 201–269) suggest that some underlying economic necessity existed that having a Korean colony helped to resolve. One of these was probably related to **iron**, which was in use in Japan as early as 300 C.E. Ironware and a manufacturing process known as *tatara-buki* were imported via the Korean peninsula from China. By the end of the 16th century, lumps of iron known as *nambanbetsu* were imported on Portuguese ships. This enabled the production of steel for swords.

Japanese pirates known as ***wako*** operated in various parts of Asia from at least the 12th or 13th century and were seen as far away as the Straits of Malacca. Whatever the nature and extent of trade during the period of the civil wars (Sengoku Jidai), trade slowly came under government control. First **Toyotomi Hideyoshi** and then **Tokugawa Ieyasu** began a system whereby limited trading activities were licensed by the government. This was known as the **Vermilion Seal Trade** (*shuinjo boeki*), which lasted until 1635, when the closed-country policy was implemented, and Japan entered nearly 300 years of international isolation (***Sakoku Jidai***). The port of Nagasaki was the only city open to any foreign shipping, and that was limited to one trading ship per year, in effect closing Japan to any serious trade.

The arrival of the ***kurofune***, the flotilla of U.S. naval vessels under the command of Commodore Matthew Perry in 1853, had, as one of its objectives, the opening of international trade with Japan. The **Meiji period** (1868–1912) government was aware of the deficiency in national resources and opened the country for trade, which had been suspended for 300 years. This gave rise to the development of the trading houses (***sogo shosha***) that in several instances, notably **Mitsubishi Corporation**, had as their primary objective the import of raw materials. In order to finance imports, Japan became an exporting nation also. The **textile industry** was the first to be developed on a large scale, although many kinds of souvenir goods made in early Meiji period Japan can be found. With the closure of most of Japan's **mining** activities, the country became a major importer of raw materials that it paid for by the export of manufactured goods, first textiles in the prewar and immediate postwar period, followed by domestic **electronic** appliances and components and subsequently **automobiles**.

The **Ministry of International Trade and Industry** (**MITI**) created the **Japan External Trade Organization** (**JETRO**) to help exporters penetrate foreign markets and was most successful in achieving its goals. By the late 1980s, the United States had lodged numerous complaints with the Japanese government, and from these came the **Structural Impediments Initiative** (**SII**) talks that were intended to facilitate access to the Japanese market. While Japan bashing over trade has been common in the postwar period, this has to be placed alongside the nation's vast imports of raw materials. While it is only Australia that has a trade surplus with Japan, data from the Japan Foreign Trade Council, Inc., suggests that Japan's dependence ratio, in percentage figures, is around 10 percent for exports and 9 percent for imports. The comparable figures for Germany in the same year were 30.9 percent for exports and 26.3 percent for imports. There is no doubt, however, that the trade imbalance with some individual countries appears serious. The United States in 2002 imported U.S.$129 million worth of goods from Japan (approximately 10 percent of its total worldwide imports). Japan in the same year imported only U.S.$57 million worth of goods. The numbers are clear, but if considered against the relative size of populations, the value of imports per head is virtually identical.

The arguments over trade will probably continue, and now that the **General Agreement on Tariffs and Trade** (**GATT**) has been superseded by the **World Trade Organization** (**WTO**), the question of managed trade, particularly between Japan and the United States, a topic raised in the late 1980s, might surface again. On the other hand, all of this may pale into insignificance as Chinese exports begin to flood world markets.

TRADEMARK LAW. The Shohyo Ho of 1959 set up a system whereby trademarks could be registered and protected. They were defined as characters, letters, figures, signs, or any combination of these used in the conduct of the various aspects of business. **Trade names** (*shogo*) are not included. To prevent unused trademarks from remaining in the registry, a potentially interested user can apply for one if it has not been used within three years of the date of registration.

TRADE NAMES. These are the name (*shogo*) under which a company trades. It may have only one, even if it has several businesses. Once registered, a trade name may not be used by anyone else. Some businesses, such as **banks** and **insurance** companies, must include the nature of the business in the registered trade name.

TRADE UNIONS. *See* LABOR UNIONS.

TRUST BANKS. Shintaku Ginko are financial institutions that have both trust business and **banking** operations, which by law must be kept in separate accounting systems. The trust business deals with the management of investments, such as money, pensions, **securities**, real estate, and other assets. The banking business handles demand deposits from major **corporations** that are lent for working capital. The seven principal trust banks are **Mitsubishi**, **Sumitomo**, **Mitsui**, **Yasuda**, Toyo, Chuo, and Nippon Shintaku Ginko. Two other banks, the Bank of Ryuku and the Bank of Okinawa, along with several foreign banks, handle trust business. The financial **deregulation** that began in 1993 permitted securities companies to set up subsidiaries to engage in trust business.

TSUKIJI SHIJO. This is the largest single wholesale fish market in Japan and probably in the world. It is located in the Tsukiji district of Tokyo, on the Sumida River a few blocks east of the Ginza, and has been there since 1923. It was moved from Nihombashi because of the great Kanto earthquake and was located immediately outside the gates of the Edo Castle. It had stood on that site since the early **Edo period** (1615–1868).

The functioning of the market is quite complex. It is fundamentally a spot market based on open auctions among licensed wholesalers. The auctions are run by seven brokerages that are the primary wholesalers (*oroshi* ***gyosha***). Seafood may be taken on consignment from local sources or from importers or bought directly from **fishing** concerns. Some of the major fishing corporations, such as Maruha, are the center of *keiretsu* that supply regional markets as well as Tsukiji. There are a designated 1,677 licenses for intermediate wholesalers (*nakaoroshi gyosha*) held by 900 companies. These wholesalers buy at the auctions according to their own specialty. The specialties include octopus, tuna, shrimp, live fish, and crab, and the most common are grouped into trade associations (*gyokai*). These trade associations distribute to the retailers and end users, also specialized according to their customers, who range from top-class sushi restaurants to supermarkets or family fishmongers.

The complexity of the **distribution** system that emanates from Tsukiji, a surviving model of the traditional system, is considered by many critics to be not only out of date but also quite contrary to the trend toward simplification and streamlining of distribution in other sectors of the economy. Since the beginning of the protracted **recession of the 1990s**, both the volume and the value of sales in the Tsukiji market have steadily decreased. It remains to be seen whether this is simply a by-product of the recession or whether it is the reflection of the more general trend toward reducing the role of wholesalers in the importing business.

TSUTSUMI FAMILY. This is the founding family of the **Seibu-Saison Group** headed by Tsutsumi Yasujiro (d. 1964), whose empire was taken over by his youngest son, Yoshyiaki (b. 1935). Another son, Kiyoshi (b. 1914), fell out with his father, and a third, Seiji (b. 1928), renounced his right of inheritance. Yoshiaki became president of Kokudo Keihaku (now Kokudo) in May 1965, the principal stockholder of **Seibu Railway**. He became president of Seibu Railway in 1973. After this, he established the Seibu Lions professional baseball club in Tokorozawa City, Saitama prefecture. His status grew, and he became, among other things, president of the Japan Olympic Committee. The rise and fall of Tsutsumi Yoshiaki has been chronicled in the Japanese press as a mirror of the era he belonged to. He was arrested on 3 March 2005 on charges relating to the falsification of financial statements of Seibu Railway and of insider trading after having stepped down as president in April 2004 because of illegal payments made to ***sokaiya***, corporate racketeers. This type of old-fashioned family-style management has in several cases been demonstrably defective in three areas, and each was a problem in the case of Tsutsumi. Basically, his business, at that time a group of 135 subsidiaries employing 30,000 people, failed to meet its social obligations. It lacked a sense of the obligation to pay **taxes**, it lacked strong corporate governance, and it lacked a sense of legal compliance. It parallels the story of **Daiei** and **Yaohan**, both of which collapsed for similar reasons. In the age of the **globalization** of Japanese business, the old "one-man" rule, as it is referred to, has become outmoded. A family dynasty running a business may succeed, provided that corporate social obligations are met, but too often the line between business and family is blurred, and from there it is a small step to the inappropriate use of corporate assets, as in the case of Tsutsumi.

– U –

UBE INDUSTRIES (UBE KOSAN). Corporation founded in 1942 through the merger of Kioyama Coal Mining (established in 1897 in Ube, Yamaguchi prefecture), Ube Iron and Steel Works (coal-mining machinery manufacturer), Ube Cement Manufacturing, and Ube Nitrogen Industry, a producer of ammonium sulfate. After 1945, with the decline in coal **mining** and related industries, the company moved into the **petrochemical** field, producing polyethylene, polypropylene, and polybutadiene. It has become a general chemical manufacturing corporation that also deals in cement and machinery. Its head office is in Tokyo.

UENO YOICHI (1883–1957). A management consultant who introduced the scientific management theories of Frederick Winslow Taylor of the United States. He graduated from the University of Tokyo as a psychology major but became interested in management in the second decade of the 20th century, when Taylor's theories had become fashionable in Japan. He began applying techniques such as time-and-motion study, job description, standardization, and other related concepts to the production systems of various manufacturers. He focused on industrial efficiency and created a federation of organizations along the lines of the modern **Japan Productivity Center** to improve efficiency. World War II saw a decline in his influence, forcing him to write rather than consult. He founded a management academy (now Sanno University). He was given a prominent position in the National Personnel Authority by the **Supreme Commander Allied Powers** (**SCAP**) after 1945.

Although Ueno was a great advocate of Taylor's methods, commentators have noted that he was not merely a blind follower and that he differed from some of Taylor's underlying assumptions about human nature, preferring to see **Confucianism** and Confucian values as able to play a role in industrial management. He objected to Taylor's stress on self-interest and emphasized the Confucian virtue of harmony and cooperation as necessary for effective management. Less well known than postwar names, he was nevertheless close to the ideals enshrined in the human resource management concept of **Matsushita Konosuke**.

UFJ BANK (UNITED FINANCE JAPAN). A new **city bank** formed on 15 January 2002 by the merger of the **Tokai Bank** and the **Sanwa Bank**, the consequence of a combination of factors including **nonperforming loans**, the general state of the economy, and pressures on the **banking system** arising from global trends.

URAGA SHIPYARDS. One of the large shipyards constructed at the close of the **Edo period** (1615–1868) and the early **Meiji period** (1868-1912) to develop a **shipbuilding** industry in Japan. Most famous of the group were **Ishikawajima, Yokusuka**, and Kawasaki, all of which continue to exist as centers of heavy industry or, in the case of Yokosuka, as a naval installation, which it had been for the pre–World War II Imperial Navy.

– V –

VENTURE CAPITAL. Unlike Western economies in which venture capital has been readily available for start-up businesses since at least the 1970s, there are structural problems as well as economic ones hindering such growth in Japan. The economy is dominated by a small number of large **corporations** that will themselves create a new subsidiary or affiliate if they deem it necessary. This in turn keeps **distribution** routes restricted to existing businesses and recognized brand names. New businesses cannot compete with older companies in hiring because they cannot match their terms and conditions.

The major obstacle, however, is acquiring the capital itself. There are three small business development companies organized by the government and the private sector jointly, namely, the Small Business Finance Corporations located in Tokyo, Osaka, and Nagoya. They provide consulting services but very little money because of limited budget. There are also around 130 private venture capital companies that are funded by **banks**, **securities** companies, and **insurance** companies. The largest, Japan Associated Finance, was founded by **Nomura Securities** in 1973, and the next largest, Nippon Investment, was founded by **Daiwa Securities** in 1982, coinciding with the emerging high-tech developments of 1982–1985. The failure of many of these start-up firms between 1985 and 1987 dried up sources of finance for this kind of business, with preference going to service sector companies.

Growth in venture capital companies revived after the over-the-counter (OTC) market opened in 1990, permitting investors to buy shares in medium-sized corporations that appeared to have growth potential. The **financial deregulation** that lowered the wall between securities companies and banks, part of the **big bang** reforms started after 1993, had the effect of these companies promoting the venture capital business through their subsidiaries.

From the early 1990s to 1995, the venture capital business expanded in response to the poor performance of the major corporations, low interest rates, and recognition on the part of the government that small companies could be innovative and should be supported. A second OTC market, the Frontier Market, with easier listing requirements, was established in 1995 for fast-growing small businesses. A hundred companies took advantage of this in 1996 and went public on the OTC market. While it appeared that venture capital was now readily available, it dried up with equal suddenness when the banking crisis started and ratios of capital to assets were being examined. To preserve assets, loans to venture companies were the first to be stopped. One knock-on effect was that the growth of new companies slowed down, and bankruptcies increased.

This situation has been heavily criticized by foreign analysts who point to the fact that the purveyors of venture capital—banks and securities companies and their subsidiaries—view the start-ups as future business for the group rather than as new enterprises with original ideas. Accordingly, they favor low-risk traditional medium-sized companies over risk-taking innovators. While this may be a valid judgment of venture capital companies strategies, it could equally be a judgment of an entire economic system that has gradually placed survival against innovation, certainly not the creed of the makers of modern Japan from the **Meiji period** (1868–1912).

VERMILION SEAL SHIP TRADE (SHUINSEN BOEKI). Government-approved international **trade** licensed by **Toyotomo Hideyoshi** in the last decade of the 16th century and continued by the Tokugawa shogunate until 1635 as part of the closed-country policy of the ***Sakoku Jidai***. Ships carried an official license (*jo*) bearing the vermilion seal (*shuin*) of the shogun. The target market was the Philippines and Southeast Asia since China had been closed to Japanese ships after an edict issued by the Chinese government in 1547. Once the trade had ended, only the port of Nagasaki remained open for one Dutch ship each year. *See also* DUTCH TRADE.

VERTICAL SOCIETY. This is an explanatory model or concept of the structure of Japanese society as a complex hierarchy. It was developed by Professor Nakane Chie of the University of Tokyo in a 1967 book titled *Tateshakai no ningen kankei* (Human Relations in a Vertically Structured Society). An English version was published in 1970. The main theme is that hierarchically structured relationships are central to work, religious, and social relations, displayed in such distinctively Japanese relational forms as ***giri-ninjo***, ***sempai-kohai***, and ***oyabun-kobun***. *See also* CONFUCIANISM.

VICTOR COMPANY OF JAPAN. This company is a wholly owned subsidiary of Victor Talking Machine Co., Ltd, of the United States (RCA), incorporated in 1927. The present name was adopted in 1945. It produces audio and video products, television sets, and CDs. The overseas brand name is JVC. The company operates nine subsidiaries in Europe, North America, and Southeast Asia. It is now owned by **Matsushita** Corporation. Its corporate headquarters are in Tokyo.

VSLI. Very Large-Scale Integrated Circuit Research Cooperative formed by the government and five major computer manufacturers between 1976 and 1980. *See also* ELECTRONICS INDUSTRY; INDUSTRIAL POLICY.

– W –

WACOAL CORPORATION. This company was founded as Tako Shoji in 1949 to retail women's accessories. It grew into a comprehensive manufacturer of high-quality women's lingerie and general apparel. Its underwear business is the largest in Japan, capitalizing on the changing trends of the postwar period. It expanded to joint ventures in Thailand, Taiwan, and South Korea in 1970 and dominated the Thai market by 1980. It entered the U.S. market in 1978 and was an early entrant to China in 1979. The head office is in Kyoto.

WAKO. This is the Japanese reading of a word used by Chinese and Korean to refer to Japanese pirates who conducted marauding raids on the coastal areas of East Asia between the 13th and the 17th centuries. *Wa* carried the meaning of dwarf, and *ko* meant bandit. The earliest use of the word dates to 414 in reference to a Korean leader who defeated an army of *wako*. Struggles between Koreans and the *wako* were sometimes on the scale of a small war. In 1380, for example, a well-equipped Korean fleet destroyed a fleet of nearly 500 *wako* ships in the estuary of the Kum River. As part of the process of unifying the nation and suppressing rivals to the government, **Toyotomi Hideyoshi** and, after him, **Tokugawa Ieyasu** began a system of **trade** licensing known as the **Vermilion Seal Trade** (*shuinjo boeki*), which lasted until 1635, when the closed-country policy was implemented, and Japan entered nearly 300 years of international isolation (***Sakoku Jidai***).

WAKON-YOSAI. This was a popular **Meiji period** (1868–1912) slogan meaning "Western techniques: Japanese Spirit." It is usually interpreted as explaining how the Japanese were trying to combine some of the characteristic Japanese ways of thinking with their imported learning and science. It could be seen as symbolic of the way in which whatever is adopted from abroad is adapted to meet Japanese needs and expectations. The adoption of Frederick Winslow Taylor's system of scientific management by **Ueno Yoichi** (1883–1957) in terms of Confucian values is a good example of how the idea was applied in practice.

WHALING INDUSTRY. This important Japanese industry dates to 1606 and started in Taji, a city now in Wakayama prefecture, with early whalers using hand harpoons. A method of whaling using a net was invented and employed successfully in 1675, after which it spread along the western coast of Japan. During the period of the closed country (***Sakoku Jidai***), whaling was confined to close coastal waters. The golden age of Japanese whaling was from 1810 to around 1850. As Western whalers began appearing in Japanese waters, the breeding of whales declined, and the Japanese industry suffered. Russian whalers with modern equipment began operating off the coast of Korea during the last decade of the 19th century.

With technology imported from the Norwegian whaling industry, the Japanese modernized and quickly created a string of whaling stations from Taiwan to the northern isles. From the 1930s, they developed a fleet of small boats to hunt for the smaller species. It was not until the first Japanese whalers went to the Antarctic in 1934 that factory-ship whaling started. Before World War II and as late as in 1940 and 1941, Japanese ships sailed to the northern waters of the Pacific Ocean. World War II almost led to the demise of the industry. All six factory ships were destroyed and most of the smaller craft with them. However, the shortage of food resulted in the resumption of coastal whaling initially and factory-ship whaling in 1946. By 1952, the North Pacific whaling was restarted. A total of seven factory-ship whaling fleets were operating by 1965, and the industry had completely revived to exceed its prewar scale.

The International Whaling Commission that began functioning in the latter half of the 1960s enforced decreased catches; as a result, by 1977, only one factory-whaling ship was operating, and only four large-scale whaling stations remained. Unlike Western nations, whose whaling is conducted to obtain whale oil, Japanese whaling is more comprehensive, making use of oil, sperm whale oil, and meat extract, which are in turn processed for sale. Nonedible parts are cooked to yield whale meat extract, animal feed (meal), and soluble fertilizer. Teeth and bones are used in making various items, as is the hide.

The Japanese language has two famous proverbs about whales, one of which states that there is no part of a whale that cannot be used. The Japanese have been criticized for eating whale meat. However, the tradition goes back centuries to the time when the only whales caught were those that had beached or had strayed into isolated bays. The good fortune at such a find is enshrined in the other proverb that "one whale can enhance the well-being of seven fishing villages." Like all ancients, they learned how to use every piece of the whale for some purpose. Whaling as an industry in conformity with world regulation is barely surviving, but the Japanese continue to wait for the whale population to increase because it remains an important source of animal protein for the Japanese diet. *See also* FISHING INDUSTRY.

WOMEN. At the end of the 20th century, almost 39 percent of the workforce of around 55 million was women. This sizable proportion, it has been argued, has never received fair treatment. This, among other factors, has heightened gender awareness in a society whose understanding of the roles of men and women differs significantly from that in Western societies. Early rumblings of the rise of gender issues came in the form of the pink power movement of the 1970s. While it achieved little, it served as a reminder that the rest of the world was changing. It was the issues of **sexual harassment** and the creation of **equal opportunity laws** in other societies, particularly in the United States, that affected Japan. The notorious case of a **Mitsubishi Bank** official who gave female staff a chocolate penis as a Christmas present sparked a court case.

A raft of various kinds of discrimination cases brought to the attention of a congressional committee in the United States during July, August, and September 1991 further highlighted the impropriety of many Japanese practices abroad. It was from there only one step to the same issues being raised domestically. These various complaints in turn led to new laws and regulations that were intended to give women workers the same rights as men.

The most important of these was the **Equal Employment Opportunity Law** of 1986. The appointment in 2005 by **Sanyo Electric** of a woman chief executive officer indicates how far gender issues have progressed. However, the level of commitment required of those entering the managerial track in Japan is such that few women would wish to undertake it. Indeed, men are now given the option in some **corporations** of a standard nine-to-five job with no promotion prospects, another indirect way of equalizing rights and roles. However, major changes will continue to be slow because of the degree to which traditional Japanese cultural thinking still exerts enormous influence. *See also* JAPANESE-STYLE MANAGEMENT; PART-TIME WORK.

WORLD TRADE ORGANIZATION (WTO). The WTO was formed in 1995 as part of the entry into force of the agreements concluded at the Uruguay Round of trade negotiations signed initially by numerous governments' ministers at Marrakesh on 15 April 1994. The WTO was the next stage in regulating world trade after the **General Agreement on Tariffs and Trade** (**GATT**), which dated back to 1947. It was intended to be, among other things, an arbitrator in the case of **trade** disputes.

However, its international image is controversial, depending on how its role is perceived. On the one hand, it is widely recognized that it was designed to regulate fair trade. Others, however, view it as a tool of richer countries to ensure that the world's economic status divide remains as it is, placing it in the same bracket at the International Monetary Fund (IMF) or other organizations that are claimed to exploit poorer nations for the benefit of the richer. Its 10th Anniversary was marked by a number of events, including a report by the Consultative Board to Director General Supachai Panitchpakd on the *Future of the WTO*. At any rate, it is a much-needed institution that has an important regulatory role that may change to meet new needs. Nevertheless, anti**globalization** protesters will doubtless continue to attack its very existence, making its work more complicated and challenging.

– Y –

YAKUZA. General name given to organized crime groups in Japan, many of which trace their roots to the **Edo period** (1615–1868). The term originated from a card game (*sanmai karutua*) in which, as in blackjack, there was a winning number, in this case 19. Someone with 8 (*ya*), 9 (*ku*), and 3 (*za*) was close but useless. The nuance of "worthless" was thus attached to the name. Japanese *yakuza*, however, have graced themselves with a so-called code of honor derived from the values of the Edo period, particularly of the **military houses**. They are also well known for their ultranationalism. However, they remain parasites, living off human weakness and exploitation. Drugs, prostitution, and real estate are typical areas of operation. For a time, they were heavily involved in small loans and consumer finance (*sarakin*) at exorbitant interest rates.

Yakuza groups also have a record of blackmailing large **corporations**. ***Sokaiya*** were often paid large sums of money for their silence, although the enforcement of the law has become stricter, but scandals involving them brought down **Tsustumi** Yoshiaki of the **Seibu Group** after revelations in 2004.

YAMAHA. Nippon Gakki was founded in 1897 by Yamaha Torakusu to produce reed organs. It grew to being a manufacturer and world leader in the marketing of musical instruments known under the brand name Yamaha. Pianos, organs, electronic organs, guitars, audio systems, keyboards, and, more recently, household items, such as mirrors, wash basins, and cabinets, plus motorcycle parts, now make up the product line. From 1900 it began producing upright pianos, and in 1932 it built Japan's first pipe organ. This was followed by the world's first electronic organ in 1959. It began its international business by exporting its Butterfly brand of harmonicas to the United States in 1915.

Postwar Japan experienced great expansion as music education developed rapidly and the culture of pop music of many genres spread worldwide. This was also aided by the technology that produced the tape recorder, the CD, and other devices for playing recorded music. Its headquarters are in Shizuoka prefecture.

YAMAICHI SECURITIES. Yamaichi Shoken was the smallest of the big four **securities** companies in Japan that collapsed on 24 November 1997. Its failure was due to a combination of bad investment policies, and this was a major event in the **banking** and finance crisis of the closing years of the 20th century.

YAMAMOTO KANSAI (1944–). He is one of the best-known postwar generation of fashion designers who achieved international recognition. He was born in Kanagawa prefecture and educated at Nippon University. He was the first designer to hold a show abroad, in his case London in 1971.

YAMAMOTO TAMESABURO (1893–1966). Entrepreneur born in Osaka who inherited a bottle-making business that he developed into Nippon Bottle Manufacturing in 1918. He became managing director of the Nippon Brewery and Mineral Water company and executive director of Dai Nippon Breweries. When Dai Nippon Breweries was split into **Asahi Breweries** and **Sapporo Breweries**, Yamamoto became president of the Asahi Company. He went on to become one of the leading figures in postwar industrial reconstruction.

YAMASHITA TARO (1889–1967). Entrepreneurial pioneer of Japan's overseas **oil** development. He was born in Akita prefecture and graduated from Sapporo Agricultural College (now the University of Hokkaido). With many young men of his generation, he went to work in Manchuria and in other parts of the Japanese Empire. In 1956, he created Japan Oil Export (now Arabian Oil Company) to engage in oil exploration in the Persian Gulf.

YAMATAKE-HONEYWELL. This is a highly regarded **electronics** manufacturer that produces air-conditioning and fuel control equipment. The company dates to 1906, when it was founded by Yamaghuchi Takehiko, and to a sales agreement with Brown Instruments of the United States made in 1920. Brown was acquired by Honeywell in 1934, and in 1952 a licensing and **joint-venture** agreement was made with Honeywell. The quality of the company's products is internationally recognized, and they are sold through Honeywell's worldwide distribution system. Yamatake-Honeywell also manufactures in Taiwan. The head office is in Tokyo.

YAMATO TAKKYUBIN. This was the first company in the field of overnight delivery of small packages and a major truck haulage business. It goes back to a company founded in 1919 at Kyobashi in Tokyo by Ogura Yasuomi. With only four trucks, he initially struggled to compete with the lower-priced horse and cart services. A 1923 contract with **Mitsukoshi Department Store**, Japan's first **department store**, gave him a solid operational base on which he developed the business. He studied road haulage in the United Kingdom and started a route between Tokyo and Yokohama in 1929 and extended it to the entire Kanto area in1935. After World War II, the company resumed in 1949 but did not enter the Tokyo-to-Osaka route until 1960, by which time competitors were in the field.

Ogura Maso succeeded his father as president in 1971 and following the United Parcel Service (UPS) model of the United States began overnight service delivery in 1976. By 1986, through a tie-up with UPS, he initiated international service. The Yamato network covered all of Japan by 1989. With the rise of convenience stores (***konbini***), the company began pickup services for suitcases, golf clubs, and skiing equipment as well as home removal services and book delivery. The service was gradually extended to include cash collection for mail-order companies, television sales, and **Internet** retailers. Others that followed in the field are Footwork and Sagawa Kyubin, making for fierce competition between rivals.

YAMAZAKI BAKING. This is Japan's largest bread-baking corporation founded in 1948 and now producing Western-style bread and Japanese-style confectionery goods. It was very successful in the immediate postwar years through mass production of bread by means of modern equipment. It expanded to 22,000 retail outlets and set up offices in New York, where Yamazaki is related to the National Biscuit Co. (Nabisco), and Paris and Taipei. Its affiliate, Kansai Yamazaki, added great strength to domestic sales and merged in 1986. It has a subsidiary created in cooperation with Nabisco of the United States, Yamazaki-Nabisco. Its headquarters are in Tokyo.

YANO TSUNETA (1865–1951). Entrepreneur and business leader born in Okayama prefecture who studied at but did not graduate from the University of Tokyo. He worked in the Ministry of Agriculture and Commerce and was responsible for drafting the Insurance Business Law (Hokengyo Ho) in 1900. He left the Ministry in 1902 and founded Daiichi Seimei, the first mutual **insurance** company in Japan. All other companies followed Daiichi Seimei's lead and became mutual insurance corporations after 1945. *See also* DAI-ICHI MUTUAL LIFE INSURANCE.

YAOHAN. An initially successful **department store** chain that collapsed due to overextension. It traces its origins to 1930 to a store opened by Wada Ryohei and his wife in Atami City. The first modern department store was established in 1962 with its head office in Numazu City in Shizuoka Prefecture. Under the leadership of Wada's oldest son, it opened its first store in Brazil in 1971, then Singapore in 1974, followed by the United States and Hong Kong. It became listed on the Tokyo Stock Exchange in 1986, after which it opened stores in Brunei, Malaysia, and Taiwan. In 1990, its head office was moved to Hong Kong with the plan of opening 2,000 stores in China. It opened branches in Thailand and in China in 1991 and in the United Kingdom in 1993, and in 1995 "Nextstage Shanghai" claimed to have the largest total counter length in Asia.

Yaohan financed itself through warrant bonds and convertible bonds issued five times, in 1990, 1992, 1993, and again in 1994. It was forced to begin restructuring in 1996 but declared bankruptcy in 1997. Its collapse is part of the story of the **bubble economy** of the period, but it has also been attributed to the worst side of Japanese management in which family management of assets preempts any kind of objective decision making or adequate external fiscal control. Wada himself was at one time feted by *Fortune International* as a model corporate president. He continues to offer his advice to fledgling businesses, although the collapse of Yaohan left his credibility open to question.

YASHICA. Camera maker incorporated in 1949. It successfully mass-produced double-lens reflex cameras and helped to popularize camera ownership. It merged in 1983 with **Kyocera Ceramic**, a producer of ceramic items for the **electronics** industry. It has manufacturing subsidiaries in Hong Kong and Brazil and has nine overseas sales companies. The corporate headquarters are in Tokyo.

YASUDA BANK. The Yasuda Ginko was founded by **Yasuda Zenjiro** in 1880 and became the centerpiece of the **Yasuda *zaibatsu***. It was renamed **Fuji Bank** after 1946 when the **Supreme Commander Allied Powers** (**SCAP**) ordered the dissolution of all the large-prewar financial combines.

YASUDA FIRE & MARINE INSURANCE. Yasuda Kasai Kaijo Hoken is one of the major sellers of non–life **insurances**. It began as a fire insurance company in 1880 and was the first company of its kind. It joined the **Yasuda *zaibatsu*** in 1893, and after a 1944 merger with two other companies, it became known by its present name. It is a member of the **Fuyo Group**, which that is made up of former Yasuda Zaibatsau concerns as well as those of the **Asano *zaibatsu***, the **Okura *zaibatsu***, and several others.

YASUDA TRUST & BANKING. Yasuda Shintaku Ginko was first organized as a **trust bank** within the **Yasuda *zaibatsu*** in 1925. The company functions as a normal **bank** but also specializes in long- and middle-term financing, annuity trusts real estate, and **securities**. It belongs to the **Fuyo Group**. It is also one of the member companies of the "Silver Service Promotional Association," set up by the Ministry of Health because of its activities in the field of finance involving trusts for the elderly. *See also* SILVER BUSINESS.

YASUDA ZAIBATSU. Business enterprise started in 1880 by **Yasuda Zenjiro** when he founded the **Yasuda Bank** that in time became the center of the financial combine of all the Yasuda-related corporations. The **holding company** was abolished in 1945 by order of the **Supreme Commander Allied Powers (SCAP)**. It was replaced after the war by a ***keiretsu*** known as the **Fuyo Group**, which that is centered on the **Fuji Bank**.

Unlike some of the other ***zaibatsu*** that had origins in **shipbuilding**, heavy industry, or **trade**, the Yasuda *zaibatsu* was made up primarily of finance-related companies, **insurance**, and real estate but with little involvement in manufacturing or heavy industry. The **bank** and the trading company he founded in 1899, Yasuda Shoji were both placed under the control of his holding company, Yasuda Honzensha. Both became **joint-stock companies** after World War I in 1919, by which time the Yasuda *zaibatsu* consisted of 17 banks and 16 other corporations, all under the holding company. When Zenjiro died in 1921, **Yuko Toyotaro** was brought in from the **Bank of Japan** to manage the holding company. He successfully merged 11 of the banks to create the Yasuda Bank, capitalized at ¥150 million and with deposits of 542 million, making it Japan's largest bank.

After the abolition of the holding company, all the individual members were made independent. However, from the 1950s, the ***keiretsu*** was loosely reformed into the Fuyo Group of 29 companies, whose presidents began meeting regularly after 1966. Because of Yasuda Zenjiro's friendship with **Asano Soichiro** and **Mori Nobuteru**, the companies of their *zaibatsu* joined the Fuyo Group in the 1950s.

YASUDA ZENJIRO (1831–1921). Founding figure of the Yasuda Bank (now Fuji Bank) and the **Yasuda *zaibatsu***. He began as a street-corner money changer in the closing decade of the **Edo period** (1615–1868) and by this means acquired capital to begin creating his empire. In 1887, he set up Yasuda Honzensha as a **holding company** to secure his family wealth. Borrowing from his own **Yasuda Bank**, he reached a capitalization of ¥1 million, a vast sum for that time. He turned the **bank** into a limited partnership in 1893 and in 1894 reorganized Yasuda Honzensha in keeping with the government's new **Commercial Code**. He formed Yasuda Shoji, a trading company (***sogo shosha***), in 1895 to manage a range of interests he had hitherto handled himself. He kept close friendly relations with **Asano Soichiro**, founder of the **Asano Zaibatsu**, and **Mori Nobuteru**, the industrialist who set up numerous companies in several industries. Zenjiro was assassinated in 1921 by a member of an ultranationalist group to which he refused to give a donation.

YASUKAWA DAIGORO (1886–1976). He was a business pioneer, born in Fukuoka, Kyushu, the son of Yasaukawa Keiichiro, a coal-mine developer. After graduating from the University of Tokyo, he founded **Yasukawa Electric** with his father and brother to manufacture engines, becoming president in 1936. After World War II, he occupied several posts, including director of the Coal Agency and subsequently the first director of Japan's Atomic Energy Research Institute in 1956. His last major task was to chair the organizing committee of the 1964 Tokyo Olympic Games.

YAWATA IRON AND STEEL WORKS. Yawata Seitetsujo was the largest steel mill built in 1896 at Yawata Mura (now part of Kita Kyushu in Fukuoka prefecture) as part of the plan to build a rich economy and a strong military (***fukoku-kyohei***) of the **Meiji** government. The project was under the direction of the Ministry of Agriculture and Commerce and was financed mostly by the sale of public bonds, with some money coming from war indemnities paid by China after the Sino-Japanese War of 1894–1895. In 1934, it merged with five other companies to form Nippon Steel (Nippon Seitetsu) and was a major arms supplier to the Japanese military. It was broken into Yawata Seitetsu and Fuji Seitetsu after World War II by order of the **Supreme Commander Allied Powers (SCAP)**. The two companies united again in 1970 to become **Nippon Steel Corporation**. *See also* IRON AND STEEL INDUSTRY.

YKK. *See* YOSHIDA KOGYO.

YODOAYA TATSUGORO. This is the inherited name of successive heads of an **Osaka merchant** family during the **Edo period** (1615–1868). The family name was Okamoto, and the founder, Tsuneyasu, moved to Osaka in 1619 and opened a lumber business under the trade name Yodoya. Gaining not only wealth but also the trust of the **Tokugawa shogunate**, the house was put in charge of the raw silk trade with China, and it also acted as agent for some regional feudal lords (*daimyo*) in the **Dojima Rice Market** in Osaka. In 1705, the fifth incumbent of the Yodoya name was censured by the shogun for being improperly extravagant in lifestyle. The house wealth was confiscated and the family banished from Osaka in a display of the kind of arbitrariness that typified the feudal system of the time. The incident was subsequently portrayed in literature and drama.

YOEKI. This is a term referring to Taika Reform of 645. Under the later **Ritsuryo Seido**, more detailed laws were formulated in the **Taiho Code** of 701. Two kinds of taxes were listed. One was *saieki*, which was levied by the central government. It was normally regulated as 10 days of labor per year or could be paid in kind by a piece of cloth around eight meters in length. The other was *zoyo*, which was levied by provincial governors, and consisted of from 15 to 60 days each year, depending on age.

YOKOHAMA MAINICHI SHIMBUN. This was the first modern Japanese daily **newspaper** started in 1871 by Iseki Moriyoshi, the governor of Kanagawa. It was bought in 1879 by a journalist who moved it to Tokyo, making it the *Tokyo-Yokohama Mainichi Shimbun*. It began to acquire a reputation for investigative reporting on various scandals and questionable business deals. It became the *Mainichi Shimbun* in 1886 and continued as the *Tokyo Mainichi Shimbun* after 1906 until it was absorbed by the *Teito Ninichi Shimbun* in 1940.

YOKOHAMA RUBBER. Founded in 1917 with capital from **Furukawa Electric** and B. F. Goodrich Company of the United States, it is a major producer of **automobile** tires and second in scale to **Bridgestone Tire**. The company also manufactures industrial products and

aircraft components. It started in its early days with tire and tubes but diversified after World War II, when it began to manufacture radial tires for ex port. The head office is in Tokyo. *See also* FURUKAWA ZAIBATSU.

YOKOHAMA SPECIE BANK. The Yokohama Shokin Ginko was a government-founded **bank** set up in 1880 to increase the supply of silver specie in Japan and to serve the needs of exporters and trading companies. It was given special status in 1887. It became a colonial bank serving Japanese interests in Manchuria after the Russo-Japanese War of 1904–1905 and was central in a consortium that lent money to China. It continued to function as an instrument of government fiscal policy until it was reorganized as a commercial bank by order of the **Supreme Commander Allied Powers** (**SCAP**) in 1945 and renamed the **Bank of Tokyo**.

YOKOSUKA SHIPYARDS. These yards were the forerunner of the Yokosuka Naval Arsenal. They were originally created in 1866 by order of the **Tokugawa shogunate** as a foundry and shipyard. A French naval engineer, François Verny (1837–1908), designed the yard and supervised construction. After the **Meiji Restoration of 1868**, the government took control and placed them under the Ministry of the Navy. The present name, Yokosuka Zosenjo, was adopted in 1871, after which it began producing ships, initially with French help but thereafter independently. It was one of the four largest naval arsenals in Japan until the end of World War II, when it came under control of the U.S. Navy and has remained so ever since.

YOMIURI SHIMBUN. Japan's most widely circulated **newspaper**, founded in 1874 by the Nisshusha newspaper company as a small daily targeting the general public that became popular and successful very quickly. In 1917, the company changed its name to the Yomiuri Shimbun Sha in line with the name of the paper. The policy of publishing only a morning edition in the 1920s almost bankrupted the *Yomiuri*, which was faced with competition from papers that also provided an evening edition. **Shoriki Matsutaro** took control of management in 1924. His revolutionary ideas ranged from sensational reporting to publishing the schedule of radio broadcasts. He brought a U.S. major league baseball team to Japan and founded the nation's professional baseball team, now known as the Tokyo Yomiuri Giants.

By 1941, the *Yomiuri* had achieved top circulation in the Tokyo area. Wartime circumstances forced a merger with the *Hochi Shimbun* to create the *Yomirui-Hochi Shimbun*. In 1946, the paper underwent an internal power struggle in which the **labor union** was defeated in an attempt to take control. The paper reverted to its old name and, by 1952, had expanded to Osaka. Its principal offices are in Tokyo, Osaka, and Kita Kyushu, with suboffices in Sapporo and Takaoka, along with 20 overseas bureaus. It also publishes an English-language daily as well as books and magazines. Its daily circulation is over 10 million copies, giving it the largest circulation in the world.

YOSHIDA KOGYO (YKK). Highly successful manufacturer of zip fasteners founded in 1945 by **Yoshida Tadao** (1908–). The company's production system was highly mechanized from the beginning, starting from raw materials to finished product. The quality of YKK products quickly became known worldwide, and it is by far the largest manufacturer in this field. The company is also active in the field of nonferrous metals for building purposes. The company is not listed on the stock exchange because the founder believed in an employee shareholding system. The head office is in Tokyo.

YOSHIDA TADAO (1908–). He is the founder of **Yoshida Kogyo,** the successful manufacturer of fasteners marketed under the brand name YKK. He was born in Toyama prefecture and received an education only to the age of 14. He worked for a trading company but started his fastener production at the age of 26. In spite of the war years from 1941 to 1945, his venture survived, and he formed Yoshida Kogyo in 1945. The company expanded through the acquisition of related companies in Japan and consequently increased production at home and abroad, all under the watchful supervision of Yoshida, who directly managed the company to a ripe old age. He passed away in 1993.

– Z –

ZA. *See* GUILDS.

ZAIBATSU. First used in the **Taisho period** (1912–1926), the term referred to large family-controlled industrial combines that began to emerge as major forces in the economy in the early years of the 20th century. They were ranked by size and influence. **Mitsui** was the largest, employing in the prewar period almost 3 million people. **Mitsubishi** was next, followed by **Sumitomo** and **Yasuda** and then the smaller ones, **Asano**, **Okura**, **Furukawa**, and **Kawasaki**. By 1930, they controlled 15 percent of the nation's joint stock capital and were able to withstand not only the effects of World War I but also those of the **Great Depression** of 1929.

The years between World War I and World War II saw the *zaibatsu* grow in power and prestige. Apart from expanding their business interests, their relations with the political system became complex and controversial. Whether through inside information or good judgment, **Mitsui Bussan**'s management believed in 1931 that because of the Great Depression, Japan would place an embargo on the export of gold and substantially devalue the yen, which in fact happened. As a result, Mitsui Bussan and Mitsui Trust bought, according to press reports, ¥10 million worth of U.S. dollars. The defense offered was the termination of the gold standard by the United Kingdom. Public disfavor over this resulted in the assassination of the leading figure of the group, Dan Takuma, in 1932.

This was part of a process that forced the *zaibatsu* as a whole to take on a more nationalistic outlook in keeping with the mood of the times and be less concerned with their profits. The Mitsubishi *zaibatsu*, like Mitsui, was forced to undergo *tenko*, a change of spiritual direction under which family interests were severely restricted, and shares (albeit a modest amount) were sold to the public as a gesture in order to spread wealth more evenly. The actual result was that the *zaibatsu*, unintentionally, came to be seen as more political and patriotic. With Mitsubishi leaning more and more to heavy industry, it became a major supplier of the Japanese military machine.

After the defeat in 1945, the *zaibatsu* were judged by the **Supreme Commander Allied Powers (SCAP)** to be a major support if not the source of the Japanese war effort and were therefore technically dismantled, with **holding companies** being abolished. Large companies were divided into smaller ones, and the democratization of industry and commerce was thought to have been achieved. How far this would have been pursued is an interesting question, but contracts to service the U.S. military during the Korean War resulted in the regrouping of companies in the interests of cooperation. The **Antimonopoly Law** (1947) was never very effective, and given the Japanese preference for structured group activity, it is hardly surprising that the former *zaibatsu* transformed themselves into industrial groups (*kigyo shudan*) known also as ***keiretsu***.

The differences between the *zaibatsu* and the *keiretsu* are substantial, the most important being that the relations are generally less formal. The **Sumitomo Group** most closely resembles the old system. In addition, new industry-centered groups emerged, the largest of which is the **Toyota Group** of over 300 companies all contributing to the core business. The lifting of the prohibition on holding companies in 1997 was dictated by the needs of the depressed economy and enabled several groups to restructure their finances to avoid complete bankruptcy.

While some observers are wary of a revival of the *zaibatsu*, others argue that the fear is exaggerated. Commerce and industry have changed such that flexibility is now a vital element of corporate strategy as much as solidarity was a century before. **Globalization** has created a new set of challenges that cannot be dealt with by structures that belong to an earlier period. The *zaibatsu* are best seen as a unique Japanese solution to the problems of socioeconomic development in the early years of the 20th century but as one that might look anachronistic in the 21st century. The Japanese preference for group activity will not change, but the form in which it expresses itself may differ in accordance with the perceived needs of the time.

ZAIGO SHONIN. These were rural merchants of the hinterlands of large cities during the late **Edo period** (1615–1868) who were originally active in farming villages and who became rich because of the cash crops of the early 18th century. This gave them considerable influence in the market economy of the period, and by the early 19th century they were well established as dealers in cotton, cottonseed, rapeseed, oils, vegetables, **rice**, and grains. The urban merchants' associations (***kabu-nakama***) initially hindered their growth because those associations were under government patronage. However, as the *zaigo shonin* became stronger, they were able to bypass the associations, and by 1841 the associations had been abolished. The *zaigo shonin* were rising in wealth and status, and some even moved into fields such as **sake** brewing. This in turn led to more rural manufacturing, which was integrated into the economy. There are various theories about the impact of these merchants, but one fact is plain, namely, that their social mobility was an important contributory element in the collapse of the **Tokugawa feudal system**.

ZAIKAI. This is a term used in journalism to refer to financial circles, business, and industry as distinct from *seikai* (political circles) and *kankai* (**bureaucratic** circles). The four main *zaikai* organizations are **Keidanren** (Federation of Economic Organizations), **Keizei Doyukai** (Japan Committee for Economic Development), **Nikkeiren** (Japan Federation of Employers' Associations), and the **Japan Chamber of Commerce and Industry**. Spokespersons for the *zaikai* in the postwar period have included the following notables: **Ishizaka Taizo**, president of Keidanren from 1956 to 1968; **Doko Toshio**, former president of **Ishikawajima-Harima Heavy Industries** and of **Toshiba Corporation** and president of Keidanren from 1974 to 1980; and **Inayama Yoshihiro**, chairman of **Nippon Steel Corporation**, who was also chairman of Keidanren from 1980 to 1987.

ZAISEI TOYUSHI. This is the name of a government investment and loan plan that was intended to mobilize surpluses from the National Treasury by using government-run savings, pensions, and life insurance programs under direction of the **Ministry of Finance**. Its purpose was to give loans to various **public corporations**, such as **Japan National Railways** (before it became privatized), **Nippon Telegraph and Telephone Public Corporation** (also before privatization), Japan Housing Corporation, and **Japan Highway Public Corporation**, and to local governments. Unlike the government budget, which required Diet approval, this program could be used at the Ministry's discretion, providing another example of the complex subtlety of the Japanese financial system.

ZAITEKU. This term is used to refer to the practice that developed from the mid-1980s as a result of the strength of the yen as an international currency and of Japanese manufacturers engaging in the investment of large amounts of money in the then-rising Japanese stock markets to increase income and enhance profits. The anticipated benefits were severely curtailed by the collapse of the markets and by the **recession of the late 1990s**. *See also* ENDAKA.

ZENIYA GOHEI (1773–1852). He was a merchant and trader of the **Edo period** (1615–1868) who was born in Kaga province (now Ishikawa prefecture) into a family engaged for several generations in the money-changing business. He developed a successful business transporting goods between what is now Hokkaido and Fukushima prefecture, owning over 20 ships that plied various routes. His wealth grew as he began lending money even to the government of Kaga. Rather like the tale of **Yodogoya Tatsugoro**, his wealth made him unpopular with officialdom. On the allegation that he had failed in a land reclamation project, his assets were confiscated, and he was imprisoned until his death in another arbitrary act of the **Tokugawa feudal system**.

Glossary 1

Business Proverbs

Japanese businessmen frequently express themselves using proverbial expressions to make a point succinctly and suggestively. These are drawn from a variety of sources, the majority of which are expressed in Japanese imagery, although many date back to the Edo period (1615–1868) or before. Not a few however, are derived from concepts or expressions found in the Chinese classics. Others are the kind of universal proverbs found in the common sense of almost all cultivated civilizations. Examples of all varieties follow.

PROVERBIAL EXPRESSIONS DERIVED FROM CHINESE CULTURE AND THE CHINESE CLASSICS

井の中の蛙 (*i no naka no kawazu*, lit. "a frog in a well") The original Chinese version was the work of Zhuang Zhu (399–295 B.C.E.), who declared that "with a frog who never leaves the well one cannot discuss the ocean," implying that experience is a precondition of understanding. The Japanese version usually refers to someone who finds him- or herself in unfamiliar surroundings. The compound of the two characters, *i* (well) and *kawazu* (frog), can also be read as *seia* and refers to someone who is narrow-minded.

兵は神速を尊ぶ (*hei wa jinsoku o tattobu*, lit. "in war, speed is of the essence") It is a way of suggesting that once a business plan is agreed, it should be implemented without delay before any rivals can develop the same strategy.

過ぎたるは及ばざるが如し (*sugitaru wa oyobazaru ga gotoshi*, lit. "going too far is as bad as not going far enough) This comes from the *Analects* of Confucius, book 11:15. When asked which of his pupils was better between Shih and Shang, he stated that one went too far but the other not far enough and that both positions are inadequate. Striking a balance in strategies is being advocated.

柳に雪折れなし (*yanagi ni yuki-ore nashi*, lit. "even heavy snow cannot snap bamboo"), suggesting that being flexible is a source of strength and that pressure can be resisted without being broken.

蛇の道はヘビ (*ja no michi wa hebi*, lit. "a serpent, or a big snake, always knows the routes taken by other snakes") An idea close to the expression "it takes one to know one" but with the more positive nuance of an expert knowing his field thoroughly being able to guide novices. One other Chinese equivalent is that rats know the way of rats.

備えあれば憂いなし (*sonae areba urei nashi*, lit. "if you are prepared, you have nothing to worry about"), used often to warn someone who is not adequately prepared. This idea belongs to the famous Chinese treatises on the art of war.

楽あれば苦あり (*raku areba, ku ari*, lit. "pain follows pleasure") is a commonsense warning that no condition is permanent. One meaning of the symbol of the *Dao* in Chinese thought (which reverses on itself) is that in times of plenty, prepare for adversity, and, likewise in times of adversity, prepare to rise again.

虎穴に入らずんば虎児を得ず (*koketsu ni- irazuneba koji wo ezu*, lit. "if you do not enter the tiger's lair, you will not capture a tiger cub") Some prized items call for risks to be taken in their procurement.

PROVERBIAL EXPRESSIONS BASED ON JAPANESE CULTURE

棚からぼた餅 (*tana kara botamochi*, lit. "a rice [*mochi*] cake fell from the shelf into his lap or hands"), used to refer to an unearned but beneficial piece of good fortune.

太鼓判を押す (*taikoban wo osu*, lit. to give a large [drum-sized] seal of approval to someone or something), used to refer to a recommendation by someone of credibility and status, a form of endorsement very important in Japanese business.

鶴の一声 (*tsuru no hito koe*, lit. "one word from the crane") Considered the most elegant of birds, the crane features in everything from sake brand names to the logo of Japan Airlines. The expression refers to pronouncements or orders issued by a superior.

暖簾に腕押し (*noren ni use oshi*, lit. "pushing through the noren"), referring to the curtain hung out in Japan to indicate that a restaurant or shop is open for business. It is pushed aside by beating the air, suggesting actions that are not really profitable.

目から鼻に抜ける (目から鼻に抜けるような人) (*me kara hana ni nukeru*, lit. "in through the eye and out through the ear"), implying someone who is very quick and clever.

娘一人に婿八人 (*musume hitori, muko hachinin*, lit. "one daughter, eight suitors"), used to refer to situations where the range of options or choices is very wide.

横車を押す (*yokoguruma wo osu,* lit. "to ride a big wagon"), implying riding roughshod over people's feelings or public opinion.

禍転じて福となす (*wazawai tenjite fuku to nasu*, lit. "making good fortune out of bad fortune"), similar to "pulling the chestnuts out of the fire."

糠に釘 (*nuka ni kugi*, lit. "hammering a nail into bean paste"), a meaningless action, used to refer to talking to people who will not listen.

あちら立てればこちら立たず (*achira tatereba kochira ga tatazu*, lit. "to save the face of one is to lose the face of another"), implying that one cannot run with the hares and chase with the hounds and is therefore unable to satisfy both sides.

縁の下の力持ち (*ennoshita no chikaramochi*, lit. "a strong man under the floorboards") comes from the passageways. It refers to someone who inconspicuously performs a thankless but important task.

鬼の目にも涙 (*oni no me ni no namida*, lit. "even a demon can shed tears"), suggesting that no one is truly heartless.

負けるが勝ち (*makeru ga kachi*, lit. "pull victory from the jaws of defeat"), referring as in English to pulling off a come-from-behind victory.

身から出た錆び (*mikara deta sabi*, lit. "rust from one's own body"), meaning to lie in the bed that one has made.

怪我の巧妙 (*kega no komyo*, lit. "a great act coming out of an injury"), meaning a lucky break.

古川に水絶えず (*furukawa ni mizu taezu*, "old rivers never really dry up"), an expression using an archaic form of Japanese, suggesting that business from old and established customers can continue, provided they are properly serviced.

人を見て法を説く (*hito o mite, ho wo toku*, lit. "see the person then teach the law") Allegedly advice from the Buddha that it is wise first to understand the audience before presenting a position.

仏作って魂入れず (*hotoke tsukutte tamashii irezu*, lit. "making a statue of Buddha but giving it no soul"), meaning that if perfection is not sought, the result will be poor.

後悔先に立たず (*kokai saki ni tatazu*, lit. "regret never precedes a bad action") Since regret is useless, it is better to avoid things that may be regretted.

先んずれば人を制す (*sakinzureba hito wo seisu*, lit. "if you take action before others, you will be in charge"), an exhortation to be proactive in daily affairs and always be ahead.

背に腹は代えられない (*se ni hara wa kaerarenai*, lit. "one cannot exchange one's stomach for the sake of one's back"), implying that during a crisis, emergency measures are necessary, even saving the stomach at the cost of the back if that is the priority.

提灯に釣鐘 (*chochin ni tsurigane*, lit. "a paper lantern and a temple bell"), suggesting the image of a match between uneven or incongruous opponents or colleagues.

石橋を叩いて渡る (*ishibashi wo tataite wataru*, lit. "tapping a stone bridge before crossing"), implying the actions of a very cautious person.

宝の持ち腐れ (*takara no mochigusare*, lit. "a treasure decayed before use"), which implies a talent wasted through lack of use.

損して特取れ(*sonshite toku tore*, lit. "small losses can lead to big profits") Used when yielding short-term concessions in the interests of long-term gain.

手玉に取る (*tedama ni toru*, lit. "the beans are in little sacks"), meaning to have control of someone just as a heavy load of beans can be carried easily if divided into small amounts.

同病相哀れむ (*dobyo ai awaremu*, lit. "people with the same illness feel sympathy"), referring to people in similar circumstances being able to understand each other.

節供働き (*sekku bataraki*, lit. "lazy people begin to work in the evening") Sekku means a festival day, and such people work after they have had the day's fun and celebration. They do not prioritize work.

ないそでは振れない(*nai sode wa furenai*, lit. "nothing comes out of the sleeve if there is nothing in it") While the Japanese image of the kimono sleeve is used, it expresses the universal principle that people get back only what they put into an endeavor.

縁は異なもの 味なもの (*En wa i na mono, aji na mono*, lit. "good fortune is great") or "Love is a many spendored thing"—now applied to mergers and acquisitions where the "*en*," or fortune through meeting, truly matches the needs of each partner.

二階から目薬 (*nikai kara megusuri*, lit. "eye drops from the second floor"), implying that there is no logistical chance of success.

盗人にも三分の理あり (*nusubito nimo sanbun no ri ari*, lit. "even a thief has a 30 percent reason for his actions"), suggesting that there is some rationale in all behavior even when bad.

能あるタカは爪 を隠す (*nou aru taka wa tsume wo kakusu*, lit. "A really sharp hawk hides his claws"), meaning a shrewd businessman who does not expose his hand.

ひょうたん駒 (*hyotan kara koma*, lit. "a horse can come out of a gourd"), meaning that the impossible sometimes happens.

花を持たせる (*hana wo motaseru*, lit. "to have someone take a flower"), meaning to let someone benefit by taking the credit for some success.

魚心あれば水心 (*uogokoro areba mizugokoro*, lit. "if the fish has a feeling of water, the water will have a feeling for the fish"), referring to mutual attraction between the sexes. It also refers to corporate cooperation.

無理が通れば道理が引っ込む (*muri ga toreba dori ga hikomu*, lit. "when force [irrationality] holds the road, reason backs off"), used when yielding to an irrational or stupid superior.

すまじきものは宮仕え (s*umajiki mono wa miyazukae*, lit. "the life of a government official is not to be envied") This famous line from Kabuki drama dates to the Edo period (1615–1868) and was widely used and understood to mean that as long as one works for another, a lot of humiliation is to be expected.

敵に塩を送る (*teki nki shio wo okuru*, lit. "let's send salt to the enemy"), a saying recalling the incident when Takeda Shingen (1521–1573) was blockaded by Uesugi Kenshin, who magnanimously sent some salt to Takeda because the blockade prevented him from receiving any. In modern times, the nuance has changed to it refer to benefits given to a country that might enable it to become hostile.

柳の下の二匹目のどうじょう (*yanagi no shita no nihikime no dojo*, lit. "a second loach found under the willow tree"), implying that one success might lead to another. The original version, however, *yanagi no shita ni itsumo dojo wa inai*, warns that finding another loach in the same place is unlikely.

PROVERBIAL EXPRESSIONS FOUND IN OTHER CULTURES

塵も積もれば山となる (*chiri mo tsumoreba, yama to naru*, lit. "piled up specks of dust can turn into a mountain") The expression can be used in two ways. Small, accumulated economies in a business can turn into big savings. It also implies that if problems are not dealt with in a timely manner, they can grow to an unmanageable scale.

二足の草鞋 (*ni-soku no waraji*, lit. "wearing of two sandals"), referring to individuals working at more than one job, similar to wearing two hats in English idiom.

餅は餅屋 (*mochi wa mochiya*, lit. "let the rice cake maker make rice cakes"), meaning every man to own profession.

手も足も出ない (*te mo ashi mo denai*, lit. "neither hand or foot can move"), referring to anyone who is completely in a bind. "Bound hand and foot" is found in English idiom.

安物買いの銭失い (*yasumonogai no zeni ishinai*, lit. "to buy cheap is to lose money"), close to the English idiom "penny wise, pound foolish."

終わりよければすべて良し (*owari yokereba subete yoshi*, lit. "all's well that ends well"). This is also the name of one of Shakespeare's plays, and the expression carries the same meaning.

それはやぶ蛇になります (*sore wa yabuhebi ni narimasu*, lit. "that will become a snake in the bush"), referring to something best not disturbed. It matches the English "let sleeping dogs lie."

笛吹けど踊らず (*fue fukedo odorazu*, lit. "I have piped, but you won't dance"), referring to people who are exorted to action but do not respond. This is found in an identical form in the New Testament of the Judeo-Christian writings (St. Matthew 11:17; St. Luke 7:32).

Glossary 2

Traditional Business Expressions

This group of expressions is derived from aspects of Japan's Edo period (1615–1868) culture: political, social, and economic. They have all acquired new usages because of the changes that have taken place in business culture since modernization began in 1868. The fact that even with modifications these expressions can still be used, albeit metaphorically, in modern business life is a reminder of the power of continuity within the process of change in modern Japan. The expressions listed here are in common use but do not fit the categories of entries in the dictionary, nor are they proverbial expressions.

ABURA WO URU (油を売る). Meaning literally "selling oil" and modeled on the rather laid-back sales style of rapeseed oil sellers of premodern times, it is used to refer to someone who does not pursue his tasks with the level of enthusiasm expected by his or her employer. It also refers to people who take longer than necessary for an outside assignment or who kill time sitting in coffee shops when they could be back at their desks.

AOTA-GAI (青田買い). "To buy a green rice paddy" was an Edo period (1615–1868) business strategy of buying rice on the stalk prior to harvesting. This enabled farmers to receive payment before delivery. It came in modern times to refer to the corporate practice of offering jobs to the best prospective graduates well in advance of graduation. While the numbers graduating have been decreasing since the mid-1990s, corporations still offer jobs to outstanding applicants up to a year in advance of graduation.

ASAMESHI-MAE (朝飯前). "Before breakfast," implying a job that is easily completed without much effort.

ATE-UMA (あて馬). Meaning "used horse," this expression referred originally to a stallion brought close to a mare to prepare her for mating. The concept that the stallion is a decoy is applied in modern business to refer to any method used to tease out the ideas, strategy, or pricing policy of another corporation. In bidding, decoy companies may be asked to tender in order to find out the objectives of the company that has been designated as the first choice.

ATO-NO-MATSURI (あとの祭). "After the festival," meaning too late to be of use or past the "sell-by" date. Also refers to something that is out of date or past the date of usefulness.

CHA-BOZU (茶坊主). Sarcastic term applied to individuals who try to find special favor with their boss. Originally referring to low-ranked samurai of the Edo period (1615–1868) who donned monastic robes and shaved their heads in order to serve tea (*ocha*) to the shogun, it came to refer to those engaged in menial tasks. But since such people had unique access to the shogun's ear, their influence could be disproportionate to their status. Whether they were modest or arrogant, they were not viewed favorably, and the term came to take on a contemptuous tone on the part of those labeling other employees as "tea-serving priests."

CHONBO (チョンボ). A term used in the Japanese game of Mahjongg that refers to a player declaring incorrectly that his or her hand has been completed, an error that breaks the rules, and for which penalties are incurred. It refers in corporate contexts to careless errors of a minor nature.

DAIKOKU-BASHIRA (大黒柱). Literally meaning the central pillar that supports a traditional-style Japanese house, the expression refers to a person who is central to an organization or a project. The expression *chushin-jinbutsu* is also used for the same purpose.

DOSA-MAWARI (ドサまわり). Referring originally to provincial tours by entertainers during the Edo period (1615–1868), it came to refer in business or bureaucracy to people who are consistently assigned to the regions and away from the head office. It can also be interpreted as a way of suggesting to an employee that there is no real place for him or her in the organization.

FUTOKORO-GATANA (懐刀). The reference is to the short dagger carried in the chest overlap of the kimono during the Edo period (1615–1868). Since it was carried in an intimate position, it was close to the heart of the owner and might be called into service in the event of unexpected danger. In modern business parlance, it refers to a right-hand man who is privy to the plans and secrets of his boss. While being a position of honor, it can also carry serious risks.

GEKO (下戸). In contrast to the rich, there were the people who were considered so poor they could not drink alcohol. People who appear to become drunk easily because they do not appear to be accustomed to alcohol are referred to in this way (lower townspeople).

GETA WO AZUKERU (下駄を預ける). Traditionally, people checked in their *geta* (Japanese wooded clogs) when entering a theater or a store. In business, it refers to someone being given the responsibility to make a decision by informing that person that he or she is being entrusted with the *geta*.

GIRI-ON (義理恩). Repayment of a debt incurred either through a relationship or a favor granted, failure to discharge which would cause loss of face or could be regarded as an insult to someone's honor.

GO-EN (御縁). A Buddhist term referring to the cycle of cause and effect that maintains the flow of life. The concept of *en* can relate past, present, and future. In the business world, it signifies a relationship between companies or that they work in the same market, often competing for market share. To have *en* with a company or a person is positive. Not to have *en* implies a negative outcome of a negotiation or a relationship.

GOMASURI (ごますり). Based on the image of grinding sesame seeds. The seeds fly around inside the earthenware bowl being used and often stick on the mortar in what looks like a cringing manner. The term *gomasuri* (someone who grinds sesame seeds) refers to anyone who is a sycophant and who crawls, flatteringly, to his superiors.

HANAMICHI-WO-KAZARU (花道を飾る). Literally, to decorate the walkway to the stage with flowers. Hanamichi refers to the stage structure of the Edo period (1615–1868) form of drama known as Kabuki, where an apron leads from the main stage through the audience to the back of the theater. It is used in some large corporations to refer to the preparations for the retirement celebrations of a president, chairman, or senior executive.

HARA (腹). Seat of the emotions in Japanese cultural anthropology. Many expressions using *hara* are found in daily usage. The most famous perhaps is *hara-kiri*, better referred to as *seppuku* but which can mean to decide radically about something. Some expressions using *hara* in Japanese can be translated using "heart" in English. *See also* SUICIDE.

HARA-NO-MUSHI (腹の虫). Literally "to have an insect or worm in one's stomach" is a way of expressing anxiety about a situation involving reassignment, a contract, or the success or failure of a project.

HASHIGO WO HAZUSARERU (はしごを外される). The ladder of corporate promotion may not necessarily advance a career. Removal of the ladder, the meaning of the expression, refers to a promotion that carries rank but no supporting staff, which is one method of weakening someone's influence in the organization.

HESO WO MAGERU (ヘソを曲げる). Literally meaning that someone's navel is off center, this expression refers to someone who is difficult, unreasonable, and uncooperative. Such a person may also be petty and consumed by trivia and problematic on a daily basis, sometimes because of what was perceived as unfair treatment.

HIDARI-UCHIWA (左うちわ). Carrying the fan in the left hand in order to let the right hand free to draw one's sword if necessary. In business parlance, it came to refer to the state of always being prepared for an emergency and having the presence of mind to deal with the unexpected. More recently, it came to carry the nuance of living worry free.

HI-NO-KURUMA (火の車). The fiery wagon used in the Buddhist hell to transport the wicked in a painful manner. It refers to any organization or individual in dire financial straits.

HIRU-ANDON (昼あんどん). Meaning a paper lantern lit in daylight, something that cannot be seen, the expression refers to someone whose presence is not conspicuous and whose value is therefore difficult to assess.

HITORI-ZUMO (一人相撲). Meaning a sumo match in which the wrestler fights with himself, it refers to someone who is facing a major task alone but, instead of concentrating on the task, is mixing his own problems into the scenario, thus making everything unnecessarily complicated.

HIYA-MESHI-KUI (冷飯食い). The "cold rice eaters" were the children of the household, or the lowest-ranked members of the household. Traditionally, the head of the house and the eldest son ate first when the rice was hot. The rest of the family ate their rice after it had become cold. In business, it refers to people whose work is not important. It can also refer to people passed over in the promotion process.

HONNE-TATEMAE (本音建前). *Tatemae* (from the terminology of building) means erecting the building framework, while *honne* (from music) means the pure sound. It is used in Japan to distinguish between what someone says and what the same person is actually thinking. It was a cultural device created to keep smooth relations between people by avoiding harsh words that might lead to future confrontational situations. Hence the preference to say, "I'll think about it," as against saying, "Absolutely no!" Among politicians in Japan, it has become an art by means of which they make pleasant gestures while concealing their personal ideas or actual intentions.

INSEI (院政). Cloistered emperor of the Heian period (894–1185) who was active behind the scenes in influencing decision making in the government. In contemporary parlance, it refers to people who have retired from a senior post but who continue to influence the organization because the new leadership is either weak or personally dependent on the retired executive. A retired president or chairman may continue as an adviser to the company for a year or two to help smooth the way for his successor.

JINGI (仁義). The five virtues taught by Confucius were humanity (sometimes benevolence), righteousness, propriety, wisdom, and sincerity. The two Chinese characters for *jin* and *gi* refer to the virtues of humanity and justice. The warrior code of the samurai stressed these two virtues as the basis of social order. The term was transformed by its use among *gumi*, or gangs, of the Edo period (1615–1868) who used it to refer to the *oyabun*, or head man, of the group.

KACHU-NO-KURI (火中の栗). Literally "chestnuts in the fire," it has the same nuance as "pulling the chestnuts out of the fire." It was most likely introduced by Jesuit missionaries when they also brought Aesop's fables.

KAKI-IRE-DOKI (書き入れ時). Literally meaning "time to write in," it referred to merchants writing up their sales ledgers, particularly at busy seasons such as midyear or end of year. It originally meant a written guarantee to provide collateral for a loan. Like many expressions, its meaning gradually evolved over time to refer to the busy periods of the business year.

KAI (甲斐). A term from antiquity referring to things perceived as worthwhile. *Iki-gai* means something worthwhile in life, such as one's work or a human relationship.

KAMIKAZE-GA-FUKU (神風が吹く). *Kamikaze*, meaning "divine wind," refers to the two occasions, in 1274 and 1281, when Mongol armies tried to invade Japan. On both occasions, typhoons foiled the invaders, and the Buddhist leader Nichiren (1222–1282) coined the expression. In business, it refers to a lucky break or a big unexpected order that gets business moving. It should be distinguished from the reference to taxi drivers who break the rules of the road to save time. That name came from the suicide pilots who crashed their aircraft into U.S. ships at the end of World War II.

KANO-DORI GA NAKU (閑古鳥が鳴く). The Japanese cuckoo is known for its plaintive cry. In the business world, it refers to times of recession or when business is poor, especially in bars and clubs, where the staff members are waiting but where there are no customers.

KATABO WA KATSUGU (片棒をかつぐ). Meaning literally "to carry one end of the pole," it referred to the way in which people of rank were carried in a private palanquin, which had a pole front and back. Because bearers often robbed customers, the expression acquired a slightly sinister nuance analogous to the English expression "partners in crime."

KATA WO IRERU (肩を入れる). The expression "putting one's shoulder under the pole" originates, as does the preceding one, from the metaphor of the palanquin bearer. This expression carries the positive nuance of helping someone's career in its early stages.

KEMU NI MAKU (煙に巻く). Meaning literally "to wrap something in smoke," the expression refers to one side taking advantage of the other's ignorance of some aspects of the proposed business in a negotiation.

KI (気). Human vitality and energy in Japanese is referred to as *ki*. It contrasts with the Chinese concept of *chi*, which uses the same character. In the Chinese tradition, it means to harness the power of heaven as in the exercises of *Tai-chi*. In Japanese culture, *ki* arises from within. *Yaru-ki*, for example, refers to a high degree of motivation. Japanese disciplines are designed to strengthen and elicit *ki* from workers and athletes, the quality that guarantees success.

KIMON (鬼門). This refers to the gate by which demons enter, usually from the northeast. Traditionally, buildings never had a gate to the northeast and never had a washroom or kitchen located there either. The same applied to the southwest. In modern use, it refers to someone's bête noire, or a weakness or lack of skill in some field.

KOGAI (子飼い). Meaning originally a domestic pet, such as a cat or dog that one has found and brought up from its infancy, the term came to refer to anyone who apprenticed himself as a child to a tradesperson during the Edo period (1615–1868). It refers now to anyone who is under the patronage of a superior from the time he joined the company.

KONJO (根性). Like *yaru-ki*, the term refers to the virtues of tenacity, determination, and will power. People with *konjo* are considered a great asset to their company.

KOSHI-KUDAKE (腰くだけ). The waist/hip area of the human body that is used in numerous expressions. This one comes from sumo, when a wrestler's waist begins to "break down" in the middle of the ring. In business it refers to someone who has a tendency to collapse at the crucial moment in a negotiation. Someone who is overwhelmed by a situation is referred to by the expression *koshi ga nukeru* (腰が抜ける), meaning that his waist is out of joint.

KUBI O KAKERU (首をかける). The neck is symbolic of status, honor, and professional reputation. Therefore, to stick out one's neck in Japanese is similar to "stake one's life" in English. *Kubi o kiru* (首を切る), to cut the neck, meant execution or, in modern business usage, dismissal.

KUGI O SASU (釘をさす). Traditional Japanese buildings such as the Grand Shrines of Ise were jointed without nails. To hammer (*sasu*) a nail (*kugi*) into a joint was intended to make it doubly secure. The expression refers to an act of confirmation of something by a telephone call or follow-up visit. It is a standard practice of Japanese businesses that many westerners find tiresome but that is expected. The expression also covered the securing of a roof so that in a typhoon it would not move. The nuance here in business refers to reminders that certain things were agreed to and that the agreement is binding.

KUROMAKU (黒幕). An image from Bunraku (puppet plays) where the puppets are moved around by stagehands dressed all in black. In modern life it refers in business or politics to backstage manipulators who cut deals and set up agreements, unseen to the public eye.

MA O MOTASU (間をもたす). The term *ma* means "space" or "interval" in the vocabulary of Japanese aesthetics. *Ma o motasu* means to fill in time if an unexpected gap appears in a program. *Ma o ireru* (間を入れる), literally to "insert an interval," is really the equivalent of "to take time out," usually for consideration of strategy before taking action.

MIYA-ZUKAE (宮仕え). *Miya* were palaces of the nobility in ancient times. *Miya-zukae* meant to serve in a palace. In modern business, it refers to anyone working under a superior who is not kind or reasonable.

NAISHOKU (内職). Traditionally the side work of a samurai or the chores of a *ronin*, a masterless samurai. It can also refer to work done at home by housewives, such as translation of books and papers, or even writing articles for payment by anyone who is working full time.

NAKAZU TOBAZU (鳴かず飛ばず). Taken from a Chinese story of a lazy king who was rebuked by a retainer who used the metaphor of a bird that neither cries nor flies, it refers to someone who has failed to meet the expectations of people who judged that person to be more able than he or she turned out to be.

NANIWA-BUSHI (なにわ節). This was the name of a famous minstrel act performed in Osaka whose old name was Naniwa. The themes were always tragedy, involving separation of parents and child or the vigilante exploits of *yakuza* in punishing corrupt officials. Anyone referred to as a "*Naniwa bushi*" is someone who has a strong sense of justice. It can also refer to someone who places emotion over reason in negotiations.

NAWABARI (縄張り). Japanese feudal castles had several gates after which came a maze of passages hung with ropes (*nawa*) to show the way. *Nawabari* came to mean the ground plan of a castle. During construction, areas of responsibility were marked with ropes. Each contractor had his own "*nawabari*," meaning now his sphere of influence. A corporate manager may take his staff to his favorite bar, his "*nawabari*," where he will be responsible for the bill.

NEWAZA-SHI (寝わざ師). In judo, the term refers to an offensive technique used by someone lying on the mat to reverse the bout. It refers to people able to spring surprises even when they appear to be almost defeated.

NIBAN-SENJI (二番せんじ). Based on a method of Chinese medicine that boils herbs in order to isolate the essence needed for treatment, the idea of boiling something twice is considered excessive and negative. It is also used as a criticism of simple imitations.

NIPPACHI (二八). Referring to the second and eighth months of the year (February and August), the coldest and hottest months of the year, the modern nuance is that of the slowest months of the business year. The business slowdown often forces enterprises to reschedule projects.

NOREN-WAKE (暖簾分け). Referring to the cloth curtain hanging over the doorway of restaurants in the Edo period (1615–1868), as it still does in modern Japan, it symbolized being open for business. To "split" the *noren* meant to give the right of franchise, name and *noren*, to a relative or long-serving employee.

NUKEGAKE (抜け駆け). This refers to the warrior who leaves his camp before an engagement and carries out a raid on the enemy camp by himself out of sheer bravado. Successful or not, it was forbidden because of the risk it entailed and because it was a breach of discipline. In modern corporate culture, it refers to glory seekers who ignore company policy and undertake something alone. Even if the result is successful, as with the original *nukegake*, it is not a popular or respected way of behaving.

ODAWARA-HYOJO (小田原評定). Recalling the 1583 siege of Odawara Castle, the headquarters of Hojo Uiyasu, by Toyotomi Hideyoshi (1536–1598), when those inside the castle could not decide whether to fight or negotiate, the expression refers to any discussion that reaches no conclusion and consequently leads to no action.

OGOSHO (大御所). The name of the residence of a retired shogun of the Edo period (1615–1868), or *insei* (retired emperor). The *ogosho* is the celebrity of the past who is still celebrated in old age because of his achievements.

OHAKO (十八番一おはこ). Read also as *juhachiban* (eighteen), it refers to the 18 most famous Kabuki plays of the Ichikawa family. It means now a person's unique skill or talent that is often called on as a party piece.

OKAME-HACHIMOKU (岡目八目). In the game of *go*, it refers to the onlooker who can see eight moves ahead of the players, the way in which an outsider can often see things better than the participants.

OMONO (大物). Also called a *daijinbutsu* (大人物), the term refers to an outstanding and recognized leader or central figure in a field. Leaders of the Meiji Restoration such as Saigo Takemori (1828–1877) or academic leaders such as Fukuzawa Yukichi (1835–1901), founder of Keio University, are typical examples.

OSUMITSUKI (御墨付き). A document bearing the seal of the shogun or a ranked feudal lord giving someone a privilege or authority to act under certain circumstances. In modern business, it refers simply to approval given to someone by a superior.

OWARAWA (おおわらわ). Literally meaning "big child," it referred to the image of a warrior whose topknot (*chonmage*) unraveled in a fight and who ended up looking like a child with his hair down. People who are so busy that they cannot take time to attend to their appearance are *owarawa*.

OYABUN-KOBUN (親分子分). Literally "parent part-child part," the expression refers metaphorically to any relationship of boss to underling, whether in work gangs (*gumi*), such as carpenters, or in criminal gangs (*yakuza*). Being part of the feudal structure of Edo period (1615–1868) society, it implied an absolute and unchangeable relationship that reflected the natural order of things and that people accepted because individual loyalty was the key to receiving the protection of the *oyabun*.

OYAKATA (親方). Term referring to the head person in an *oyabun–kobun* relationship. In modern times, sumo stable heads are referred to as *oyakata*.

SEKIGAHARA (関ヶ原). Japanese fondness for dramatizing situations by means of historical analogies gives rise to numerous metaphors. At Sekigahara, Tokugawa Ieyasu (1546–1616) eliminated his final rivals to become master of Japan and imperially appointed shogun. In contemporary business, it refers to corporate conflicts for market share.

SHAKUN (社訓). Following the Edo period (1615–1868) merchant house constitutions, many modern corporations have their policy stated as precepts to be followed by all members. These are often recited at the morning assembly.

SHAZE (社是). Usually written on a *kakejiku*, a hanging scroll, the *shaze* symbolizes the corporate ideal. It may also be displayed at special events such as days when new staff join the organization at a special ceremony for that purpose.

SHIO (塩). Salt is traditionally a purifying agent used in Shinto rituals. Many restaurants place two piles of salt outside their entrance, one on each side, hoping to keep misfortune out and good customers in.

SHIRAHA-NO-YA (白羽の矢). White feather (*shiraya*) and arrow (*ya*) refers to a legend of a divine being (*kami*) who identified a girl he wanted by placing a white feathered arrow on the roof of her house. The *shiraha-no-ya* was the sacrifice in days gone by. It now means someone who has been selected for a special duty. Such a person is never spoken of directly or even congratulated in these terms because of the past sad nuance.

SODE-NO-SHITA (袖の下). Literally meaning "under the sleeve," this expression refers to underhanded, or "under the table," activities, such a bribery.

TANABOTA (棚ぼた). A lucky windfall.

TANA-OROSHI (棚下ろし). Literally to take down from the shelf, it refers to stocktaking or inventory checking.

TARAI-MAWASHI (たらいまわし). A circuslike act in which a wooden vat (*tarai*), about 120 centimeters in diameter, is twirled around (*mawashi*) by an acrobat laying on his back with his legs in the air. It refers to a situation where something goes round and round without ever achieving anything. It can refer to negotiations or more frequently to political deliberations.

TATAKI-AGE (叩きあげ). Traditionally a term used to refer to hammering metal, including steel for swords, into shape. It describes someone who has starts from humble status and who by developing solid character rises to a highly respected position.

TATAKI-DAI (たたき台). At festivals, a merchant may bang (*tataki*) his table (*dai*), reducing his price in order to make a sale. In business parlance, it means to place something on the table for study or discussion. While the concept is old, the usage dates to the 1960s.

TEN-NOZAN (天王山). A 1583 battle that changed the course of Japanese history. Modern confrontations between labor unions and corporate management climax in the "*Ten-nozan*," the last decisive conflict before a pay settlement is reached.

TONOSAMA-SHOBAI (殿様商売). Feudal nobility did not engage in any trade but had to deal with merchants in the course of managing their domains. Having no experience, they were frequently cheated. The image of people who were robbing him while bowing to him was ironic. When companies begin to depend on reputation and not on products, they are accused of being like feudal lords trying to do business.

TOZAMA (外様). The feudal lords of the Edo period (1615–1868) who were not part of the shogun's inner circle were known as *Tozama*, the independent lords. In modern business, it refers to people who come into a corporation in midcareer and who are therefore not purebred members of the organization.

UCHI-AGE (打ち上げ). Normally used to means the close of a performance, it has come to refer to a drinking party held to celebrate a business success. It also helps to deepen the esprit de corps of the company staff.

UMI-SEN YAMA-SEN (海千山千). According to a Chinese legend, a snake that has lived one thousand years in the sea (*umi-sen*) and another thousand years on a mountain (*yama-sen*) will become transformed into a dragon that can fly to heaven. It refers to someone well versed in the ways of the world who rarely loses a negotiation. It denotes someone who will be difficult to deal with at any level.

YAKUTOKU (役解). The receiving of a gift because of one's position. For example, as a buyer, receiving a midyear or end-of-year gift is *yakutoku*. If the gift is disproportionately large or the official hints at wishing a more expensive gift, *yakutoku* can shade into bribery. In any gift-giving context in Japan, the gift should be in proportion to the situation.

Glossary 3

Modern Business Expressions

This list of expressions is mostly post–Meiji Restoration (1868) and developed during the Taisho (1912–1926), Showa (1926–1989), and Heisei (1989–) periods, reflecting business usages and customs that grew up as Japan underwent modernization and, since 1945, increasing degrees of internationalization. However, similar to any Western ideas they may seem to be, there is always a residual nuance that remains Japanese or that reflects some aspects of Japan's unique practices or perspectives.

AISATSU MAWARI (挨拶まわり). Following the formal New Year's greetings by a company president to all staff, employees begin to make a round of customers and clients after visiting different sections of the company. Not only New Year's visits but also courtesy visits both inside and outside the company made by an executive after arriving in a new post are referred to by this term.

AKA-CHOCHIN (赤ちょうちん). Literally "red lantern," it is the sign of an informal restaurant where workers can meet causally, eat a variety of small dishes, and open their hearts to each other over a few drinks or have one for the road before boarding their train home.

APOINTO (アポイント). Traditionally, employees of one company could drop in unannounced citing a reason, such as passing through the district. *Appointo*, short for "appointment," means that the intention of a visit is announced. The window of time may be flexible. Visits to senior executives may be referred to as *yakusoku* and are for specific times.

BANZAI! BANZAI! (ばんざい). A celebratory expression used on special occasions such as victory, ending of a party, and even sending off newlyweds on their honeymoon. Literally "ten thousand years," the phrase originates in classical Japanese literature and implies a wish for longevity, success, and prosperity.

BENKYO SHINASAI (勉強しなさい). Although meaning literally "study hard," this has become an idiomatic way of asking for a discount in the process of bargaining, "*benkyo shimasen ka*?" (Won't you consider reducing the price a little please?). Merchants seeking volume turnover would normally agree to "*niju-en benkyo*," namely, a ¥20 discount or whatever they judged appropriate. While this kind of bargaining is not common and prices are normally regarded as set at the most competitive levels, discounts to regular customers are quite common, particularly in sushi restaurants, where prices are frequently unpublished and where bills can be expensive. Some restaurant chains and supermarkets use point cards, which accumulate with each visit and which can lead to modest savings over a period.

BONEN-KAI (忘年会). The end-of-year office party that encourages people to "forget the old year," as the title implies. Staff eat and drink and are encouraged to become intoxicated in order to wash away the memories they wish to forget as well as say "*Banzai*" over moments of success. The corresponding post–New Year's event is the *shinen-kai*.

CHARAN-PORAN (ちゃらんぽらん). Referring to undependable people who avoid difficult situations by either telling a lie or blaming others. Its origin is uncertain.

-CHON (-チョン). Someone assigned to a city away from home and without family. Saka-chon, means someone sent to Osaka, and Nago-chon refers to someone living in Nagoya. The general name for this kind of person is *tanshin-funin*.

CHOREI (朝礼). The company morning assembly at which the president or section leader gives greetings and an exhortation for the day. This may also include some physical exercises to music, singing the company anthem (*shaka*), or reciting the company creed (*shakun*).

CHOTTO-IPPAI (ちょっと一杯). A request from a colleague to join him or her for a quick drink after work, usually to troubleshoot a problem that cannot be conveniently discussed in the office or in front of other staff members. Not infrequently, these meetings take place at an *aka-chochin*.

DAME-OSHI (だめ押し). The process of reconfirmation of attendance at a meeting or delivery of goods. Normally done on the day, in the case of meetings, or one or two days before delivery is due, either by sender or by receiver, to confirm that goods will be delivered as promised. The purpose is to ensure that everything will go smoothly and according to plan.

DOKI (同期). Relationship among those entering a company (or school) at the same time. *Doki* frequently meet formally or informally to maintain contact and exchange information. *Doki no Sakura* is the name used to refer to contemporaries who became *kamikaze*.

DOSOKAI (同窓会), DOSOSEI (同窓生). College graduates of the same year whose continuing relationship can be very important for business. Meetings are occasions for exchanging news and information about current business trends.

EN-MAN-TAISHA (円満退社). Leaving the service of a company amicably after submitting a letter of resignation.

GAKUREKI (学歴). The personal history that includes all important information about high school and university, facts that determine the pedigree of a prospective employee.

GASHI-KOKAN (賀詞交換). The exchanging of greetings and name cards during the first few days of the New Year. This is done at reception parties organized for the purpose by various organizations. It is convenient for businessmen to meet many people at one time.

HAENUKI (はえぬき). People who join a company upon graduation and remain with it their entire working life.

HANKO (はんこ). The personal seal of an individual used instead of a signature. In the processes of administration, the *hanko* of all relevant officials is required, with the president being the final one. This ensures the orderly circulation of information towards final approval.

HARAGEI (腹芸). The *hara* (stomach) is the seat of the emotions. *Hara-gei* refers to nonverbal "stomach communication" between people who have a basic understanding of the subject under discussion.

HIJIKAKE-ISU (肱かけ椅子). The large chair with armrests that marks the managerial rank from lower ranks, accompanied usually by a larger desk.

HIKINUKI (引き抜き). Someone recruited by a company for a special purpose outside the normal annual hiring time.

ISHIN-DENSHIN (以心伝心). Expression referring to people's ability to communicate without words, slightly similar to the idea of *haragei*.

JIGYOKA (事業化). Term referring to industrialization or commercialization.

JIGYOKA (事業家). Entrepreneur or business innovator used particularly of the early modern period after the Meiji Restoration of 1868.

JIHYO (辞表). The formal letter of resignation submitted by an employee who wishes to leave. Verbal intimation to leave is not acceptable. The company may refuse for a number of reasons, and therefore departure should be negotiated in a way that is satisfactory all round.

JIKISO (直訴). Once a proposal for a project has been passed over by the immediate superior of the person who proposed it, he or she may take it directly (*jikoso*) to the president or managing director. This is an action that calls for a strong spirit, good timing, and a sound sense of judgment.

JIKO-TAISHOKU (次子退職). A request to retire from a company for personal reasons, a request that may or may not be well received by the management.

JINJI-IDO (人事異動). During March of each year, decisions are made about corporate staffing arrangements for the ensuing year. Staff changes in departments, overseas assignments, transfers between branches, and major reassignments are all decided before the new fiscal year commences on 1 April. "Staff movement" is not merely a personnel issue. It is also a human resources policy designed to upgrade all round versatility, a concept central to Japanese corporate culture. A supplementary *jinji-ido* may also be scheduled in October.

JIN-MYAKU (人脈). *Myaku* means a vein that links things or people. *Jin-myaku* means personal connections, a vital part of business culture.

JIREI (辞令). The official document, ceremonially presented that states the appointment, promotion, transfer, dismissal, or retirement of an individual. These are most frequently issued early in April or once *jinji-ido* decisions have been made.

JITSUGYOKA (実業家). Industrialist, leading businessman, or captain of industry, a term referring to current business leadership.

KABAN MOCHI (鞄持ち). Baggage carrier, implying someone whose role is minor, particularly on a business trip.

KABU GA AGARU (株が上がる). "Stock value rising" is a metaphor referring to the rise of an individual's reputation or value to an organization. The opposite, *kabu ga sagaru*, refers to a reversal in fortune.

KABU GA SAGARU (株が下がる). "Stock value declining" when used of an individual means that the individual's reputation, popularity, or esteem in the company or in society is going down. It carries a heavy and negative nuance.

KAKI-KYUKA (夏季休暇). The annual summer vacation, scheduled around the time of the Buddhist *Obon* rituals to permit people to return to their home towns to take part in ancestral observances.

KAKUSHI-GEI (かくし芸). Meaning literally "hidden entertainment," it refers to the assumed ability of every businessman to be able to perform a party piece in public for the amusement of other staff or for customers. Such talents may range from singing a popular *karaoke* song to magic tricks.

KANGEI-KAI (歓迎会). A party to welcome new staff to a company or people transferred or reassigned to a new section or branch. These are occasions to integrate new staff after the *jinji-ido* staff reassignment in March and part of the nationwide Japanese corporate policy of building solidarity within the labor force.

KARAOKE (カラオケ). Literally "without an orchestra," the word was invented to refer to people singing songs to recordings of music. Use of CD audiovisual support was introduced as soon as CDs went on sale. Originally confined to clubs for business entertainment, *karaok*e quickly spread to all age-groups, and the expensive club atmosphere was replaced by the *karaok*e box, rooms of various sizes fully equipped with *karaoke* machines and microphones and appropriately soundproofed and supplied with liberal amounts of beer and other beverages. Since the 1990s, *karaoke* has spread beyond Japan and has become popular in many countries.

KATA-TATAKI (肩たたき). The "tap on the shoulder" expresses the manner in which a superior will approach someone about to become 55 years of age with the information that his services will no longer be required by the organization. Most companies have a retirement age of 55. If someone has been evaluated as an asset, that person may be promoted or given a higher position in a subsidiary in the case of a large company. Government civil servants are not retired by age, but if their usefulness has ended, they may receive the *kata-tataki*. Most people concede and try to get the best arrangement possible in terms of retirement allowances. High-ranking people in the civil service are often hired by companies in the business field with which they are familiar.

KIBO TAISHOKU (希望退職). Voluntary resignation has been welcomed in companies going as far back as the oil shock of 1972 and again after the bubble economy burst in 1990. Retirement allowances are calculated according to the employee's basic salary and years of service, normally one month's basic salary multiplied by the number of years of service. This may be reduced in the case of someone leaving before the mandatory retirement age for personal reasons or increased if it is in the company's interest to release an employee.

KOSAI-HI (交際費). This is the company budget allotted for entertainment of guests and maintaining good public relations. More money is spent on this in Japan than in any other business culture, and consistently the amount spent nationwide exceeds the national defense budget.

MADOGIWA-ZOKU (窓際族). The *zoku* ending refers to a group or gang. In this case, it is the group that sits beside the window. It refers to people managed out to the fringe of the organization, literally, often beside a window. They are usually assigned relatively meaningless tasks in order to justify drawing a salary since dismissing staff can become extremely difficult. It is sometimes translated as "the windowsill tribe."

MAE-DAOSHI (前倒し). This occurs when passengers lurch forward in a bus or car that brakes suddenly. It became a government term used to refer to the often-used strategy of spending money on public works projects to stimulate the economy. In the private sector, it refers to the advancing of a schedule, which calls for tremendous efforts within the company to complete the project within the new time frame.

MAI-CAR SHUGI (マイカー主義). In the 1970s and 1980s, owning a car was a dream. Car ownership expanded dramatically, and with the launch of small cars aimed at the housewives market, such as the Suzuki Alto or the Nissan Marche, many Japanese became two-car families. These K-jidosha, as they are called in Japanese, pay a lower rate of road tax and consume less fuel, in effect doubling the domestic car market in just over a decade.

MAI-HOME SHUGI (マイホーム主義). A 1970s and 1980s expression of the dream of many Japanese to own a home at a time when costs were prohibitive. The expansion of condominiums (known in Japanese as "mansions") has enabled many people to purchase and own a home. Compared to the United States or Europe, however, these homes are quite small and eventually require regular maintenance. For that reason, many people still prefer to rent.

MEISHI KOKAN (名刺交換). The ritual exchange of business cards at a first meeting or at any social event when such opportunity arises. Weddings are such occasions, especially if the bride and groom come from families that are high in the corporate hierarchy. Even when the meal is being served, people get up and "work the room," exchanging business cards with people they want to meet and whose place they can find from the seating plan conveniently laid out on every table.

MIYAKU WO MIRU (脈を見る). To "take the pulse" of a plan or project to see if it is still viable or if it has senior executive support.

MIZU SHOBAI (水商売). "Water trade" refers to the restaurants and bars where corporate entertainment takes place. Although they perform an invaluable service, many customers do not hold bar owners in high esteem, often because of underworld connections.

MIZUHIKI-TORIHIKI (水引取引). This refers to a transaction that entails a small loss in order to make a greater profit at a later date.

MIZU-KAKE-RON (水賭け論). Literally, "water dousing argument," this expression refers to an inconclusive argument.

MIZU NI NAGASU(水に流す). To let the water wash away the past after an incident to permit "bygones to be bygones."

MORETSU (モーレツ). A 1960s buzzword referring to the almost fanatical way in which Japanese workers slaved from early morning until late at night in order to rebuild the nation. The "*moretsu shain*" were known internationally as "workaholics," the generation that drove Japan to rapid economic growth rates in the late 1960s, lifting the nation to become the second-largest economy after the United States.

NAKATTA-KOTO NI SURU (なかったことにする). Meaning to start over by reverting to the situation before anything took place. For example, if two companies make an agreement but have not yet signed a contract and one is forced to renege, that company asks the other to agree that there was no such agreement. The side that benefits most from *nakatta-koto* incurs an obligation (*giri*) that may be called at some time in the future.

NAKI (泣き). *Naku* means to cry, not a posture, usually associated with Japanese businessmen. However, various metaphors about crying are used in business to cover a range of situations where failure or disappointment are experiences. *Naki-neiri*, "to cry oneself to sleep," may be used when a project is taken away unexpectedly and there is no one to consult. *Naki wo ireru* means to make a crying plea to a superior. *Naki-dokoro*, or "crying place," refers to someone's weak point.

NEGAI (願い). In order to receive permission to travel, attend a funeral, or even have annually approved leave, a *negai* (request) must be formally submitted to the immediate superior, and thereafter it finds its way to the president's desk for final approval. There is a correct form to be filled in for everything from office supplies to maternity leave. *Negai* means "request."

NIGIRI-TSUBUSHI (握りつびし). This term refers to a proposal submitted to a superior who simply ignores it, "crushing it in his hand," so to speak. *Nigiri-tsubusareta* means that the project has been totally rejected, opening the way for a direct appeal.

NURUMA-YU (ぬるま湯). A lukewarm bath can refer metaphorically to the situation of someone whose workplace offers no surrounding stimulus and whose overall situation is neither good nor bad and who finds no motivation to change jobs or look for new challenges. It is like sitting in a comfortable bath.

OBUROSHIKI (大風呂敷). The *furoshiki* is the cloth sheet that is used to wrap and carry gifts. The big *furoshiki* was used to carry goods for sale during the Edo period (1615–1868). Salesmen often boasted of how big was the *furoshiki* that they were carrying. This led to referring to people who exaggerated as *oburoshiki*.

OL. "Office lady" refers to the young women who work in companies. Originally, in parallel with businessmen, they were referred to as BG (business girls). Because the term in English had a quite different meaning, BG was replaced by OL, which seemed less offensive. OL normally refers to younger women, perhaps up to the age of marriage or late thirties. "Career woman" has been introduced to refer to women who pursue a career in a manner similar to their male counterparts.

ONAJI KAMA NO MESHI (同じ釜のメシ). Literally "eating rice from the same bowl," this refers to people not of the same family but who have lived together and shared similar experiences. Company retreats, dormitory life, and evening drinks and dinner are all designed to reinforce solidarity.

OTEMORI (お手盛り). Referring to someone who fills his or her bowl rather than having it filled by another. When Japan was rebuilding after the war in the Pacific that ended in 1945, food was in short supply. People would fill their own bowls to collect as much as they could. Because of this, it came to refer to self-centered and greedy behavior. Executives giving themselves large bonuses when the company is not making money, as often happens in the United States, is an example of this.

OYAKATA-HINOMARU (親方日の丸). "Godfather" "big boss" and "Rising Sun flag," taken together, refer to the Japanese government much in the way Americans speak of "Uncle Sam," particularly where the government pays various subsidies from the public purse to support even failing public corporations. Private sector corporations often criticize public corporations because they are protected by the government. *Oyakata-hinomaru* is a critical way of referring these companies.

SABISU (サービス). This refers to anything value added given to customers, such as a towel or T-shirt, as appreciation for being a regular customer.

SABISU-GYO (サービス業). Collective term for service industries, such as travel and leisure.

SAJI O NAGERU (匙を投げる). Like "throw in the towel," to throw away the spoon suggests the image of a physician who has given up on a patient. In business it is used when a negotiation has reached an impasse if one party quits.

SASEN (左遷). Meaning "lowering in the seating order," this refers to someone being lowered in rank or transferred to a branch or subsidiary with no staff or real authority.

SEIFUKU (制服). Corporate uniforms worn by women workers in banks, department stores, supermarkets, and many other businesses where uniforms tell customers who are staff. Men wear the company badge on their lapels. Airlines use top fashion designers, adding prestige to the organization. Many Japanese prefer to work for a company that has a uniform because it gives them a sense of added status.

SEIRI-KYUKA (生理休暇). A monthly leave for women provided by the Labor Standards Law. It was an early attempt to treat women fairly, but in many cases it has created other problems concerning which many female workers are critical. Chauvinistic men who are posted out of town (*tanshin-funin*) refer to their odd days at home as male *seiri-kyuka*. Elsewhere than in Japan, this would be considered improper humor.

SENPAI-KOHAI (先輩後輩). Cultural term for a human relationship that refers to those who have joined an organization first and those who came after, it is one way of ranking the members by seniority. Once a person has become *kohai* to someone, that person is expected to be respectful and obedient in return for guidance and protection. The senior–junior relationship never changes throughout life despite changes in rank or status. It is found in companies, universities, high schools, clubs, and other organizations. It is a function of Japan's legacy of Confucianism and an important component of the vertical structure of the social order.

SHAFU (社風). This means "company atmosphere," referring to manners, style, corporate customs, and behavior associated with members of a company. In an informal and unwritten way learned from seniors that guides employees how and how not to behave in public.

SHA-GAI-HI (社外秘). Stamped on official documents, it means that the contents are confidential and therefore "secret outside the company."

SHAKA (社歌). While not necessarily sung every day, although some companies do so, the company song is normally sung by all employees at New Year's, on founding day, on the admission of new staff, and whenever the company expands to a new location. Company flags and banners bearing he corporate logo are also widely used.

SHA-NAI (社内). "Inside the company," in-house, refers to internal corporate matters and is part of the group identification, the habits and style of Japanese corporations, and, indeed, all organizations. The opposite, *sha-gai*, refers to what is outside and does not relate to company life or values.

SHA-NAI-KEKKON (社内結婚). The marriage of two employees to each other (in-house wedding).

SHAI-NAI RYOKO (社内旅行). A company trip of all employees or an employees-only group tour.

SHA-NAI-YOKIN (社内預金). Company savings plan (in-house savings plan). Usually rates are higher than at banks, but it adds to the company's working capital.

SHINEN-KAI (新年会). A New Year's party, similar to the *bonen-kai*.

SHINTAI-UKAGAI (進退伺い). In the event of an employee making a serious misjudgment or being involved in a scandal, that person will submit a letter asking if he or she should resign. It is a tacit admission of responsibility that will be dealt with less severely than if no remorse is shown. This is one mechanism in Japanese culture for avoiding extreme reactions. Voluntarily expressed remorse is generously received. Convicted criminals in courts of law who show no remorse during the trial are normally punished with very severe sentences.

SHIRI (尻). The buttocks/hip region in Japanese culture is symbolic of many aspects of human behavior. The following listings indicate the versatility of the expression as it is used to characterize certain kinds of businesspeople.

SHIRI GA KARUI (尻が軽い). "Hip is light," meaning lacking seriousness, referring to someone who is a "lightweight" or a reference to a women of easy virtue.

SHIRI GA NUGUI (尻が拭い). To mend matters after someone has made a serious error.

SHIRI GA OMOI (尻が重い). "Hip is heavy," meaning a slow starter.

SHIRI NI HI GA TSUKU (尻に火がつく). "Hip caught fire," meaning that until someone lit a fire under him, he did not take action.

SHIRI NO ANA GA CHIISAI (尻の穴が小さい). "Small" in this case denotes weakness and nervousness.

SHIRI O MAKURU (尻をまくる). "Hip is standing," referring to a defiant posture.

SHIRI O MOCHIKOMU (尻を持ち込む). This means to ask some third party to intervene when problems arise.

SHUKKO-SHAIN (出向社員). Someone transferred to another company on loan or for some specific purpose. A bank often assigns a senior executive to supervise the finances of a company it is supporting.

SOBETSU-KAI (送別会). Farewell party before someone leaves on a trip or is transferred or reassigned to a new location.

TAIGU (待遇). Referring literally to the quality of treatment a customer receives in a restaurant while being dined on business, it is also used as a designation on a business card to denote someone who has the salary, rank, and title of a manager but with no supporting staff. It enables such a person to receive managerial status in line with the seniority system but without the functional authority that would normally accompany it.

TAISHOKUKIN (退職金). The lump sum normally paid to an employee on his or her retirement, equal to one month's basic pay (*honpo*) for each year of service. The size of some of these in the public sector has been the subject of controversy.

TAMAMUSHI-IRO (玉虫色). Similar to the variable color the beetle called *tamamushi* may have, depending on the angle from which it is observed, this expression refers to a statement that is sufficiently unclear to be interpreted in various ways. Japanese politicians' answers in the National Diet are usually cited as prime examples.

TANSHIN-FUNIN (単身赴任). Japanese companies often post male staff to different parts of the country without their families, usually because the children of high school age do not want to change schools. Estimates vary, but it is generally thought that in 2004 the number was over 450,000.

TEATE (手当). Allowances paid to employees on top of their basic monthly salary for various reasons such as transport to and from work, lunch allowance, uniform allowance, and numerous other reasons often peculiar to individual companies.

TEINEN (定年). The mandatory retirement age, which may vary from one corporation to another. When the age limit has been reached, individuals must retire according to company regulations.

TENBIKI（天引き). The system under which various deductions are made from the employee's monthly salary for tax, health insurance, rent of a company apartment, and so on. Most employees find this system convenient because it relieves them of the chore of making these payments.

TODOKE (届け). Forms reporting anything in a company, such as change of address, family circumstances, or information about a business trip. A request form (*negai*) is required even if an employee is ordered to make a trip. This keeps bookkeeping smooth and information flowing within the system.

UCHI/SOTO (内・外). This distinction between "inside" and "outside" is a basic concept that runs consistently through all aspects of Japanese culture. Whether company or club, people who are outsiders can never become insiders. The characters may also be read as *nai* and *gai*. The word for "country" tagged onto *gai* (*gaikoku*) creates the term "foreign country," and for "person" it becomes *gaijin*, or "foreigner." The same *koku* plus *nai* means "domestic." This style of thinking has been identified as one source of Japan's tribal mentality.

YOKO-MESHI (横めし). Literally meaning "horizontal" and "meal," it combines the image of Western horizontal script with eating to imply a business lunch or dinner with a guest from abroad.

YUKYU-KYUKA (有給休暇). The official paid leave given to all employees in addition to weekends and national holidays. Usually it is around 20 days, and frequently employees do not take all the permitted days off.

ZANGYO (残業). The standard term for overtime work for which a *zangyo teate* (special overtime allowance) is paid.

Bibliography

CONTENTS

Introduction 360
General Studies 361
  Japanese Economy and Economic History 361
  Japanese Society, Culture, and Politics 364
Historical Studies 367
  Pre-Edo Period and Edo Period (1615–1868) 367
  Meiji Period (1868–1912), Modernization, Taisho, and Showa Periods (to 1945) 368
  Business Leaders 369
  Studies of Business Houses and Major Corporations 369
Management and Production 370
  Japanese-Style Management 370
  Production Systems 372
  General Trading Houses and Industrial Groupings 373
Government and Legal 374
  Amakudari 374
  Bureaucracy 375
  Commercial Law and Economic Policy 375
  Employment, Labor, and Unions 376
  Foreign Business and International Trade 378
  Government Ministries 379
  Industrial Structure and Policy 379
Selected Sector Studies 380
  Accounting 380
  Agriculture 381
  Airline Industry 381
  Automobile Industry 382
  Banking and Finance 382
  Communications and Electronics 384
  Construction 385
  Food and Beverages 385
  Insurance 385
  Railways 386
  Shipbuilding 386
  Steel 386
  Telecommunications 386

INTRODUCTION

The bibliography is subdivided into what are intended to be convenient reference categories. However, some observations on the nature of the literature are called for by way of preliminary explanation.

A large amount of the early business literature on Japan was prompted by trader issues and soon after by an interest in aspects of Japanese manufacturing and production systems. Study missions from the United States and to a lesser extent from Europe visited Japan in order to study Japanese methods and the concepts related to them such as just-in-time, total quality control, *kamban*, and *kaizen*. This literature was more edifying and more balanced than the earlier ephemeral and contentious debate on trade issues. There also emerged a genre of writing that was in essence uncritical and indeed sycophantic, typified by Chalmers Johnston's book *MITI and the Japanese Miracle*. The pinnacle was Ezra Vogel's *Japan as No. 1: Lessons for America*, which was appropriately critiqued by Jon Woronoff's *Japan as Anything but Number 1*.

While the number of book-length studies of various sectors and subjects appears to be steadily increasing, there are still too many areas of Japanese business and the Japanese economy that are lacking in-depth studies. Covering these are numerous texts in Japanese, but it is obvious that many Western writers have had little access to them. Further to this is the phenomenon found in other areas of Asian studies in general, namely, that Western-style conclusions among even Asians tends to be the result of these scholars having studied in Western institutions. This often reinforces Western misunderstandings about Japan and can lead to misguided or inappropriate strategies being developed.

This latter problem combines with the degree to which a great deal of research appears to be conducted from secondary sources, frequently English-language newspaper articles. While the *Nikkei Weekly* is a respectable and reliable source of information, a sound understanding of the Japanese background is a prerequisite to understanding what is being stated in English. In Japanese, perhaps more so than in some other languages, too much is lost in translation. It can only be hoped that that number of thoroughly researched works will increase in volume to match the quality of other areas of Japan studies. Authors whose books and articles are well researched and highly informative include Dr. James C. Abegglen, who was feted at a publication party for his new book *21st Century Japanese Management: New Systems, Lasting Values*, on 4 March 2005 at the International House in Tokyo, as well as Ronald P. Dore and Michael Cusumano of the Massachusetts Institute of Technology on the automobile industry. Hirschmeier and Yui are sound reading on the history of Japanese business, and publications from the Japan Management Association and the Japan Productivity Center supplement them. Ohmae Ken'ichi offers a hybrid Japanese–Western perspective on many issues. Pascale and Athos and, also from an older generation, Mikchael Yoshino, still make useful reading on Japanese management, provided that they are put into perspective. Among Japanese who have written from the inside are notably Matsushita Konosuke and Morita Akio of Sony. These come immediately to mind as representative of subjects and period. As within all bibliographies, readers should scan the literature for themselves.

GENERAL STUDIES

Japanese Economy and Economic History

Abe Makoto. *A Monetary Model of the Japanese Economy*. Ann Arbor: University Microfilms International, 1969.

Ackerman, Edward A. *Japan's Natural Resources and Their Relation to Japan's Economic Future*. Chicago: University of Chicago Press, 1953.

Adams, T. F. M. *A Financial History of Modern Japan*. Tokyo: Research (Japan) Ltd, 1965.

Adams, T. F. M., and Iwao Hoshii. *A Financial History of the New Japan*. Tokyo: Kodansha International, 1972.

Adams, T. F. M., and Kobayashi Noritake. *The World of Japanese Business*. Tokyo: Kodansha International, 1969.

Allen, G. C. *A Short Economic History of Modern Japan*. London: George Allen & Unwin, 1962.

Balassa, Bela, and Maru Noland. *Japan in the World Economy*. Washington, D.C.: Institute for International Economics, 1988.

Beed, C. S. "The Separation of Ownership from Control." *Journal of Economic Studies* 11 (1996): 29–46.

Bestor, T. C. *Tokyo's Marketplace*. Berkeley: University of California Press, 2002.

Bieda, K. *The Structure and Operation of the Japanese Economy*. Sydney: John Wiley & Sons, 1970.

Boltho, Andrea. "A Century of Japanese Business Cycles: Did Policy Stabilize Activity?" *Journal of the Japanese and International Economies* 5, no. 3 (1991): 282–97.

Broadbridge, Seymour. *Industrial Dualism in Japan: A Problem of Economic Growth and Structural Change*. London: Frank Cass, 1966.

Brzezinski, Z. *The Fragile Blossom: Crisis and Change in Japan*. New York: Harper & Row, 1972.

Carlile, L., and Tilton, M., eds. *Is Japan Really Changing Its Way? Regulatory Reform and the Japanese Economy*. Washington, D.C.: Brookings Institution, 1998.

Caves, Richard E., and Uskasa Masu. "Industrial Organization." In *Asia's New Giant: How the Japanese Economy Works*, edited by Hugh Patrick and Henry Rosovsky. Washington, D.C.: Brookings Institution, 1976.

Hoshii Iwao. *The Dynamics of Japan's Business Evolution*. Philadelphia: Orient-West Publishers, 1969.

———. *Japan's Business Concentration*. Philadelphia: Orient-West Publishers, 1969.

Imai Kenichi and Komiya Ryutaro, eds. *Business Enterprises in Japan: Views of Leading Japanese Economists*. Cambridge, Mass.: MIT Press, 1994.

Ishi Hiromatsu. *The Japanese Tax System*. Oxford: Oxford University Press, 1993.

Ito Takatoshi. *The Japanese Economy*. Cambridge, Mass.: MIT Press, 1992.

Kahn, Hermann. *The Emerging Japanese Superstate: Challenge and Response*. Harmondsworth: Penguin Books, 1973.

Kahn, Hermann, and Thomas Pepper. *The Japanese Challenge: The Success and Failure of Economic Success*. Tokyo: Charles E. Tuttle, 1980.

Kaplan, Eugene J. *Japan: The Government-Business Relationship: A Guide for the American Businessman*. Washington, D.C.: U.S. Department of Commerce, Bureau of International Commerce, 1972.

Kester, W. C. *Japanese Takeovers: The Global Contest for Corporate Control*. Boston: Harvard Business School, 1991.

Komiya Ryutaro. *The Japanese Economy: Trade, Industry, and Government*. Tokyo: University of Tokyo Press, 1990.

Larke, R. *Japanese Retailing*. London: Routledge, 1994.

Lockwood, William W. *The Economic Development of Japan: Growth and Structural Change 1868–1938*. Princeton, N.J.: Princeton University Press, 1954.

———. *The State and Economic Enterprise in Japan: Essays in the Political Economy of Growth*. Princeton, N.J.: Princeton University Press, 1965.

Matsukata Masayoshi. *Report on the Adoption of the Gold Standard in Japan*. Tokyo: Japanese Government Press, 1899.

Mizoguchi Toshiyuki. *Personal Savings and Consumption in Postwar Japan.* Tokyo: Kinokuniya Bookstore, 1970.

Morgan Guaranty Trust Co. *The Financing of Business in Japan.* Tokyo: Morgan Guaranty Trust Co., 1965.

Nakamura Takafusa. *The Postwar Japanese Economy: Its Development and Structure.* Translated by Jaqueline Kaminski. Tokyo: University of Tokyo Press, 1981.

Nakao Shigeo. *The Political Economy of Japanese Money.* Tokyo: University of Tokyo Press, 1995.

Noda K. *Economic Growth in Postwar Japan.* Berkeley: University of California Press, 1966.

Ohkawa Kazushi, and Henry Rosovsky. *Japanese Economic Growth-Trend Acceleration in the Twentieth Century.* Stanford, Calif.: Stanford University Press, 1973.

Ohmae Ken'ichi. *The Borderless World: Power and Strategy in the Interlinked Economy.* New York: McKinsey & Co., 1991.

———. *The Invisible Continent: Four Strategic Imperatives of the New World Economy.* New York: HarperCollins, 2000.

———. *The Mind of the Strategist: The Art of Japanese Business.* New York: McGraw-Hill, 1982.

Patrick, Hugh, ed. *Japanese Industrialization and Its Social Consequences.* Berkeley: University of California Press, 1976.

———. *Monetary Policy and Central Banking in Contemporary Japan.* Bombay: University of Bombay, 1962.

Pempel, T. J. *Regime Shifts: Comparative Dynamics of the Japanese Economy.* Ithaca, N.Y.: Cornell University Press, 1988.

Schumpeter, E. B., ed. *The Industrialization of Japan and Manchukuo, 1930–1940.* New York: Macmillan, 1940.

Shibata Tokue, ed. *Japan's Public Sector: How the Government Is Financed.* Tokyo: University of Tokyo Press, 1993.

Shinohara Miyohe. *Structural Changes in Japan's Economic Development.* Tokyo: Hitotsubashi University, Economic Research Series No. 11, 1970.

Smith, Thomas C. *Political Change and Industrial Development in Japan: Government Enterprise, 1868–1880.* Stanford, Calif.: Stanford University Press, 1955.

Taira Koji. *Economic Development and the Labor Market in Japan.* New York: Columbia University Press, 1970.

Takenaka Heizo. *Contemporary Japanese Economy and Economic Policy.* Ann Arbor: University of Michigan Press, 1991.

Teranishi Juro and Kosai Jutaka. *The Japanese Experience of Economic Reforms.* New York: St. Martin's Press.

Trezise, Philip H., and Suzuki Yukio, "Politics, Government and Economic Growth in Japan." In *Asia's New Giant: How the Japanese Economy Works*, edited by Hugh Patrick and Henry Rosovsky. Washington, D.C.: Brookings Institution, 1976.

Tsuru Shigeto. *Japan's Capitalism: Creative Defeat and Beyond*. Cambridge: Cambridge University Press, 1993.

UNESCO. *History of Industrial Education in Japan 1868–1900*. Tokyo: Japan National Commission for UNESCO, 1959.

Uriu, R. *Troubled Industries: Confronting Economic Change in Japan*. Ithaca, N.Y.: Cornell University Press, 1996.

West, Kenneth D. "Sources of Cycles in Japan, 1975–1987." *Journal of the Japanese and International Economies* 6, no. 1 (1992): 71–98.

Whittaker, D. H. *Small Firms in the Japanese Economy*. Cambridge: Cambridge University Press, 1997.

Wolferen, Karl von. *The Enigma of Japanese Power.* New York: Vintage, 1990.

Woronoff, Jon. *Asia's "Miracle" Economies*. Tokyo: Lotus Press, 1986.

———. *Japan: The Coming Economic Crisis*. Tokyo: Lotus Press, 1979.

———. *Japan's Commercial Empire*. Tokyo: Lotus Press; New York: Praeger, 1984.

Yamamura Kozo. *Economic Policy in Postwar Japan*. Berkeley: University of California Press, 1967.

Yamanaka Tokutaro. *Small Business in Japan's Economic Progress*. Tokyo: Asahi Evening News, 1971.

Yoshikawa H., and Ohtake, F. "Postwar Business Cycles in Japan: A Quest for the Right Explanation." *Journal of the Japanese and International Economies* 1 (1987): 373–407.

Yuzawa Takeshi, ed. *Japanese Business Success: the Evolution of a Strategy*. London: Routledge, 1994.

Japanese Society, Culture, and Politics

Akita, George. *Foundations of Constitutional Government in Modern Japan 1868–1900*. Cambridge, Mass.: Harvard University Press, 1967.

Allinson, Gary D., and Sone Yasunaori, eds. *Political Dynamics in Contemporary Japan*. Ithaca, N.Y.: Cornell University Press.

Bellah, Robert. *Tokugawa Religion: the Values of Pre-Industrial Japan*. Boston: Beacon Press, 1957.

Benedict, Ruth. *The Chrysanthemum and the Sword: Patterns of Culture*. Tokyo: Charles E. Tuttle, 1954.

Clammer, J. *Contemporary Urban Japan*. Oxford: Blackwell, 1975.

Cousins, Steve. "Culture and Self-Perception in Japan and the United States." *Journal of Personality and Social Psychology* 56, no. 1 (1989): 124–31.

De Vos, George A. *Socialization for Achievement: Essays on the Cultural Psychology of the Japanese*. Berkeley: University of California Press, 1975.

Doi, Takeo. *Anatomy of Dependence*. Tokyo: Kodansha International, 1973.

———. *The Anatomy of the Self: The Individual versus Society*. Tokyo: Kodansha International, 1985.

Dore, Ronald P., ed. *Aspects of Social Change in Modern Japan*. Princeton, N.J.: Princeton University Press, 1967.

———. *City Life in Modern Japan*. Berkeley: University of California Press, 1960.

———. *Land Reforms in Japan*. Oxford: Oxford University Press, 1959.

Hall, John Whitney, Nagahara Keiji, and Yamamura Kozo, eds. *Japan before Tokugawa: Political Consolidation and Economic Growth, 1500–1650*. Princeton: Princeton University Press, 1981.

Hase Akihasa. *Japan's Modern Culture and Its Roots*. Tokyo: International Society for Educational Information, 1982.

Kaplan, David E., and Alec Dubro. *Yakuza*. Reading, Mass.: Addison-Wesley, 1986.

Keifer, C. W. "The Psychological Interdependence of Family, School, and Bureaucracy in Japan." *American Anthropologist* 72 (1970): 66–75.

Mishima Yukio. *On Hagakure: The Samurai Ethic and Modern Japan*. Translated by Kathryn Sparling. Tokyo: Charles E. Tuttle, 1978.

Morris, Ivan. *Nationalism and the Right Wing in Japan; A Study of Post-War Trends*. London: Oxford University Press 1960.

———. *The Nobility of Failure*. New York: Meridian Books, 1976.

Nakamura Hajime. *Development of Japanese Thought*. Tokyo: Japan Society for the Promotion of Science, 1976.

———. *Ways of Thinking of Eastern Peoples*. Honolulu: East-West Center Press, 1973.

Nakane Chie. *Japanese Society*. Berkeley: University California Press, 1970.

———. *Kinship and Economic Organization in Rural Japan*. New York: Humanities Press, 1967.

Nitobe Inazo. *Bushido: The Soul of Japan*. New York, 1905.

Picken, Stuart D. B. "The Role of Traditional Values in Contemporary Japanese Society" *University of Stirling Centre for Japanese Studies Discussion 8 Paper 4*. Shell International Conference on Continuity and Innovation in

Japanese Society, June 1984.

Reischauer, Edwin O. *Japan: Past and Present.* New York, 1946.

———. *Japan: Tradition and Transformation.* With Albert M. Craig. Tokyo: Tuttle, 1978.

———. *The Japanese.* Tokyo: Tuttle, 1978.

Reischauer, R. K. *Early Japanese History.* 2 Vols. Princeton, N.J.: Princeton University Press, 1937.

Sansom, Sir George. *History of Japan.* 3 Vols. New ed. Tokyo: Tuttle, 1979.

———. *Japan: A Short Cultural History.* New York: Century, 1951.

Sethi, S. Prakash. *Japanese Business and Social Conflict: A Comparative Analysis of Response Patterns with American Business.* Cambridge, Mass.: Ballinger, 1975.

Smith, Robert J. *Ancestor Worship in Contemporary Japan.* Stanford, Calif.: Stanford University Press, 1974.

Smith, Robert J., and Richard K. Beardsley, eds. *Japanese Culture: Its Development and Characteristics.* Chicago: Aldine, 1962.

Smith, Warren W., Jr. *Confucianism in Contemporary Japan.* Tokyo: Hokuseido Press, 1973.

Taira Koji. *Economic Development and the Labor Market in Japan.* New York: Columbia University Press, 1970.

Tsunoda Ryusaku, William, Theodore de Bary, and Donald Keene, eds. *Sources of the Japanese Tradition.* New York: Columbia University Press, 1958.

Varley, Pail, with Ivan and Nobuko Morris. *The Samurai.* London: Penguin Books, 1974.

Vogel, Ezra. *Japan as No. 1: Lessons for America.* Cambridge, Mass.: Harvard University Press, 1979.

———. *Japan's New Middle Class.* Berkeley: University of California Press, 1963.

Whiting, Robert. *The Chrysanthemum and the Bat.* Tokyo: The Permanent Press, 1977.

Woodliwiss, Anthony. *Law, Labor, and Society in Japan.* London: Routledge, 1992.

Woronoff, Jon. *Japan as Anything but Number One.* London; Macmillan, 1991.

———. *Japan: The Coming Social Crisis.* Tokyo: Lotus Press, 1980.

Yamamoto Tsunemoto. *Hagakure: The Book of the Samurai.* Translated by William Scott Wilson. Tokyo: Kodansha International, 1979.

Yanaga Chitoshi. *Big Business in Japanese Politics.* New Haven, Conn.: Yale University Press, 1968.

HISTORICAL STUDIES

Pre–Edo Period and Edo Period (1615–1868)

Bolitho, Harold, *Treasures among Men: The Feudal Daimyo in Tokugawa Japan*. New Haven: Yale University Press, 1974.

Hauser, William B. *Economic Institutional Change in Tokugawa Japan*. London: Cambridge University Press, 1974.

Henderson, Dan Fenno. *Village "Contracts" in Tokugawa Japan*. Seattle: University of Washington Press, 1975.

Hirschmeier, Johannes, and Yuii Tsunehiko. *The Development of Japanese Business 1600–1973*. London: George Allen & Unwin, 1975.

Horie Yasuzo, "Clan Monopoly Policy in the Tokugawa Period." *Kyoto University Economic Review* 17, no. 1 (1942).

Miller, John Holmes. *Social Disorder in Late Tokugawa Japan*. Ann Arbor, Mich.: University Microfilms International, 1985.

Nakane, Chie, and Shinzaburo Oishi, eds. *Tokugawa Japan*. Tokyo: University Press, 1990.

Ooms, H. *Tokugawa Ideology*. Princeton, N.J.: Princeton University Press, 1986.

Prasad, S. A. *The Patriotism Thesis and Argument in Tokugawa Japan*. 3 Vols. Delhi: Guntur, 1975–1984.

Schaede, U. "Forwards and Futures in Tokugawa-Period Japan: A New Perspective on the Dojima Rice Market." *Journal of Banking and Finance* 13 (1989): 487–513.

———. "The Historical Development of Self-Regulation in Japan's Trade Associations." In *Cooperative Capitalism: Self-Regulation, Trade Associations, and the Antimonopoly Law in Japan*. Oxford: Oxford University Press, 2000.

Sheldon, C. D. *The Rise of the Merchant Class in Tokugawa Japan 1600–1868: An Introductory Survey*. New York: Russell & Russell, 1973.

Smith, Thomas C. *The Agrarian Origins of Modern Japan*. Stanford, Calif.: Stanford University Press, 1959.

———. "'Merit' as Ideology in the Tokukawa Period." In *Aspects of Social Change in Modern Japan*, edited by Ronald P. Dore. Princeton, N.J.: Princeton University Press, 1967.

———. *Political Change and Industrial Development in Japan: Government Enterprise 1868–1880*. Stanford, Calif.: Stanford University Press, 1955.

Toyoda Takeshi. *A History of Pre-Meiji Commerce in Japan*. Tokyo: Kokusai Bunka Shinkokai, 1969.

Yamamura Kozo. "The Development of *Za* in Medieval Japan." *Business History Review* 47 (1973): 438–65.

———. *A Study of Samurai Income and Entrepreneurship*. Cambridge, Mass.: Harvard University Press, 1974.

Meiji Period (1868–1912), Modernization, Taisho, and Showa Periods (to 1945)

Black, C. K. E. *The Dynamics of Modernization*. New York: Harper & Row, 1966.

Blumenthal, Tuvia. "The Japanese Shipbuilding Industry." In *Japanese Industrialization and Its Social Consequences*, edited by Hugh Patrick. Berkeley: University of California Press, 1976.

Brunton, Richard Henry. *Building Japan 1868–1876*. Kent: Japan Library, 1991.

Burks, Ardath W., ed. *The Modernizers : Overseas Students, Foreign Employees, and Meiji Japan*. Boulder, Colo.: Westview Press, 1985.

Eisenstadt, S. N. *Modernization: Growth and Diversity*. Bloomington, Department of Government, Indiana University, 1963. *Indiana Quarterly* 20 (January–March 1964): 17–42.

Fujita, Fumiko. *Boys, Be Ambitious!: American Pioneers on the Japanese Frontier, 1871–1882*. Ann Arbor, Mich.: University Microfilms International, 1988.

Gerstle, C. Andrew, ed. *18th Century Japan*. Sydney: Allen & Unwin, 1989.

Henderson, Dan Fenno. *Conciliation and Japanese Law: Tokugawa and Modern*. Seattle: University of Washington Press, 1965.

———. *Village "Contracts" in Tokugawa Japan*. Seattle: University of Washington Press, 1975.

Hirschmeier, Johannes. *The Origins of Entrepreneurship in Meiji Japan*. Cambridge, Mass: Harvard University Press, 1964.

Horie Yasuzo. "Entrepreneurship in Meiji Japan." In *The State and Economic Enterprise in Japan*, edited by William W. Lockwood. Princeton, N.J.: Princeton University Press, 1965.

Jansen, Marius. *The Modernization of Japan and Russia*. New York: Macmillan, 1975.

Lebra, Joyce C., ed. *Japan's Greater East Asia Co-Prosperity Sphere in World War II: Selected Readings and Documents*. New York: Oxford University Press, 1975.

Marsh, Robert M., and Mannari Hiroshi. *Modernization and the Japanese Factory*. Princeton, N.J.: Princeton University Press, 1976.

Marshall, Byron K. *Capitalism and Nationalism in Prewar Japan: The Ideology of the Business Elite 1868–1941*. Stanford, Calif.: Stanford University Press, 1967.

Pyle, Kenneth P. *The New Generation in Meiji Japan: Problems of Cultural Identity, 1885–1895*. Stanford, Calif.: Stanford University Press, 1969.

Ranis, Gustav. "The Community-Centred Entrepreneur in Japanese Development." *Exploration of Entrepreneurial History* 3, no. 2 (December 1955).

Rosovzky, Henry. *Capital Formation in Japan, 1868–1940*. Glencoe, Ill.: Free Press, 1961.

Sainai, I. Robert. *The Challenge of Modernization: The West's Impact on the Non-Western World*. London: Chatto & Windus, 1964.

Samuels, R. *Rich Nation, Strong Army: National Security, Ideology, and the Transformation of Japan*. Ithaca, N.Y.: Cornell University Press, 1994.

Shively, Donald H. *Tradition and Modernization in Japanese Culture*. Princeton, N.J.: Princeton University Press, 1971.

Business Leaders

Hirschmeier, Johannes. "Shibusawa Eiichi: Industrial Pioneer." In *The State and Economic Enterprise in Japan: Essays in the Political Economy of Growth*, edited by William W. Lockwood. Princeton, N.J.: Princeton University Press, 1965.

Mannari Hiroshi. *The Japanese Business Leaders*. Tokyo: University of Tokyo Press, 1974.

Morita Akio. *Made in Japan: Akio Morita and Sony*. New York: E. P. Dutton, 1986.

Obata Kyugoro. *An Interpretation of the Life of Viscount Sbibusawa*. Tokyo: Diamondo Jigyo Corporation, 1937.

Studies of Business Houses and Major Corporations

Alletzhauser, A. J. *The House of Nomura: The Inside Story of the Legendary Japanese Financial Dynasty*. New York: Arcade/Little, Brown, 1990.

Arai, R. T. *The Real Ability of the Lion, Fuji Film*. Tokyo: Nikkan Kogyo Shinbun, 1995.

Fitzgibbon, J. E., Jr. *Deceitful Practices: Nomura Securities and the Japanese Invasion of Wall Street*. New York: Carol Publishing Group, 1991.

Fruin, Mark. *Kikkoman: Company, Clan, and Community*. Cambridge, Mass.: Harvard University Press, 1983.

Fuji Photo Film. *50 Years of Fuji Photo Film*. Tokyo: Fuji Shoshun Fuirumu KK, 1984.

Gould, Rowland. *The Matsushita Phenomenon*. Tokyo: Diamondosha, 1970.

Havens, Thomas R. H. *Architects of Influence: The Tsutsumi Family and the Seibu-Saison Enterprises in Twentieth Century Japan*. Cambridge, Mass.: Harvard University Press, 1997.

Lynch, S. *Arrogance and Accords: The Inside Story of the Honda Scandal*. Dallas: Pecos Press, 1997.

Lyons, N. *The Sony Vision*. New York: Corona Publishers, 1976.
Mizoue U. *Daiei VS Ito-Yokado*. Tokyo: Baru Shuppan, 1998.
Nathan J. *Sony: The Private Life*. New York: Houghton Mifflin, 1999.
Nelson, D., P. E. Moody, and R. Mayo. *Powered by Honda: Developing Excellence in Global Enterprise*. New York: John Wiley & Sons.
Nomura Securities Company. *Beyond the Ivied Mountain*. Tokyo: Nomura Securities, 1986.
Otsuki S., F. Tanaka, and Y. Sakurai. *Good Mileage: The High-Performance Business Philosophy of Soichiro Honda*. New York: Weatherhill, 1996.
Roberts, John G. *Mitsui: Three Centuries of Japanese Business*. New York: Weatherhill, 1973.
Sakiya, T. *Honda Motor: The Men, the Management, the Machines*. Tokyo: Kodansha International, 1982.
Sandoz, P. *Canon*. London: Penguin Books, 1997.

MANAGEMENT AND PRODUCTION

Japanese-Style Management

Abegglen, James C., and George Stalk Jr. *Kaisha: The Japanese Corporation*. New York: Basic Books, 1985.
Aoki Masahiko and Ronald Dore, eds. *The Japanese Firm: Sources of Competitive Strength*. Oxford: Oxford University Press, 1994.
Ballon, Robert J., and Iwao Tomita. *The Financial Behavior of Japanese Corporations*. Tokyo: Kodandha International, 1988.
Clark, Rodney. *The Japanese Company*. New Haven, Conn.: Yale University Press, 1979.
Gregory, Gene. "Pickens Prescription: A Hard Pill to Swallow." *Japan Times*, December 1990.
Gundling, Ernest, "Ethics and Working with the Japanese: The Entrepreneur and the 'Elite Course.'" *California Management Review* 33, no. 3 (1991): 25–39.
Hasegawa Keitaro. *Japanese-Style Management: An Insider's Analysis*. Tokyo: Kodansha International, 1986.
Hayashi, S. *Culture and Management in Japan*. Tokyo: University of Tokyo Press, 1988.
Inohara, H. *Human Resource Development in Japanese Companies*. Tokyo: Asian Productivity Organization, 1990.
Liker, J. K., W. E. Fruin, and P. S. Adler. *Remade in America: Transplanting and Transforming Japanese Management Systems*. New York: Oxford University Press, 1999.

Marsh, Robert M., and Mannari Hiroshi. "Lifetime Commitment in Japan: Roles, Norms and Values." *American Journal of Sociology* 76 (1971): 795–812.

———. "A New Look at 'Lifetime Commitment' in Japanese Industry." *Economic Development and Cultural Change* 20 (1972): 611–30.

Nonaka, I., and H. Takeuchi. The Knowledge Creating Company: *How Japanese Companies Create the Dynamics of Innovation.* Oxford: Oxford University Press, 1998.

Ouchi, William G. *Theory Z.* Reading, Mass.: Addison-Wesley, 1981.

Ozaki, Robert. *Human Capitalism.* New York: Penguin Books, 1991.

Pascale, R. T., and A. G. Athos. *The Art of Japanese Management.* New York: Simon & Schuster, 1981.

Picken, Stuart D. B. "Values and Value Related Strategies in Japanese Corporate Culture." *Journal of Business Ethics* 6, no. 2 (February 1987): 137ff.

Pickens, T. Boone. *Fortune International,* December 31, 1990, in *Letters to Fortune* under the heading "They Don't Love What Toyota Does."

Prestowitz, Clyde V., Jr. *Trading Places.* New York: Basic Books, 1988.

Rohlen, Thomas P. *For Harmony and Strength: Japanese White-Collar Organization in Anthropological Perspective.* Berkeley: University of California Press, 1974.

Sai Yasutaka. *Eight Core Values of the Japanese Businessman.* Binghamton, N.Y.: International Business Press, 1995.

Sakai Kuniyasu. "The Feudal World of Japanese Manufacturing." *Harvard Business Review* 68, no. 6 (November–December 1990): 38–49.

Smith, L. "Japan's Autocratic Managers," *Fortune,* January 7, 1985.

Sullivan, Jeremiah J. "Japanese Management Philosophies: From the Vacuous to the Brilliant." *California Management Review* 34, no. 2 (winter 1992): 66–87.

Takamiya Susumu. *Background, Characteristics and Recent Trends in Japanese Management.* London: British Institute of Management, 1970.

Thurow, L. *The Management Challenge: Japanese Views.* Cambridge, Mass: MIT Press, 1985.

Vogel, Ezra F. *Modern Japanese Organization and Decision-Making.* Berkeley: University of California Press, 1975.

Whitehill, A. M. *Japanese Management: Tradition and Transition.* New York: Routledge, 1991.

Winsbury, Rex. *The Managers of Japan.* London: British Institute of Management, 1970.

Yoshimura Noboru. *Inside the Japanese Kaisha: Demystifying Japanese Business Behavior.* Boston: Harvard Business School Press, 1997.

Yoshino, M. Y. *The Japanese Marketing System: Adaptations and Innovation.* Cambridge, Mass.: MIT Press, 1971.

———. *Japan's Managerial System: Tradition and Innovation*. Cambridge, Mass.: MIT Press, 1968.

Production Systems

Abo, T., ed. *Hybrid Factory: The Japanese Production System in the United States*. New York: Oxford University Press, 1994.

Feigenbaum, Armand. *Quality Control*. New York: McGraw-Hill, 1983.

Frank, Jeffrey. *The Teamwork Advantage: An Inside Look at Japanese Product and Technology Development*. Cambridge, Mass.: Productivity Press, 1992.

Fujimoto T. *The Evolution of a Manufacturing System at Toyota*. New York: Oxford University Press, 1999.

Goto A., and H. Odagiri. *Innovation in Japan*. New York: Oxford University Press, 1997.

Herbig, Paul. *Innovation Japanese-Style: A Cultural and Historical Perspective*. Westport, Conn.: Quorum Books, 1995.

Ishikawa K. *Guide to Quality Control*. Tokyo: Asian Productivity Organization, 1976.

———, ed. *Quality Control Circles at Work: Cases from Japan's Manufacturing and Service Sectors*. Portland, Ore.: Productivity Press, 1984.

———. *What Is Total Quality Control? The Japanese Way*. Translated by D. Lu. Englewood Cliffs, N.J.: Prentice Hall, 1985.

Itagaki, H., ed., *The Japanese Production System: Hybrid Factories in East Asia*. London: Macmillan 1997.

Japan Management Association. *Canon Production System: Creative Involvement of the Total Workforce*. Cambridge, Mass.: Productivity Press, 1984.

Japan Productivity Center. *The Productivity Movement in Japan: The Basic Concept of Productivity and the Development of the Productivity Movement*. Tokyo: Japan Productivity Center, 1983.

———. *A Visual Review: Productivity Movement*. Tokyo: Japan Productivity Center, 1983.

Liker, J. K., K. J. Ettlie, and J. C. Campbell. *Engineered in Japan: Japanese Technology Management Practices*. New York: Oxford University Press, 1995.

Lilllrank, P., and N. Kano. *Continuous Improvement: Quality Circles in Japanese Industry*. Ann Arbor: Center for Japanese Studies, University of Michigan, 1989.

McIntyre, J. R. *Japan's Technical Standards: Implications for Global Trade and Competitiveness*. Westport, Conn.: Quorum, 1997.

Monden, Y. *Toyota Production System: An Integrated Approach to Just-in-Time*. Atlanta: Institute of Industrial Engineers, 1998.

Nakamura, S. *The New Standardization: Keystone of Continuous Improvement in Manufacturing*. Translated by B. Talbot. Portland, Ore.: Productivity Press, 1998.

Nemoto, M. *Total Quality Control for Management: Strategies and Techniques from Toyota and Toyota Gossei*. Translated by D. Lu. Englewood Cliffs, N.J.: Prentice Hall, 1987.

Noble, G. W. "Standard Setting and R & D Consortia in Japan's Video Industry." In *Collective Action in East Asia: How Ruling Parties Shape Industrial Policy*. Ithaca, N.Y.: Cornell University Press, 1998.

Onglatco, Mary Lou Uy. *Japanese Quality Control Circles: Features, Effects and Problems*. Tokyo: Asian Productivity Organization, 1988.

Ono Taiichi. *Kanban and Just-in-Time at Toyota*. Tokyo: Japan Management Association, 1989.

Shingo Shigeo. *A Revolution in Manufacturing*. Cambridge, Mass.: Productivity Press, 1986.

———. *The Sayings of Shigeo Shingo: Key Strategies for Plant Improvement*. Cambridge, Mass.: Productivity Press, 1987.

———. *Study of Toyota Production System*. Cambridge, Mass.: Productivity Press, 1987.

———. *Zero Quality Control: Source Inspection and the Poka-Yoke System*. Cambridge, Mass.: Productivity Press, 1987.

Sugimori, Y., K. Kusonoki, E. Cho, and S. Uchikawa. "Toyota Production System and Kanban System: Materialization of Just-In-Tine and Respect for Human System." *International Journal of Production Research* 15, no. 6 (1997): 553–64.

Takeuchi, H., and I. Nonaka. "The New Product Development Game." *Harvard Business Review* 64, no. 1 (1986): 137–46.

Wilkinson, B. *The Japanization of British Industry: New Developments in the 1990s*. Oxford: Blackwell, 1992.

General Trading Houses and Industrial Groupings

Arai, S. Shoshaman. *A Tale of Corporate Japan*. Berkeley: University of California Press, 1991.

Bisson, T. A. *Zaibatsu Dissolution in Japan*. Berkeley: University of California Press, 1954.

Eli, Max. *Global Strategies of Japanese Trading Corporations*. New York: McGraw-Hill, 1990.

Flath, D. "The Keiretsu Puzzle." *Journal of the Japanese and International Economies* 10 (1996): 101–21.

Gerlach, M. *Alliance Capitalism: The Social Organization of Japanese Business*. Berkeley: University of California Press, 1993.

Hadley, Eleanor M. *Antitrust in Japan*. Princeton, N.J.: Princeton University Press, 1970.

Iwao Ichiishi. "Soga Shosha: Meeting New Challenges." *Journal of Japanese Trade and Industry*, no. 1: 16–18, 19.

Lincoln, James R., Michael Gerlach, and Christina L. Ahmadjian. "Keiretsu Networks and Corporate Performance in Japan." *Review of Economics and Statistics* 75 (1993): 249–58.

Miyazaki, Y. "Rapid Growth in Postwar Japan—with Special Reference to 'Excessive Competition' and the Formation of 'Keiretsu.'" *The Developing Economies* 5 (1967): 329–50.

Sumiya Fumio. "Trading Titans: Agile Enough to Thrive?" *Nikkei Weekly*, July 26, 1993, 1.

Tilton, M. *Restrained Trade: Cartels in Japan's Basic Materials Industries*. Ithaca, N.Y.: Cornell University Press, 1996.

Tokyo Economic Information Service, ed. *Sogo-shosha Nenkan*. Tokyo: Nihon Kogyo Shinbunsha. Annual.

Yonekawa Shinichi, ed. *General Trading Companies: A Comparative and Historical Study*. Tokyo: United Nations University Press, 1990.

Yonekawa Shinichi and Yoshihara Hidedki, eds. *Business History of General Trading Companies*. Tokyo: University of Tokyo Press, 1987.

Yoshino, M. Y. *Japan's Multinational Enterprises*. Cambridge, Mass.: Harvard University Press, 1976.

Yoshino, M. Y., and T. B. Lifson. *The Invisible Link: Japan's Sogo Shosha and the Organization of Trade*. Cambridge, Mass.: MIT Press, 1986.

Young, Alexander K. *The Sogo Shosha: Japan's Multinational Trading Companies*. Boulder, Colo.: Westview Press, 1979; Tokyo: Charles E. Tuttle, 1982.

GOVERNMENT AND LEGAL

Amakudari

Blumenthal, T. "The Practice of *Amakudari* within the Japanese Employment System." *Asian Survey* 25, no. 3 (1985): 310–21.

Calder, K. "Elites in an Equalizing Role: Ex-Bureaucrats as Coordinators and Intermediaries in the Japan Government-Business Relationship." *Comparative Politics* 21, no. 4 (1989): 379–404.

Johnson, C. "The Reemployment of Retired Government Bureaucrats in Japanese Big Business." *Asian Survey* 14 (1974): 953–965.

Kim, H., et al., eds. *The Japanese Civil Service and Economic Development*. Oxford: Clarendon Press, 1995.

Schaede, U. "The 'Old Boy' Network and Government-Business Relationships in Japan." *Journal of Japanese Studies* 21, no. 2 (1995): 293–317.

Usui, C., and R. Colingon. "Government and Elites and Amakudari in Japan, 1963–1992." *Asian Survey* 35, no. 7 (1995): 682–98.

Bureaucracy

Gyosei Shido. "Inside Japanese Bureaucracy." *Tokyo Business Today*, January 1986, 34–37.

Kubota, A. *Higher Civil Servants in Postwar Japan: Their Social Origins, Educational Backgrounds, and Career Patterns*. Princeton, N.J.: Princeton University Press, 1969.

Commercial Law and Economic Policy

Coleman, Rex, and John O. Haley. *An Index to Japanese Law: A Bibliography of Western Language Materials (1867–1973)*. Tokyo: Japanese American Society for Legal Studies, 1975.

Foster, Richard, and Ono Masao, trans. *The Patent and Trademark Laws of Japan*. Tokyo: Asahi Evening News, 1970.

Hadley, Eleanor. *Antitrust in Japan*. Princeton, N.J.: Princeton University Press, 1970.

Idei, Y. "Corporate Chiefs Ready to Face Strong-Arm *Sokaiya*." *Japan Economic Journal*, May 4, 1991, 6.

Itoh Yoshiaki. "Anti-Gang Law Wracks Mob Ranks." *Nikkei Weekly*, March 22, 1993, 1, 12.

Iyori Hiroshi. *Antimonopoly Legislation in Japan*. New York: Federal Legal Publications, 1969.

Iyori Hiroshi, and A. Uesugi. *The Antimonopoly Law and Policies of Japan*. New York: Federal Legal Publications, 1994.

Kanabayashi Masayoshi and Marcus W. Bracuhli. "Japanese Gangsters' Expanding Role in the Economy Worries Law Enforcement Government Officials." *Asian Wall Street Journal Weekly*, June 10, 1991, 11.

Kawamoto Ichiro and Monma Ittoku. "Sokai-ya in Japan." *Hong Kong Law Journal* 6 (1976): 179–88.

Kishimoto Eitaro. "Labor-Management Relations and the Trade Unions in Postwar Japan." *Kyoto University Economic Review* 38 (1968): 1–35.

Large, Stephen S. *The Rise of Labor in Japan: The Yuaikai 1912–1919*. Tokyo: Sophia University Press, 1972.

Levine, Stephen S. *Industrial Relations in Postwar Japan*. Urbana: University of Illinois Press, 1958.

Lincoln, Edward. "Crackdown Won't Open Japan's Corporate Closets." *Asian Wall Street Journal Weekly*, November 24, 1997, 21.

Matsushita Mitsuo. *International Trade and Competition Law in Japan*. Oxford: Oxford University Press, 1993.

Matsushita Mitsuo and John Davis. *Introduction to Japanese Antimonopoly Law*. Tokyo: Yukihaku Publishing, 1990.

Michida Shin'ichiro. "The Legal Structure for Economic Enterprise: Some Aspects of Japanese Commercial Law." In *Law in Japan: The Legal Order of a Changing Society*, edited by Arthur Taylor von Mehren. Cambridge, Mass.: Harvard University Press, 1963.

Morishita Kaoru. "Scandals Put Corporate Culture on Trial." *Nikkei Weekly*, June 23, 1997, 4.

Oda Hiroshi, ed. *Japanese Commercial Law in an Era of Internationalization*. London: Graham & Trotman/Martinus Nijhoff, 1994.

Ramseyer, M. "The Costs of Consensual Myth: Antitrust Enforcement and Institutional Barriers to Litigation in Japan." *Yale Law Journal* 94, no. 3 (1985): 604–5.

Szmkowiak, K. "Sokaiya: An Examination of the Social and Legal Development of Japan's Corporate Extortionists." *International Journal of Sociology of Law* 22 (1994): 123–43.

Wanner, Barbara. "*Sokaiya* Scandals, Economic Woes Spotlight Japanese Corporate Governance." *JEI Report* 3A, January 23, 1998.

West, M. D. "Information, Institutions and Extortion in Japan and the United States: Making Sense of Sokaiya Racketeers." *Northwestern University Law Review* 93 (1999): 767–817.

Employment, Labor, and Unions

Abegglen, James. *Management and Workers: The Japanese Solution*. Tokyo: Sophia University, 1973.

Ayusawa, Iwao F. *A History of Labor in Modern Japan*. Honolulu: East-West Center Press, 1966.

Ballon, Robert J. *The Japanese Employee*. Tokyo: Sophia University Press, 1969.

Brown, C., Y. Nakata, M. Reich, and L. Ulman. *Work and Pay in the United States and Japan*. New York: Oxford University Press, 1997.

Brown, W., R. Lubove, and E. Kalwasser. *Karoshi: Alternative Perspectives on Japanese Management Styles*. Greenwich, Conn.: Business Horizons, 1994.

Cole, Robert. *Japanese Blue Collar: The Changing Tradition*. Berkeley: University of California Press, 1971.

———. *Work, Mobility, and Participation*. Berkeley: University of California Press, 1979.

Cook, Alice H. *An Introduction to Japanese Trade Unionism*. Ithaca, N.Y.: Cornell University Press, 1966.

Dore, Ronald. *British Factory-Japanese Factory: The Origins of National Diversity in Industrial Relations*. Berkeley: University of California Press, 1973.

Garon, S. *The State and Labor in Modern Japan*. Berkeley: University of California Press, 1987.

Gordon, A. *The Evolution of Labor Relations in Japan: Heavy Industry 1853–1955*. Cambridge: Cambridge University Press, 1985.

Kawanishi Hirosuke. *Enterprise Unionism in Japan*. Translated by Ross E. Mouer. London: Kegan Paul International, 1992.

Koike Kazuo. *Understanding Industrial Relations in Modern Japan*. London: Macmillan, 1988.

Lo, L. J. *Office Ladies/Factory Women: Life and Work at a Japanese Company*. New York: M. E. Sharpe, 1990.

Marsh, Robert, and Hiroshi Mannari. "Lifetime Commitment in Japan: Roles, Norms and Values." *American Journal of Sociology* 76 (1971): 795–812.

Ministry of Labor. *Basic Survey on Labor Unions*. Tokyo: Ministry of Labor. Annual.

Ogasawara, Y. *Office Ladies and Salaried Men: Power, Gender, and Work in Japanese Companies*. Berkeley: University of California Press, 1998.

Okochi Kazuo. *Labor in Modern Japan*. Tokyo: Science Council of Japan, 1958.

Palumbo, F., and A. Herbig. "Salaryman Sudden Death Syndrome." *Employee Relations* 1991: 554–61.

Price, J. *Japan Works: Power and Paradox in Postwar Industrial Relations*. Ithaca, N.Y.: Cornell University Press, 1997.

Sako, M., and H. Sato,. eds. *Japanese Labor and Management in Transition*. London: Routledge, 1997.

Saso, Mary. *Women in the Japanese Workplace*. London: Hilary Shipman, 1990.

Shirai Taishiro, ed. *Industrial Relations in Japan*. Madison: University of Wisconsin Press, 1984.

Smith, P. "Tougher Than the Rest." *Management* 1998: 42–47.

Sugeno Kazuo. *Japanese Labor Law*. Translated by Leo Kanowitz. Tokyo: University of Tokyo Press, 1912.

Tachibanaki, T. *Wage Determination and Distribution in Japan*. New York: Oxford University Press, 1996.

Taira Koji. "Characteristics of Japanese Labor Markets." *Economic Development and Cultural Change* 10 (1962): 150–68.

Tominaga Ken'ichi. "Occupational Mobility in Japanese Society: Analysis of the Labor Market in Japan." *Journal of Economic Behavior* 2, no. 2 (1962): 1–37.

Wilkinson, Thomas O. *The Urbanization of Japanese Labor, 1868–1955*. Amherst: University of Massachusetts Press, 1965.

Woronoff, Jon. *Japan's Wasted Workers*. Tokyo: Lotus Press, 1982.

Foreign Business and International Trade

Allen, G. C. *Western Enterprises in Far Eastern Development: China and Japan*. London: George Allen & Unwin, 1954.
Ballon, Robert J. *Doing Business in Japan*. Tokyo: Sophia University and Charles E. Tuttle, 1968.
———. *Japan's Market and Foreign Business*. Tokyo: Sophia University, 1971.
———. *Joint Ventures and Japan*. Tokyo: Sophia University, 1967.
Ballon, Robert J., with Tomita Iwao and Usami Hajime. *Financial Reporting in Japan*. Tokyo: Sophia University, 1976.
Ballon, Robert J., and Eugene H. Lee, eds. *Foreign Investment and Japan*. Tokyo: Tokyo, Sophia University, 1972.
Henderson, Dan Fenno. *Foreign Enterprise in Japan: Laws and Policies*. Tokyo: Charles E. Tuttle, 1973.
Ho, Alfred. *The Far East in World Trade*. New York: Praeger, 1967.
Huddleston, Jackson N. *Gaijin Kaisha: Running a Foreign Business in Japan*. Armonk, N.Y.: M. E. Sharpe, 1990.
Huh, Kyungn-Mo. *Japan's Trade in Asia*. New York: Praeger, 1966.
Kang, T. W. *Gaishi: The Foreign Company in Japan*. New York: Basic Books, 1990.
Kapla, Eugene J. *Japan: The Government-Business Relationship: A Guide for the American Businessman*. Washington, D.C.: U.S. Bureau of International Commerce, 1972.
Kishi Naganmin and David Russell. *Successful Gaijin in Japan: How Foreign Companies Are Making It in Japan*. Lincolnwood, Ill.: NTC Business Books, 1996.
Kojima Kiyoshi. *Japanese Direct Foreign Investment: Model of Multinational Business Operations*. Tokyo: Charles E. Tuttle, 1978.
Matsushita Mitsuo. *International Trade and Competition Law in Japan*. Oxford: Oxford University Press, 1993.
Norbury, Paul, and Geoffrey Bownas, eds. *Business in Japan: A Guide to Japanese Business Practice and Procedure*. Boulder, Colo.: Westview Press, 1980.
Ozaki, Robert S. *The Control of Imports and Foreign Capital in Japan*. New York: Praeger, 1972.
Tsurumi Yoshi. *Japanese Business: A Research Guide with Annotated Bibliography*. New York: Praeger, 1978.
———. *Multinational Management: Business Strategy and Government Policy*. Cambridge, Mass.: Ballinger, 1977.
Wilkinson, Endymion. *Japan versus Europe: A History of Misunderstanding*. Harmondsworth: Penguin Books, 1981.

Government Ministries

Johnson, Chalmers. "MITI and Japanese International Economic Policy." In *The Foreign Policy of Modern Japan*, edited by Robert A. Scalapino. Berkeley: University of California Press, 1977.

———. *MITI and the Japanese Miracle*. Stanford, Calif.: Stanford University Press, 1982.

Kerbo, H. R., and J. A. McKinstry. *Who Rules Japan: The Inner Circles of Economic and Political Power*. Westport, Conn.: Praeger, 1995.

Koh, B. C. *Japan's Administrative Elite*. Berkeley: University of California Press, 1991.

Okimoto, Daniel I. *Between MITI and the Market*. Stanford, Calif.: Stanford University Press, 1989.

Industrial Structure and Policy

Calder, K. *Strategic Capitalism: Private Business and Public Purpose in Japanese Industrial Finance*. Princeton, N.J.: Princeton University Press.

Callon, S. *Divided Sun: MITI and the Breakdown of Japanese Hi-Tech Industrial Policy*. Stanford, Calif.: Stanford University Press, 1995.

Caves, Richard E., and Uekusa Masu. *Industrial Organization in Japan*. Washington, D.C.: Brookings Institution, 1966.

Dore, Ronald. *Flexible Rigidities: Industrial Policy and Structural Adjustment in the Japanese Economy, 1970–1980*. Stanford, Calif.: Stanford University Press, 1986.

Fruin, Mark. *The Japanese Enterprise System-Competitive Strategies and Cooperative Structures*. Oxford: Oxford University Press, 1991.

Gruvoyannis, Elias. *Current Issues in Monetary Policy in the United States and Japan: The Predictability of Money Demand*. New York: Praeger, 1992.

Imai Ken'ichi. "Japan's Industrial Organization." *Japanese Economic Studies*, spring–summer 1978.

Johnson, C. *Japan's Public Policy Companies*. Washington, D.C.: American Enterprise Institute for Public Policy Research, 1978.

Kaplan, Eugene J. *Japan: The Government-Business Relationship*. Washington, D.C.: U.S. Bureau of International Commerce, 1972.

Mannari Hiroshi. *Nihon ni okeru Keiseisha no Joken* (The Business Elite). Tokyo: Kodansha, 1965.

Matsumoto Koji. *The Rise of the Japanese Corporate System*. London: Kegan Paul International, 1991.

McGraw, Thomas K., ed. *America vs. Japan: A Comparative Study of Business-Government Relations Conducted at the Harvard Business School*. Boston: Harvard Business School Press, 1986.

Nakamura Hideichiro. "Japan Incorporated and Postwar Democracy." *Japan Economic Studies*, spring–summer 1978.

Okimoto, D. *Between MITI and the Market: Japanese Industrial Policy for High Technology*. Stanford, Calif.: Stanford University Press, 1989.

Ramseyer, J. Mark, and Frances M. Rosenbluth. *Japan's Political Marketplace, the Politics of Oligarchy: Institutional Choice in Imperial Japan*. Cambridge: Cambridge University Press, 1996.

Schaede, U. *Cooperative Capitalism: Self-Regulation, Trade Associations, and the Antimonopoly Law in Japan*. Oxford: Oxford University Press, 2000.

Singleton, Kenneth J., ed., *Japanese Monetary Policy*. Chicago: University of Chicago Press, 1993.

Sumiya, M. *A History of Japanese Trade and Industry Policy*. Oxford: Oxford University Press, 2001.

Uekasa Masu. "Industrial Organization: The 1970s to the Present." In *The Political Economy of Japan*, vol. 1, *Domestic Transformation*, edited by Yamamura Kozo and Yasuba Yasukichi. Stanford, Calif.: Stanford University Press, 1987.

Ueno Hiroya. "Conception and Evaluation of Japanese Industrial Policy." *Japanese Economic Studies*, winter 1976–1977.

Vogel, S. "Can Japan Disengage? Winners and Losers in Japan's Political Economy, and the Ties That Bind Them." *Social Science Japan Journal* 2 (1999): 3–21.

———. *Freer Markets, More Rules: Regulatory Reform in the Advanced Industrial Countries*. Ithaca, N.Y.: Cornell University Press, 1996.

Wilks, Stephen, and Maurice Wright, eds. *The Organization and Regulation of Industry in Japan*. London: Macmillan, 1991.

Woronoff, Jon. *Inside Japan, Inc*. Tokyo: Lotus Press, 1984.

Yoshikawa Hiroshi. "Monetary Policy and the Real Economy in Japan." In *Japanese Monetary Policy*, edited by Kenneth J. Singleton. Chicago: University of Chicago Press, 1993.

Yoshino, M. Y. *The Japanese Marketing System*. Cambridge, Mass.: MIT Press, 1971.

SELECTED SECTOR STUDIES

Accounting

Arai Kiyomitsu. *Accounting in Japan*. Tokyo: Institute for Research in Business Administration, Waseda University, 1994.

Ballon, Robert J., with Iwao Tomita and Hajime Usami. *Financial Reporting in Japan*. Tokyo: Kodansha International, 1976.

DuBois, Donald A., and Kyojiro Someya. "Accounting Development in Japan." *The Accountant*, May 5, 1977.
Gomi Yuji. *Guide to Japanese Taxes*. Annual. Tokyo: Zaikeishohosha.
KPMG Peat Marwick. *Comparison of Japanese and U.S. Reporting and Financial Practices*. Tokyo: Peat Marwick, 1993.
Ministry of Finance. *An Outline of Japanese Taxes*. Tokyo: Okura Zaimu Kyokai. Annual.
Mueller, Gerhard G., and Yoshi Hiroshi. *Accounting Practices in Japan*. Seattle: Graduate School of Business Administration, University of Washington, 1968.

Agriculture

Havens, T. R. H. *Farm and Nation in Modern Japan: Agrarian Nationalism*. Princeton, N.J.: Princeton University Press, 1974.
———. "Religion and Agriculture in Nineteenth-Century Japan: Ninomiya Sontoku and the Hotoku Movement." *Japan Christian Quarterly* 38, no. 2 (1972).
Hayami Yujiro. *Japanese Agriculture under Siege: The Political Economy of Agricultural Policies*. London: Macmillan, 1988.
Hayami Yujiro, and Yamada Saburo. *The Agricultural Development of Japan: A Century's Perspective*. Tokyo: University of Tokyo Press, 1991.
Longford, Joseph H. "Note on Ninomiya Sontoku." *Transactions of the Asiatic Society of Japan* 22, pt. 1 (1894): 103–8.
Moore, Richard M. *Japanese Agriculture: Patterns of Rural Development*. Boulder, Colo.: Westview Press, 1990.
Ohsawa Shinichi. "Agri-Business and Agricultural Reform in Japan." *Japan Research Quarterly* 6, no. 33 (1997) :100–130.
Reich, Michael, Endo Yasuo, and C. Peter Timmer. "Agriculture: The Political Economy of Structural Change in *America versus Japan* (ed. Thomas K. McCraw)." Boston: Harvard Business School Press, 1986.

Airline Industry

Hasegawa Mina. "JAL Restructuring: Will It Fly?" *Nikkei Weekly*, March 8, 1993.
Japan Air Lines. *A More Competitive JAL Group*. Tokyo: Japan Air Lines, 1999.
Japan Economic Almanac. "Airlines" Tokyo: *Nikkei Shimbun*. Annual.
Saito, M. "Challenges to Human Factors Issues in JAL Maintenance." In *Human Factors in Aviation*. Montreal: International Air Transport Association, 1993.
Ujimoto, K. V. "Changes, Challenges, and Choices in the Japanese Aviation Industry: The Development of Crew Resource Management in Japan Airlines."

In *Japan at Century's End*, edited by H. Millward and J. Morison. Halifax: Fernwood, 1997.

Yamamori, H. "Keeping CRM Is Keeping the Flight Safe." In *Cockpit Resource Management*, edited by E. L. Weiner, B. G. Kanki, and R. L. Helmrich. New York: Academic Press, 1999.

Automobile Industry

Clark, Kim B., and Fujimoto Takahiro. *Product Development Performance, Organization, and Management in the World Auto Industry*. Boston: Harvard Business School Press, 1991.

Cusumano, Michael A. *The Japanese Automobile Industry: Technology and Management at Nissan and Toyota*. Cambridge, Mass.: Council on East Asian Studies, Harvard University, 1989.

———. "Manufacturing Innovation: Lessons from the Japanese Auto Industry." *Sloan Management Review* 30 (1988): 29–39.

Cusumano, Michael A., and K. Nobeoka. "Strategy, Structure, and Performance in Product Development: Observations from the Auto Industry." In *Managing Product Development*, edited by T. Nishiguchi. New York: Oxford University Press, 1994.

Garrahan, Phillip, and Paul Stewart. *The Nissan Enigma: Flexibility at Work in a Local Economy*. London: Mansell, 1992.

Japan Automobile Manufacturers' Association. *The Motor Industry of Japan*. Tokyo. Annual.

———. *Motor Vehicle Statistics of Japan*. Tokyo: Japan Motor Industrial Federation. Annual.

Pasacale, E., and T. Rohlen. "The Mazda Turnaround." *Journal of Japanese Studies* 9, no. 2 (1983): 219–63.

Sako Mari. "Suppliers Association in the Japanese Automobile Industry: Collective Action for Technology Diffusion." *Cambridge Journal of Economics* 20 (November 1996): 651–71.

Shibata Yasuhiko. "Japan's Changing Automotive Industry." *Journal of Japanese Trade and Industry*, no. 1 (1995): 19–21.

Toyoda Tatsuro. "The Strength of the Japanese Auto Industry." *Japan Echo* 21, no. 2 (1994): 19–22.

Banking and Finance

Aggarwal, R., ed. *Restructuring Japanese Business for Growth*. Boston: Kluwer Academic, 1999.

Aoki Masahiko and Hugh Patrick, eds. *The Japanese Main Bank System*. Oxford: Oxford University Press, 1994.

Arora, D. *Japanese Financial Institutions in Europe: International Competitiveness of Japanese Banks and Securities Companies*. Amsterdam: Elsevier, 1995.
Elton, Edwin, and Martin J. Gruber, eds. *Japanese Capital Markets*. New York: Harper & Row, 1990.
Fabozzi, Frank J., ed. *The Japanese Bond Markets: An Overview and Analysis*. Chicago: Probus, 1990.
Federation of Bankers in Japan. *The Banking System of Japan*. Tokyo: Zenkoku Ginko Kyokai, 1994.
———. *Japanese Banks*. Annual. Tokyo: Zenkoku Ginko Kyokai.
Feldman, Robert. *Japan's Financial Markets*. Cambridge, Mass.: MIT Press, 1986.
Fuji Bank. *Banking in Modern Japan*. Tokyo: Fuji Bank, 1967.
Hanazaki M., and A. Horiuchi. "Is Japan's Financial System Efficient?" *Oxford Review of Economic Policy* 16, no. 2 (2000): 61–73.
Hayakawa Shigenobu, ed. *Japanese Financial Markets*. Cambridge: Gresham Books, 1996.
Horiuchi Akiyoshi. "An Evaluation of Japanese Financial Liberalization: A Case Study of Corporate Bond Markets." In *Financial Deregulation and Integration in East Asia*, edited by Ito Takatoshi and Anne O. Krueger. Chicago: University of Chicago Press, 1996.
Hoshi T., and A. Kas Ghyap. "The Japanese Banking Crisis: Where Did It Come from and How Will It End? " *NBER Macroeconomic Annual* 1999: 129–301.
Hurwitz, S. L. *The Japanese Venture Capital Industry*. Cambridge: MIT Japan Program, Center for International Studies, Massachusetts Institute of Technology, 1999.
Kitagawa Hiroshi and Kurosawa Yoshitaka. "Japan: Development and Structural Change of the Banking System." In *The Financial Development of Japan, Korea, and Taiwan*, edited by Hugh Patrick and Yung Chul Park. New York: Oxford University Press, 1994.
Motonish, Li T., and H. Yashikawa. "Causes of the Long Stagnation of Japan during the 1990s: Financial or Real?" *Journal of Japanese and International Economies* 12, no. 2 (1999): 1801–2000.
Nomura Hidekazu, ed. *Seiko: A Comprehensive Analysis of Consumer Cooperatives in Japan*. Tokyo: Otsuki Shoten, 1993.
Presssnell, L. S., ed. *Money and Banking in Japan*. London: Macmillan, 1973.
Rose, Peter S., *Japanese Banking and Investment in the United States*. New York: Quorum Books, 1991.
Rosenblush, Francis M. *Financial Politics in Contemporary Japan*. Ithaca, N.Y.: Cornell University Press, 1989.
Sasaki Toyonari. "Bank Regulation." In *Capital Markets and Financial Services in Japan*. Tokyo: Japan Securities Research Institute, 1992.

Scher, M. J. *Japanese Interfirm Networks and Their Main Banks*. London: Macmillan; New York: St. Martin's Press, 1996.

Scher, M. J., and S. L. Beechler. "Japanese Banking in the U.S.—From Transient Advantage to Strategic Failure." Working Paper Series. New York: Columbia University Center on Japanese Economy and Business, 1994.

Schiffer, Hubert F. *The Modern Japanese Banking System*. New York: University Publishing, 1962.

Suzuki Yoshio, ed. *The Japanese Financial System*. Oxford: Oxford University Press, 1987.

Tatewaki Kazuo. *Banking and Finance in Japan*. London: Routledge, 1991.

Tatsuta Misao. *Securities Regulations in Japan*. Tokyo: University of Tokyo Press, 1970.

Tokyo Stock Exchange. *Tokyo Stock Exchange History, Organization, Operation*. Tokyo: Tokyo Stock Exchange, 1972.

Tsuru Shigeto. *Japan's Capitalism: Creative Defeat and Beyond*. Cambridge: Cambridge University Press, 1993.

Walter, I., and T. Hiraki. *Restructuring Japan's Financial Markets*. Homewood, Ill.: Irwin, 1993.

Yamashita Takeji. *Japan's Securities Markets: A Practitioners' Guide*. Singapore: Butterworths, 1989.

Zelinski, Robert, and Nigel Holloway. *Unequal Equities: Power and Risk in Japan's Stock Market*. Tokyo: Kosansha International, 1991.

Zemba, William T., and Sandra L. Schwartz. *Invest Japan*. Chicago: Probus, 1992.

Communications and Electronics

Anchordoguy, M. *Computers, Inc.: Japan's Challenge to IBM*. Cambridge, Mass.: Harvard University Press, 1989.

———. "Japanese-American Trade Conflict and Supercomputers." *Political Science Quarterly* 109 (1994): 35–80.

———. "Japan's Software Industry: A Failure of Institutions?" *Research Policy* 29 (2000): 391–408.

Aoyama Y. *Ka-den* (Home Electronics). Tokyo: Nippon Keizei Shimbun, 1991.

Craig, Tim. "The Japanese Beer Wars: Initiating and Responding to Hypercompetition in New Product Development." *Organization Science* 7, no. 3 (1996): 302–21.

Cusumano, Michael. *Japan's Software Factories*. Oxford: Oxford University Press, 1991.

Fransman, M. *Japan's Computer and Communications Industry: The Evolution of Industrial Giants and Global Competitiveness*. Oxford: Oxford University Press, 1995.

Japan Electronics and Information Technology Industrial Association. *Industry Review: Electronics and Information Technology Industries in Japan.* Tokyo. Annual. www.jeita.or.jp.

Japan Fact Book: Guide to Japan's Electronics Manufacturers and Industry. Tokyo: Dempa Publications. Annual.

Japan Information Processing Center. *The Computer White Paper.* Tokyo: Japan Information Processing Development Center. Annual.

Lynn, L. "The Commercialization of the Transistor Radio in Japan: The Functioning of an Innovation Community." In *IEEE Transactions of Engineering Management.* New York: Quorum, 1998.

Partner S. *Assembled in Japan: Electrical Goods and the Making of the Japanese Consumer.* Berkeley: University of California Press, 1999.

Construction

Coaldrake, W. *The Way of the Carpenter: Tools and Japanese Architecture.* Tokyo: Weatherhill, 1990.

Hasegawa, S., and the Shimizu Group. *Built by Japan: Competitive Strategies of the Japanese Construction Industry.* New York: John Wiley & Sons, 1988.

Levy, Sydney M. *Japanese Construction: An American Perspective.* New York: Van Nostrand Reinhold, 1990.

———. *Japan's Big Six: Inside Japan's Construction Industry.* New York: McGraw-Hill, 1993.

Woodall, B. *Japan under Construction: Corruption, Politicism and Public Works.* Berkeley: University of California Press, 1996.

Food and Beverages

Bestor, Theodore C. *Tokyo's Marketplace.* Berkeley: University of California Press, 2002.

O'Rourke, A. Desmond, ed. *Understanding the Japanese Food and Agrimarket: A Multi-Faceted Opportunity.* New York: Food Products Press, 1994.

Insurance

Ministry of Finance. *Finance Review.* Tokyo. Annual.

Ostrom, Douglas. "From Colossus to Casualty: The Transformation of Japan's Insurance Industry." *JEI Report* 2A, January 16, 1998.

———. "Japan's Sleeping Insurance Giants." *JEI Report* 17A, May 1, 1992.

Yamamoto Yuri. "Insurer Performance Mixed in Deregulation." *Nikkei Weekly*, June 16, 1997, 13.

———. "Life Insurers Falling Behind in Money-Management Race." *Nikkei Weekly*, June 15, 1998, 1.13.

Railways

Choy, Jon. "Tokyo Concerned with Runaway Railroad Debt." *JEI Report* 33B, August 30, 1996, 8–10.

Fukui Koichiro. *Japanese National Railways Privatization Study: The Experience of Japan and Lessons for Developing Countries*. Washington, D.C.: World Bank, 1992.

Noda M., K. Harada, F. Aoki, and Y. Oikawa. *Japanese Railway: The Establishment and Development*. Railway History Series. Tokyo: Nihon Keizei Shimbun-sha, 1990.

"Private Rails Make Headway." *Nikkei Weekly*, April 18, 1992, 1.

Suzuki Yumiko. "Railway Debt Could Cost Taxpayers Trillions of Yen." *Nikkei Weekly*, April 1, 1996, 1.19.

———. "Railway Spinoffs Chug Ahead with Improvements." *Nikkei Weekly*, April 7, 1997, 1.21.

Shipbuilding

Shipbuilding in Japan. Tokyo: Shipbuilders Association of Japan. Annual.

Yonezawa Yoshie. "The Shipbuilding Industry." In *Industrial Policy of Japan*, edited by ed. Komiya Ryutaro. Tokyo: Academic Press, 1988.

Steel

Hasegawa Harsukiyo. *The Steel Industry in Japan: A Comparison with Britain*. London: Routledge, 1996.

Japan Iron and Steel Federation. *The Steel Industry of Japan*. Annual. Tokyo: Japan Iron and Steel Federation.

Klamann, Edmund. "MITI Steel Cartel Fades, yet Stable Order Intact." *Nikkei Weekly*, August 3, 1991, 10.

Komatsu Naoki. "Japan's Steel Industry Is Restructuring Its Way Back to Profitability," *Tokyo Business Today*, November 1989, 40–45.

Yonekura Seiichiro. *The Japanese Iron and Steel Industry, 1850–1990: Continuity and Discontinuity*. New York: St. Martin's Press, 1994.

Telecommunications

Ogawa, Joshua. "Restructuring Would Put NTT into Hot Global Arena." *Nikkei Weekly*, December 9, 1996, 1, 8.

About the Author

Stuart D. B. Picken was educated at Allen Glen's School, Glasgow, and the University of Glasgow, where he majored in philosophy and divinity. He served on the faculty of the International Christian University in Tokyo for 25 years prior to moving to Nagoya University of Commerce and Business Administration. He served as dean of the faculty of Foreign Languages and Asian Studies since its inception in 1988 and also as dean of the Graduate School of Global Business Communication since its opening in 2002. His prior books include *Shinto: Japan's Spiritual Roots* (1979), *The Essentials of Shinto* (1994), and *Historical Dictionary of Shinto* (2002). He is also the author of over 200 academic papers and articles. From 1985 to 1988, he served as director of the Centre for Japanese Studies at the University of Stirling in Scotland and was instrumental in founding the Japan Society of Scotland. In Japan, he served as a council member of the Japan-British Society from 1981 to 2001. He has been actively involved in interreligious dialogue at many levels and in promoting the better understanding of Shinto and Japanese culture in international Asia and in the West. He served as a special adviser to the president of the International Association for Religious Freedom between 1997 and 2000. He also maintains close connections with the Japan Research Center of the Chinese Academy of Social Science in Beijing. Outside academia, he has functioned as a consultant to various major Japanese corporations, including Mutsui Mining and Smelting Corporation, Kobe Steel, and the Japan Airlines Group. He retired early in 2004 and now lives in Perthshire in Scotland, where he devotes time to research and writing.